HOW TO PROTECT YOUR CHILDREN FROM CHILD ABUSE:

A Parent's Guide

Cómo Proteger a Sus Hijos del Abuso Infantil: Una Guía Para los Padres

Disponible en español en su oficina local de Boy Scouts of America o ir a *www.scouting.org/pubs/ypt/pdf/46-072.pdf.*

BOY SCOUTS OF AMERICA

INTRODUCTION

Our children are often faced with choices that affect their development and safety. As parents, we can do our best to provide education and guidance to prepare them to make the best decisions. One way we do this is to talk with our children. Some subjects are easy to discuss with them—sports, their grades in school, their friends, and many other features of our daily lives. Other things are more difficult for us to discuss, including child abuse—especially child sexual abuse.

Although discussing child abuse with your children may be difficult for you, it is very important. Perhaps the most important step parents can take to protect their children from abuse is to have open communication in the home. Research has shown that children whose parents talk to them about preventing abuse are more effective at fending off assaults. Your role is very important.

More than 3 million reports of child abuse are received each year nationally, including half a million reports of child sexual abuse. As a major youth-serving organization, the Boy Scouts of America has a unique opportunity to help protect the youth of our nation. This booklet is designed to give you essential information that should help you teach your children how to protect themselves.

If your son is a new Boy Scout, this might be the first time that you have seen this *Parent's Guide*. If you have other sons in Scouting, or if your son has advanced in Boy Scouting, we hope that you are familiar with this guide and have discussed its contents with your children. In either case, we encourage you to make this information part of a continuing family effort that reinforces the concepts included in this guidebook.

We do not expect that your son will become a victim of child abuse. It is extremely important, however, that if he is ever confronted with an abusive situation, he will know that there are adults in his life who will listen and respond in a supportive manner. The purpose of this booklet is to help you and your son establish, or reinforce, open communication on this sensitive topic.

SECTION I. INFORMATION FOR PARENTS

**Youth Protection Joining Requirement:
For your son to join a Boy Scout troop,
he must complete the exercises included
in Section II of this pamphlet.**

Using This Booklet

This booklet is divided into two sections. The first section contains information about child abuse and provides some tips to help parents talk with their Boy Scout–age sons about child abuse. The second section is for you to share with your son. Some of the activities listed in the second section are requirements your son needs your help to complete before he can join his Boy Scout troop.

It is important that you read the entire booklet before you and your son do any of the exercises together. You might be tempted to hand this booklet to your son and tell him to read it. We urge you to resist this temptation. Your son needs to know that he can openly discuss difficult topics with you.

CHILD ABUSE:
BASIC INFORMATION FOR PARENTS

An abused or neglected child is a child who is harmed, or threatened with physical or mental harm, by the acts or lack of action of a person responsible for the child's care. There are several forms of abuse: physical abuse, emotional abuse, and sexual abuse. Child neglect is a form of abuse that occurs when a person responsible for the care of a child is able, but fails, to provide necessary food, clothing, shelter, or care. Each state has its own definitions and laws concerning child abuse and child neglect.

Child abuse and neglect are serious problems for our society. The number of cases reported has increased each year since 1976, when statistics were first kept. Brief discussions of each form of abuse are presented below.

Neglect

A child is neglected if the people this child depends on do not provide food, clothing, shelter, medical care, education, and supervision. When these basic needs are deliberately withheld, not because the parents or caregivers are poor, it is considered neglect. Often parents or caregivers of neglected children are so overwhelmed by their own needs that they cannot recognize the needs of their children.

Physical Abuse

Physical abuse is the deliberate injury of a child by a person responsible for the child's care. Physical abuse often stems from unreasonable punishment, or by punishment that is too harsh for the child. Sometimes it is the result of a caregiver's reaction to stress. Drinking and drug abuse by caretakers have become more common contributing factors in physical abuse cases.

Physical abuse injuries can include bruises, broken bones, burns, and abrasions. Children experience minor injuries as a normal part of childhood, usually in predictable places such as the shins, knees, and elbows. When the injuries are in soft-tissue areas on the abdomen or back, or don't seem to be typical childhood injuries, physical abuse becomes a possibility.

Physical abuse happens to children of all age groups; however, youth ages 12 to 17 have the highest rate of injury from physical abuse. This is possibly due to increasing conflict between parents and children as children become more independent.

Emotional Abuse

Emotional abuse is harder to recognize but is just as harmful to the child as other forms of abuse. Emotional abuse damages the child's self-esteem and, in extreme cases, can lead to developmental problems and speech disorders. A child suffers from emotional abuse when constantly ridiculed, rejected, blamed, or compared unfavorably with brothers or sisters or other children.

Expecting too much from the child in academics, athletics, or other areas is a common cause of emotional abuse by parents or other adults. When a child can't meet these expectations, the child feels that he or she is never quite good enough.

Sexual Abuse

When an adult or an older child uses his or her authority over a child to involve the child in sexual activity, it is sexual abuse, and that person is a child molester. The molester might use tricks, bribes, threats, or force to persuade the child to join in sexual activity. Sexual abuse includes any activity performed for the sexual satisfaction of the molester, including acts ranging from exposing his or her sex organs (exhibitionism), observing another's sex organs or sexual activity (voyeurism), to fondling and rape.

Here are a few facts you should know about child sexual abuse:

▶ Child sexual abuse occurs to as many as 25 percent of girls and 14 percent of boys before they reach 18 years of age.

▶ Boys and girls could be sexually abused at any age; however, most sexual abuse occurs between the ages of 7 and 13.

▶ Children are most likely to be molested by someone they know and trust.

▶ Eighty to 90 percent of sexually abused boys are molested by acquaintances who are nonfamily members.

▶ Females perform 20 percent of the sexual abuse of boys under age 14 (prepubescents).

▶ Few sexually abused children tell anyone that they have been abused. Children are usually told to keep the abuse secret. This could involve threats, bribes, or physical force.

▶ Children might feel responsible for the abuse and fear an angry reaction from their parents.

Sexual Molestation by Peers

Approximately one-third of sexual molestation occurs at the hands of other children. If your child tells you about club initiations in which sexual activity is included, or if your child tells you about inappropriate or tricked, pressured, or forced sexual activity by other children, this is a form of sexual abuse and you need to take steps to stop the activity. This kind of sexual misconduct is serious and should not be ignored.

Children who molest other children need professional help. They are much more likely to respond to treatment when young than are adults who were molesters as children and received no treatment, and continue to molest children as adults.

Parents and other adults who work with children need to distinguish between sexual behavior that is a normal part of growing up, and sexual behavior that is abusive. If you find your child has engaged in sexual behavior that might not be abusive, but which bothers you, use the opportunity to discuss the behavior and help your child understand why it bothers you.

Preteen and teenage boys are especially at risk for sexual abuse. The physical and hormonal changes caused by puberty, and their natural curiosity about their new emotions and feelings, make these youth likely targets for child molesters. The normal desire of boys this age to show their independence from their parents' control adds to the risk. This combination might keep boys this age from asking their parents for help when faced with sexual abuse.

Signs of Sexual Abuse

The best sign that a child has been sexually abused is his statement that he was. Children often do not report their abuse, so parents should be alert for other signs.

These are some signs to watch for:

▶ *Hints, indirect messages*—Refusing to go to a friend's or relative's home for no apparent reason; for example, "I just don't like him anymore."

▶ *Seductive or provocative behavior*—Acting out adult sexual behavior or using sexual language a child his age is unlikely to know.

▶ *Physical symptoms*—Irritation of genital or anal areas.

The following are common signs that children are upset. If present for more than a few days, these signs could indicate that something is wrong and your child needs help and parental support. They might also be signs that your child is being sexually abused:

▶ *Self-destructive behavior*—Using alcohol or drugs, deliberately harming himself, running away, attempting suicide, or sexual recklessness or promiscuity.

▶ *Unhappiness*—Undue anxiety and crying, sleep disturbances or loss of appetite.

▶ *Regression*—Behaving like a younger child, thumb sucking, or bed-wetting.

▶ *Difficulty at school*—Sudden drop in grades, behavioral problems, or truancy.

PREVENTING CHILD ABUSE

Except for sexual abuse of boys, the great majority of child abuse occurs within families. Prevention efforts for emotional and physical abuse as well as neglect generally focus on helping abusers, often the parents, change their behavior.

Some physical and emotional abuses are reactions by parents to the stresses in their lives. By learning to recognize these stresses, and then taking a time-out when the pressures mount, we can avoid abusing those we love. The next page lists some alternatives to physical and emotional abuse for overstressed parents. These suggestions come from the National Committee to Prevent Child Abuse.

In addition to the alternatives on the next page, parents and other child caregivers may want to think about the following questions suggested by Douglas Besharov, the first director of the U.S. National Center on Child Abuse and Neglect, regarding the methods of discipline they use.

▶ Is the purpose of the punishment to educate the child or to vent the parent's anger?

▶ Is the child capable of understanding the relationship between his behavior and the punishment?

▶ Is the punishment appropriate and within the bounds of acceptable discipline?

▶ Is a less severe, but equally effective, punishment available?

▶ Is the punishment degrading, brutal, or extended beyond the limits of what the child can handle?

▶ If physical force is used, is it done carefully to avoid injury?

These questions help to define the boundaries between acceptable discipline and child abuse. Other causes of child abuse inside the family might be much more complex and require professional help to resolve.

Alternatives to Child Abuse

The next time everyday pressures build up to the point where you feel like lashing out—*Stop!* Try any of these simple alternatives. You'll feel better . . . and so will your child:

- Take a deep breath. And another. Then remember you are the adult.
- Close your eyes and imagine you're hearing what your child is about to hear.
- Press your lips together and count to 10, or, better yet, to 20.
- Put your child in a time-out chair. (Remember this rule: One time-out minute for each year of age.)
- Put yourself in a time-out chair. Think about why you are angry: Is it your child, or is your child simply a convenient target for your anger?
- Phone a friend.
- If someone can watch the children, go outside and take a walk.
- Splash cold water on your face.
- Hug a pillow.
- Turn on some music. Maybe even sing along.
- Pick up a pencil and write down as many *helpful* words as you can think of. Save the list.

Few parents mean to abuse their children. When parents take time out to get control of themselves before they grab hold of their children, everybody wins.

Talking With Your Child About Sexual Abuse

Some parents would almost rather have a tooth pulled than talk with their children about sexual abuse. This reluctance seems to increase with the age of the child. To help you in this regard, the information in Section II focuses on sexual abuse prevention.

The following information should help you and your child talk about sexual abuse prevention:

▶ **If you feel uncomfortable discussing sexual abuse with your child, let him know.** When you feel uncomfortable discussing sexual abuse with your children and try to hide your uneasiness, your children might misinterpret the anxiety and be less likely to approach you when they need help. You can use a simple statement like, "I wish we did not have to talk about this. I am uncomfortable because I don't like to think that this could happen to you. I want you to know that it's important and you can come to me whenever you have a question or if anybody ever tries to hurt you."

▶ **Children at this age are developing an awareness of their own sexuality and need parental help to sort out what is and is not exploitive.** Children at this age need specific permission to ask questions about relationships and feelings. Nonspecific "good touch, bad touch" warnings are insufficient, since most of the touching they experience might be "confusing touch." Adolescents also need parental help to set boundaries for their relationships with others—an awareness of when they are being controlling or abusive.

▶ **Many children at this age feel it is more important to be "cool" than it is to ask questions or seek parental assistance.** Your son might resist discussing the material in this booklet with you. He might be giggly, unfocused, or restless. He might tell you that he already knows about sexual abuse. That's all right. The point of discussing sexual abuse with him is to let him know that if and when he has questions or problems he can't handle by himself, you will help him. If he tells you he already knows about sexual abuse, you can ask him to tell you what he knows.

Today's teenagers and preteens receive a lot of misinformation about sexuality, relationships, and sexual abuse. Their role models are likely to be rock stars and other media personalities. As influential as these are, surveys of young people indicate that parents continue to be a strong influence in their lives.

WHEN A CHILD TELLS YOU ABOUT ABUSE

If your child becomes a victim of abuse, your first reaction can be very important in helping him through the ordeal. The following guidelines may help you:

▶ *Don't* panic or overreact to the information your child tells you.

▶ *Don't* criticize your child or tell your child he misunderstood what happened.

▶ *Do* respect your child's privacy and take your child to a place where the two of you can talk without interruptions or distractions.

▶ *Do* reassure your child that he is not to blame for what happened. Tell him that you appreciate being told about the incident and will help to make sure that it won't happen again.

▶ *Do* encourage your child to tell the proper authorities what happened, but try to avoid repeated interviews that can be stressful to the child.

▶ *Do* consult your family doctor or other child abuse authority about the need for medical care or counseling for your child.

You should show real concern, but NOT alarm or anger, when questioning your child about possible sexual abuse.

Finally, if your child has been sexually abused, do not blame yourself or your child. People who victimize children are not easy to identify. They come from all walks of life and all socioeconomic levels. Often they have a position of status—they go to church, hold regular jobs, and are active in the community. Child molesters are sometimes very skilled at controlling children, often by giving excessive attention, gifts, and money.

Child molesters use their skills on parents and other adults, disguising their abusive behavior behind friendship and care for the child.

RESOURCES

BSA Youth Protection Materials

A Time to Tell is a video produced by the BSA to educate boys 11 to 14 years of age about sexual abuse. This video introduces the "three R's" of Youth Protection. Boy Scout troops are encouraged to view the video once each year. It is available from your BSA local council. A meeting guide supporting its use can be found in the *Scoutmaster Handbook*.

For Scouting's leaders and parents, the BSA has a video training program, *Youth Protection Guidelines: Training for Volunteer Leaders and Parents*. This is available from your BSA local council, and regular training sessions are scheduled in most districts. It is also available online on your local council's Web site. It addresses many questions that Scout volunteers and parents ask regarding child sexual abuse.

In addition to these materials, the BSA sometimes provides Youth Protection information to its members and families through *Boys' Life* and *Scouting* magazines.

Other Sources of Child Abuse Prevention Information

National Clearinghouse on Child Abuse and Neglect Information
330 C St., SW
Washington, DC 20447
800-394-3366 or 703-385-7565
Fax: 703-385-3206
E-mail: nccanch@caliber.com
Web site: *http://nccanch.acf.hhs.gov*

Prevent Child Abuse America
200 South Michigan Ave., 17th Floor
Chicago, IL 60604-2404
312-663-3520
Fax: 312-939-8962
Web site: *www.preventchildabuse.org*

National Center for Missing and Exploited Children
699 Prince St.
Alexandria, VA 22314-3175
800-843-5678
Fax: 703-274-2200
Web site: *www.missingkids.org*

SECTION II. INFORMATION FOR YOUTH
(Youth Protection Troop Joining Requirements)

The *Child's Bill of Rights* outlines some specific strategies your child can use to protect himself. You should discuss these and the "three R's" of Youth Protection with your child before completing the Youth Protection joining requirements. These could provide the information that your son needs to help him respond to the situations in the exercises.

Child's Bill of Rights

When feeling threatened, you have the right to:

- Trust your instincts or feelings.
- Expect privacy.
- Say no to unwanted touching or affection.
- Say no to an adult's inappropriate demands and requests.
- Withhold information that could jeopardize your safety.
- Refuse gifts.
- Be rude or unhelpful if the situation warrants.
- Run, scream, and make a scene.
- Physically fight off unwanted advances.
- Ask for help.

It's important to remember that these are protective actions that will give your son the power to protect himself.

The Boy Scouts of America bases the Youth Protection strategies it teaches its members on the "three R's" of Youth Protection.

The "three R's" of Youth Protection provide a useful tool for parents when they talk with their 11- to 14-year-old children about sexual abuse. Children of this age are less apt than younger children to respond to a list of child safety rules. They need to develop the problem-solving skills necessary to evaluate situations and come up with their own responses. Parents need to help their children develop these skills.

You can help your children develop their personal safety skills. Read the following material with your son. Use the "three R's" of Youth Protection and the *Child's Bill of Rights* as references.

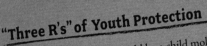

"Three R's" of Youth Protection

Recognize that anyone could be a child molester and be aware of situations that could lead to abuse.

Resist advances made by child molesters to avoid being abused.

Report any molestation or attempted molestation to parents or other trusted adults.

Personal Protection Rules for Computer Online Services

When you're online, you are in a public place, among thousands of people who are online at the same time. Be safe by following these personal protection rules and you will have fun.

▶ Keep online conversations with strangers to public places, not in e-mail.

▶ Do not give anyone online your real last name, phone numbers at home or school, your parents' workplaces, or the name or location of your school or home address unless you have your parent's permission first. Never give your password to anyone but a parent or other adult in your family.

▶ If someone shows you e-mail with sayings that make you feel uncomfortable, trust your instincts. You are probably right to be wary. Do not respond. Tell a parent what happened.

▶ If somebody tells you to keep what's going on between the two of you secret, tell a parent.

▶ Be careful who you talk to. Anyone who starts talking about subjects that make you feel uncomfortable is probably an adult posing as a kid.

- ▶ Pay attention if someone tells you things that don't fit together. One time an online friend will say he or she is 12, and another time will say he or she is 14. That is a warning that this person is lying and may be an adult posing as a kid.

- ▶ Unless you talk to a parent about it first, never talk to anybody by phone if you know that person only online. If someone asks you to call—even if it's collect or a toll-free, 800 number—that's a warning. That person can get your phone number this way, either from a phone bill or from caller ID.

- ▶ Never agree to meet someone you have met only online any place off-line, in the real world.

- ▶ Watch out if someone online starts talking about *hacking*, or breaking onto other people's or companies' computer systems; *phreaking* (the "ph" sounds like an "f"), the illegal use of long-distance services or cellular phones; or viruses, online programs that destroy or damage data when other people download these onto their computers.

- ▶ Promise your parent or an adult family member and yourself that you will honor any rules about how much time you are allowed to spend online and what you do and where you go while you are online.

1. CHILD ABUSE AND BEING A GOOD SCOUT

When a boy joins the Scouting program, he assumes a duty to be faithful to the rules of Scouting as represented in the Scout Oath, Scout Law, Scout motto, and Scout slogan.

The rules of Scouting don't require a Scout to put himself in possibly dangerous situations—quite the contrary, we want Scouts to "be prepared" and to "do their best" to avoid these situations.

We hope that you will discuss these rules with your Scout and be sure that he understands that he should not risk his safety to follow the rules of Scouting.

The Scout Oath includes the phrase, "To help other people at all times." The Scout Law says that "A Scout is helpful," and the Scout slogan is "Do a Good Turn Daily." There are many people who need help, and a Boy Scout should be willing to lend a hand when needed.

Sometimes people who really do not need help will ask for it in order to create an opportunity for abuse. Boy Scouts should be very familiar with the rules of safety so that they can recognize situations to be wary of. For example:

▶ It is one thing to stand on the sidewalk away from a car to give directions, and something else to get in the car with someone to show them the way. A Scout should never get into a car without his parent's permission.

▶ It may be OK for a Scout to help carry groceries to a person's house, but he should never enter the house unless he has permission from his parents.

The Scout Law also states that a Scout is obedient—but a Scout does not have to obey an adult when that person tells him to do something that the Scout feels is wrong or that makes the Scout feel uncomfortable. In these situations, the Scout should talk with his parent about his concerns.

Mario's Story

I am a 13-year-old boy with a problem—my 17-year-old uncle, Joe. Joe stays with me when my parents go out of town. The last time, he started to act really strange. He wouldn't let me out of his sight. Even when I took a shower, he insisted that I keep the bathroom door open. When I turned around, Joe was taking a picture of me in the shower. He told me there wasn't any film in the camera and that it was a joke. I don't think it was funny, though. On the last night he was there, he told me to come into his bedroom and watch TV with him—only it wasn't TV, it was sex stuff. He told me not to tell anyone because if I did he would be in trouble *and so would I.*

Does the fact that Joe is a member of Mario's family and only 17 years old mean that he could not be a possible child molester?

— Remember that a child molester could be anyone. Most are family members or someone else the child knows.

— Many child molesters begin molesting others when they are teenagers

Does the fact that Joe has not touched Mario mean that sexual abuse did not happen?

— Joe violated Mario's privacy by taking a picture that Mario did not want taken—this is one form of abuse.

— Showing Mario pornographic videos is a form of sexual abuse and is usually a forerunner of sexual contact.

Should Mario get into trouble if he tells on Joe?

— Mario should not be blamed.
  He did nothing wrong.

— Anytime that sexual abuse occurs, the abuser is the one who is responsible.

Steven's Story

My name is Steven. I go to junior high school and make pretty good grades, so I'm not stupid. But the other day something happened that made me feel really dumb. A group of guys decided that they wanted to start a secret club. Only a few kids would be able to join their club. It was a fun thing, and the only way that you could join was to be asked by one of the members of the club. Well, one of my friends belonged and asked me to join. I was really flattered, and I really wanted to join. He told me that the club was meeting in one of the storage buildings on campus and that we could get high and have some fun—then he grabbed my crotch and laughed.

What do you suppose Steven's friend meant when he said, "We could get high and have some fun," and then grabbed Steven's crotch?

— Secret clubs are often used by child molesters to gain access to unsuspecting boys.

— Using drugs and alcohol to lower resistance to sexual abuse also is quite common.

Suppose that Steven went to the club meeting and ended up being sexually molested by one of the other guys there. How do you think he would feel?

— A lot of boys feel very embarrassed when they realize that they have been fooled. Often they are afraid that others will think that they are homosexual if they have been sexually abused by another guy.

— Embarrassment might cause Steven and other boys in his situation to not report their abuse.

Family Meeting
(Not Part of Joining Requirement)

A child must feel comfortable telling his parent about any sensitive problems or experiences in which someone approached him in an improper manner, or in a way that made him feel uncomfortable. Studies have shown that more than half of all child-abuse incidents are never reported because the victims are too afraid or too confused to report their experiences.

Your children need to be able to talk freely about their likes and dislikes, their friends, and their true feelings. You can create open communication through family meetings where safety issues can be talked about by the entire family. The Youth Protection materials could be discussed in a family meeting.

BOY SCOUTS OF AMERICA
1325 West Walnut Hill Lane
P.O. Box 152079
Irving, Texas 75015-2079
www.scouting.org

100-015
2009 Printing

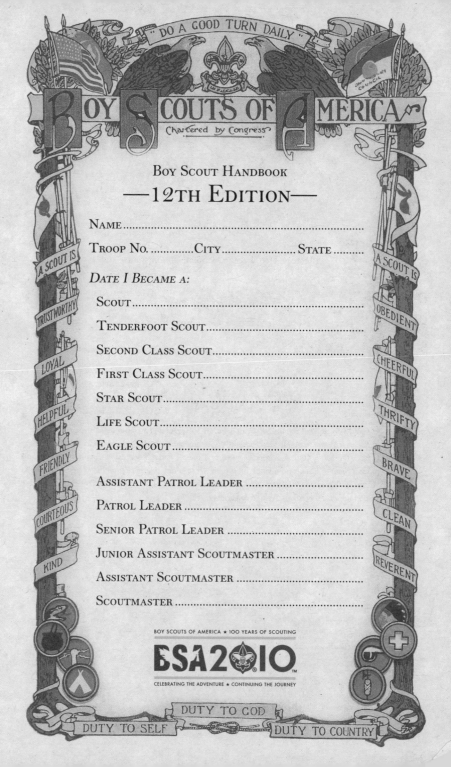

"DO A GOOD TURN DAILY"

BOY SCOUTS OF AMERICA

Chartered by Congress

BOY SCOUT HANDBOOK

—12TH EDITION—

NAME...

TROOP NO. ....CITY......................STATE ....

DATE I BECAME A:

SCOUT...

TENDERFOOT SCOUT..

SECOND CLASS SCOUT.......................................

FIRST CLASS SCOUT...

STAR SCOUT...

LIFE SCOUT...

EAGLE SCOUT...

ASSISTANT PATROL LEADER ....

PATROL LEADER ....

SENIOR PATROL LEADER ....

JUNIOR ASSISTANT SCOUTMASTER ....

ASSISTANT SCOUTMASTER ....

SCOUTMASTER ....

A SCOUT IS — TRUSTWORTHY — LOYAL — HELPFUL — FRIENDLY — COURTEOUS — KIND

A SCOUT IS — OBEDIENT — CHEERFUL — THRIFTY — BRAVE — CLEAN — REVERENT

BOY SCOUTS OF AMERICA ★ 100 YEARS OF SCOUTING

BSA2010

CELEBRATING THE ADVENTURE ★ CONTINUING THE JOURNEY

DUTY TO GOD

DUTY TO SELF

DUTY TO COUNTRY

Dedicated to the American Scoutmaster,
who makes Scouting possible.

This handbook, the official BSA manual, is based
on the experience of the Boy Scouts of America
in the United States since its founding in 1910
and is administered under the leadership of

John Gottschalk, *President*

Hector "Tico" Perez, *National Commissioner*

Robert J. Mazzuca, *Chief Scout Executive*

Mixed Sources
Product group from well-managed
forests, controlled sources and
recycled wood or fiber
www.fsc.org   Cert no. BV-COC-080733
© 1996 Forest Stewardship Council

Text pages printed on Rolland Enviro 100 Print, which is 100 percent post-consumer waste recycled paper,
processed chlorine free, and manufactured within the Environmental Choice Program guidelines. This stock
was produced in Quebec by Cascades using biogas energy, and the Forest Stewardship Council has tracked the
paper through a chain of custody from forest through printer to ensure that stock from these forests is managed
correctly. Cover stock printed on 12 pt. Kallima Coated one-side cover, FSC certified as a mixed-sources piece,
containing a minimum 30 percent recycled wood or fiber.

Copyright ©2009
Boy Scouts of America
Irving, Texas
Printed in U.S.A.
No. 34554

Twelfth Edition
Total copies of twelfth edition—700,000
Total printing since 1910—39,470,000

Library of Congress Cataloging-in-Publication Data

Boy Scouts of America.
        Boy Scout handbook.— 12th ed.
        p.   cm.
    Includes bibliographical references and index.
    ISBN 978-0-8395-3102-9 (alk. paper)
    1. Boy Scouts of America—Handbooks, manuals, etc. 2. Boy
Scouts—United States—Handbooks, manuals, etc. I. Title.
HS3313.B69 2009
369.43—dc22

2009005531

FROM THE CHIEF SCOUT EXECUTIVE

In some ways, my first *Boy Scout Handbook* was much different from the book you're holding now. In the front were instructions for flying the 48-star United States flag, which didn't yet include Alaska and Hawaii. In the back were requirements for merit badges like Pigeon Raising and Signaling, and advertisements for official Boy Scout shoes.

But like this centennial-edition *Handbook*, that old Scout manual promised me fun, adventure, leadership, and service. And boy did it deliver.

The pages of this book, your own *Boy Scout Handbook*, offer those same adventures to you. I wish you a lifetime of watching them unfold.

Good luck and good Scouting!

Robert J. Mazzuca
Chief Scout Executive
Boy Scouts of America

BOY SCOUTS OF AMERICA

100 YEARS OF SCOUTING

Origins of Scouting, 1899–1909

1899—Baden-Powell launches the Scouting movement by hosting a camp at Brownsea Island near England's southern coast.

Scouting for Boys, Baden-Powell's book of activities for young people, promotes the creation of Scout patrols throughout England.

1909—A British Boy Scout helps American businessman William D. Boyce find his way on a foggy London street, sparking Boyce's interest in bringing Scouting to the United States.

Original Edition, 1910–1911
Boy Scouts of America Official Handbook

- Called A Handbook of Woodcraft, Scoutcraft, and Life-craft
- Written by the BSA's first Chief Scout, Ernest Thompson Seton
- Includes sections on the American flag, organizational structure and rank advancement, camping, finding directions and signaling, and Scouting games
- Serves as the official handbook of the BSA into its second year

First Edition, 1911–1914
The Official Handbook for Boys

- Becomes the official manual for Boy Scouts
- Teaches Scouts how to find their way using the North Star
- Includes the American Morse Code
- 313,500 copies printed

Second Edition, 1914–1927
The Official Handbook for Boys

- Adds descriptions of map and compass skills, conservation and nature, woods tools, troop leader positions, the Scout handclasp, and proper uniform wear
- More than 2 million copies printed

Third Edition, 1927–1940
Revised Handbook for Boys

- First of many Handbook covers by Norman Rockwell
- First major content revision
- Introduces proper wear of the neckerchief

Fourth Edition, 1940–1948
Revised Handbook for Boys

- Cover art The Scouting Trail by Norman Rockwell
- 39 printings of the third and fourth editions

Fifth Edition, 1948–1959
Handbook for Boys

- Covers new advancement requirements and a new joining age (11)
- Teaches Scouts to "Do a Good Turn Daily"
- Change in cover art brought about by uniform change to overseas caps
- Introduces lashings and the taut line hitch

Sixth Edition, 1959–1965
Boy Scout Handbook

- The only cover painted by Norman Rockwell specifically for a Handbook, in honor of the BSA's 50th anniversary
- Written by William "Green Bar Bill" Hillcourt
- Omits requirements for all merit badges

Seventh Edition, 1965–1972
Boy Scout Handbook

- Much the same as the sixth edition, except for requirements changes

Eighth Edition, 1972–1979
Scout Handbook

- Complete revision reflects a revamped Boy Scouting program
- Second cover features Joseph Csatari painting All Out for Scouting
- Introduces "skill awards"

Ninth Edition, 1979–1990
Official Boy Scout Handbook

- Written by "Green Bar Bill" Hillcourt
- Features a return to traditional Scouting skills
- Artwork in the fourth printing was redrawn to depict a new uniform design

10th Edition, 1990–1998
Boy Scout Handbook

- First cover to feature color photographs
- Introduces Scouts to low-impact camping skills
- Introduces Venture and Varsity programs, as well as Varsity Scouting

11th Edition, 1998–2009
Boy Scout Handbook

- Introduces a new Scout skill: using GPS to find your way
- Recommends Leave No Trace's low-impact camping principles
- First cover to show Scouts dressed in activity wear rather than full uniform

12th Edition, 2009–today
Boy Scout Handbook

- First "green" edition—printed on recycled paper with environmentally friendly processes
- Commemorates the centennial anniversary of the Boy Scouts of America
- Illustrated with art elements borrowed from previous editions

Visit www.bsahandbook.org for more information on the history of the Boy Scout Handbook.

Color-coding throughout the sections and chapters will help you navigate.

A HANDBOOK FOR THE PAST AND THE FUTURE

You hold in your hands a century of Scouting. In addition to being a reference for the youth of Scouting's second century, this 12th edition of the *Boy Scout Handbook* also honors the heritage of Scouts who came before you. It combines art from previous editions with modern illustrations, photographs, and information—it even leaves opportunity to reach into the future with continuous updates through the World Wide Web.

As you browse through its pages, take note of the elements that make this edition special.

Quotes from past and present BSA leaders and literature will inspire you and remind you that Scouting's values are timeless.

Vintage artwork from Handbooks past will help you understand how Scouting skills have changed very little from a century ago. Curious about where the illustrations came from? Art credits begin on page 448.

"In This Chapter" boxes will give you an idea of what you can expect, as well as a quick index when you're looking for specific information.

"To take over hills and through deep valleys, under big trees and along murmuring streams is one of life's real pleasures."
—*Boy Scout Handbook*, 1939

HIKING

One of the best sights in Scouting is the beginning of an open trail. Lace up your boots, swing your pack onto your back, and set off toward adventure. Leave roads and automobiles behind—and sometimes the towns and cities, too. Go without mobile phones, electronic games, and music players. What lies ahead are possibilities, discoveries, and a closeness with nature that you earn one footstep at a time.

Hiking has always been among the Boy Scouts of America's great adventures. On trails, across open country, and along city streets, traveling by foot is a terrific way to get out with your friends and see the world.

Every season is special when you are hiking, and so is every place you go. Roam the backcountry with a map and compass to guide you. Walk through urban parks and neighborhoods. Follow a pathway to the summit of a mountain or along the banks of a river. Everywhere you hike will offer much to learn and enjoy as you...

IN THIS CHAPTER
- The Scout Basic Essentials
- Food and water for a hike
- Making a trip plan
- Appropriate clothing
- Leave No Trace hiking
- Pace
- Trail manners
- Cross-country hiking
- Hiking and weather safety
- Staying found

The skills you practice on even the shortest hike can prepare you for longer journeys.
- Clothing and rain gear for hiking are the same you'll need for camping and backpacking.
- The Scout Basic Essentials are items to take whenever you go to the backcountry.

Photography is essential to a beautiful book. Three of the five professional photographers who worked on this edition are Eagle Scouts; one was a Life Scout and now has worked professionally for the BSA for 30 years; and the fifth is an adult Scouter! You might have seen them at work—the photos in this book were taken at BSA local council events and camps across the nation from June 2007 to February 2009.

ABOUT THIS BOOK

When you see this symbol, check the *Handbook* Web site, *www.bsahandbook.org*, for more information. You'll find the latest information on related topics, as well as video, interactive demos, and other stuff we just couldn't fit on paper. The site is truly the Web's version of the *Boy Scout Handbook*, and it will change frequently. For example, when you get ready to plan for summer camp, check the *Handbook* site for information about where to go and what to pack this year.

These icons alert you to information you need to complete a rank requirement.

The BSA's First Green Handbook

The 12th edition of the Boy Scout Handbook is the embodiment of the BSA's longstanding tradition of being a good steward of Earth's natural resources. You'll see these symbols printed in this book as a testament to our commitment to going green.

 The Universal Recycling Symbol denotes that the book is printed on 100 percent post-consumer-waste recycled paper. It contains wood fiber that has been recuperated entirely from paper used by consumers through recycling programs and has been de-inked.

 The Chlorine Free Products Association logo ensures that the paper was produced with advanced technologies free of chlorine chemistry. This stock is certified Processed Chlorine Free.

 The Environmental Choice Program logo, EcoLogo, identifies this book as being manufactured and supplied by companies that produce environmentally preferred products and services.

 The Biogas logo certifies that gas used in the paper-making process was produced from the decomposition of waste in a landfill and transported to the mill. Using this green energy substantially reduces greenhouse gas emissions.

 The Forest Stewardship Council logo certifies that the FSC has tracked the paper through a chain of custody, meaning that product and content come from well-managed and controlled sources.

This 12th edition is a tribute to 100 years of the *Boy Scout Handbook*, celebrating the historical significance of *Handbooks* past and present. As you progress through the ranks of Scouting, you will use this book as your guide. You will remember your youth and your adventures as a Scout, and you will cherish this book as a collectible.

 Watch the paper for this book being made and its pages being printed on the *Handbook* Web site, *www.bsahandbook.org*.

CONTENTS

Introduction   12

Your Adventure Begins   16

Scoutcraft

1. Leadership   44
2. Citizenship   66
3. Fitness   90
4. First Aid   122
5. Aquatics   178

Woodcraft

6. Nature   204
7. Leave No Trace   242

Campcraft

8. Hiking   260
9. Camping   284
10. Cooking   312
11. Navigation   344
12. Tools   376

Your Adventure Continues   418

Rank Requirements   432

Acknowledgments   448

Index   462

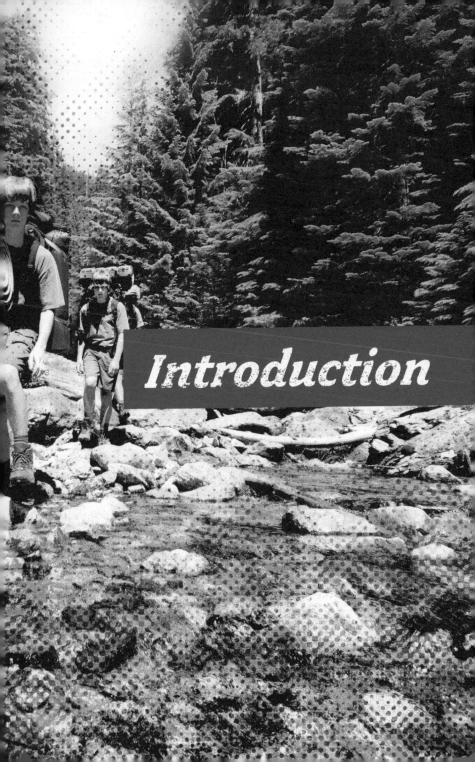

Introduction

"In these pages and throughout our organization we have made it obligatory upon our scouts that they cultivate courage, loyalty, patriotism, brotherliness, self-control, courtesy, kindness to animals, usefulness, cheerfulness, cleanliness, thrift, purity and honor. No one can doubt that with such training added to his native gifts, the American boy will in the near future, as a man, be an efficient leader in the paths of civilization and peace."

—From the preface to *Handbook for Boys*, 1911

INTRODUCTION

WELCOME TO SCOUTING'S SECOND CENTURY!

A hundred years ago, the first edition of the *Boy Scout Handbook* asked: "Would you like to be an expert camper who can always make himself comfortable out of doors, and a swimmer that fears no waters? Do you desire the knowledge to help the wounded quickly, and to make yourself cool and self-reliant in an emergency?"

The book went on to ask: "Do you believe in loyalty, courage, and kindness? Would you like to form habits that will surely make your success in life?"

Millions of boys through the decades have answered "Yes." They have laced up their hiking boots and set off on great adventures in the outdoors. They have served their families, their communities, and the nation. The values of Scouting have encouraged them to do their best with their abilities and have given them a foundation for success throughout their lives.

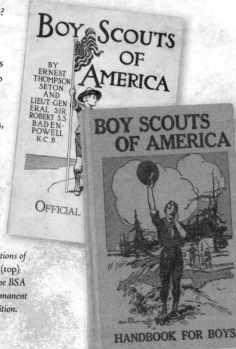

Shown here are both the original and the first editions of the Boy Scout Handbook. *The original edition (top) was intended as a temporary Handbook until the BSA could standardize the program and publish a permanent Handbook (right), known as the official first edition.*

The *Handbook* you are reading today is the first edition for Scouting's second century. It is asking the same kinds of important questions as that book from long ago:

▶ Are you ready to become an expert hiker and camper, to explore the natural world, and to meet challenges with good judgment and skill?

▶ Are you eager to make the most of yourself and succeed in the best ways possible?

▶ Do you want to become a leader and do all you can for your family, your neighborhood, and America?

▶ Would you like to develop lifelong friendships and a set of values that can guide you through the years to come?

▶ Do you want to understand your duties to your religious beliefs and your responsibilities in caring for the environment?

If you answered "Yes," then Scouting is for you. Join a troop and soon you will be hiking in open country and camping under the stars. You will learn first aid, become stronger physically and mentally, and practice leading yourself and others. The places you explore will become familiar as you discover plants, wildlife, and all else nature offers. You'll also learn how to enjoy the outdoors leaving no trace that you were ever there.

The *Boy Scout Handbook* is a guide to all of that and to much more. Throughout your life, you will face challenges as great as any you meet while camping and hiking. The Scout Oath and Scout Law provide guidelines for doing the right thing. As a Scout, you will be surrounded by friends and leaders who share your values.

Scouting has changed a great deal since the Boy Scouts of America was founded a hundred years ago. Camping gear is lighter and easier to use. Troop members set off on high adventures their grandfathers could not have even imagined. Scouts today use computers to plan their activities and Global Positioning System receivers to help find their way. The earliest Scouts could earn merit badges in Bee Farming, Blacksmithing, and Signaling. Scouts today can work on Cinematography, Nuclear Science, Oceanography, and plenty of other merit badges well-suited for the 21st century.

Not everything has changed, though. The Boy Scout pocketknife still looks the same and is used in the same way. The Scout Oath and Law are the same, too. Scouts still prepare themselves to do their best in emergencies and to care for their communities and the environment with Good Turns and other service projects. As steady as the Big Dipper and the North Star, the Scout Oath and Law have shown the way for millions of boys and men during their time as Scouts and throughout the rest of their lives.

The first edition of the *Boy Scout Handbook* divided Scouting's message into three parts—Scoutcraft, Woodcraft, and Campcraft. This centennial edition of the *Handbook* is organized the same way.

Scoutcraft Preparing for Scouting's adventures and for life

Woodcraft Understanding, appreciating, and caring for nature while you travel and live in the outdoors

Campcraft Learning skills useful along the trail, in camp, and beyond

Scouting continues to be an adventure that is filled with opportunities to learn, to have fun, and to become the best person possible. The pages ahead will lead you deep into Scouting. The more you learn, the more exciting and challenging your adventures will be. Together, Scoutcraft, Woodcraft, and Campcraft will guide you through much of what Scouting has to offer and will help you establish habits of success for the years to come.

More than 1 billion boys around the world have answered the call of Scouting over the last hundred years. You can be among the first Scouts of the BSA's second century. The challenge and adventure of Scouting are as strong as they have always been, and now you're invited.

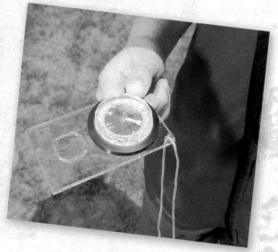

Adventure, learning, challenge, and responsibility—the promise of Scouting is all this and more. If you are ready for the adventure to begin, then let's get started.

PROGRAMS OF THE BSA

The Boy Scouts of America has programs that are just right for young people ages 7 and older. Adults can become involved as leaders and in other support roles with local Scouting units. At all levels, Scouting helps youth achieve the aims of strengthening character, physical and mental fitness, and good citizenship.

Cub Scouting is a year-round family program designed for boys who are 7 through 10 years old. Parents, leaders, and organizations work together to help Scouts learn and have fun.

Boy Scouting is a year-round program for boys ages 11 through 17. Through the Boy Scouting program, young men can achieve Scouting's aims through methods that include the ideals of the Scout Oath and Scout Law, patrols, outdoor adventures, advancement, association with adults, personal growth, leadership development, and the uniform.

Varsity Scouting is a program for young men who are at least 14 years old but not yet 18. They work toward the same ranks and merit badges as Boy Scouts, but they also participate in high-adventure activities and sports.

Venturing is for young men and women who are about 14 through 20 years of age. Venturing's purpose is to prepare young people to become responsible and caring adults.

Become a Scout.
Grow from the past.
Achieve today.
Be the future.

The mission of the Boy Scouts of America is to prepare young people to make ethical and moral choices over their lifetimes by instilling in them the values of the Scout Oath and Scout Law.

For up-to-date membership requirements for each program, visit www.scouting.org.

YOUR ADVENTURE BEGINS

A Scout troop is a group of boys and adult leaders taking part in the Scouting program. You might know of a troop chartered by a place of worship or an organization in your community. Maybe an older brother or some of your friends are already in a troop.

Troops within an area belong to one of more than 300 BSA local councils. Your local council can help you find a troop near your home. With your parent's permission, you can find your local council through the Boy Scouts of America's Internet Web sites: *www.scouting.org* (click "Local Councils" at the top of the page) or *www.thescoutzone.org* (select the "Troop Locator" link).

The Scoutmaster and Scouts of a troop you visit will welcome you and talk about the exciting activities in store for you. If you decide to become a member, they can guide you through the BSA's joining requirements.

Joining Requirements

☐ **Meet the age requirements.**
Be a boy who is 11 years old, or one who has completed the fifth grade or earned the Arrow of Light Award and is at least 10 years old, but is not yet 18 years old.

☐ Find a Scout troop near your home.

☐ Complete a Boy Scout application and health history signed by your parent or guardian.

☐ Repeat the Pledge of Allegiance. *(Page 19)*

☐ Demonstrate the Scout sign, salute, and handshake. *(Page 20)*

☐ Demonstrate tying the square knot (a joining knot). *(Page 21)*

☐ Understand and agree to live by the Scout Oath or Promise, Scout Law, motto, and slogan, and the Outdoor Code. *(Page 22)*

☐ Describe the Scout badge. *(Page 31)*

☐ Complete the pamphlet exercises. *(Page 34)*
With your parent or guardian, complete the exercises in the pamphlet How to Protect Your Children From Child Abuse: A Parent's Guide.

☐ Participate in a Scoutmaster conference. *(Page 34)*
Turn in your Boy Scout application and health history form signed by your parent or guardian, then participate in a Scoutmaster conference.

Tell Your Friends

Scouts who are already on the trail to Eagle can use this section of the *Handbook* as reference when introducing other boys to Scouting.

That's all there is to it! Your Scoutmaster and the Scouts in your troop will welcome you as a new member, and you can proudly wear the badge and uniform of the Boy Scouts of America.

 The BSA application form and health history form can be downloaded from the *Handbook* Web site: *www.bsahandbook.org.*

Repeat the Pledge of Allegiance

The pledge of allegiance is recited on many occasions where Americans honor their flag.

Pledge of Allegiance

I pledge allegiance to the Flag of the United States of America, and to the Republic for which it stands, one Nation under God, indivisible, with liberty and justice for all.

What the Pledge Means

I pledge allegiance . . . you promise to be loyal

to the Flag . . . to the symbol of your country

of the United States of America, . . . a nation of 50 states and several territories, each with certain rights of its own

and to the Republic . . . a country where the people elect representatives from among themselves to make laws for everyone

for which it stands, . . . the flag represents the values of our form of government, in which everyone is equal under the law

one Nation under God, . . . a country formed under God whose people are free to believe as they wish

indivisible, . . . the nation cannot be split into parts

with liberty and justice . . . with freedom and a system of law

for all. . . . for every person in the nation, regardless of their differences

Practice saying "one Nation under God" without hesitating in the middle of the phrase.

Demonstrate the Scout Sign, Salute, and Handshake

Scouts greet one another and show they are members of the BSA with the Scout sign, salute, and handshake.

Scout Sign

Make the Scout sign by covering the nail of the little finger of your right hand with your right thumb, then raising your right arm with your elbow at a right angle and holding the three middle fingers of your hand upward.

The three fingers stand for the three parts of the Scout Oath:

▶ **Duty to God and country**

▶ **Duty to others**

▶ **Duty to yourself**

Your thumb and little finger touch to represent the bond uniting Scouts throughout the world.

Give the Scout sign each time you say the Scout Oath and Scout Law. When a Scout or Scouter raises the Scout sign, all Scouts should make the sign, too, and come to silent attention.

Scout Salute

Form the Scout sign with your right hand, then finish the salute by bringing that hand up, palm down, until your forefinger touches the brim of your hat or the tip of your right eyebrow.

The Scout salute is a form of greeting that also shows respect. Use it to salute the flag of the United States of America. You may also salute other Scouts and Scout leaders.

Scout Handshake

Extend your left hand to another Scout and firmly grasp his left hand. Made with the hand nearest your heart, the Scout handshake signifies friendship.

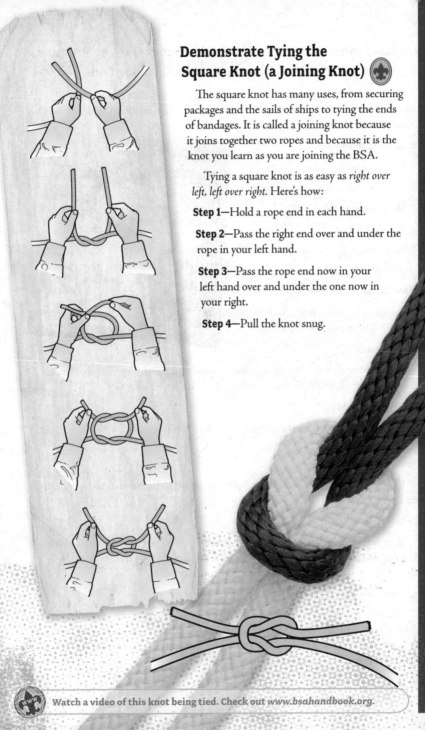

Demonstrate Tying the Square Knot (a Joining Knot)

The square knot has many uses, from securing packages and the sails of ships to tying the ends of bandages. It is called a joining knot because it joins together two ropes and because it is the knot you learn as you are joining the BSA.

Tying a square knot is as easy as *right over left, left over right*. Here's how:

Step 1—Hold a rope end in each hand.

Step 2—Pass the right end over and under the rope in your left hand.

Step 3—Pass the rope end now in your left hand over and under the one now in your right.

Step 4—Pull the knot snug.

Watch a video of this knot being tied. Check out *www.bsahandbook.org*.

Understand and Agree to Live by the Scout Oath or Promise, Scout Law, Motto, and Slogan, and the Outdoor Code

Every Scout for a hundred years has pledged to guide his thoughts and actions according to the Scout Oath, Scout Law, motto, and slogan, and the Outdoor Code. Now it is your turn.

Scout Oath or Promise

On my honor I will do my best

To do my duty to God and my country

and to obey the Scout Law;

To help other people at all times;

To keep myself physically strong,

mentally awake, and morally straight.

What the Scout Oath or Promise Means

Before you agree to the Scout Oath or Promise, you must know what it means.

On my honor ...

Honor is the core of who you are—your honesty, your integrity, your reputation, the ways you treat others, and how you act when you are on your own.

I will do my best ...

Do all you can to live by the Scout Oath, even when you are faced with difficult challenges.

To do my duty ...

Duty is what others expect of you, but more importantly it is what you expect of yourself.

to God ...

Your family and religious leaders teach you about God and the ways you can serve. You can do your duty to God by following the wisdom of those teachings and by defending the rights of others to practice their own beliefs.

and my country ...

Help the United States continue to be a strong and fair nation by learning about our system of government and your responsibilities as a citizen. When you do all you can for your family and community, you are serving your country. Making the most of your opportunities will help shape our nation's future.

and to obey the Scout Law; . . .

In your thoughts, words, and deeds, the 12 points of the Scout Law will lead you toward doing the right thing throughout your life.

To help other people at all times; . . .

By helping out whenever you can, you are making the world better. "At all times" is a reminder to help even when it is difficult and even without waiting to be asked.

To keep myself physically strong, . . .

Taking care of your body prepares you for a lifetime of great adventures. You can build your body's strength and endurance by eating nutritious foods, getting enough sleep, and being active. You should also avoid tobacco, alcohol, illegal drugs, and anything else that might harm your health.

mentally awake, . . .

Develop your mind both in and outside of the classroom. Be curious about everything around you, and never stop learning.

and morally straight.

Your relationships with others should be honest and open. Respect and defend the rights of all people. Be clean in your speech and actions and faithful in your religious beliefs. Values you practice as a Scout will help you shape a life of virtue and self-reliance.

Scouting's adventures will help you fulfill the last part of the Oath—staying strong and fit.

ArrowCorps⁵, 2008

Scout Law

A Scout is trustworthy, loyal, helpful, friendly, courteous, kind, obedient, cheerful, thrifty, brave, clean, and reverent.

What the Scout Law Means

The Scout Law will show you how to live as a boy and as a man.

A Scout is trustworthy. A Scout tells the truth. He is honest, and he keeps his promises. People can depend on him.

A Scout is loyal. A Scout is loyal to those to whom loyalty is due.

A Scout is helpful. A Scout cares about other people. He helps others without expecting payment or reward. He fulfills his duties to his family by helping at home.

A Scout is friendly. A Scout is a friend to all. He is a brother to other Scouts. He offers his friendship to people of all races, religions, and nations, and respects them even if their beliefs and customs are different from his own.

A Scout is courteous. A Scout is polite to people of all ages and positions. He understands that using good manners makes it easier for people to get along.

A Scout is kind. A Scout treats others as he wants to be treated. He knows there is strength in being gentle. He does not harm or kill any living thing without good reason.

A Scout is obedient. A Scout follows the rules of his family, school, and troop. He obeys the laws of his community and country. If he thinks these rules and laws are unfair, he seeks to have them changed in an orderly way.

A Scout is cheerful. A Scout looks for the bright side of life. He cheerfully does tasks that come his way and tries his best to make others happy, too.

A Scout is thrifty. A Scout works to pay his way and to help others. He saves for the future. He protects and conserves natural resources. He is careful in his use of time and property.

A Scout is brave. A Scout faces danger even if he is afraid.

A Scout is clean. A Scout keeps his body and mind fit. He chooses friends who also live by high standards. He avoids profanity and pornography. He helps keep his home and community clean.

A Scout is reverent. A Scout is reverent toward God. He is faithful in his religious duties. He respects the beliefs of others.

What the Scout Motto Means

Be Prepared. That's the Boy Scout motto.

"Be prepared for what?" someone once asked Robert Baden-Powell, the founder of Scouting.

"Why, for any old thing," he replied.

Training in Scoutcraft, woodcraft, and campcraft will help you live up to the Scout motto. You will be prepared if someone is hurt, because you know first aid. Because you will have practiced lifesaving skills, you might be able to save a nonswimmer struggling in deep water. Whenever leadership is needed, you will understand what to do.

Baden-Powell wasn't thinking only of being ready for emergencies. His idea was that Scouts should prepare themselves to become productive citizens and strong leaders and to bring joy to other people. He wanted each Scout to be ready in mind and body and to meet with a strong heart whatever challenges await him.

Be prepared for life—to live happily and without regret, knowing that you have done your best. Being prepared financially is a particularly important skill you can practice by saving at least half of what you earn.

What the Scout Slogan Means

The Scout slogan is *Do a Good Turn daily.* That means doing something to help others each day without expecting anything in return. It means doing your part to care for your community and the environment, too.

Keep a Good Turn coin like this in your pocket to help you remember the Scout slogan.

Some Good Turns are big—service after floods or other disasters, rescuing someone from a dangerous situation, recycling community trash, or completing conservation projects with your patrol.

Good Turns also can be small, thoughtful acts—helping a child cross a busy street, going to the store for an elderly neighbor, cutting back weeds blocking a sign, or doing something special for a brother or sister.

From recycling to helping conserve America's natural resources, opportunities for Good Turns are everywhere.

The Importance of a Good Turn

A Good Turn was what brought Scouting to America. More than a hundred years ago on the foggy streets of London, England, American businessman William Boyce lost his way. A boy walked up and asked if he could help. Mr. Boyce explained where he wanted to go, and the boy led him there. The grateful American wanted to give the boy some money, but the boy said, "No, thank you, sir. I am a Scout. I won't take anything for helping."

Mr. Boyce was so impressed by the boy's actions that he learned more about the Boy Scout movement that was just beginning in Great Britain and about its founder, Robert Baden-Powell. Mr. Boyce realized that many boys in the United States would want to be Scouts, too.

On February 8, 1910, Mr. Boyce and a group of businessmen, educators, and political leaders founded the Boy Scouts of America. Today, Scouts celebrate that date as the birthday of the BSA.

No one knows what happened to the boy who guided Mr. Boyce through the London fog, but he will never be forgotten. Like many acts of kindness, what was done proved to be far more important than who did it. In helping bring Scouting to America, the boy's simple Good Turn has been multiplied millions of times over as Scouts through the decades have followed his example.

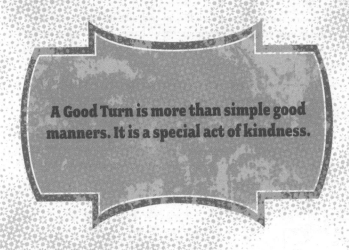

A Good Turn is more than simple good manners. It is a special act of kindness.

Outdoor Code

As an American, I will do my best to

Be clean in my outdoor manners,

Be careful with fire,

Be considerate in the outdoors,

and

Be conservation-minded.

What the Outdoor Code Means

The Outdoor Code reminds Scouts of the importance of caring for the environment. Its ideals take on special meaning whenever you are camping, hiking, and taking part in other outdoor events.

Being clean in your manners, careful with fire, and considerate means you can enjoy the outdoors in ways that do the environment no harm. For example, using the principles of Leave No Trace, you can hike and camp in an area without leaving any signs that you were there.

Being conservation-minded encourages the protection and thoughtful use of natural resources. You also can do your part in service projects that improve the condition of wildlife, water, air, forests, and the land itself.

Wisdom you gain about the outdoors through your Scouting experiences can direct your actions wherever you are, whatever you do, and at every stage of your life. Your commitment to the Outdoor Code will make a positive difference in the quality of the environment today and for generations to come.

Scout Spirit

You show Scout spirit by making the Scout Oath, Scout Law, motto, and slogan part of your life. Many of the requirements for Scout ranks can be measured by other people. When you set out to swim 25 yards for the Second Class swimming requirement, anyone can see that you have covered the distance.

How well you live the Scout Oath and Scout Law can be judged by you and by others. You know when you are being kind and when you are helpful and a good friend. You know when you are trustworthy and reverent. You know how you act when no one is around to see what you do.

Do your best to live each day by the Scout Oath and Scout Law. You may look back on some of your decisions and wish you had acted differently, but you can learn from those moments and promise yourself to do better in the future.

As you use the Scout Oath and Scout Law for guidance, don't be surprised when others recognize those values in you and respect you for it. When a non-Scout tells you that you are behaving like a Boy Scout, that's a good sign that you have Scout spirit. Set high standards for yourself and strive to reach them. Ask nothing less of yourself, and no one can ask anything more of you.

"You prove that you have caught this spirit by the way you help in patrol, troop, home, school, church or synagogue, and community and your habits of caring for your own things and protecting the properties of others."

—*Boy Scout Handbook*, 6th ed., 1959

The Scout Oath and Scout Law are not meant just to be recited at troop meetings, and they are not to be obeyed just while you are wearing a Scout uniform. The spirit of Scouting is always important—at home, at school, and in your community.

The standards set by the Scout Oath and Scout Law are very high. Strive to reach them every day, and you will find that they become as natural for you to live by as they are for you to say.

Describe the Scout Badge

The Scout badge is shaped like the north point on an old compass. The design is also known as a trefoil (a flower with three leaves) or a fleur-de-lis (the French name for an iris flower). It is the basic shape of the badges worn by Scouts in other countries, too.

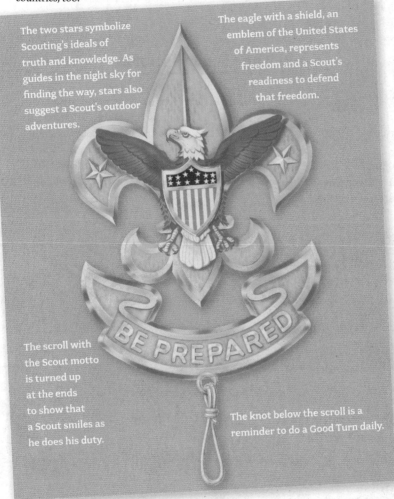

The two stars symbolize Scouting's ideals of truth and knowledge. As guides in the night sky for finding the way, stars also suggest a Scout's outdoor adventures.

The eagle with a shield, an emblem of the United States of America, represents freedom and a Scout's readiness to defend that freedom.

BE PREPARED

The scroll with the Scout motto is turned up at the ends to show that a Scout smiles as he does his duty.

The knot below the scroll is a reminder to do a Good Turn daily.

The shape of the Scout badge signifies a Scout's ability to point the right way in life just as a compass does in the wilderness. The three points of the trefoil, like the three raised fingers of the Scout sign, represent the three parts of the Scout Oath—duty to God and country, duty to others, and duty to yourself.

"Putting on the uniform does not make a fellow a Scout, but putting on the uniform is a sign to the world that one has taken the Scout obligations and folk expect Scout-like acts from one wearing it."

—*Handbook for Boys*, 1927

Your Scout Uniform

The Scout uniform is a symbol of the BSA. It tells others that you are a Scout and represents Scouting's history of service to the nation and the world. Wearing uniforms allows Scouts to show that they are equals and that they share values and beliefs. Your uniform is also a sign that you are a person who can be trusted and that you will lend a hand whenever help is needed. Dressed as a Scout, you will want to act as a Scout.

Whether your uniform includes a Scout neckerchief is up to the troop. To wear a neckerchief, first roll the long edge to about 6 inches from the tip. Place the neckerchief smoothly around your neck, either over or under the collar, depending on your troop's custom. Hold the neckerchief in place with a neckerchief slide.

 For more about how to properly wear the official uniform, visit the *Handbook* Web site: www.bsahandbook.org.

The BSA's official uniform includes a Scout shirt, Scout pants or Scout shorts, Scout belt, Scout socks, and shoes or hiking boots. Your troop may also elect to wear a cap or broad-brimmed hat. Your uniform may be brand-new, or it might have been worn by others for many troop activities. Proudly wear your uniform to troop meetings, ceremonies such as courts of honor, and most other indoor troop functions. When you're headed outdoors, you can pull on a T-shirt with Scout pants or shorts, or wear other clothing that is right for the events of the day.

With Your Parent or Guardian, Complete the Exercises in the Pamphlet *How to Protect Your Children From Child Abuse*

Inside the cover of this *Handbook* is a pamphlet that is part of the BSA's commitment to ensuring the safety of young people wherever they may be. The pamphlet is meant to be shared by a Scout and his parent or guardian.

Participate in a Scoutmaster Conference

The last joining requirement instructs you to participate in a Scoutmaster conference. Your Scoutmaster will visit with you after you finish the requirements for each Scout rank.

Every Scoutmaster conference is an opportunity for you to review how you are doing and to begin planning your next steps. You can ask questions, share what you like about being a Scout, and figure out ways to make your Scouting experience even better.

YOUR TROOP

The troop you are joining is an organization of boys enjoying the challenges of Scouting. Your Scoutmaster and other adult leaders will help Scouts become good leaders, then will step back and allow the troop's youth leaders to take charge of planning and carrying out activities.

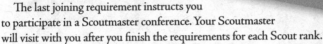

A GOOD TURN DAILY

The chart that follows shows how a large Scout troop is organized. Your troop might be big like this one, or quite a bit smaller. It might have a long history or could be brand new. Leaders might have years of experience or could be learning their roles as they go. Whatever your troop is like, you can proudly wear its number on the sleeve of your uniform and know that everyone is working along with you to make the troop a success.

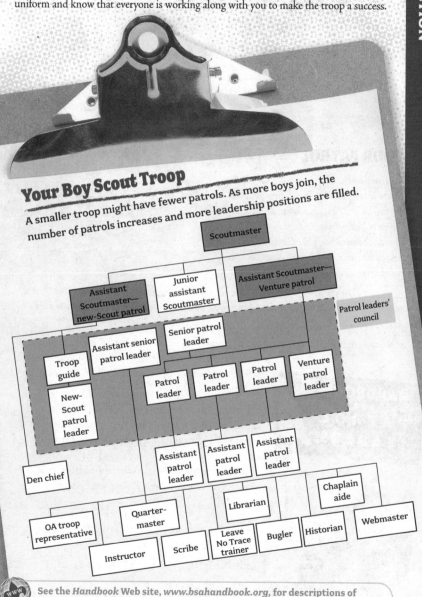

Your Boy Scout Troop

A smaller troop might have fewer patrols. As more boys join, the number of patrols increases and more leadership positions are filled.

See the *Handbook* Web site, *www.bsahandbook.org*, for descriptions of these troop leadership positions.

YOUR PATROL

The Boy Scout troop you join will be made up of patrols. Your patrol will be a team of young men who make things happen. You will learn together, make plans, and turn your ideas into action. Together, your patrol can achieve much more than each of you would on your own.

A patrol of six to eight Scouts is the right size for many outdoor adventures. A few tents will shelter everyone on camping trips, and a couple of backpacking stoves are enough for cooking patrol meals.

Patrols are so important to Scouting that most troop meetings include time for each patrol to meet by itself. Other patrol meetings might take place at a special patrol site or in the home of one of its members.

Everyone in your patrol will have skills and knowledge to share. You can teach one another what you know. Hikes and campouts give your patrol a chance to put its knowledge to good use. As friends, you can look out for one another. Friendship, fun, and adventure—that's what a Scout patrol is all about.

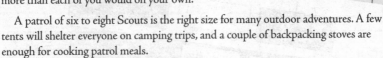

"A good Patrol is a gang of good friends, standing shoulder to shoulder whatever comes. 'All for One—One for All'—that's the spirit of a Scout Patrol."

—*Handbook for Patrol Leaders*, 1950

In 1907, Robert Baden-Powell hosted Scouting's first camp on Brownsea Island off the coast of England. The boys were divided into four patrols—the Ravens, Wolves, Curlews, and Bulls.

Kinds of Patrols

A Scout troop can have three kinds of patrols:

New-Scout Patrols—The new-Scout patrol is made up of guys who have just become Scouts. An experienced Scout, called a troop guide, helps show the way. An assistant Scoutmaster assigned to the patrol gives it added support.

Members of a new-Scout patrol choose their patrol leader and plan what they want to do. They take part in troop meetings and activities. As they learn hiking and camping skills, they also will start completing requirements for the Tenderfoot, Second Class, and First Class ranks.

Regular Patrols—Scouts who hold the rank of First Class or higher can be members of regular patrols. Older Scouts who have not yet reached First Class also may join a troop's regular patrols and continue to complete the First Class requirements.

Venture Patrols—Many troops have a Venture patrol for older Scouts who are eager to set out on rugged, high-adventure activities. Being part of a Venture patrol gives older Scouts the opportunity to stay active in their troops. They also may use their knowledge to enrich the Scouting experience for themselves and for other troop members.

Your Patrol's Name, Flag, and Emblem

Your patrol can also choose a name for itself. You might name your patrol after an animal, as the Brownsea Island Scouts did. Through the years, many patrols have named themselves for trees (the Pine Tree Patrol) or people (the Baden-Powell Patrol, perhaps, or the Daniel Boone Patrol). You can do that, too, or you might want to be known by a name special to members of your patrol—the Mechanics Patrol, for example, or the Superstars, the Brainiacs, or something else that says something about who you all are.

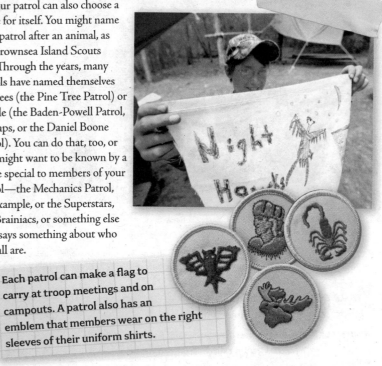

Each patrol can make a flag to carry at troop meetings and on campouts. A patrol also has an emblem that members wear on the right sleeves of their uniform shirts.

Patrol Yell

Patrols have yells, too. If your patrol is named for an animal, you can use that animal's sound—the howl of a wolf, for example, or the hoot of an owl. Any patrol might choose an animal's call or decide on some other shout that identifies it. Members can give the patrol yell whenever the patrol does well in a troop competition or reaches an important goal, and even when they're ready to chow down on a camp meal.

Patrol Leaders' Council

Your patrol will elect a leader to help the patrol reach its goals. The senior patrol leader, the chief youth leader of the troop, gives guidance, too. The patrol leaders will meet with the senior patrol leader and his assistants at a patrol leaders' council to plan the troop's programs and activities. Your patrol leader will represent the wishes of your patrol as decisions are being made. High on the list of things discussed at patrol leaders' council meetings are upcoming adventures—that often means going camping.

YOUR FIRST SCOUT CAMPOUT

Soon after you join a troop, you'll be on your way to your first campout. You might go to a park near your home or to a Scout camp far away. Perhaps you'll be surrounded by mountains, farm fields, or the skyline of your city. The campsite might be near a road, or you might have to carry a backpack and hike a few miles down a trail to get there. Wherever you go, expect to find plenty of challenge and adventure.

BUDDY SYSTEM

For many outdoor activities, Scouting uses the buddy system to help ensure everyone's safety. You and a buddy can watch out for each other during a campout by checking in now and then to be sure everything is all right.

YOU'RE ON YOUR WAY!

Going to meetings and camping with your troop and patrol will give you an idea of all that you can do as a Scout. You'll also discover that your troop's leaders and Scouts are there to guide you along the way. You're going to have great times together!

Write a few notes on this page so that you will always remember where your adventures as a Boy Scout began.

My First Campout

Date: _____

Where did we go? _____

_____

_____

_____

_____

Who came along? _____

_____

_____

_____

_____

What did we see? _____

_____

_____

_____

_____

What did we eat? _____

_____

_____

_____

_____

How was the weather? _____

_____

_____

What did I like most about the campout? _____

_____

_____

_____

What did I not like? _____

_____

_____

_____

What did I learn that I will use on future campouts? _____

_____

_____

_____

_____

In the back of this *Handbook*, you'll find a page you can use to record your Scout campouts and service projects.

▶ Scout Camping Log, pages 444, 446

▶ Scout Service Log, pages 445, 447

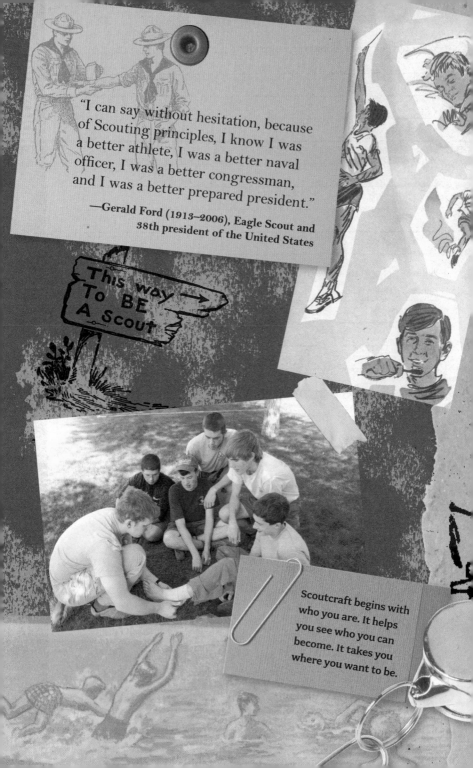

"I can say without hesitation, because of Scouting principles, I know I was a better athlete, I was a better naval officer, I was a better congressman, and I was a better prepared president."

—Gerald Ford (1913–2006), Eagle Scout and 38th president of the United States

This way → To BE A Scout

Scoutcraft begins with who you are. It helps you see who you can become. It takes you where you want to be.

Scoutcraft is what you do to prepare yourself to be the best Scout you can be. It's about making the most of your talents to become an effective leader and a good citizen. It means getting into good physical shape so that you are ready for the outdoors, for sports, and for remaining healthy.

Scoutcraft also means staying mentally awake by understanding how you learn and by exploring the world around you. It includes understanding how to get along with others and using good judgment to make wise decisions.

Mastering the first-aid skills of Scoutcraft will help you manage risk and act effectively during an emergency. Once you pass the BSA swimmer test, for example, you'll be prepared for Scouting's aquatics activities and journeys on rivers and lakes.

Scoutcraft skills provide the building blocks you need to become a responsible young man. They will help you apply the Scout Oath and Scout Law in your daily life. They can guide you as you become a leader in your patrol and troop, and in your responsibilities as a member of your family and a citizen of your community and nation.

Leadership

LEADERSHIP

Leadership starts with leading the person you know best—yourself. You might be surprised to learn that you've already developed some important leadership skills.

Before you joined your troop, you thought about what being a Scout is like. Maybe you imagined hitting the trail with your friends. You could almost see yourself arriving at a campsite, pitching your tent, and settling in for a night under the stars.

With that picture in mind, you figured out the steps to make it happen. First, you had to find a neighborhood Boy Scout troop. Next, you recited the Scout Oath and Scout Law, tied a square knot, and completed the other joining requirements before helping your patrol plan your first campout.

You completed those steps one at a time. Locating a troop was as easy as calling your BSA local council or visiting a troop you knew about. You might have asked an older Scout to teach you to tie a square knot. Scouts in your troop helped you with the other joining requirements and showed you how to get ready for camping.

Before long, you were hiking into camp with a big grin on your face. You had an idea of what your first Scouting adventure would look like, and now it was happening. You took responsibility for leading yourself to an experience you wanted to have. You followed through until you were right in the middle of that picture.

IN THIS CHAPTER

▶ Self-leadership

▶ Forming, researching, and achieving your vision of success

▶ Leading others in your troop, your family, and your community

▶ Stages of leadership

▶ Making good choices

Self-Leadership Is...

▶ Having a vision of where you want to be

▶ Figuring out the steps to get there

▶ Completing those steps one at a time

Growth of a Leader (1966), by Norman Rockwell

47

WHERE DO YOU WANT TO BE?

You are a collection of wonderful talents, ideas, and experiences. Your skills and interests are possibilities. They are hints of where you can go, what you can accomplish, and who you will become.

What do you want your future to look like tomorrow? Next week? Ten years from now? Success begins with a vision—picturing yourself where you want to be.

Perhaps you have seen someone doing something you would love to do—handling a sailboat, constructing a snow cave, designing a Web site, building a tree house, or climbing a mountain. Do you enjoy writing stories or doing science experiments? Are you in a choir or a band? Your teachers, coaches, teams, and clubs might help you see yourself becoming a better athlete, playing first-rate chess, speaking another language, mastering mathematics, or pursuing other areas you like. Maybe learning about the people and cultures of other countries interests you, and you'd like to visit those countries someday.

Scouting will open many doors to learning for you. As a Scout, you'll meet people who have interesting careers. While training in first aid, you might meet medical professionals and emergency responders. While hiking in parks and forests, you'll meet rangers, wildlife experts, and others who are doing exciting work you might like to learn.

Scouting's merit badge program will encourage you to sample more than a hundred subjects—everything from American Business, Archery, and Automotive Maintenance to Weather, Wilderness Survival, and Woodwork. You'll have a great time discovering new skills. You might even find yourself launched on a lifelong interest that could become a career.

DOING THE RESEARCH

When you picture what you want to accomplish, you can start making that vision real. You'll need good information to make that happen, which means you're going to have to do some research. Doing research is part of making success happen, and it's part of the fun, too.

Ways to research information include:

▶ Observing

▶ Asking and listening

▶ Reading

▶ Writing

▶ Teaching

Requirements for all merit badges can be found at *www.scouting.org/BoyScouts/AdvancementandAwards/MeritBadges.aspx*, and the most current merit badge pamphlets are available at *www.scoutstuff.org*.

Observing

Observation skills are important in many pursuits. For example, you can make sense out of a map only if you pay attention to landmarks. When you notice changes in the clouds, you can set up your tent before a storm breaks. When you sit quietly in the woods, you might observe animals that would otherwise stay hidden.

The same is true of anything you want to learn about. Observe how someone paddles a canoe so that it glides straight across the water. Watch the way a crew repairs a street or carpenters put up a house. Notice where birds are nesting and what they are doing. Pay attention as Scouts teach campcraft skills, and you will understand much more than you did before.

Asking and Listening

When you are curious about something, ask. When you don't understand, ask. When you want additional information, ask. When you aren't sure what to do next, ask. Asking questions like, "Could you show me how this works?", "Can you please tell me why this happens?", and "Is there a better way to get this done?" can save you from wasting time and effort.

People generally are pleased to share what they know. Ask politely, then give them all of your attention as you listen to their answers. If someone is busy, you might need to find another time for him or her to talk with you. But there are no silly questions or questions that are too simple. Unless you ask, you might never know.

Reading

Through the magic of reading, you can imagine what it would be like to strap yourself into a rocket and blast into space. Reading can take your imagination to many places. You might find yourself hoisting the anchor of a pirate ship and sailing across the sea or shrinking to the size of a blood cell and swimming through the human body. You might even watch dinosaurs stride across prehistoric lands.

Books can be flying carpets, time machines, and telescopes. Open a book and travel to the far reaches of Earth, to the inside of an atom, and to the most distant stars. Visit famous men and women throughout the centuries, or read about what's on the minds of young people all over the world.

Books also teach. Do you know what makes a computer work? Can you perform two really good magic tricks or juggle three balls at once? Do you know how to find a summer job? Would you like to be able to say "hello" in a different language? Books can teach you all that and much more. They can spark your imagination and increase your understanding of what is possible. Reading helps you develop a bigger picture of what you would like to do and where you want to be.

Librarians at your school and in public libraries can help you find books about subjects you like—just ask. They'll guide you to videos and DVDs, audio recordings, and plenty of other electronic resources. Get a library card and you can take home books and other library materials that interest you.

The Internet is a tremendous source of reading material. Computer search engines can take you directly to information you are seeking and link you to related subjects. For example, the *Boy Scout Handbook* Web site—*www.bsahandbook.com*—is a good way to begin exploring a wealth of Scouting knowledge and lore. (Be sure to get your parent's permission before exploring the Internet.)

Reading is a window to the past and the future. It is a doorway to discovery. Read, read, and read some more. It will entertain you, expand your mind, and introduce you to fresh possibilities you can explore.

Internet Tips

Follow these three guidelines whenever you go online.

▶ Don't respond to messages or Web sites that you know are meant only for adults or that make you feel uneasy.

▶ Don't share personal information such as your address, telephone number, school name, or your parent's work address or telephone number. Never send photos via the Internet without your parent's permission.

▶ Never meet anyone who has contacted you online unless your parent or guardian goes with you.

 Visit *www.bsahandbook.com* to learn how to recognize legitimate sites and avoid cyberbullies.

Writing

Writing is a terrific way to organize information you've researched or learned in a way that makes sense to you and to others. It is an important leadership tool for developing a vision of future success and for setting goals. Putting words on paper can be very satisfying and a lot of fun.

Explorers and travelers often record what they see by writing in a journal. Scientists take notes about experiments they conduct. Sailors keep a ship's log. Many Scout patrols have a trip book in which they write about each of their campouts and hikes.

Try keeping a journal of your own. Use a notebook and write a little every day about what you have seen and done. Include drawings, photos, stories from newspapers or magazines, and anything else that interests you. If you prefer, use a computer to keep a journal or Internet blog. A blog also is a great way to record and share your Scouting activities and to stay in touch with your patrol between meetings.

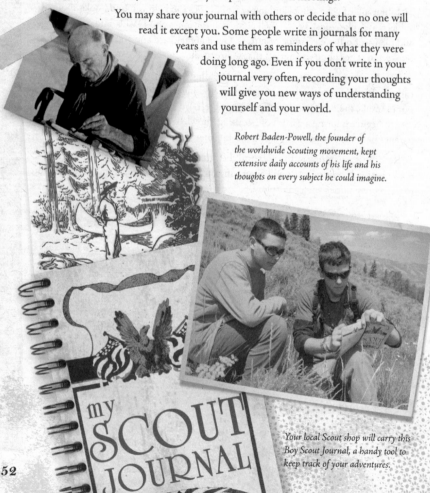

You may share your journal with others or decide that no one will read it except you. Some people write in journals for many years and use them as reminders of what they were doing long ago. Even if you don't write in your journal very often, recording your thoughts will give you new ways of understanding yourself and your world.

Robert Baden-Powell, the founder of the worldwide Scouting movement, kept extensive daily accounts of his life and his thoughts on every subject he could imagine.

Your local Scout shop will carry this Boy Scout Journal, a handy tool to keep track of your adventures.

Scouting's Teaching EDGE

Use the Teaching **EDGE** to teach others a skill.

▶ **E**xplain how it is done.

▶ **D**emonstrate the steps.

▶ **G**uide learners as they practice.

▶ **E**nable them to succeed on their own.

Teaching

A Scout is helpful. Scouts live up to that point of the Scout Law by sharing what they know. Teaching someone helps you to become better at using a skill, too. You can think of it as hands-on research.

You can use Scouting's Teaching EDGE any time you are helping others learn. First, think carefully about how to explain to others the way the skill is done. Then demonstrate the steps and guide them as they practice. Lastly, provide the support they need to enable them to use the new skill on their own.

That's what happened when you learned to tie the square knot as you were joining your troop. Another Scout explained the knot to you and then demonstrated how to tie it. Then he gave the rope to you and guided you through the steps. The two of you kept at it until he had enabled you to tie a square knot by yourself.

Two leadership training courses for Boy Scouts teach how to put the EDGE method into practice. Visit *www.bsahandbook.com* for more information on National Youth Leadership Training (NYLT) and National Advanced Youth Leadership Experience (NAYLE).

REACHING YOUR GOALS

The world is full of exciting opportunities. By forming a vision of what you want to do and where you want to be, you'll be well on your way to achieving a goal.

Scouting's trail to Eagle is a good example of how self-leadership can help you make great things happen. Seeing yourself as an Eagle Scout begins to make earning Scouting's highest rank a real possibility for you. By committing yourself to becoming an Eagle, you can figure out the steps to get from where you are now to where you want to be.

There are dozens of requirements to fulfill to become an Eagle Scout. Of course, you aren't going to be able to complete them all at once. You can begin with the requirements for Tenderfoot and take them on one at a time.

Scout

You'll need to manage your time, stay motivated by the progress you are making, and ask for help when you need it. You will find plenty of satisfaction in your Scouting experiences along the trail to Eagle. You'll also know that you really are advancing toward that vision of success you've set for yourself. One day you'll be standing before your troop at a court of honor receiving your Eagle Scout medal.

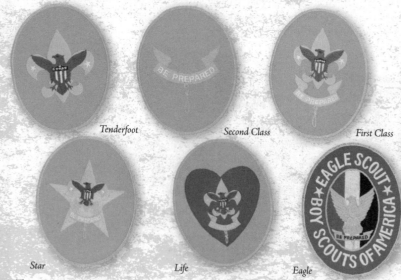

Tenderfoot   *Second Class*   *First Class*

Star   *Life*   *Eagle*

The steps to earn the Eagle Scout Award are the requirements for each of Scouting's ranks.

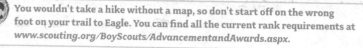

You wouldn't take a hike without a map, so don't start off on the wrong foot on your trail to Eagle. You can find all the current rank requirements at *www.scouting.org/BoyScouts/AdvancementandAwards.aspx.*

Boards of Review

Once you complete all the requirements to advance one rank and have participated in a Scoutmaster conference, your Scoutmaster will arrange a board of review for you. The review board usually is made up of members of the troop committee. The purpose of the review is to give you the opportunity to talk about how you are getting along in the troop, and to review the rank requirements to ensure that they have been met.

You can use the same method to move toward any goal you want to reach. Break down a big challenge into small steps, then complete them one at a time.

Eagle
Scout
Award

Short-Term and Long-Term Goals

Some goals—short-term goals—can be reached quickly. For example, suppose you are leading a game at a troop meeting. You might take the following steps:

1. Read about games in a book or on the Internet.

2. Choose a game for the troop.

3. Gather any materials that you will need.

4. Get everyone together and explain the rules.

Bigger goals—long-term goals—may require weeks, months, or even years to reach. Do you dream of being an airline pilot? A marine biologist? A guitarist? A basketball player? All these goals require considerable time to learn to do well, but this doesn't mean you can't achieve them. Follow the same plan you would with a short-term goal. Figure out the steps leading toward what you want to do. Stick with your plan, taking it step by step, and you will reach your goal.

Sometimes the hardest part of accomplishing something is just getting started. Ask people how you can achieve something that interests you. Their suggestions will help you see the pathway to follow. Open a book and start reading, and you'll find that the ideas will begin to flow. Stand at a trailhead with your pack on your shoulders, and take that first step. Nothing can hold you back.

"To make our way, we must have firm resolve, persistence, tenacity. We must gear ourselves to work hard all the way. We can never let up."

—Dr. Ralph Bunche (1903–1971), recipient of the Nobel Peace Prize for his efforts on behalf of the United Nations and of the Silver Buffalo Award, Scouting's highest honor, for his extraordinary service to youth

Silver Buffalo Award

LEADING OTHERS

You will have many opportunities as a Scout to lead members of your patrol and troop. Perhaps you've been part of a flag ceremony opening a troop meeting. Maybe you led the troop in reciting the Scout Oath and Scout Law. You might have helped your patrol plan and pack food for your first campout. You may already be using a map and compass or a GPS receiver to help lead the way during hikes.

Leading others means wanting them to succeed and then doing what you can to help them reach their goals. That's as true for a flag ceremony as for a backpacking trip. Guiding people toward their visions of success is good for them, and for you, too. When your patrol does well, everybody moves ahead. As your troop progresses, each of you wins.

The Silver Buffalo Award is the BSA's most prestigious honor for adults. To learn more about it and other BSA awards like the Silver Beaver and Silver Antelope, visit *www.bsahandbook.com*.

For example, your patrol might decide it's time for another camping trip. This time the patrol's vision of a successful adventure includes hiking, fishing, and learning about constellations in the night sky.

To do all of that, you'll want to figure out the steps to make the picture real. You'll need to decide where to go and what to take. You will have to gather your fishing tackle, find star charts, and map out a hiking route. Then you'll need to complete each step as part of your preparation for the trip. Your efforts to support and guide your patrol every step of the way are signs of leadership.

Your troop uses the same leadership methods. Patrol leaders get together with the senior patrol leader and adult leaders—the patrol leaders' council. They consider ideas from all the Scouts and develop a vision for what the troop can achieve in the weeks and months ahead. The patrol leaders' council will lay out the steps that lead toward that vision and decide how to complete each step to keep the troop moving toward its goals.

STAGES OF LEADERSHIP

Leadership and teaching are closely related. Think again about learning to tie a square knot. Another Scout used Scouting's Teaching EDGE to explain, demonstrate, guide, and enable you to tie the knot.

A good leader can help a group such as a Scout patrol work through the same stages with a project that the patrol members are doing. At the beginning, the patrol's enthusiasm is high, but it can turn to discouragement as the work becomes hard. A leader can help by explaining and demonstrating what to do. This encourages group members not to give up while at the same time showing them how to tackle difficulties. As the group's skills and motivation increase, the leader can step back and guide the group as it begins to succeed. When the group members have the ability and enthusiasm to move ahead on their own, the leader enables them to keep going by providing support when they ask for it.

The *Handbook* Web site—*www.bsahandbook.com*—will help you learn more about how the patrol leaders' council works.

LEADERSHIP IN YOUR PATROL AND TROOP

Some of your fellow Scouts wear leadership patches on the sleeves of their uniform shirts. Your patrol leader wears one with two green bars. The senior patrol leader's patch has three bars. There are patches identifying your troop's scribe, quartermaster, and chaplain. Adult leaders—Scouters—also have special patches.

Descriptions of all the troop and patrol positions of responsibility can be found at *www.bsahandbook.com*.

The patches let you know that these people are ready to help your patrol and troop move ahead. But leadership is not just about earning a patch. What really matters is how Scouts and Scouters show leadership by sharing knowledge and offering guidance and encouragement to others.

You can step forward to become a leader of your patrol. You can even take on some of the leadership responsibilities for your whole troop. You will find it challenging and fun, and it will provide you with a great learning experience. Along the way you will discover the satisfaction of seeing how your leadership efforts allow your patrol and troop to succeed.

Scouting's Leading EDGE

Use Scouting's Leading EDGE to help a group work toward its goal.

Where the Group Is	What a Leader Can Do
Starting out— Skills are low; enthusiasm is high.	**E**xplain
Becoming discouraged— Skills and enthusiasm are low.	**D**emonstrate
Making progress— Skills and enthusiasm are rising.	**G**uide
Finding success— Skills and enthusiasm are high.	**E**nable

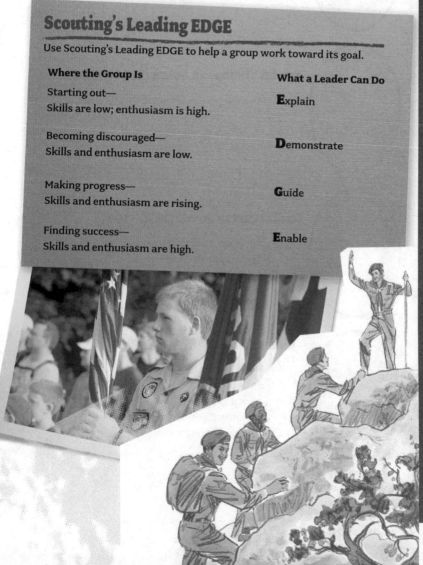

Scouting's Founding Leaders

Robert Baden-Powell (1857–1941)

In 1907, Robert Baden-Powell began the worldwide Scouting movement in Great Britain. He had developed his leadership skills during a long career in the British military. He saw Scouting as a way to help boys become young men of good character, virtue, and ability.

Ernest Thompson Seton (1860–1946)

The first Chief Scout of the Boy Scouts of America, Ernest Thompson Seton was a well-known author, artist, and naturalist who made nature study an important part of the Scouting program.

Daniel Carter Beard (1850–1941)

A woodsman in a buckskin shirt, "Uncle Dan" Beard encouraged boys to learn outdoor skills that are still at the heart of Scouting.

James E. West (1876–1948)

Dr. James E. West overcame physical disabilities, ill health, and a childhood in an orphanage to earn a law degree. He went on to lead the Boy Scouts of America through its first three decades as it grew into a strong national organization.

Learn from history! Check out www.bsahandbook.com for more about Scouting's founding leaders.

MAKING GOOD CHOICES

Common sense, ethics, wisdom, and good judgment help you make good choices and allow you to do your best with what you know. The skills you have can prepare you for what lies ahead. Self-leadership will help you develop a vision of what is right and the steps for getting there. The Scout Oath and Scout Law will provide guidance along the way.

Good Judgment in Choosing Friends

Your friends are among the most important people in your life. You enjoy being with them and going places together. They understand you. You depend on one another to be there for you through good times and bad. Good friends can be with you for many years to come.

Choose friends whose values you share and admire. Be open to those who are not just like everyone else you know. Differences in race, culture, and language may keep some people at a distance, but those differences can also be doorways for you to expand your understanding of other people and of the world. Disabilities might seem to be barriers to friendship, too, but look beyond what seems to separate you. You might be surprised to discover how much you have in common with others and how much you can share with one another.

Peer Pressure

At some point while you are growing up, you could discover that friends or acquaintances are doing something you know is wrong. They might be using tobacco, alcohol, or illegal drugs. They might be cheating on tests, stealing, or being unkind to others. They may want you to join them, even though you believe what they are doing is not right. When you refuse, they might say that they'll stop being friends with you.

Real friends will not ask you to do anything that could put you at risk. If those who say they are your friends are smoking, drinking, using drugs, watching pornography, using profanity, or doing anything else that is unwise, you don't have to go along with them. You might need to look for new friends who are interested in healthier activities. Don't worry, they are out there. Be true to your values, and you will find them.

Online Citizenship

The Internet is a great resource, but like any other community, it has dangers, too. Cyberbullies use the Internet and text messaging to harass or threaten other people. Being online gives these bullies a false sense of security, but they can be found out, caught, and even punished. If you feel you are the victim of a cyberbully, do not retaliate. In a private message, calmly ask the cyberbully to stop and let the bully know that you will take other steps if the abuse does not stop. If that does not help, tell your parent or guardian right away.

Bullying and Hazing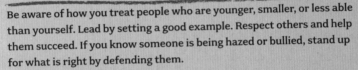

Be aware of how you treat people who are younger, smaller, or less able than yourself. Lead by setting a good example. Respect others and help them succeed. If you know someone is being hazed or bullied, stand up for what is right by defending them.

Sometimes it might seem easy to respond to someone's poor behavior with angry words or physical force, but there are always better ways to handle difficult situations. When dealing with peer pressure, bullying, hazing, and other challenges, use the Scout Oath and Scout Law as reliable guides for making good decisions.

LEADERSHIP AND YOUR FAMILY

A family provides belonging, support, and love. For many Scouts, a family is made up of parents and brothers and sisters all under the same roof. Grandparents, aunts, uncles, and cousins might live nearby or they might be far away, even in other countries.

Perhaps yours is a family with a single parent. Maybe you share time with a father and mother who live in different places. Perhaps your family is made up of other relatives or guardians who want the best for you. What makes a family is not the number of people in it or whether they are related. More important is that they care for each other and hope to share their lives with one another.

Of course, there may be times when you feel that others in your family don't understand you. You might disagree with the way they do some things. As you grow older, you will want to be more independent. The changes you are going through as you become an adult might cause strain at home, but by being patient and putting energy into developing healthy relationships with family members, you can make the most of family life.

The leadership skills you are learning as a Scout can be helpful, too. When you have a vision of where you want to be as a family member, you can figure out the steps to get there and then complete them one at a time.

Family members can sometimes offer good solutions to problems you are facing. You might be having difficulty with a subject in school. Maybe you don't understand why your friends are acting a certain way. If you ask the adults in your home and your older brothers and sisters, they will usually be able to give you a hand.

Helping Your Family

On patrol campouts, patrol members work together to set up tents, cook meals, and leave a clean campsite. Doing your part goes a long way toward an adventure's success. The same can be true at home. Running a household takes a lot of hard work and cooperation. You might already keep your room neat, do your own laundry, care for pets, and clear the table after meals. Don't wait to be asked. Remember: A Scout is helpful. Notice what needs to be done and then lend a hand.

Use this example to start your own list of important telephone numbers. Keep the list in a safe, convenient place near the telephone, and program the numbers into your mobile phone, too.

Emergency response: _____

Parent or guardian at work: _____

Parent's or guardian's mobile phone: _____

Nearest relative: _____

Neighbor: _____

Family friend: _____

Taking Care of Yourself When You Are Alone

Another of your family responsibilities could be taking care of yourself when your parents or guardians are away from home. That might happen once in a while when they are gone for an afternoon or an evening, or you could be on your own for a few hours every day after school.

Discuss with your family what they expect of you when you are on your own. An important step can be making a list of phone numbers and keeping it near a telephone. You also might program the numbers into a mobile phone for quick dialing in an emergency. Keeping these numbers handy will give you plenty of trusted people you can call if you have questions or need help.

Your parents or guardians may set guidelines for you to follow when you are at home by yourself. Perhaps they'll ask that you not invite friends over during those hours. They may ask that you call them if you plan to leave. Remember: A Scout is trustworthy. Show by your actions that you can be trusted.

Remember the Three R's

Be aware of the three R's to help ensure your personal safety and to help protect yourself.

▶ **Recognize** that anyone could be a child molester. Child molesters can be very skilled at influencing children, so be aware of situations that could lead to abuse.

▶ **Resist** advances made by child molesters to avoid being abused. Just say no, and don't be embarrassed to run away, scream, or cause a commotion.

▶ **Report** any molestation or attempted molestation to parents or other trusted adults. Anytime someone does something to you that your instincts tell you is wrong, or that makes you feel threatened or uncomfortable, tell someone you trust. It's OK to ask for help.

PUTTING IT ALL TOGETHER

Leadership begins with leading yourself and continues with leading others. Scouting will show you how. By knowing where you are headed, you can develop confidence in your abilities and do what is right.

Your Scout troop is organized so that you can practice leading others, too. You can become an elected leader of your patrol and troop. Along with your fellow Scouts, you can decide where you want your troop and patrol to go, the steps to get there, and the ways to complete each step. Helping others succeed is leadership at its best, as you do your part for other Scouts, your community, your family, and your nation.

Citizenship

> "The Boy Scouts of America will prepare every eligible youth in America to become a responsible, participating citizen and leader who is guided by the Scout Oath and Scout Law."
>
> —Boy Scouts of America vision statement

CITIZENSHIP

For more than a century, every Boy Scout has pledged on his honor to do his duty to his country. Each Scout reciting the Scout Law has promised to be loyal, helpful, obedient, and brave. The words come easily, but what does it really mean to be a good citizen? How can you fulfill the promises of the Scout Oath and Scout Law, and your promise to America?

To find the answer, start learning about your community, state, and nation and how they are governed. Along the way, you will discover that you and other Americans have certain rights and responsibilities that make our nation unique in the history of humanity. You will learn that citizenship means doing all you can to be aware of what is going on around you, thinking for yourself, and acting to defend and advance your country.

AN ONGOING EXPERIMENT

The idea of citizenship started more than 2,500 years ago in the ancient Greek city-states of Athens and Sparta. Spartans lived under the rule of a king who decided what people could do. Citizens of Athens ruled themselves. They held meetings to vote on the laws that would guide them.

Since then, groups of people have tried many different ways to organize and govern themselves. Some forms of government, such as the democracy of Athens, enjoyed much success. Other governments, especially those that limited the rights of individuals, did not.

The United States of America is an ongoing experiment in how people can work together for the good of all. As an American, you are a member of a nation with tremendous possibilities. You have certain rights that are guaranteed by the United States Constitution. You also have duties and responsibilities to fulfill if America is to continue.

The word "citizen" comes from a very old word meaning "a member of a city."

HOW OUR NATION CAME TO BE

The United States of America was born out of a desire for freedom. Colonists who settled much of the eastern coast of North America were ruled by a British government that limited the liberties the colonists believed they should have. The colonists had to obey British laws and pay British taxes even though they had no legal way to make changes when they felt those laws and taxes were unfair.

Many colonists wanted to govern themselves. They proclaimed their freedom from Great Britain on July 4, 1776, with the Declaration of Independence. Britain did not want America to slip out of its control, so it sent armies to put down the rebellion. The Revolutionary War dragged on for five years until a treaty signed in 1781 brought an end to the war. The United States became an independent nation.

Representatives of the 13 Colonies gathered to write the Constitution—the plan for governing the new nation—calling for a form of government in which citizens would elect officials to represent them. A country governed in this way is called a republic.

IN THIS CHAPTER

▶ How citizenship began

▶ Our nation's history

▶ Your rights and duties as a citizen

▶ The American flag

▶ Your community and you

▶ Serving your community

▶ Knowing your state, your nation, and the world

Get the scoop on the Constitution from its birth to how it affects America today. Visit the National Constitution Center at *www.constitutioncenter.org*.

The United States Constitution, adopted on Sept. 17, 1787, lays out the rules for how America's citizens are to govern themselves. The authors of the Constitution designed a government flexible enough for a nation that would be growing and changing. They also guaranteed that the United States would be a land where every citizen would have certain rights and certain duties.

YOUR RIGHTS AS AN AMERICAN

Do you like to get together with your friends? Read whatever you wish? Live in a home no one can enter unless invited? Those are rights that are guaranteed by the Constitution and shared by all Americans. You also have the right to practice any religion you want, and your freedom of speech is protected.

It doesn't matter where we live, how much money we have, the color of our skin, whether we are male or female, or what we believe—the Constitution states that all Americans are equal under the law. Never in human history have the rights of every person been so respected.

The Bill of Rights

Known as the Bill of Rights, the first 10 amendments to the United States Constitution spell out basic rights of every American. The Bill of Rights guarantees Americans the right to keep and bear arms, the right of private property, fair treatment for people accused of crimes, protection from unreasonable search and seizure, freedom from self-incrimination, a speedy and impartial trial by jury, and representation by legal counsel.

See *www.bsahandbook.org* for the full text of the Constitution and Bill of Rights.

CHALLENGES AND CHANGES TO THE CONSTITUTION

The strength of the Constitution has been tested many times. A difficult struggle for the young nation was the question of slavery. When the Constitution was written, many people believed slaves did not have the same rights as free Americans. Other people were certain that slavery was wrong and that the Constitution should grant the same rights to all people, regardless of their race.

In 1861, the states supporting slavery and the rights of states to determine their own laws tried to break away from the United States to form a separate country. Citizens of the other states fought to hold the nation together. When the Civil War ended in 1865, America was still united.

Through the Emancipation Proclamation and the addition of the 13th Amendment to the Constitution, liberties were extended to people of all races, but those bloody years of war will always be a dark reminder that our freedoms have a high price. Throughout our history, hundreds of thousands of Americans have paid that price by giving their lives to defend the Constitution.

WHAT YOUR NATION ASKS OF YOU

America is your land. Its soil grows food that feeds you. Its communities offer support, safety, and services. Its laws protect your rights. By defending the Constitution, you preserve those rights. As a citizen, you should defend these same rights for others, even when you do not agree with the ways in which they exercise them.

Written by our elected representatives, the laws of our communities, states, and nation guide much of what we do every day. You can help your government respond to the needs of the people by learning about laws and obeying them. When you disagree with a law, seek to improve it through constitutional processes.

America relies on its citizens to protect it. The men and women of the armed forces guard the nation against threats from beyond our borders. Ignorance, prejudice, and indifference are enemies of our country, too. Do your part to defeat those threats by taking advantage of educational opportunities and by standing up for the rights of others.

A strong America exists only if its citizens are informed. Read about our nation's history and about how our government works. Learn about current issues and how your representatives are making decisions for you. When you are old enough, it will be your right and your responsibility to cast an informed vote during elections, to serve on juries, and to fulfill other duties to America.

Our country also needs dedicated teachers, engineers, scientists, writers, bus drivers, farmers, and merchants. The nation counts on capable coaches, pilots, soldiers, computer programmers, and business leaders. It depends upon people committed to protecting the environment, caring for the sick, and assisting others in need.

America especially needs young people who are doing something good with their lives. You are the future of your country, and you can contribute right now. When you do your best in school and are of service to your family and community, you are strengthening America. Be engaged. Be aware. Learn what is going on around you and develop the ability to think for yourself.

An excellent way to explore your role as a citizen is by earning the BSA merit badges for Citizenship in the Community, Citizenship in the Nation, and Citizenship in the World.

Citizenship in the Community

Citizenship in the Nation

Citizenship in the World

THE AMERICAN FLAG

The flag of the United States is much more than just red, white, and blue cloth. As the symbol of America, it stands for the past, present, and future of our country. It represents our people, our land, and our many ways of life.

Honoring the flag offers all of us a time to think about what it means to be Americans and to pledge ourselves to making our country the best it can be. Perhaps you recite the Pledge of Allegiance each day at your school. Before sporting events and at other public gatherings, you might stand and put your hand over your heart for the singing of "The Star-Spangled Banner," the national anthem. Boy Scout troops open many of their meetings with a flag ceremony. In Scout camp, you can join with others to raise the flag each morning and in the evening to retire it.

While you are wearing your Scout uniform, greet the flag with a Scout salute. Do this whenever you see the flag being hoisted or lowered, when you pass it or it passes you, and during the playing of the national anthem. Give the Scout salute as you recite the Pledge of Allegiance, too. Greet the flag when you are not in uniform by removing your hat, if you are wearing one, and placing your right hand over your heart.

The Story Behind the Anthem

During the War of 1812, a British fleet attacked Fort McHenry near Baltimore, Maryland. A young man named Francis Scott Key watched as the bombardment lasted through the night. He did not know if the American fortress could withstand the assault.

When the smoke cleared the next morning, Key saw the United States flag—the Star-Spangled Banner—still flying over the fort. He wrote down the feelings he'd had during the night and his trust in America's future in a poem he called "Defence of Fort McHenry." Soon the words were being sung throughout the country. Francis Scott Key had written the lyrics to the song that has become known as "The Star-Spangled Banner"—our national anthem.

The Star-Spangled Banner

O! say can you see, by the dawn's early light,

What so proudly we hailed at the twilight's last gleaming,

Whose broad stripes and bright stars through the perilous fight,

O'er the ramparts we watch'd, were so gallantly streaming?

And the Rockets' red glare, the Bombs bursting in air,

Gave proof through the night that our Flag was still there;

O! say does that star-spangled Banner yet wave,

O'er the Land of the free, and the home of the brave?

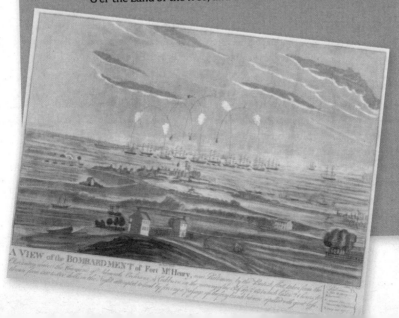

A VIEW of the BOMBARDMENT of Fort M!Henry,

Flying the Flag

The flag of the United States may be flown every day. Flags are usually flown from sunrise to sunset. Properly lit, they can be flown at night, too. The flag should fly on all national and state holidays and on other days proclaimed by the president of the United States.

When the American flag is displayed with flags of other nations, each national flag must be flown from a separate staff of the same height. When the American flag is displayed with other types of flags, such as state flags or the flags of organizations, the national flag is given the position of honor (to its own right) and should be flown above the others. If flags are displayed at equal heights, the United States flag is either out in front or farthest to its own right. The American flag is hoisted first and lowered last.

Hoisting the Flag

> The United States flag should never be flown upside down except as a distress signal to call for help.

To hoist a flag on a flagpole, hold the folded flag and prevent it from touching the ground. A second person should attach the flag to the flag line (called a halyard), then briskly raise the flag, keeping the line tight. When the flag is flying freely, step back and salute as the other person ties the halyard to the flagpole.

Lowering the Flag

Loosen the halyard from the pole and slowly lower the flag. A second person salutes until the flag is within reach, then gathers the flag into his arms. Remove the flag from the halyard and tie the halyard to the pole.

The Flag at Half-Staff

Fly the flag at half-staff to show sorrow following a national tragedy, the death of a president or other national or state figure, or to honor those who have sacrificed their lives for their country. Hoist the flag to the top of the pole, hold it there for an instant, and then lower it to a point halfway between the top and the bottom of the pole. Take it down by first raising the flag to the top of the pole and then lowering it slowly. On Memorial Day, fly the flag at half-staff until noon and then hoist it to full-staff.

Visit www.USHistory.org, which has a ton of information about—what else?—our nation's history. Check out the site's Flag Rules and Regulations page.

Folding the Flag

Hold the flag at waist level between yourself and another person, and then fold the flag in half lengthwise and then again in half lengthwise. Keep the blue field on the outside. While you hold the flag by

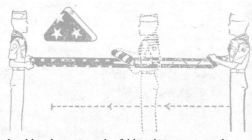

the blue field, the other person should make a triangular fold in the opposite end. Continue folding the flag in triangles until only the blue field is visible.

Displaying the Flag

The flag may be carried on a staff in parades, at Scout meetings, and during other ceremonies and patriotic events.

Displayed from a staff in an auditorium or place of worship, the flag of the United States of America holds the position of honor to the right of a speaker as he or she faces the audience. Any other flags should be placed to the speaker's left.

When displaying a flag horizontally or vertically against a wall, the blue field should be at the top and at the flag's own right (to your left as you look at the flag).

To display a flag over a street, hang it vertically with the blue field to the north on an east-west street or to the east on a north-south street.

Retiring Worn-Out Flags

As a Good Turn, Scouts can volunteer to help replace faded and tattered flags in their communities with new ones and to conduct flag retirement ceremonies for those that have been taken down. A national flag that is worn beyond repair may be burned in a fire. The ceremony should be conducted with dignity and respect and the flag burned completely to ashes.

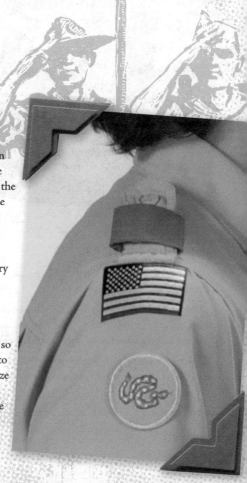

Flags on Uniforms

Every Boy Scout uniform shirt has an embroidered American flag sewn on the right sleeve. Following the guidelines of the U.S. Flag Code, it is placed with the blue field (the "union") to the flag's own right (to the left, as someone views it).

You might have noticed that the flag patch on the right sleeves of U.S. military uniforms places the blue field to the observer's right. According to current Department of the Army regulations, "When worn on the right sleeve, it is considered proper to reverse the design so that the union is at the observer's right to suggest that the flag is flying in the breeze as the wearer moves forward." Either method of displaying the flag on a sleeve is correct, depending on the regulations or code that one follows.

KNOW YOUR COMMUNITY

Scouting prepares you to explore the outdoors and understand the natural world all around. Just as important is the BSA's encouragement that you know your community, learn how people can cooperate to improve their neighborhoods, and find out how you can do your part.

Your Community's History

Many American towns and cities are hundreds of years old. They might be near rivers and harbors, or they may have sprung up long ago along trails and railroad lines that crossed the continent. Other communities are much younger. They may have started at the edges of cities or close to industrial, commercial, or agricultural centers.

Find resources on the Internet or in your library to discover why your hometown is located where it is, who started it, and how it has changed over the decades. Visit museums and monuments that honor local historical events. People who have lived in your neighborhood for a long time might share their memories of what your community was like in years gone by.

My community's name: _____

Why my community has that name: _____
_____
_____

Names of people who founded my community: _____
_____
_____

Important events in my community's history: _____
_____
_____
_____

My community's population: _____

Names of elected leaders of my community: _____
_____
_____
_____

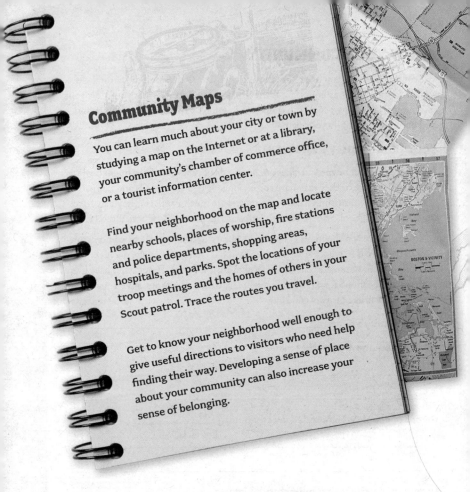

Community Maps

You can learn much about your city or town by studying a map on the Internet or at a library, your community's chamber of commerce office, or a tourist information center.

Find your neighborhood on the map and locate nearby schools, places of worship, fire stations and police departments, shopping areas, hospitals, and parks. Spot the locations of your troop meetings and the homes of others in your Scout patrol. Trace the routes you travel.

Get to know your neighborhood well enough to give useful directions to visitors who need help finding their way. Developing a sense of place about your community can also increase your sense of belonging.

GETTING TO KNOW YOUR NEIGHBORS

Your city or town is more than a collection of buildings and streets. The people living there turn a spot on the map into a community. Neighbors are the people in homes near yours, on farms down the road, or in apartments in your building. You probably already know some of them. Along with a parent, a guardian, or Scout leaders, you can introduce yourselves to others. Explain that you are a Scout who lives nearby and that you would be pleased to learn about them. Everyone has interesting stories to tell and something to add to your community.

Senior Citizens

Older Americans can draw on decades of experience to help solve community problems. If they are retired, they might have extra time to devote to their neighborhood. Many appreciate the friendship of others and especially of young people.

People With Special Challenges

We all wish we could have perfect health and awareness. However, illnesses and accidents can leave people of any age with challenges. Perhaps you or another Scout in your troop gets around with crutches or in a wheelchair. Some of your neighbors might have poor hearing or eyesight. Others could have faced physical or mental challenges since birth. The effects of many disabilities are not visible. Understanding more about the challenges confronting others is a step toward getting to know people for who they really are.

Other Cultures

Each of us has a cultural background. Your parents, grandparents, or other ancestors might have come from Africa, Asia, Europe, South America, or another part of the world. Perhaps your family arrived in America hundreds of years ago. Maybe you and your family have lived in the United States just a few months. If you are an American Indian, you may be a member of a tribe that has been in North America for thousands of years.

Americans believe in a nation where people of all backgrounds and races can live together and succeed. We also take pride in our different histories. Our languages and religious beliefs, music, clothing, and foods help each of us identify with our past. Festivals and holidays encourage us to celebrate our cultures and to enjoy the heritages of our neighbors. By accepting the differences among us, we can experience the variety and strength that all people can bring to a community.

WHAT A COMMUNITY GIVES YOU

Are you proud of the troop number on the sleeve of your Scout shirt? That's because you know you belong. You can feel the same way about the community where you live. You are glad to say, "I am from this place." It is your home, and it provides you with support, safety, and services.

Support

If you play on a sports team, you know how good it feels to have local fans cheer you on. When you do your best in school, your teachers, family, and neighbors will give you a pat on the back. In your Scout troop, religious groups, community clubs, and other local organizations, you can find people with values and interests that you share.

People in a community support one another through bad times as well as good times. You might know a family whose home was damaged by fire, a flood, or some other disaster. Neighbors brought them food, blankets, spare clothing, and other items they needed. Some may have pitched in to repair the damage and raised money to help the family get started again. That's what a community can do.

Safety

People who care about their neighbors and the places they live want to keep their communities safe. You can play a role, too. You can shovel snow from sidewalks, sweep glass out of a street, cut brush that is hiding a stop sign, paint over graffiti, or report a broken streetlight. With your knowledge of first aid, you are ready to assist injured people if an accident occurs. You can also support the police, fire departments, and rescue squads that handle more serious safety matters. They are part of your community, too.

Services

If there were no communities and your family lived alone, you would need to find your own food and water every day. At night you could burn a candle or a lantern, but there probably would be no other light. If you became sick, you would have to heal yourself.

Thanks to our communities, though, clean water is as close as the nearest faucet. Electric lights come on at the flip of a switch. If someone becomes injured or ill, he or she can get treatment at clinics and hospitals. School systems provide educational opportunities for young people and for adults eager to gain new knowledge.

Fresh water, electrical power, medical attention, education, and dozens of other services exist because people in a community work together. By sharing the labor and the cost, you and your neighbors provide yourselves and others with many necessities of life.

Whenever you dive into a public swimming pool, visit a museum or a zoo, or read a book in a library, you are enjoying community resources. The same is true of local hiking trails and bike paths, beaches, sports fields, parks, and picnic areas.

To learn more about how a community supports its citizens, your patrol or troop can visit a fire department, police station, sewage-treatment plant, utility, or other public service.

COMMUNITY GOVERNMENT

Large cities have full-time governments. But officials in a small town might be men and women who serve part-time, often as volunteers. In either case, the people of the community elect a council of citizens and a mayor, town manager, or tribal leader to look after local affairs.

City council meetings are often open to the public. County, state, and federal sessions of elected officials are often public as well. By watching government bodies in session and reading about meetings in newspapers, you can see how lawmakers make decisions. That's one of the ways you can decide whether officials are making choices you feel are best for everyone.

Visit a Community Leader

Many people are dedicated to public service. Talking with them will help you understand the challenges and rewards of their work. You might also discover some of the ways that you can be of service to your neighborhood and your community.

Public officials appreciate meeting with people they represent. They often have busy schedules, so write or call their offices to make an appointment. Before you visit, make notes about the subjects you would like to discuss. You may wish to find out what young people can do to prepare themselves for public service. Perhaps you have seen a problem in your neighborhood that you feel a community leader should know about, and you want to suggest a solution. By answering your questions and by supporting your interests, leaders are helping to build a better community for tomorrow.

A Visit With a Community Leader

In the spaces below, write about your visit with an elected official, judge, attorney, civil servant, principal, teacher, or other community leader.

Date: _____

Person's name and occupation: _____

_____

Questions you asked: _____

_____

_____

What the leader suggested you can do to help your community: _____

_____

_____

_____

Volunteer Organizations

A mayor or city council member will tell you that government cannot provide every service a community needs. That's where volunteer organizations step in. Volunteer organizations are groups whose members give time and energy to get things done. A good example is the parent-teacher organization your parents or guardian might attend at your school. They know that working together with teachers can make your school an even better place for you to learn.

Your Scout troop is a volunteer organization, too. Adults interested in BSA programs help organize and support your troop. They find ways to pay for camping gear and cover other expenses. On their own time, your Scout leaders receive training and take part in troop meetings and Scouting adventures with you and your fellow Scouts.

Religious organizations often help with community needs, and so do volunteer fund-raising organizations such as the United Way. Neighborhood awareness groups do much to involve everyone in the safety of homes and businesses. In smaller towns, the fire department and rescue squad are often staffed by trained volunteers who have other careers but are ready to go to someone's assistance.

You can be a volunteer, too. Perhaps you belong to a school organization that informs students about the dangers of using alcohol, tobacco, and illegal drugs. You and your friends might spend a Saturday collecting food and used clothing for people in need, helping out at a home for senior citizens, working on environmental protection efforts, or completing projects at a place of worship. Scout patrols and troops can plan and complete many service projects that will benefit their communities and the environment.

"I have never forgotten my days as an Eagle Scout. I didn't know it at the time, but what really came out of my Scouting was learning how to lead and serve the community."

—Lloyd Bentsen (1921–2006), an Eagle Scout, U.S. Senator, and U.S. Representative who received the Army Air Corps' Distinguished Flying Cross for heroism

CITIZENSHIP AND SERVICE PROJECTS

A service project is a special Good Turn that puts Scout spirit into action. Projects can take many forms. You might take part in a community cleanup; repair a place of worship, a museum, or the home of an elderly person; improve a wildlife habitat; volunteer at a hospital or with a public safety group; organize a recycling effort; or conduct a clothing pickup or food drive.

Service projects for your community improve the lives of those around you. They will also enrich your life as you discover that what you do makes a real difference. The more you give, the more you get back in satisfaction, in accomplishment, and in understanding that you have done the right thing. Service to others, to your community, and to the environment becomes a habit that you will want to practice often.

Service Project Leadership

Service projects are ideal opportunities for Scouts to use the skills of self-leadership and leading others.

▶ **Have a vision of what a successful project will look like.**

▶ **Figure out the steps to get there.**

▶ **Complete those steps one at a time.**

BE PREPARED TO HELP OTHER PEOPLE AT ALL TIMES

Service Project

Write a short description of a service project you have helped plan and complete. _____
_____
_____
_____
_____
_____
_____

Your vision of a successful project: _____
_____
_____
_____
_____
_____
_____

The steps to make it happen: _____
_____
_____
_____
_____
_____

How you completed those steps: _____
_____
_____
_____
_____
_____

KNOW YOUR STATE

Fifty states share America's national history. Each of us is proud of what makes our own state special. The name of your state often holds clues to its origin, as does your capital city. A state flag, motto, song, bird, and flower further identify each state.

Do a little research at the library or on the Internet to discover the emblems of your state. Write them here. What do they tell you about your home?

My state's name: _____

My state's capital city: _____

My state's motto: _____

My state's flower: _____

My state's bird: _____

My state's song: _____

KNOW YOUR NATION

The United States of America embraces 3.5 million square miles. Ours is a country of enormous variety. It stretches from Arctic tundra to tropical wetlands, from sun-baked desert to old-growth forest, and from great cities to prairies, farmlands, and mountain ranges.

Americans are as different from one another as the land upon which we live. Even so, when we work together we have the energy, optimism, and ability to accomplish almost anything we set out to do. We have sent astronauts to the moon, for example, and built remarkable school systems and transportation networks. We work together to help fellow citizens in need after hurricanes, fires, tornadoes, earthquakes, and other natural disasters. We also come together to fight diseases, poverty, unemployment, and crime.

We remember the sacrifices and achievements of Americans with federal holidays, including observances of the birthdays of George Washington, Abraham Lincoln, and Dr. Martin Luther King Jr.; Memorial Day; Independence Day; Labor Day; and Veterans Day. America has many unsung heroes as well. It has become a strong nation because of the efforts of every person living upon its soil. Its future depends on the ways each American contributes in the years to come.

Guam, the United States Virgin Islands, and American Samoa are territories that are part of our nation. They have some degree of self-government and limited representation in the U.S. Congress. Commonwealths such as Puerto Rico and the Northern Mariana Islands are also associated with the United States but are self-governing. The programs of the Boy Scouts of America are available to the youth of all U.S. territories and commonwealths.

Our Nation's Motto: In God We Trust

In 1861, U.S. Treasury Secretary Salmon D. Chase wrote a letter to the director of the U.S. Mint. "No nation can be strong except in the strength of God, or safe except in His defense," Chase wrote. "The trust of our people in God should be declared on our national coins." A vote of Congress made the secretary's suggestion law, and in 1864 the motto "In God We Trust" began to appear on coins of the United States.

American's Creed

"I believe in the United States of America, as a government of the people, by the people, for the people; whose just powers are derived from the consent of the governed; a democracy in a republic; a sovereign Nation of many sovereign States; a perfect union, one and inseparable; established upon those principles of freedom, equality, justice, and humanity for which American patriots sacrificed their lives and fortunes. I therefore believe it is my duty to my country to love it, to support its Constitution, to obey its laws, to respect its flag, and to defend it against all enemies."

—William Tyler Page, 1917

87

"Our patriotism should be of the wider, nobler kind which recognizes justice and reasonableness in the claims of others and which leads our country into comradeship with . . . the other nations of the world."

—Robert Baden-Powell

WORLD COMMUNITY

In 1920—only 13 years after he had launched Scouting in Great Britain—Robert Baden-Powell helped host the first of many world Scout jamborees. More than 8,000 Scouts from 34 countries gathered in London to share the fellowship of Scouting.

More than 28 million youths and adults currently hold membership in the Scouting organizations of 155 nations. As Baden-Powell explained during that first jamboree, Scouts around the globe form a world brotherhood of Scouting that is committed to do its share in developing peace and happiness in the world and goodwill among people everywhere.

We are living at a time when the world seems to be getting smaller. Economies, businesses, and organizations are increasingly global, and communication is instantaneous at almost every point in the world. Gaining an understanding of other nations is vital to our shared success.

The more we discover how much people beyond our borders are contributing to the good of the world community, the more possibilities we can see for international cooperation. People all over the world can pull together whenever drought, flood, earthquake, or famine threatens some part of the planet. Nations that have available resources can send food, supplies, and medical aid to people in trouble.

Many problems the people of the world face today cannot be solved by one nation. The list is long—pollution, AIDS, the destruction of rain forests, the endangering of wildlife, and threats posed by nuclear weapons are just a few. The challenges are difficult, but they all have solutions.

You might someday help find some of the answers. Begin by learning about people around the world. Meeting people who have immigrated to the United States from foreign countries is one way to learn about the cultures, histories, religions, and languages of others.

Be willing throughout your life to make this a better place—not just for yourself and other Americans, but for everyone. That is what good citizens of the world can do. That is what can truly build a healthy community, a strong nation, and a peaceful world.

21st World Scout Jamboree, 2007
Chelmsford, England

Fitness

> "To secure endurance, physical power, physical courage, and skill, the first thing needful is to take stock of one's physical make-up, put the body in the best possible condition for doing its work and then keep it in good order."
>
> —*Handbook for Boys,* 1911

FITNESS

What does fitness mean to you? For many Scouts, it's an inviting trail and a day to go exploring. It might mean a challenge from another patrol to a game of basketball. Perhaps it is the goal of earning the BSA's Mile Swim Award, or an all-day bicycle ride, a backpacking trip, or a long canoe journey. Being prepared for the adventures of Scouting means taking care of your body. Exercising regularly and eating a nutritious diet can help you be physically fit for challenges now and in the future.

There is also fitness of the mind. Diet and exercise are important for your brain as well as for your muscles. Training yourself to learn, to lead, and to solve problems is a large part of building mental strength. Developing a positive attitude is part of it, too, and finding the good in what happens every day.

Making ethical decisions is a third kind of fitness. The ways in which you treat other people and the world around you are choices to think about seriously, and so is the respect you have for yourself and the decisions you make that can affect your health and your future.

Whenever you recite the Scout Oath, you pledge to do your best to keep yourself physically fit, mentally awake, and morally straight. That's Scouting's idea of fitness—fitness of your body, fitness of your mind, and fitness in making moral choices. They are among the most important building blocks of a young man.

You can do a lot to develop your fitness in all three areas by using self-leadership as a way to accomplish great things. Self-leadership is especially valuable for laying out a plan to improve your physical fitness and then sticking with that plan as good things begin to happen.

 Visit the *Handbook* Web site at *www.bsahandbook.org* for the requirements for the Mile Swim and other awards that test your level of fitness.

IN THIS CHAPTER

▶ Envisioning physical fitness

▶ Completing the steps to better fitness

▶ Tenderfoot fitness checklist

▶ Stretching

▶ Healthy eating and the food guide pyramid

▶ Maintaining the proper weight

▶ Getting enough sleep

▶ Taking care of and protecting your body

▶ Avoiding tobacco, alcohol, and drugs

▶ Staying mentally awake and morally straight

A VISION OF FITNESS

When you imagine yourself being physically fit, what picture do you see? Perhaps your idea of physical fitness is to be as healthy as possible and to have the strength and endurance to take part in all the Scout adventures and school activities that interest you. Your vision also can include regular exercise and a good diet that will lay a foundation of health for years to come.

Each of us is born with a body of a certain type. We can't change how tall we are or whether we are naturally slender, stocky, or somewhere in between, but we can do a lot to care for the bodies that we have. If you're already in good shape, see what more you can do. If you have physical disabilities, you can explore ways to strengthen yourself and be as healthy as you can. If a health professional has advised you to lose some weight, begin doing something about the extra pounds.

Whatever your starting point, you have great potential. Develop a vision of what being physically fit will look like, and then start taking the steps to make that vision real.

Self-Leadership Is ...

▶ Having a vision of where you want to be

▶ Figuring out the steps to get there

▶ Completing those steps one at a time

To Keep Myself
Physically Strong
(1964), by
Norman Rockwell

Before beginning any exercise routine, it's a good idea to have a physical examination. Your doctor can answer any questions you might have and can provide guidance for you to undertake the activities you are planning. He or she also can help you learn how to reach and maintain the weight that is right for you.

STEPS TO BETTER FITNESS

Break down your vision of lifelong fitness into challenges that you can manage one at a time. The steps leading toward being physically fit include:

▶ Getting plenty of exercise

▶ Eating a healthy diet

▶ Sleeping enough

▶ Guarding against injury and illness

COMPLETING THE STEPS

The human body thrives on exercise. Being active for 30 to 60 minutes most days is good for muscles and organs. It pushes you to become stronger. It helps with circulation and digestion. Walking, bicycling, mowing lawns, and playing sports are all terrific ways to give your body exercise. Of course, hiking, backpacking, swimming, canoeing, climbing, and many other Scouting adventures are excellent choices, too. To give all parts of your body a good workout, add push-ups, chin-ups, and a few other exercises.

You can use the Tenderfoot fitness checklist to chart your progress in becoming fit. Recording your best efforts will help you see where you are right now. Exercising for a month and then testing yourself again will show you how much you have improved.

Tenderfoot Fitness Checklist

Record your best in the following tests.

Exercise	Date	Date (30 days later)
Push-ups	_____	_____
Pull-ups	_____	_____
Sit-ups	_____	_____
Standing long jump	_____	_____
500-yard walk/run	_____	_____

Show improvement in the activities listed above after practicing for 30 days.

To build strength, complete three sets of each of these exercises three or four times a week. For example, do as many sit-ups as you can, then rest for a minute. That's one set. Do a second set of sit-ups, rest again, then finish with a third set. Keeping a notebook of your workout progress can encourage you to keep at it regularly.

Push-Ups

Push-ups build the muscles of the arms, chest, and shoulders.

How to do them:

Lie facedown on the floor with your arms bent and the palms of your hands flat against the floor. Keeping your neck, spine, and knees straight, push yourself upward until your arms are fully extended. Slowly lower yourself toward the floor, then repeat.

For less demanding push-ups, use your knees rather than your toes for balance. Remember to keep your spine and thighs in a straight line. As your strength increases, shift to the regular push-up position with your weight on your hands and toes.

Pull-Ups

Pull-ups strengthen the muscles of the arms, back, and shoulders.

How to do them:

Grasp a pull-up bar with your palms facing forward. Pull yourself upward until you can touch the bar with your chin, then slowly return to the starting position.

If you bend your legs before starting a pull-up, a friend grasping your ankles can help you complete the exercise without as much effort. That can be a good way for your body to begin building enough strength to complete regular pull-ups.

Sit-ups

Sit-ups are great for strengthening the muscles of the abdomen.

How to do them:

Lie on your back with your knees flexed and your arms crossed over your chest. Ask a friend to hold your feet down. Curl up toward the sitting position until your elbows touch your thighs. Slowly return to the starting position.

Crunches are a variation on sit-ups that produce good results. Begin in the same way as for regular sit-ups, but come up just until your shoulder blades are clear of the floor. Slowly lower yourself to the starting position, then repeat. Try doing crunches without anyone holding your feet.

Standing Long Jump

The standing long jump works muscles in the legs, hips, and torso.

How to do it:

Choose a place with a safe landing area—a soft lawn, the sand pit at a running track, or a gymnastics mat, for example. Stand with your toes against a line at the edge of the landing area. Flex your legs and then leap forward with both feet leaving the ground at the same moment. Use the strength of your legs and a swing of your arms to go as far as possible. Have someone watch where you touch the ground at the end of your jump, and then measure from there back to the starting line. Record the best of three jumps.

500-Yard Walk/Run

Walking and running strengthen the heart, lungs, and muscles of the legs and hips.

How to do it:

Five hundred yards is one lap of a standard running track plus an additional 60 yards—about halfway down the track's straightaway or around one of the curves, depending on where you start. Run or walk the distance as quickly as you can, but remember to pace yourself so you have energy to make a strong finish as you complete the walk/run.

STRETCHING

Take a few minutes to stretch before beginning a sports event, an exercise routine, a hike, or other physical activity. Stretching relaxes the tendons and ligaments in your joints. It warms the muscles and gets them ready to work. It makes your body more flexible and reduces the chances of injury. Stretching after a strenuous activity might help keep your muscles and joints from becoming stiff and sore.

Try the following stretches, doing each with just enough effort to put a little tension on your muscles. Stretch without bouncing. At first you might feel tight, but over time your range of motion will increase.

Thigh Stretch

Place your left hand on a wall or tree for support. Grab your right ankle with your right hand and gently pull your heel toward your buttocks. Hold for 30 seconds, and then repeat with your hand on your left ankle.

Achilles Tendon and Calf Stretch

Stand about 3 feet from a wall or tree and place your palms flat against it. Keep your heels on the ground and your back straight as you lean closer to the wall. Hold that position for 30 seconds, feeling the stretch of your calf muscles and Achilles tendons.

Straddle Stretch

Sit on the ground and spread your legs, and then lean forward as far as you can while reaching out with your arms. Hold the position for 30 seconds. The straddle stretch is good for the muscles in your back and the backs of your legs.

Lower Back Stretch

Lying on your back, bend a leg toward your chest, interlace your fingers around your knee, and gently pull it closer to your torso. After 15 to 30 seconds, release your hold and then perform the stretch with your other leg.

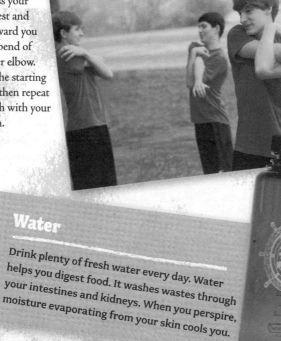

Shoulder Stretch

Hold one arm across your upper chest and pull it toward you with the bend of your other elbow. Reverse the starting position, then repeat the stretch with your other arm.

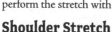

Water

Drink plenty of fresh water every day. Water helps you digest food. It washes wastes through your intestines and kidneys. When you perspire, moisture evaporating from your skin cools you.

Visit the *Handbook* Web site, *www.bsahandbook.org*, for more on exercise and nutrition.

EAT A HEALTHY DIET

Choosing healthy foods and avoiding those that aren't good for you can make a big difference in how you feel and how fit you are. Food you eat should do three things:

▶ Build up your body and keep it in good repair.

▶ Provide the vitamins, minerals, fiber, and bulk that your body needs.

▶ Serve as a source of energy for everything you do.

THE FOOD GUIDE PYRAMID

The food guide pyramid developed by the United States Department of Agriculture can help you understand what to eat to be healthy.

The colored stripes forming the pyramid represent different food groups:

▶ Orange—grains

▶ Green—vegetables

▶ Red—fruits

▶ Yellow—fats and oils

▶ Blue—milk and other dairy products

▶ Purple—meat, beans, fish, and nuts

The width of each stripe suggests the amount of food from that group to eat every day. The person climbing the pyramid stairway is a reminder of the importance of being active. It encourages you to make healthy changes one step at a time.

MyPyramid.gov
STEPS TO A HEALTHIER YOU

Grain Group
Make half your grains whole

Vegetable Group
Vary your veggies

Fruit Group
Focus on fruits

Milk Group
Get your calcium-rich foods

Meat & Bean Group
Go lean with protein

 MyPyramid.gov has extensive information on the food guide pyramid and government nutrition guidelines.

Grains

Grains include cereals, breads, crackers, rice, and pasta. Grains are a major source of *carbohydrates* that fuel you through the day. *Whole-grain* foods such as oatmeal, whole-wheat bread, and brown rice have more fiber, vitamins, and minerals than foods made from grains that are highly processed (white breads, white rice, many breakfast cereals). Choose whole grains whenever you can.

Vegetables

Vegetables are loaded with vitamins, minerals, and other nutrients important for good health. They can be eaten raw, steamed, or cooked in a microwave. (Boiling them can cause some loss of vitamins and other nutrients.)

Among the most nutritious vegetables are broccoli, spinach, and other leafy greens that are high in vitamin A, vitamin C, and important minerals. (Often the darker the color of a green vegetable, the more nutrients it contains.) Carrots, sweet potatoes, and other orange vegetables also are good sources of vitamin A.

Fruits

Apples, oranges, blueberries, bananas, and other fruits are tasty, ready to eat, and filled with vitamins and minerals. As snacks and desserts, they are hard to beat.

Milk

Low-fat milk, yogurt, pudding, cheese, ice cream, and other dairy products are rich in vitamins and in calcium, an essential building block for strong bones.

If you don't or can't consume dairy products, choose lactose-free products or other sources of calcium such as fortified foods and beverages.

Meat and Beans

Fish, poultry, beef, and other meats can provide your body with protein for building tissues.

For meats, choose poultry, fish, and lean red meats. To avoid adding unnecessary fat to your diet, it is better to eat meats that have been baked, broiled, or grilled instead of deep-fat fried, cooked in lots of butter, or prepared with heavy sauces.

Beans and other legumes such as peas and lentils are sources of protein that also add fiber, vitamins, and minerals. Nuts and seeds such as almonds, walnuts, pecans, cashews, hazelnuts, pistachios, and sunflower seeds also provide protein.

Fats

Foods with lots of fat often taste good. However, your body processes fat slowly, and eating too much fat can cause weight gain. Over time, certain kinds of fats can clog arteries, leading to heart problems. Minimize these dangers by:

▶ Getting most of your fat from fish, nuts, and vegetable oils.

▶ Going easy on solid fats—butter, stick margarine, shortening, and lard— as well as foods that contain solid fats or have been cooked in these fats.

Take responsibility every day for making good decisions about what you eat and drink and in what amounts. Remember your vision of being healthy and the goal of sticking with foods and beverages that are good for you. The more often you make wise choices about food, the easier it becomes. You'll feel better and be stronger as you get into the habit of smart eating.

Sugar and Caffeine

Sugar is found in many candies, breakfast cereals, and other foods, often in the form of *high-fructose corn syrup*. Sugary foods and sodas can give you a quick burst of energy, but the feeling wears off quickly and can leave you tired and cranky. Try to limit the amount of sugary foods and beverages you eat and drink. Fresh fruits and juices can be nutritious substitutes.

Sodas, some energy drinks, coffee, and tea often contain *caffeine*, which temporarily stirs up the nervous system and speeds the heart. Caffeine might make you irritable and make it hard to sleep. These drinks should be consumed only in moderation. Water, some fruit juices, and milk are usually better choices.

Checking the Nutrition Facts Label

Check the nutrition facts label on packaged foods to learn the amount of fat, sugar, caffeine, salt, and other ingredients in a food. The daily value percentage gives an idea of how much of your daily intake of a nutrient is contained in one serving of that food. This information can help you make healthy choices about what you eat each day.

1 Start here.

2 Check the calories.

3 Limit these nutrients.

4 Get enough of these nutrients.

5 Check the footnote.

6 5 percent or less of daily value is low; 20 percent or more is high.

Nutrition Facts

Serving Size 1 cup (228g)
Servings Per Container 2

Amount Per Serving

Calories 250   Calories from Fat 110

                      % Daily Value*

Total Fat 12g	18%
Saturated Fat 3g	15%
Trans Fat 3g	
Cholesterol 30mg	10%
Sodium 470mg	20%
Potassium 700mg	20%
Total Carbohydrate 31g	10%
Dietary Fiber 0g	0%
Sugars 5g	
Protein 5g	

Vitamin A	4%
Vitamin C	2%
Calcium	20%
Iron	4%

* Percent Daily Values are based on a 2,000 calorie diet. Your Daily Values may be higher or lower depending on your calorie needs.

	Calories:	2,000	2,500
Total Fat	Less than	65g	80g
Sat Fat	Less than	20g	25g
Cholesterol	Less than	300mg	300mg
Sodium	Less than	2,400mg	2,400mg
Total Carbohydrate		300g	375g
Dietary Fiber		25g	30g

Special Diets and Food Allergies

Many people choose not to eat certain foods because of family background, religious beliefs, medical restrictions, or personal choice. Vegetarians, for example, avoid meat, but combinations of grains, beans, and other ingredients can give them plenty of protein. People allergic to dairy products, nuts, shellfish, or other foods must be especially careful in their food choices and may need to carry emergency kits to be used in case of an allergic reaction.

 For more information about packaging emblems such as kosher or non-dairy, visit www.bsahandbook.org.

HOW MUCH SHOULD YOU WEIGH?

Your weight depends on many factors, including how quickly your body uses the food you eat and on the build of your body. You are growing rapidly, too, and your body is changing. Eat nutritious foods in reasonable amounts and get plenty of exercise most days, and your body will probably find its own ideal weight. If you have concerns about how much you weigh, a family doctor can provide the answers you need. He or she might provide a height/weight chart for you to use. A good example of such a chart is the one used by Philmont Scout Ranch to help Scouts and their leaders prepare for backcountry treks.

Philmont Weight Limits for Backcountry Participation

Each participant in a Philmont trek must not weigh more than the maximum acceptable limit in the weight-for-height chart below. The right column shows the maximum acceptable weight for a person's height in order to participate in a Philmont trek. Those who fall within the limits are more likely to have an enjoyable trek and avoid risking their health.

Height		Weight (pounds)	
Feet	Inches	Recommended	Maximum
5	0	97—138	166
5	1	101—143	172
5	2	104—148	178
5	3	107—152	183
5	4	111—157	189
5	5	114—162	195
5	6	118—167	201
5	7	121—172	207
5	8	125—178	214
5	9	129—185	220
5	10	132—188	226
5	11	136—194	233
6	0	140—199	239
6	1	144—205	246
6	2	148—210	252
6	3	152—216	260
6	4	156—222	267
6	5	160—228	274
6	6	164—234	281
6	7	170—240	295

This table is based on the revised Dietary Guidelines for Americans from the U.S. Department of Agriculture and the Department of Health and Human Services.

Take pride in caring for your body. The habits of eating right and being active will benefit you throughout your life. Whether you are a youth or an adult, it's never too late to begin making yourself more fit.

For good health and to maintain the right weight for your body type:

▶ Eat enough of a balanced diet for your daily needs, but don't overeat.

▶ Be physically active for 30 to 60 minutes or more on most days.

"To carry out all the duties and work of a Scout properly a fellow has to be strong, healthy, and active. And he can make himself so if he takes a little care about it."

—Robert Baden-Powell, *Scouting for Boys*, 1915

GETTING ENOUGH SLEEP

Sleep is one of the most important ways of renewing your energy. Rest also gives your body a chance to replace old tissues and build new muscle. Much of the growth you are experiencing now happens while you are asleep. Most boys of Scouting age need nine to 10 hours each night.

On campouts, there will be so much to do during the day that you will almost always find yourself tired by bedtime. Crawl into your sleeping bag and you will probably fall right asleep and not wake up until dawn.

Sleep routines can be different at home. With schoolwork, sports, meetings, and family activities, there often is much to do after school and in the evening. Sometimes sleep might not seem very important. Organize your time, though, so that you can get the rest you need.

▶ Plan your schedule so that you go to bed at the same time each night and get up at the same time each morning.

▶ Enjoy some physical activities during the day.

▶ Avoid soft drinks that contain caffeine as well as sugary foods and drinks in the evening.

▶ The bright lights of televisions and computer screens can prevent your brain from quieting down for sleep, so set aside quiet time as you are getting ready for bed.

TAKING CARE OF YOUR BODY

Regular exercise, a healthy diet, drinking plenty of water, and getting enough sleep are all steps toward good health. In addition, take care of the following.

Skin—The skin is the body's largest organ. It is the outer armor protecting you from injury and illness. In addition, sweat glands in the skin help control body temperature. Nerve endings in the skin are sensitive to heat, cold, and touch.

When you will be in the sun, protect your skin from harmful rays by applying plenty of sunscreen. If your skin becomes dry or irritated, soothe it with lotion.

Bathe regularly—every day, if you can. A shower or bath is best, or you can wash yourself with a wet cloth. In camp and on the trail, carry water at least 200 feet (75 steps) from lakes, streams, and springs before washing.

Teeth—Your teeth can last a lifetime if you protect them. Gently brush them with toothpaste in the morning and at bedtime to remove sticky, colorless *plaque* that causes tooth decay and gum disease. Flossing once a day loosens food particles and plaque from between your teeth. A well-balanced diet helps keep teeth healthy, too. Having a dentist check and clean your teeth every six months is important long-term maintenance.

Eyes—Your eyes should be clear and bright. If they are often red or they ache, it might be a sign of strain caused by wind or smoke, lack of sleep, or staring too long at a television or computer. It also could mean you need glasses. Have your eyes checked by an eye doctor if you have concerns.

Rest your eyes when you are reading or working at a computer by looking out of a window now and then and focusing on distant objects. Wear sunglasses in bright light, especially on open water and snow. Goggles or a snorkel mask will keep swimming-pool chemicals from irritating your eyes. Put on safety goggles whenever you use power tools.

Ears—Very loud noises can damage your hearing. Wear ear protection around machinery and on firing ranges. Keep the volume of music players at a reasonable level, especially if you are listening with headphones. An earache, constant ringing, or fluid running out of an ear are all signs of trouble. See a doctor if you have any of these symptoms.

Lungs—The air you breathe provides oxygen your body must have. Breathe the cleanest air you can by staying away from exhaust fumes, smoke, and chemical vapors. Use paints, glues, and sprays only outside or in well-ventilated areas. Refuel and light camp stoves and lanterns outdoors, and never bring them into a tent.

Lifting and Sitting

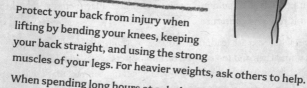

Protect your back from injury when lifting by bending your knees, keeping your back straight, and using the strong muscles of your legs. For heavier weights, ask others to help.

When spending long hours at a desk studying or doing computer work, guard your back from strain by sitting upright with your feet on the floor. Take breaks now and then to walk around and stretch. Best of all is getting outdoors and doing something active.

PROTECTING YOURSELF AGAINST INJURY AND DISEASE

It doesn't take much skill to cross a railroad track, but if a train is coming, common sense tells you to wait. It is common sense to use a sturdy stepladder instead of a wobbly chair when you have to reach something from a high place, to wear a helmet while bicycling, and to fasten your seatbelt when you get into a car. It is good judgment to stay away from unfamiliar dogs and to sweep up broken glass before someone steps on it and is hurt.

Be on the lookout for dangerous situations and do what you can to correct them. Is a campfire growing too large? Douse it. Is a sidewalk crowded? Walk your bicycle or keep your skateboard under your arm.

When it comes to avoiding injury, you can reduce risk in almost everything you do. Learn and follow the rules of the activities you enjoy. Hike and camp with care. Any time you aren't sure how to do something safely, ask. Understand the dangers of an activity and know how to minimize them.

TOBACCO, ALCOHOL, AND DRUGS

On a hike, you can rely on your map and compass to show you the way. When it comes to tobacco, alcohol, and drugs, you can trust that part of the Scout Oath in which you promise to keep yourself physically strong, mentally awake, and morally straight. Choosing not to use tobacco, alcohol, and drugs is a perfect example of ethical decision-making in how you care for your body and your mind.

Tobacco

Tobacco contains *nicotine*, a powerful drug that raises blood pressure and increases the heart rate. Smokers get in the habit of expecting these changes and become uncomfortable without nicotine. Once they have started using tobacco, many people find it is an *addiction*—a habit that is very hard to quit.

Advertisements often pretend smoking is exciting and attractive. You might have friends who think smoking makes them look grown-up. Don't be fooled. Smoking makes it harder for you to breathe and to be good at sports. Tobacco smoke coats your lungs with sticky tars that can lead to cancer and emphysema, diseases that cause misery and death for hundreds of thousands of people every year. Chewing tobacco and snuff can lead to mouth sores, gum disease, and cancers of the mouth, tongue, and throat.

For more information on avoiding the dangers of tobacco, alcohol, and drugs, visit the *Handbook* Web site, *www.bsahandbook.org.*

Effects of Smoking

If you begin smoking cigarettes, expect the following:

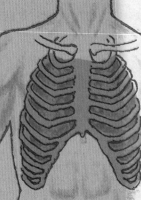

Right Now

▶ Your breath will be bad.

▶ Your clothes will smell.

▶ Your hair will stink.

▶ Your teeth will become yellow.

Soon

▶ You will have more colds and breathing problems than nonsmokers.

▶ Your lungs will become damaged, and your arteries will start to narrow and harden.

▶ You won't be as good at sports.

▶ You will have less endurance when hiking, bicycling, and taking part in other challenging activities.

▶ You will find it hard to quit smoking.

In the Future

▶ Your overall health will be poor.

▶ You might need to use an oxygen tank wherever you go, breathing from it through a mask.

▶ You will be at greater risk of dying of lung cancer.

▶ If you smoke a pack of cigarettes or more a day, you will likely live seven years less than people who have never smoked.

There's an easy way to avoid all of this. Do the smart thing and just don't start using tobacco. If you are smoking, make the ethical choice for your future and those who care for you by stopping now.

YOUR BODY UP IN SMOKE!

Alcohol

Commercials for beer, wine, and other alcoholic drinks are all around. But flashy images don't change the fact that drinking can cloud your thinking and affect your judgment. Alcoholism—a dependence on liquor—destroys many people's lives. The craving for alcohol saps their resources and their health, ruins families, and can lead to an early death.

For young people, it's best to avoid alcohol. Adults who choose to use alcohol need to be responsible in their choices, both in being safe and in setting a good example for others.

Be aware of the dangers of drinking and driving. Consuming alcohol can make a person an unsafe driver, and the results are sometimes tragic. Never ride in a car driven by someone who is under the influence of alcohol. You can always find another way home, but you might not live through a crash caused by an alcohol-impaired driver.

Talk with your parents or guardian about what to do if you ever find yourself in a situation that could involve a driver who has been drinking. Have a plan ready with a responsible adult you can always call for a ride home if you need it. That's self-leadership at its best—seeing the future you want and taking steps to make it happen.

Drugs

Drugs change the chemistry of your body. When you are ill, medicines prescribed by your doctor can help you get well. Unfortunately, many young people use illegal drugs that don't come from a doctor, or they take drugs that have been prescribed for someone else. If the amount of a drug someone swallows, smokes, inhales, or injects is not controlled by a doctor, a user never knows how much of a drug he or she is taking. An overdose can lead to serious illness or death.

Many drugs are addictive. Those who begin using a drug can soon find that they want more and that trying to stop is physically and emotionally painful. They might lie, cheat, and steal to get drugs. Using drugs can become more important to them than their friends, their families, and even their own lives.

Marijuana, meth, ecstasy, cocaine, crack, codeine, inhalants, depressants, LSD, and heroin have harmful effects on the mind. Protect your health by avoiding these and all other illegal drugs.

STAYING AWAY FROM
TOBACCO, ALCOHOL, AND DRUGS

Because tobacco, alcohol, and illegal drugs can have such dangerous effects, why would anyone ever start using them? Here are some reasons users might give you and some ways you can respond.

"All my friends are doing it." It might seem that some people you like are doing something that isn't wise. To be like them, you may be tempted to try it, too. But if their actions are wrong, you don't have to follow the crowd. Sometimes real leadership means simply doing what is right. Show your friends there's a better way to live. Get more involved in Scouting, school activities, sports, and worthwhile clubs. If you have to, find new friends who aren't developing dangerous habits.

"I want to get away from problems." Scouts learn on campouts that life in the outdoors is not always easy. Perhaps you've been caught in a thunderstorm. Maybe someone fell and twisted his ankle. You didn't run away from those problems. Instead, you used your skills to make a safe camp or to give first aid. You faced the tough times squarely and made the best of them.

At home and in school, demands can seem very heavy. You might feel as though there's a lot of weight on your shoulders or that parents and teachers expect too much of you. Instead of turning to drugs, tobacco, and alcohol to escape, use your skills to find solutions. You don't have to do it all alone. Friends, parents, teachers, school counselors, and religious leaders might all be able to help.

"I want to feel grown up." Because of the way they are often shown in movies and on television, smoking, drinking, and using drugs might seem like adult things to do. But hurting your body and your future is very childish.

Prove you are becoming an adult by accepting worthwhile responsibilities. Helping with household chores shows you are doing your part to make family life better for everyone. Advancing in Scouting's ranks and holding troop leadership positions are signs you are maturing. Doing your best in class and in school activities also shows your maturity. These are the real ways to let the world know you are becoming a respected adult.

"There's nothing else to do." Some young people say they use drugs, alcohol, and tobacco because they are bored. What they are really saying is that they are too lazy to take part in the real excitement of being alive.

If you look around, boredom should be the farthest thing from your mind. Athletics, books, Scouting, school projects, music, exercise, helping others—the world is full of great things to do. Look at life as full of possibilities for constant growth, and embrace the opportunities all around you.

IV. DUTY TO SELF

For more tips on staying away from tobacco, alcohol, and drugs, visit the *Handbook* Web site, *www.bsahandbook.org.*

Finally, you can simply turn your back on anything that would harm you, demonstrating ethical decision-making and courage. Nobody can force you to do something wrong if you don't agree to do it. With a strong body and clear mind, you will be far ahead of those who choose to risk their friends, their families, and their lives with the very real dangers of tobacco, drugs, and alcohol.

Baden-Powell's Advice

Robert Baden-Powell, Scouting's founder, had faith that Scouts were smart enough to figure out what is healthy and right. He urged Scouts not to let others pressure them into harming themselves with drugs, alcohol, or tobacco. "And if you have been foolish," he said, "there is no law that says you must stay that way."

MENTALLY AWAKE

Eating the right foods, getting enough sleep, and protecting yourself from tobacco, alcohol, and drugs are important habits for staying healthy. They can all help keep your mind strong and alert, too.

That's a good start. Staying mentally awake requires exercise, just as physical fitness does. You can exercise your mind every day at school and by learning all you can about what's going on in your community, your state, and your nation. You can look at homework as an opportunity to build your brain.

Scouting offers plenty of opportunities for your mind to grow. Advancing through Scouting's ranks and completing the requirements for BSA merit badges will challenge you to think and learn. Being a leader in your patrol and troop can stretch your mind as you practice new skills. Every Scout adventure presents opportunities to solve problems and figure out the best ways of doing things.

MORALLY STRAIGHT

The third part of the Scout Oath's fitness promises is that you will do your best to keep yourself morally straight. This idea has been at the heart of Scouting since the beginning. Early editions of the *Boy Scout Handbook* encouraged Scouts to model themselves after the knights of old. At the heart of that belief was *chivalry*—living by a code that was a guide to behaving at all times with honor. The 1914 *Handbook* explained it this way:

A Scout Is Chivalrous

"Obviously a boy scout must be chivalrous. That is, he should be as manly as the knights or pioneers of old. He should be unselfish. He should show courage. He must do his duty. He should show benevolence and thrift. He should be loyal to his country. He should be obedient to his parents, and show respect to those who are his superiors. He should be very courteous to women. One of his obligations is to do a good turn every day to some one. He should be cheerful and seek self-improvement, and should make a career for himself."

—*Handbook for Boys*, 2nd ed., 1914

We are far beyond the age of knights, but the idea of being guided by a moral code is as important today as it has ever been.

Who you are is built on the values of your family, friends, religious denomination, and community. The Scout Oath and Scout Law put those values into words that can be recited easily and understood by everyone. Helping others at all times. Doing your best to be trustworthy, loyal, and helpful. Acting with kindness to others. Being brave in doing what is right, and being reverent in your beliefs.

With the Scout Oath and Scout Law to guide you, you can make ethical decisions even when problems are difficult and even if you must stand alone. There might be times when peer pressure could tempt you to bend the rules, but you know you won't because that's not the way you want to live.

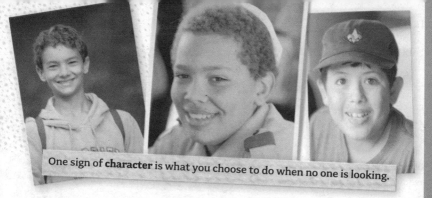

One sign of **character** is what you choose to do when no one is looking.

The self-leadership that is helping you become physically strong and mentally awake also can guide you in making moral choices. When you are faced with a tough decision, begin by forming a picture in your mind of what the right outcome will be for you and others who are involved.

When you can see the goal you want to reach, figure out the steps to get there. This might require getting more information and talking with others. You could discover that there are several pathways you might follow. If so, measure each against the Scout Oath and Scout Law to learn which one holds up.

Then you can put the steps in action, knowing that you are doing the right thing. Despite what others might think, you will be making good choices and strengthening your moral fitness as you continue toward the larger goal of always being an ethical person.

Consider the following situations:

▶ A school classmate has a paper you can copy and turn in as your own. No one will know except you and your classmate. Do you do it?

▶ On a busy street, you find a wallet with money in it. No one sees you pick it up. Do you keep it or take steps to return it to its owner? If you do return it, should you keep some of the money as a reward?

▶ Some boys your age are bullying a younger boy on the playground. Do you do something about it or pretend you haven't seen anything and walk away?

Decisions you make throughout life will come in many forms. Some will be very tough, but they will have one thing in common. You will know how you acted. You will be aware of the times when you did the right thing and realize that you've strengthened your moral fitness. You'll also know when you should have made a better choice, and you can learn from that experience, too.

Many ethical decisions involve small choices—being courteous to other people, for example, and helping out whenever you can. Other decisions can have lifelong consequences. One that you might confront in your teenage years is the matter of sexual responsibility.

Sexual Responsibility

As you grow into manhood, you are maturing sexually and are capable of becoming a father. Fatherhood is a responsibility with powerful consequences in your life and in the lives of others. The choices you make require your very best judgment.

People around you are also changing. Girls you know are becoming young women. They are maturing physically and emotionally. Your relationships with them will become closer and more meaningful, both to you and to them.

Sex is not the most important or grown-up part of a relationship. Having sex is never a test of manliness. True maturity comes from acting ethically in the following ways:

▶ *Your responsibility to women.* Whenever you like to be with someone, you want the best for that person. A healthy relationship is supportive and equal. You can have terrific times together enjoying life and growing emotionally. However, the difficulties created by an unplanned pregnancy can be very complicated. Don't burden someone you care for with a child neither of you is ready to raise.

▶ *Your responsibility to yourself.* An understanding of wholesome sexual behavior can bring lifelong happiness. Irresponsibility or ignorance, however, can cause a lifetime of regret. Diseases spread by sexual contact could threaten your health and that of others. Having a baby before you are ready might severely limit your chances for education, occupations, and travel.

▶ *Your responsibility to your beliefs.* For the followers of most religions, sex should take place only between people who are married to each other. To do otherwise may cause feelings of guilt and loss. Waiting until marriage is a wise course of action.

You owe it to yourself to enter adulthood without extra hurdles to overcome. Learn what is right. Your religious leaders can give you guidance for making ethical choices. Your parents, guardian, or a sex-education teacher can provide the basic facts about sex.

LIFELONG FITNESS

Each time you say the Scout Oath, you promise to keep yourself physically strong, mentally awake, and morally straight. These are more than just words. They are a pledge to do your best to develop healthy habits that lead to fitness of your body, your mind, and your character.

This might seem like a lot to do right now, but the important thing is to get started. Picture what fitness will look like for you in the months and years ahead, then lead yourself in the right direction. Be true to your vision of becoming the best person that you can be, and the rest will fall into place.

"One step toward happiness is to make yourself healthy and strong while you are a boy, so that you can be useful, and so can enjoy life when you are a man."

—Robert Baden-Powell

First Aid

FIRST AID

A Scout on a campout falls against a rock. He shouts for help. His head is bleeding and his arm is bent at an odd angle. *What do you do?*

Walking home from school, you hear the squeal of tires and turn to see a car knock a man to the ground. He is unconscious. Blood is spurting from a gash in his leg. You don't think he is breathing. *What do you do?*

A small child complains that he feels sick. You see a box of rat poison spilled on the floor and think the child might have eaten some. *What do you do?*

What you do is give first aid.

The Goals of First Aid

▶ Protect a person who is injured or ill from further harm.

▶ Stop life-threatening medical emergencies.

▶ Get the person under professional medical care.

IN THIS CHAPTER

▶ The goals of first aid and why first aid is important

▶ Personal and group first-aid kits

▶ First-aid method

▶ Basic first-aid techniques

▶ First aid for hurry cases

▶ Moving an ill or injured person

WHY FIRST AID IS IMPORTANT

First aid is the first help given to someone who has had an accident or other health emergency. If more attention is needed, first-aid treatment helps keep an injured or ill person as safe as possible until medical personnel arrive.

First aid has always been important to the Boy Scouts of America. It is part of being a good citizen. Learning first-aid skills is a way to put into action the Scouting ideal of doing Good Turns.

You could be the first to arrive at an accident scene and the first to offer assistance. Even if other people are around, you might be the one most able to help. On Scout trips, at home, and in your school and community, you'll want to be ready to do the best you can in any situation.

Knowing how to treat injured or ill people also is part of being prepared. The Scout motto—Be Prepared—asks that you do all you can to avoid injuries and illnesses in the first place. Good planning of hikes and campouts means that you and others in your patrol will know what to expect along the way. You'll have clothing and shelter to match the weather, and you will be careful with stoves, pocketknives, and other woods tools. You can watch out for one another.

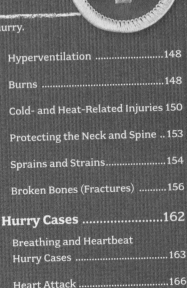

Chapter Quick Index

Use this index to find first-aid advice in a hurry.

First-Aid Kits **127**

    Personal First-Aid Kit 127

    Home or Patrol/
    Troop First-Aid Kit 128

First-Aid Method **129**

    The Steps of the First-Aid Method ..130

Basic First Aid **136**

    Simple Cuts and Scrapes 136

    Blisters 137

    Nosebleeds 138

    Poisonous Plants 138

    Animal Bites 140

    Spider and Insect Bites
    and Stings 142

    Object in the Eye 145

    Puncture Wounds 145

    Dehydration 147

Hyperventilation 148

Burns 148

Cold- and Heat-Related Injuries 150

Protecting the Neck and Spine ..153

Sprains and Strains.................... 154

Broken Bones (Fractures) 156

Hurry Cases **162**

    Breathing and Heartbeat
    Hurry Cases 163

    Heart Attack 166

    Severe Bleeding 167

    Ingested Poisoning 169

    Shock 170

**Other First-Aid
Emergencies** **172**

**Moving an Ill or
Injured Person** **173**

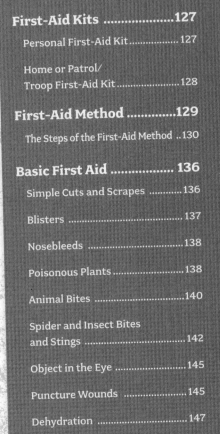

FIRST-AID KITS

Being prepared for first aid means having the necessary supplies on hand. A personal first-aid kit will help you treat scrapes, blisters, and other minor injuries. Carry a personal first-aid kit on hikes and campouts. Fit everything in a resealable plastic bag and take it with you whenever you set out on a Scout adventure. Preparing a larger first-aid kit for your patrol or troop can be useful in treating many injuries and illnesses. Everyone should know who is carrying the kit and where it is stored so that it can be located quickly.

Personal First-Aid Kit

- [ ] 6 adhesive bandages
- [ ] 2 sterile, 3-by-3-inch gauze pads
- [ ] A small roll of adhesive tape
- [ ] A 3-by-6-inch piece of moleskin
- [ ] A small bar of soap or small bottle of alcohol-based hand sanitizing gel
- [ ] A small tube of triple antibiotic ointment
- [ ] Scissors
- [ ] Disposable nonlatex gloves
- [ ] CPR breathing barrier
- [ ] Pencil and paper

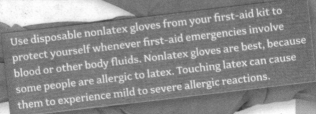

Use disposable nonlatex gloves from your first-aid kit to protect yourself whenever first-aid emergencies involve blood or other body fluids. Nonlatex gloves are best, because some people are allergic to latex. Touching latex can cause them to experience mild to severe allergic reactions.

Visit www.bsahandbook.org for downloadable checklists for personal and home/troop first-aid kits.

Home or Patrol/Troop First-Aid Kit

A more comprehensive group first-aid kit can contain the following items.

- [ ] A 2-inch roller bandage
- [ ] 2 1-inch roller bandages
- [ ] A roll of 1-inch adhesive tape
- [ ] 24 alcohol swabs
- [ ] A box of assorted adhesive bandages
- [ ] 2 3-inch-wide elastic bandages
- [ ] 12 sterile, 3-by-3-inch gauze pads
- [ ] 4 3-by-6-inch pieces of moleskin
- [ ] 2 packets of gel pads for blisters and burns
- [ ] A tube of triple antibiotic ointment
- [ ] 4 triangular bandages
- [ ] A small bar of soap, or a travel-sized bottle of alcohol-based hand sanitizing gel
- [ ] Scissors
- [ ] Tweezers
- [ ] 12 safety pins
- [ ] 6 pairs of nonlatex disposable gloves
- [ ] Protective goggles/safety glasses
- [ ] CPR breathing barrier
- [ ] Pencil and paper

These optional items also are recommended:

- [ ] An instant cold compress
- [ ] A space blanket
- [ ] A SAM® Splint

Be Prepared . . . for Emergencies

Use the contents list of the home or patrol/troop first-aid kit to build your own home first-aid kit. With the help of your parents or guardian, your home first-aid kit can become part of a larger emergency-preparedness kit that includes flashlights, a battery- or crank-powered radio, and a three-day supply of drinking water and nonperishable food. Having these items on hand will better prepare your family for storms, floods, power outages, and other emergencies.

FIRST-AID METHOD

Most first aid is for simple injuries and illnesses. There's usually plenty of time to decide what to do when you need to treat a minor cut, a rash from poison ivy, most insect bites and stings, or frostbite. However, when injuries or illnesses are more serious, using a first-aid method will guide you to do the right things in the right order in an emergency. When you use a first-aid method, you follow the same steps every time you practice first aid.

1. Check the scene.
2. Call for help.
3. Approach safely.
4. Provide urgent treatment.
5. Protect from further injury.
6. Treat every accident victim for shock.
7. Make a thorough examination.
8. Plan a course of action.

MERIT BADGE SERIES

EMERGENCY PREPAREDNESS

The Emergency Preparedness merit badge pamphlet has more detailed information about making an emergency-preparedness kit for your home.

The requirements for the Emergency Preparedness merit badge can be found on the *Handbook* Web site, www.bsahandbook.org.

The Steps of the First-Aid Method

An accident scene can sometimes be scary and confusing. An injured person might be crying or screaming. The sight of blood could startle you. Other people may be too stunned to help. You should stay as calm as you can and focus your attention on making people safe as you carry out the steps of the first-aid method.

1. Check the Scene

Before doing anything, stop for a moment to look over the entire scene and collect your thoughts. Consider the following questions:

▶ What caused the accident or illness?

▶ Are there dangers in the area? Should the victim be moved?

▶ How many victims are there?

▶ If there are other people nearby, can they assist with first aid or with getting help?

▶ Will bystanders need guidance so that they do not become victims themselves?

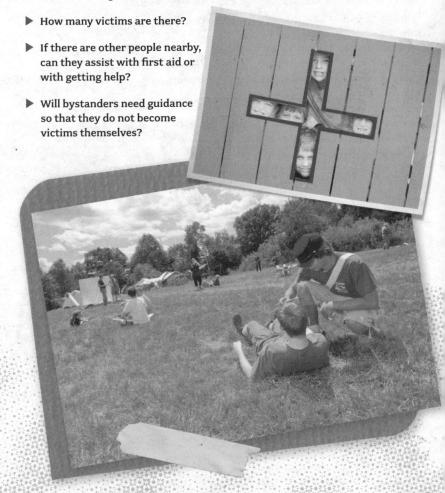

2. Call for Help

Whenever someone has anything more than a minor illness or injury, act quickly to get them medical help. In much of the United States, you can dial 911 to reach emergency services. Some communities use other emergency-alert systems such as dialing 0 or calling a local sheriff's office or fire department. Send a bystander or other first-aider to call for help immediately.

When camping or traveling through the backcountry when a serious injury or illness occurs, send two or more people for help with as much of the following information as possible:

▶ Location of the victim

▶ Description of the injuries or illness

▶ Time the injuries or illness occurred

▶ Treatment the victim has received

▶ Number of people with the victim and their general skill level for first aid

▶ Requests for special assistance or equipment, including food, shelter, or care for nonvictims

3. Approach Safely

Keep your own safety in mind. At the scene of a car accident, watch for other cars and trucks on the road. In the backcountry, be aware of falling rocks, slippery footing, steep slopes, and other hazards.

Tell the injured or ill person, "My name is _____ and I know first aid. May I help you?" If someone is unconscious or so badly hurt that he or she cannot respond, you can assume the person wants help.

4. Provide Urgent Treatment

Any situation where a victim requires urgent treatment is considered a *hurry case*, and *bleeding* and *breathing* are the immediate concerns. When you approach an ill or injured person, take 15 to 20 seconds to survey the victim's condition to find out the following:

▶ **Is the person conscious and breathing? Is the heart beating?**

▶ **Is there severe bleeding?**

▶ **Are there other contributing factors like allergies, diabetes, or other possible causes of an emergency situation? Is there evidence of pills, chemicals, or other poisons?**

5. Protect From Further Injury

Avoid moving someone who is injured unless it is impossible to perform urgent first aid or the victim is in a dangerous location. If the person's position must be adjusted, do so carefully with the minimum amount of movement—with the help of a fellow first-aider or bystander, stabilize the victim's head and neck. *Never* move a person with a suspected spinal injury unless it is absolutely necessary.

6. Treat Every Accident Victim for Shock

When a person is injured and under great stress, the circulatory system might not provide enough blood and oxygen to the body tissues. This condition is called *shock*. It requires quick and effective treatment.

See page 170 for information on treating shock.

7. Make a Thorough Examination

When professional medical help will be delayed, check the victim for other injuries. Check the victim from head to toe. If the victim is alert, ask for information about how an injury occurred. Ask where it is painful and whether the victim can move arms, legs, and so on. Pay attention to how a victim is responding as well as what he or she is saying. Open rain gear, jackets, and outer clothing that might be hiding other wounds.

8. Plan a Course of Action

If medical assistance is on the way, keep the victim comfortable. When help will be delayed, decide on a clear course of action. A victim who can walk alone or with some support may be able to hike to a road. If injuries are serious, though, it is almost always better to send two people to get medical help. Keep checking the injured person's condition and be ready to respond to any changes.

The First-Aid Method in Action:
Caring for Someone Who Is Choking

The following scenario shows how you could use the steps of the first-aid method to take care of a person who is experiencing a choking emergency.

Suppose that during a meal you notice that a man at the table is in trouble. His face is turning red. It looks as though he is choking, and he grabs his throat with his hands. Take a moment to recognize what is happening—a man is choking. Ask someone to call 911. Then tell the choking man that you know first aid and that you are there to help.

If the choking man can cough, speak, or breathe, you'll know that some air is getting into his lungs. Encourage him to cough up whatever is blocking his airway. If he is coughing weakly or making high-pitched noises, or if he can't cough, speak, or breathe, you will need to help him clear the object from his throat by using the following method.

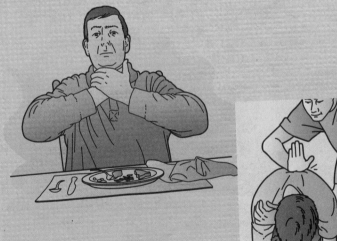

Step 1—If the man is conscious, stand behind him and place your arm across his chest. Lean him forward and firmly strike his back with the heel of your hand five times. If he still cannot breathe, continue to steps 2 and 3.

Step 2—Stand behind the victim, put your arms around his waist and clasp your hands together. The knuckle of one thumb should be just above the navel but below the rib cage.

Step 3—Thrust your clasped hands inward and upward with enough force to pop loose the object that is blocking the airway. Repeat up to five times.

Repeat steps 1 through 3 until the object is coughed up, medical help arrives, or the person becomes unconscious.

Once you have restored breathing, treat the man for shock while waiting for help to arrive. Treat any injuries he might have suffered during the choking episode. If medical help is delayed, decide how to care for the choking victim while waiting for emergency personnel. You might decide to comfort him and watch his condition closely so that you can offer additional first aid if needed.

Your first-aid method guided you to treat the choking man correctly.

▶ **Check the scene.** You took a moment to figure out that the man was choking.

▶ **Call for help.** You asked someone to call 911.

▶ **Approach safely.** You carefully made your way to the choking man and introduced yourself.

▶ **Provide urgent treatment and protect from further injury.** You saw that the man could not breathe normally, and you took steps to help him.

▶ **Treat every accident victim for shock.** Once breathing was restored, you treated the man for shock as you waited for help to arrive.

▶ **Do a thorough examination.** You checked to see if the man suffered any injuries that needed attention.

▶ **Plan a course of action.** You monitored the man's condition while waiting for medical help so that you could provide additional first aid if needed.

BASIC FIRST AID

Other chapters of the *Boy Scout Handbook* include plenty of information about getting ready for time in the outdoors. The skills of Scouting can go a long way in helping you keep yourself and others safe and managing the risks that might arise when you are out hiking or camping. Basic first-aid skills can be used to treat a wide range of minor injuries and illnesses, whether they occur on an outdoor adventure or when you are closer to home.

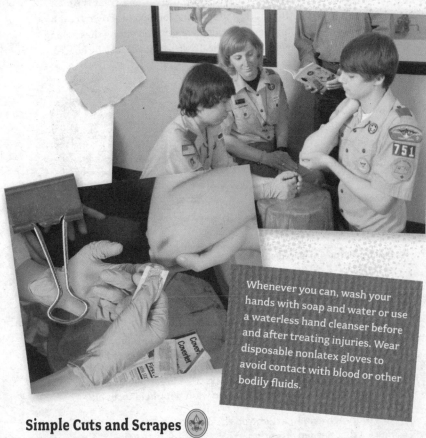

Whenever you can, wash your hands with soap and water or use a waterless hand cleanser before and after treating injuries. Wear disposable nonlatex gloves to avoid contact with blood or other bodily fluids.

Simple Cuts and Scrapes

Small cuts and scrapes and other openings in the skin can allow bacteria to enter the body and cause infection. Wash scrapes and minor cuts with soap and water. Apply triple antibiotic ointment and cover with a dry, sterile dressing or an adhesive bandage to help prevent infection and protect the wound. Clean and rebandage wounds each day.

For more detailed instructions on treating minor injuries, visit the *Handbook* Web site, *www.bsahandbook.org*.

Dealing With Hot Spots

Pay attention to how your feet feel. A *hot spot*—an area of skin that becomes tender as a blister starts to form—is a signal to stop and treat the hot spot immediately before it becomes a blister. Cover the area with a piece of moleskin larger than the hot spot.

Blisters

To help prevent blisters on your feet when hiking, wear shoes or boots that fit well and that have been broken in. Change your socks if they become sweaty or wet. Wearing work gloves can help lessen the chances of developing blisters on your hands when you are working outdoors.

If you do develop a blister, don't pop it. Breaking a blister increases the chances of infection by bacteria.

If a blister forms on your foot while hiking, apply a piece of moleskin cut slightly larger than the blistered area. Use several layers if necessary. The moleskin will take the pressure from your boot off the blister.

Nosebleeds

A bloody nose that is not caused by an accident might look bad, but the bleeding will usually stop in a few minutes. Have the person sit leaning forward so that the blood does not run down the inside of the throat. Ask the person to pinch the nose firmly but gently, and apply pressure on the upper lip, just below the nose. Hold a cold compress against the nose and surrounding area.

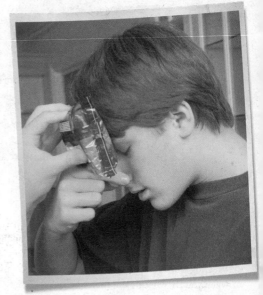

After about 10 minutes, instruct the person to slowly release the nose pinch. Check to see if the bleeding has stopped. If not, have him or her again pinch the nose and apply pressure. After the bleeding stops, instruct the person not to irritate or blow the nose. If bleeding continues for more than 15 minutes, seek medical attention.

Poisonous Plants

Poison ivy, poison oak, and poison sumac are the most common poisonous plants in the United States. Contact with oily sap in their leaves, stems, and roots may irritate your skin and cause itching. The sap must be on the skin for 10 to 20 minutes before it begins causing problems.

If you think you have touched a poisonous plant, begin first aid by washing the area immediately with soap and water. Rubbing alcohol, calamine lotion, and other nonprescription treatments might help relieve itching. Try not to scratch. If the reaction is severe, if the eyes or genital area is affected, or if plant parts were chewed or swallowed, seek immediate medical attention.

When you are out hiking and camping, knowing how to identify poisonous plants will help you avoid them and the problems they may cause.

Sap on your clothing can affect your skin later, so if you come in contact with a poisonous plant, change clothes as soon as you can and wash the affected clothes separately from other items.

Poison oak

Poison ivy

Poison sumac (spring)

Poison sumac (fall)

For more information on identifying poisonous plants, visit the *Handbook* Web site, *www.bsahandbook.org*.

Animal Bites

The bite of a warm-blooded animal such as a dog, cat, skunk, raccoon, fox, or bat is a serious puncture wound. To treat an animal bite, wash the wound and flush it with water for several minutes. Control bleeding and cover the wound with a sterile bandage.

Opossum

Bats

Skunk

Rabid Animals

Warm-blooded animals may have rabies, a deadly illness that can be spread through their saliva. For this reason, the person who was bitten must see a doctor who can determine whether to administer rabies shots.

An unprovoked attack could be a sign that an animal is rabid. Report all animal bites to your local public health authorities or the police. Do not kill the animal unless necessary, and do not put yourself at risk by trying to catch the animal. Call the police, rangers, or animal control officers, who are trained to do the job safely. Suspicious animals may be confined and observed, or destroyed so that their brains can be tested for rabies.

If the bite was caused by a pet, write down the owner's name, address, and telephone number. If the injury was caused by a wild animal, write a description of the animal and where it was last seen. This will help public health authorities take action.

Snakebites

Snakes are common in many parts of the country, but bites from them are rare. Snakebites seldom result in death. Some snakes are *nonvenomous*. Others are *venomous*.

Nonvenomous Snakebites—The bite of a nonvenomous snake requires only ordinary first aid for small puncture wounds. Wash the bitten area with soap and water, apply an antibiotic ointment, and cover with a sterile bandage. Snakes are not warm-blooded, so they cannot carry rabies.

Venomous Snakebites—The venomous snakes of North America are pit vipers and coral snakes. *Pit vipers* (including rattlesnakes, copperheads, and cottonmouths) have triangular heads with pits on each side in front of their eyes. *Coral snakes* have black snouts and are marked with red and yellow bands, separated by bands of black.

Copperhead

Rattlesnake

Cottonmouth moccasin

Coral snake

Remember this ditty for safety around coral snakes: red and black—friendly jack; red and yellow—deadly fellow.

141

Follow these steps for treating the bite of a venomous snake.

Step 1—Remove rings and other jewelry before the injury swells.

Step 2—Get the victim under a doctor's care as soon as possible. Someone who has been bitten by a venomous snake might not be affected by the venom for an hour or more. Within that time, the closer to medical attention you can get the victim, the better off he or she will be. The person might be able to walk. If not, you and one or more others may be able to carry the victim.

Step 3—If the victim must wait for help to arrive, wash the wound. For the bite of a coral snake, wrap the area snugly but comfortably with an elastic roller bandage.

Step 4—Have the victim lie down with the bitten limb lower than the rest of the body. Encourage the person to stay calm. He or she might be frightened, so keep assuring the victim that you are there and are providing care.

Step 5—Treat for shock but don't elevate the affected limb.

Being able to identify venomous snakes is a good first step toward staying safe in areas where they live. If you leave snakes alone, they are likely to avoid you, too. Use a hiking stick to poke among stones and brush ahead of you when you walk through areas where snakes are common. Be careful where you put your hands as you collect firewood or climb over rocks and logs.

Spider and Insect Bites and Stings

The bites or stings of ticks, chiggers, spiders, and insects can be painful. Some might cause infection. Protect yourself from bites and stings by wearing long pants and a long-sleeved shirt whenever you are in woodlands and fields that might be infested. Button your collar and tuck your pant cuffs into your boots or socks. Insect repellents also can be effective. Inspect yourself daily, especially the hairy parts of your body.

Tick Bites—Ticks are small, hard-shelled creatures that bury their heads in the skin. To remove a tick, put on nonlatex first-aid gloves and then use tweezers to grasp the tick close to the skin. Gently pull until the tick comes loose. Don't squeeze, twist, or jerk the tick. Doing so may cause the tick's mouthparts to break off in the skin. Wash the wound with soap and water and apply antiseptic. Wash your hands after dealing with a tick. Ticks sometimes spread Lyme disease, Rocky Mountain spotted fever, and other serious illnesses. If you develop a rash or flulike symptoms or otherwise feel ill in the next days or weeks after being bitten by a tick, talk to your doctor.

Tick

Chigger Bites —Chiggers are almost invisible. They burrow into skin pores, causing itching and small bumps on the skin. Try not to scratch chigger bites. You might find relief from the itching by covering a chigger bite with calamine lotion or by dabbing it with clear fingernail polish.

Spider Bites—The bites of most spiders cause only minor pain and itching that go away in a fairly short amount of time. However, several kinds of spiders pose a more serious threat to humans. The bite of a female black widow spider might cause redness and sharp pain at the wound site. The victim can suffer sweating, nausea and vomiting, stomach pain and cramps, severe muscle pain and spasms, and shock. Breathing may become difficult.

Black widow spider (enlarged)

A brown recluse spider bite may not hurt right away, but within two to eight hours there can be pain, redness, and swelling at the wound. An open sore is likely to form. The victim may suffer fever, chills, nausea, vomiting, joint pain, and a faint rash.

Anyone who has been bitten by a spider should be seen by a doctor as soon as possible. Treat for shock.

Insect Stings—To treat a bee or hornet sting, remove the stinger by scraping it out with the side of a knife blade. Don't squeeze the stinger, because that can force more venom into the skin. Applying an ice pack might help reduce pain and swelling.

Anyone who begins to experience difficulty breathing after having been stung by an insect must be treated immediately for anaphylactic shock. Call 911 or your community's local emergency number. If the person is carrying a kit for treating anaphylactic shock, follow the instructions.

Brown recluse spider (enlarged)

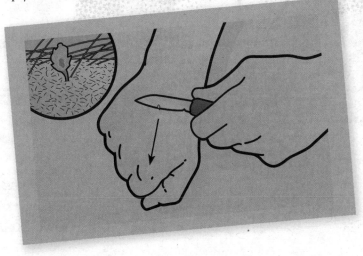

Anaphylactic Shock

For most people, insect or jellyfish stings cause pain, mild swelling, and perhaps a few days of itching. For others, these stings can cause a life-threatening allergic reaction called *anaphylactic shock.* Symptoms of anaphylactic shock may include swelling of throat tissues that makes breathing difficult or even impossible. For this reason, anaphylactic shock is a first-aid *hurry case,* that is, a condition that threatens a person's life.

Insect and jellyfish stings aren't the only triggers of anaphylactic shock. People who are allergic to peanuts, dairy products, and certain other foods also can go into anaphylactic shock if they eat or touch these items. Some people have a similar reaction when coming in contact with latex. With the help of their parents or guardian, Scouts with allergies should discuss their conditions with troop leaders and review what to do if an allergy emergency occurs.

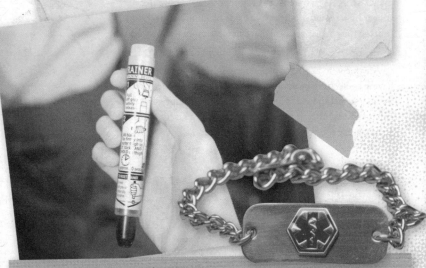

People who know they have severe allergies often carry treatment kits, such as the epinephrine injection shown here, to use in case of an emergency. They could be wearing a medical alert bracelet or necklace with emergency information. They might have a card that instructs others to call for help by dialing 911 (or another local emergency number) and lists the steps to take while waiting for emergency medical technicians to arrive.

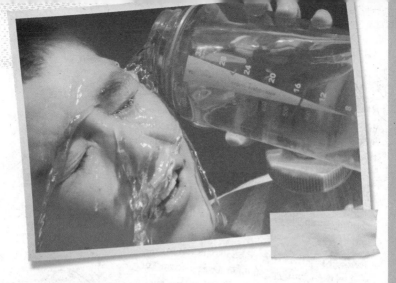

Object in the Eye

Protect your eyes by wearing safety glasses or goggles when using power tools, lawn and garden equipment, and other machinery that might throw off particles or other debris. If something does get into someone's eye, encourage him or her not to rub it. Persons who wear contact lenses should remove them. Ask the person to blink the eyes rapidly. This might allow tears to wash the eye clear. Flushing the eyes with clean water from a faucet, cup, or water bottle is another option for clearing a foreign particle from the eye. If the object will not wash out, cover the injured eye with a dry, sterile gauze pad and get the person to a doctor.

Puncture Wounds

Pins, splinters, fishhooks, cactus spines, and other sharp objects can cause *puncture wounds*. These types of wounds can trap bacteria that may cause infection. Flush a puncture wound with clean water squeezed from a water bottle or a sturdy plastic bag with a very small hole punched in one corner with a pencil or sharpened twig. Using this kind of setup will create a high-pressure stream of water that will help flush bacteria out of the wound. Repeat several times to clean the puncture wound as thoroughly as possible.

If a large object is embedded in the flesh—a nail, for example—do not try to remove it. Gently wash the area with soap and water, apply a sterile bandage, and seek medical attention.

After you've cleaned the wound, control the bleeding by applying a sterile bandage, then get the victim to medical attention as soon as possible. Because puncture wounds pose a high risk of infection, a doctor may want to prescribe antibiotics.

Fishhook Wounds

A fishhook stuck in the skin is a type of puncture wound that may occur during a fishing trip. Cut the fishing line and, whenever possible, let a doctor remove the hook from the flesh. If the hook has lodged so that the barb is visible above the skin and you have the right tools, you might be able to remove it in the field.

Step 1—Wrap a 3-foot length of fishing line around the bend of the hook, as shown, and securely wrap the ends around your index or middle finger.

Step 2—Keep the affected body part flat and stable, then gently push down on the shank to free the barb from the injured tissue. The shank should be parallel to the injured tissue.

Step 3—Keep bystanders well away from the area. While maintaining pressure on the shank, give the line a quick, sharp jerk. Be careful to avoid getting snagged by the outcoming hook.

Step 4—Wash and bandage the injury, and keep the wound clean. Apply triple antibiotic ointment if there are no known allergies or sensitivities to the medication. See a doctor as soon as possible, because the risk of infection is high with this type of injury.

Do not try to remove a fishhook from the face or from an eye or an earlobe. The chance of additional injury to these areas is too great. That is a task for a doctor.

Dehydration

Water is necessary for nearly every bodily function, including producing heat and staying cool. Moisture can be lost through breathing, sweating, digestion, and urination. A person giving off more water than he or she takes in becomes dehydrated. When this happens, the body might have a difficult time regulating core temperature. Hypothermia, heat exhaustion, and heatstroke can all be worsened by dehydration.

Signals of dehydration may include:

▶ **Severe thirst**

▶ **Dark urine, decreased urine production**

▶ **Tiredness, weakness**

▶ **Dry skin and lips, decreased sweating**

▶ **Nausea, fainting, loss of appetite**

▶ **Headache, body aches, muscle cramps**

▶ **Confusion, dizziness**

Protect yourself from dehydration by drinking plenty of fluids *before* you feel thirsty. Take in enough fluids so that your urine stays clear. This is easy to remember to do on hot days. It is just as important in cold weather when you may not feel like drinking.

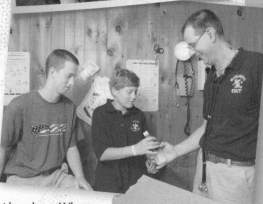

If someone shows signs of becoming dehydrated, encourage him or her to drink fluids and rest. When the weather is hot, get the person to a shaded place or into an air-conditioned vehicle or building. In cold weather, be sure he or she is wearing enough dry clothing. Help the person reach the shelter of a tent and sleeping bag or a warm building. Keep checking his or her condition, and be ready to provide further first-aid treatment.

Hyperventilation

Someone who is anxious or frightened might react by breathing too quickly. When rapid breathing continues too long, it can upset the balance of oxygen and carbon dioxide in the bloodstream. The person could feel as though he or she is suffocating and might become dizzy, disoriented, and fearful.

Treat hyperventilation by talking quietly to the victim and encouraging him or her to calm down and breathe slowly. While hyperventilation is usually not a deep concern, it is sometimes a signal of a more serious medical condition. Dizziness and anxiety, for example, can be warning signals of a heart attack. For these reasons, someone who has experienced hyperventilation should be checked by a physician.

Burns

A spark from a campfire, boiling water spilled from a pot, a bolt of lightning, toxic chemicals, a live electrical line—the causes of burns are many. First-aid treatment for a burn depends upon how serious it is. Burns usually are characterized by the severity of the skin and tissue damage.

Minor Burns or Scalds

Touch a hot stove and you could suffer a *superficial burn* (also known as a *first-degree burn*). Skin will be tender, and it also might become red. Treat a superficial burn by holding the injured area under cold water or applying cool, wet compresses until there is little or no pain.

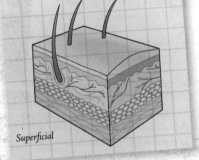

Superficial

Serious Burns

First-degree burns generally only need treatment with cold water or cool, wet compresses. However, second-degree and third-degree burns can be very serious and even life-threatening. Use the following steps to treat a burn victim:

Step 1—Take a moment before doing anything to size up the situation, and then decide what to do.

Step 2—Approach with care so you don't become a burn victim yourself.

Step 3—If a person must be moved away from a source of heat, do so only if you will not put yourself at risk.

Step 4—Treat hurry cases of stopped breathing or heartbeat and severe bleeding, and keep the victim's airway open. Then treat the burn itself.

Step 5—Get immediate medical treatment for the victim if the burns:

▶ Cause trouble breathing.

▶ Might have injured the airway (for example, if the mouth and nose have been burned).

▶ Affect the head, neck, hands, feet, or groin.

▶ Are third-degree (full-thickness) burns.

▶ Are the result of chemicals, explosions, or electricity.

Second-Degree Burns (Partial-Thickness Burns)

Medical professionals refer to second-degree burns as *partial-thickness burns* because the injury goes partway toward the tissue beneath the skin. Blisters are a sign of a second-degree burn.

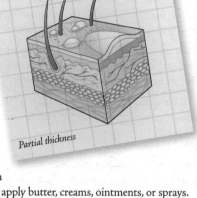

Place the injured area in cool water or apply wet cloths until the pain goes away. Allow the injury to dry, then protect it with a sterile gauze pad. Be careful not to break any blisters. Broken blisters are open wounds and could become infected. Don't apply butter, creams, ointments, or sprays. They are difficult to remove and may slow the healing process.

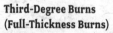
Partial thickness

Third-Degree Burns (Full-Thickness Burns)

Third-degree burns damage the skin and the tissue beneath it. They are also known as *full-thickness burns*. Skin might be burned away and flesh blackened. Third-degree burns injure nerves, so the victim may feel no pain. Do not try to remove clothing; it might be sticking to the flesh. Call 911 and ask for emergency assistance. Do not apply creams, ointments, or sprays. Wrap a clean cloth around the injury and treat the person for shock until professional medical help arrives.

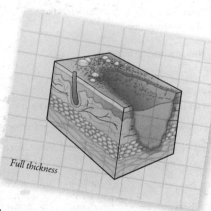
Full thickness

Cold- and Heat-Related Injuries

The human body is remarkable in its ability to stay at a constant temperature. When the weather is hot, we perspire to stay cool. When cold winds blow, we burn more calories to make heat.

What is most important is that our *core temperature*—the warmth of the organs in our bodies and our brains—stays close to 98.6 degrees. If the body's ability to cool or warm itself is overworked, the core temperature can rise or fall into dangerous zones. The results are cold- and heat-related emergencies that might become life-threatening.

Sunburn

Most sunburns are superficial burns, although more serious sunburns include the blisters of a partial-thickness burn. Repeated sunburns can cause skin damage and increased risk of skin cancer.

Guard against injury from the sun by using sunscreen when you are outdoors, or by wearing a long-sleeved shirt, long pants, and a hat with a broad brim.

Treat sunburn by applying cool, damp cloths and by protecting the skin from further exposure to the sun.

Heat Exhaustion

Heat exhaustion happens when the body's cooling system becomes overworked and struggles to keep up. Dehydration can be a factor in bringing on heat exhaustion. Hot weather, exertion, or a hot, stuffy room also can play a role. Signals of heat exhaustion include:

▶ Skin that is pale and clammy from heavy sweating

▶ Nausea and tiredness

▶ Dizziness and fainting

▶ Headache, muscle cramps, and weakness

Follow these steps to treat someone suffering from heat exhaustion.

Step 1—Have the victim lie in a cool, shady place with the feet raised. Remove excess clothing.

Step 2—Cool the victim by applying wet cloths to the body and by fanning.

Step 3—If the person is fully alert, let him or her sip some water.

Recovery should be rapid. If symptoms remain, call for medical help.

Heatstroke

Heat exhaustion left untreated can develop into *heatstroke*. The body's cooling system begins to fail, and the person's core temperature rises to life-threatening levels (above 105 degrees). In simple terms, the body's air conditioner is broken.

Signals of heatstroke can include the following:

▶ Skin that is very hot to the touch

▶ Skin that is red and either dry or damp with sweat

▶ Rapid pulse and quick, noisy breathing

▶ Confusion and unwillingness to cooperate with treatment

▶ Unconsciousness

Call for medical assistance, then follow these steps to treat heatstroke.

Step 1—Move the person to an air-conditioned or shady area.

Step 2—Loosen tight clothing and further cool the skin by fanning and applying wet cloths.

Step 3—If you have ice packs, wrap them in a T-shirt, towel, or other thin barrier and place them under the person's armpits and against the neck and groin.

Step 4—If the person is able to drink, give small amounts of cool water.

Regularly check on the victim's condition. Be ready to provide further first aid if the person's temperature goes up again or if he or she starts vomiting. You also might need to perform rescue breathing.

Frostbite

Frostbite occurs when skin and tissue become cold enough to freeze. A frostbite victim might complain that the ears, nose, fingers, or feet hurt or have become numb. Sometimes, though, a victim of frostbite will not notice anything unusual. Grayish-white patches on the skin are warning signs that ice crystals are beginning to form.

Treat frostbite by moving the victim into shelter such as a tent or building. When an ear or cheek is affected, remove a glove and warm the injury with the palm of your hand. Slip a frostbitten hand under your clothing and against warm skin.

If you suspect that frostbite is severe, help the person get into dry clothing, wrap the injured area in a blanket, and get to a doctor as soon as possible. Do not rub a frostbitten limb with your hands or with snow. When there is no chance that a frostbitten area will refreeze, rewarm the injury by placing it in warm water (warm to the touch—not hot) until normal color returns. If the frostbite injury is on a hand or foot, place dry, sterile gauze between the fingers or toes and apply a loose bandage.

Hypothermia

Hypothermia can develop when a person's body is losing more heat than it is able to produce, which causes the core temperature to drop. This may happen to anyone who is not dressed warmly enough or whose clothing is no longer dry. Wind, rain, hunger, exhaustion, and dehydration increase the danger. Temperatures do not need to be below freezing, either. A hiker caught in a cool, windy rain shower without rain gear can be at great risk for hypothermia. A swimmer in chilly water or a boater who capsizes might also fall victim to hypothermia.

Someone who is becoming hypothermic may:

▶ Feel cold and numb.

▶ Become tired and unable to think straight.

▶ Shiver uncontrollably.

▶ Make poor decisions.

▶ Become irritable.

▶ Stumble and fall or lose consciousness.

First aid for hypothermia begins with preventing a victim from getting colder. It continues with helping him or her bring the body temperature up to normal. Try any or all of the following treatments:

▶ Move the person into a shelter such as a building or a tent. Remove wet clothing and get him or her into dry, warm clothes. Wrap the person in a sleeping bag, blankets, jackets, or anything handy that could be used.

▶ If fully conscious and able to swallow, have the person drink warm liquids (soup, fruit juices, or water).

▶ Put towels or T-shirts around water bottles filled with warm water, then position the bottles in the armpit and groin areas.

▶ Watch the person closely for any change in his condition. Call for help.

Protecting the Neck and Spine

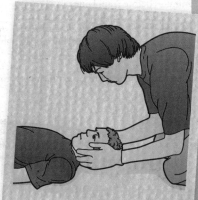

The backbone (spinal column) is made up of small bones called *vertebrae* that surround and protect the spinal cord. If a vertebra is broken or dislocated, the spinal cord could be injured.

Whenever someone has fallen, been in a car accident, or suffered a blow to the head, assume there is an injury to the head, neck, or back. If you come upon an unconscious person but do not know what caused the emergency, you should also make the assumption that the head, neck, or back has been injured and take these steps to protect the neck and spine.

▶ Stabilize the neck and spine by holding the person's head in the position found until medical personnel can determine whether the spinal column has been harmed. Another first-aider or a bystander can hold the victim's head and neck steady while you provide urgent treatment if necessary.

▶ If the victim is having trouble breathing, gently adjust the position of the head and neck just enough to maintain an open airway. Do not put a pillow under the head.

▶ Treat for shock but do not unnecessarily change the victim's position.

When the person must be moved out of the path of danger, organize other Scouts or bystanders to help so that the victim's body can be lifted all at once without causing it to twist or bend. One person should continue to hold the neck and head in a stable position throughout any move.

Sprains and Strains

A *sprain* occurs when an ankle, wrist, or other joint is twisted or bent far enough to overstretch the *ligaments*—the tough bands that hold joints together. A *strain* happens when muscles are stretched too far, causing tears in the muscle fibers. A sprained or strained joint will be tender and painful when moved and might be swollen and discolored. Strained backs, arms, and legs also will be tender and can hurt if activity continues.

Treat sprains and strains with **RICE**—**R**est, **I**ce, **C**ompression, and **E**levation:

Rest—Keep weight off injured joints or muscles to give them time to heal. Do not try to move or straighten the injured limb. Cover open wounds with a sterile dressing.

Ice—Apply ice packs or cold compresses to the affected area. To protect bare skin, put a thin towel, T-shirt, or some other cloth around the ice pack and leave the ice in place for no more than 20 minutes at a time. If continued icing is needed, remove the pack for 20 minutes before reapplying.

Compression—Wrap the injury with an elastic bandage. The bandage should be snug enough to provide support, but not so tight that it cuts off circulation—you should be able to slip a couple of fingers under it.

Elevation—For sprains or strains to an arm or leg, keep the limb raised.

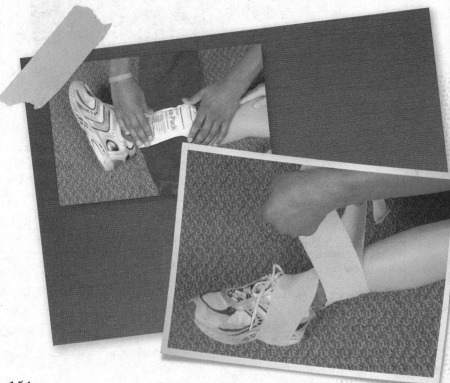

Sprains and Strains While Hiking

If someone suffers a mild ankle sprain during a hike and can walk without much discomfort, he or she can continue the hike. If walking causes pain, however, the person shouldn't walk any farther. Other Scouts can help with a walking assist or a two-person carry. Don't try to move or straighten an injured limb if doing so causes pain. Seek medical treatment whenever pain is constant or severe.

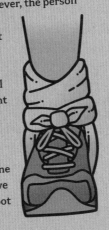

You can give support to a sprained ankle by wrapping it, boot and all, with a bandage, neckerchief, or some other strip of cloth. When you arrive at your destination, take off the boot and treat the injury with RICE.

Head Injuries

A head injury can be very serious and should be handled with extreme urgency and care. A cut to the head can cause severe bleeding; call for help immediately. If the victim is bleeding but conscious, have the victim hold a clean cloth over the wound and apply pressure. Keep the victim as comfortable as possible and wait for help to arrive. Use the triangular bandage when the entire scalp must be covered.

Broken Bones (Fractures)

A fall, a violent blow, a collision—all of these can cause a *fracture*, that is, a broken bone. When a fracture has occurred, a bone or joint will often have an abnormal shape or position. There also may be swelling or a bluish color at the site of the injury.

Ask the victim the following questions to help find out if he or she has a fracture:

▶ "Did you hear or feel a bone snap?"

▶ "Do you feel pain when you press on the skin over the injured area?"

▶ "Are you unable to move the injured limb?"

If the victim answers "yes" to these questions, he or she probably has a fracture. When you suspect a fracture, do not move the person.

First aid for fractures varies somewhat depending on whether an injury is a closed fracture or an open fracture. A *closed fracture* (also known as a *simple fracture*) is a broken bone that does not cut through the skin. An *open fracture* (also known as a *compound fracture*) is a broken bone that cuts through the skin and creates an open wound.

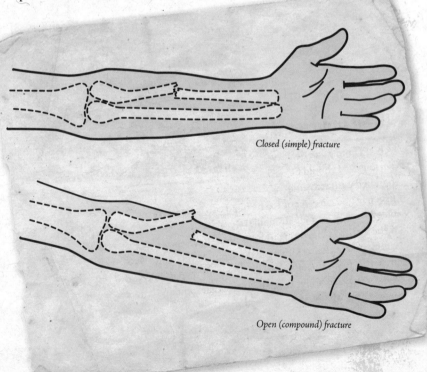

Closed (simple) fracture

Open (compound) fracture

First Aid for a Closed Fracture

▶ Call 911 or your local emergency response number.

▶ Treat hurry cases of stopped breathing, stopped heartbeat, and serious bleeding.

▶ Protect the spinal column by supporting the victim's head and neck in the position found.

▶ Treat for shock, but don't raise a leg that might be broken.

First Aid for an Open Fracture

▶ Call 911 or your local emergency response number.

▶ Treat hurry cases of stopped breathing, stopped heartbeat, and serious bleeding.

▶ Protect the spinal column by supporting the victim's head and neck in the position found.

▶ Control bleeding by placing sterile gauze around the wound. Use direct pressure only when there are no other ways to stop serious bleeding.

▶ If medical help will not arrive within an hour, carefully clean the wound with a stream of water squeezed from a water bottle or a sturdy plastic bag with a small hole punched in one corner.

▶ Treat for shock, but don't raise a leg that might be broken.

Do not move the victim unless the place is not safe and there is danger to the victim or to rescuers. Regularly check his or her condition and be ready to provide additional first-aid treatment while waiting for medical professionals to arrive.

Cravat Bandages

A *cravat bandage* has many first-aid uses, from securing splints and supporting a sprained ankle to holding a compress in place over a bleeding wound. Make a cravat bandage from a triangular bandage. Stock your family and patrol/troop first-aid kits with four triangular cloth bandages that are about 40 inches on the long side. Use the following method to make a cravat bandage:

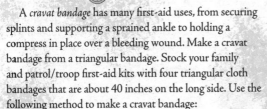

Step 1—Fold the point of a triangular bandage up to the long edge.

Step 2—Fold the bottom edge several times toward the top edge.

Step 3—Tie all bandages in place with square knots.

Splinting

Splinting the broken bone of an accident victim who must be moved relieves pain and reduces the chances of additional injury. Splinting also can lessen the discomfort of a fracture for someone who must wait a long time for professional medical help to arrive.

You can make splints from whatever is handy—boards, branches, hiking sticks, ski poles, shovel handles, or tent-pole sections. Folded newspapers, magazines, pieces of cardboard, or a sleeping pad will work, too.

Padding allows a splint to fit well and increases comfort. Cushion a splint with clothing, blankets, pillows, crumpled paper, or other soft material. Hold splints and padding in place with neckerchiefs, handkerchiefs, cravat and roller bandages, or other wide strips of cloth.

Splint suspected fractures in the same position as you found them. Do not try to straighten or reposition an injured bone. While applying the splint, keep the area above and below the injury motionless and minimize movement. Extend splints beyond the joint above and the joint below the suspected break. Tie splints in place with bandages, neckerchiefs, or other wide strips of cloth. Tie at least one above the injured area and one below, but do not tie bandages directly over the injury itself.

After the splint is in place, periodically recheck for circulation farther out on the injured arm or leg by doing the following.

▶ Gently squeeze and then release a fingernail or toenail beyond the splint. The pink color should return in one or two seconds.

▶ Ask the person to wiggle the fingers or toes.

▶ Ask the person if he or she can feel you touching the tips of his or her fingers or toes.

If any of these tests has a negative result, the splint may be too tight. Adjust it and check again for circulation.

A SAM® splint is a commercially made splint carried in many first-aid kits. It can be molded to form support for injured hands, arms, and legs.

Splinting a Lower-Leg Fracture—Use splints that are long enough to reach from the middle of the thigh to past the heel. Place one padded splint on each side of the injured limb and bind them together.

Splinting an Upper-Leg Fracture—The thigh bone (femur) is the largest bone in the leg. If it is broken, the muscles of the upper leg are strong enough to pull the jagged ends of the fractured bone into the flesh and blood vessels. This could cause internal bleeding that can threaten the victim's life. A femur fracture must be treated as a hurry case.

▶ Call for medical help immediately.

▶ Keep the victim still and quiet.

▶ Treat for shock, but do not move the injured leg.

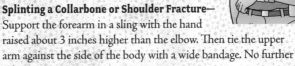

Someone who has suffered a femur fracture should not be moved until a traction splint has been applied by trained medical personnel.

Splinting an upper-leg fracture is early emergency care that might help immobilize (hold in place) the injury until medical help arrives. Apply one padded splint outside the leg extending from heel to armpit, and another inside the leg from the heel to the crotch. Bind the splints together.

Splinting an Upper-Arm Fracture—Tie a splint to the outside of the upper arm. Place the arm in a sling with the hand raised about 3 inches above level. Then use a bandage to hold the upper arm against the side of the chest. The body will act as a splint to keep the elbow and shoulder from moving.

Splinting a Collarbone or Shoulder Fracture—Support the forearm in a sling with the hand raised about 3 inches higher than the elbow. Then tie the upper arm against the side of the body with a wide bandage. No further splinting is necessary.

Splinting a Lower-Arm Fracture—Splint to hold the hand and forearm motionless. A piece of cardboard folded to support the arm, wrist, and hand can be a good splint for a forearm. Use a T-shirt or other cloth to pad the splint, and hold it in place with several bandages. Placing the splinted arm in a sling with the hand slightly raised also can help keep the elbow joint immobilized.

Slings

Slings help support an injured hand, arm, collarbone, or shoulder by stabilizing it and protecting it from further damage.

To make a sling from a large triangular bandage:

Step 1—Support the injured limb above and below the injury.

Step 2—Check the injured area for circulation (feeling, warmth, and color).

Step 3—Position a triangular sling, such as a neckerchief or triangular bandage, across the chest. Bring the upper free end of the sling behind the neck and the lower free end up, and tie the ends with a square knot.

Step 4—With a second triangular bandage, bind the sling to the chest to better help stabilize the injury.

Step 5—Recheck the injured area for feeling warmth, and color.

After Hours (1980), by Joseph Csatari

 Artist Joseph Csatari trained with Norman Rockwell and has a long history with the BSA. Learn more about him at www.bsahandbook.org.

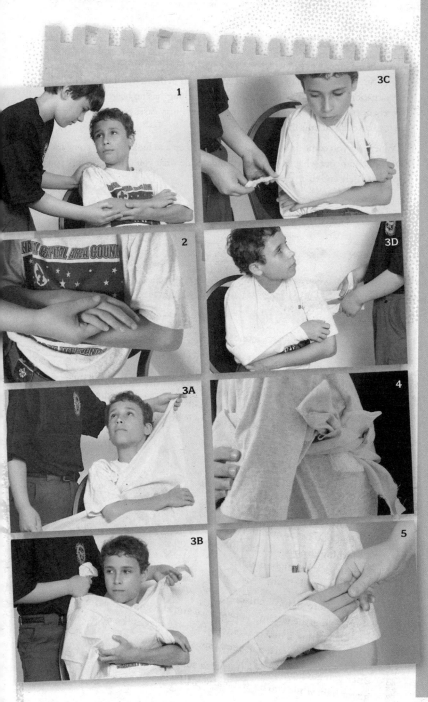

HURRY CASES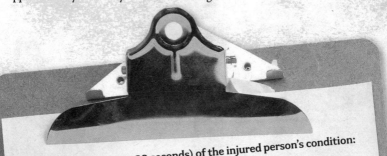

A choking emergency in which a person has stopped breathing is an example of a *hurry case*—a condition or injury that could result in death if not treated quickly. Any situation in which a victim has stopped breathing, has no heartbeat, is bleeding severely, or has ingested poison is a hurry case. All hurry cases require quick action in order to save the victim's life.

Whenever you come upon an injured person, stop and look over the scene for a moment. Figure out what has happened and decide what you can do. Be sure you can approach safely and that you won't be in danger.

Do a quick survey (15 to 20 seconds) of the injured person's condition:

1. **Is the person breathing?** If the person appears to be unconscious, pat him or her on the shoulder and ask if everything is OK. If the person doesn't respond, place your ear near the mouth and nose. Listen and feel for the movement of air and watch for the chest to rise and fall—signals that the person is breathing.

2. **Is the heart beating?** Feel for a pulse in the artery beneath the ear and just under the jawbone (the carotid artery).

3. **Is there severe bleeding?** Open rain gear and outer clothing to check for bleeding injuries that might have been hidden by clothing.

4. **Are there signs of poisoning?** Consider the victim's appearance and behavior. Look for clues (pill bottles, a fuel container, etc.) that suggest he or she might have swallowed a poisonous substance.

Once you have completed the quick survey, have someone telephone or go for help while you begin treatment.

Breathing and Heartbeat Hurry Cases

A person might stop breathing because of a heart attack, electrical shock, suffocation, drowning, smoke inhalation, and other health conditions or injuries. Brain damage or death can occur minutes after a person stops breathing and the heart stops beating. Quick, effective first aid is essential.

An easy way to remember the steps for treating the emergencies of no breathing and/or no heartbeat is **A-B-C-D**:

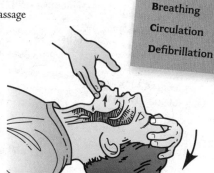

Airway

Breathing

Circulation

Defibrillation

A Is for Airway—The airway is the passage that allows air entering the mouth or nose to reach the lungs. If a victim is unconscious, place the person on his or her back, protecting the head and neck if you must roll the person over. Open the airway by pressing on the forehead with one hand and lifting the chin with the other to tilt back the head. This will keep the tongue from blocking the airway.

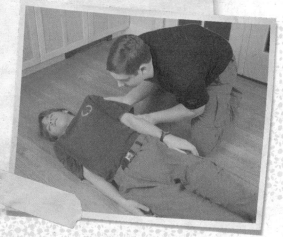

Always protect the airway of any accident victim. If he or she begins to vomit, turn the person onto the side so the vomit comes out of the mouth and is not inhaled into the lungs.

B Is for Breathing—After opening the victim's airway, see if the person can breathe normally. Place your cheek in front of the victim's mouth (about 1 to 2 inches away). Look, listen, and feel for movement and breathing for no more than 10 seconds. If the person is breathing, you will feel and hear the airflow on your cheek and see and feel the chest rising and falling. If there are no signals that a person is breathing, give two rescue breaths. Use the procedures described on the next page.

Rescue Breathing

Step 1—Place a CPR breathing barrier over the victim's mouth to protect both of you from diseases that can be spread by mouth.

Step 2—While maintaining the head-tilt, pinch the victim's nostrils, seal your mouth over his or her mouth, and blow into it to fill the lungs. The breath should last about one second. Watch to see if the person's chest rises. Remove your mouth and then give another rescue breath.

Step 3—**For an adult:** If the victim does not start breathing again after two rescue breaths, immediately begin *cardiopulmonary resuscitation (CPR)*. **For a child or an infant:** After two rescue breaths, check for a pulse for no more than 10 seconds by placing your fingers against the carotid artery just below the ear and jawbone.

If there are still no signals of breathing, resume rescue breathing (1 breath about every 3 seconds). Recheck for breathing and pulse every 2 minutes.

If there are no signs of a heartbeat, begin CPR.

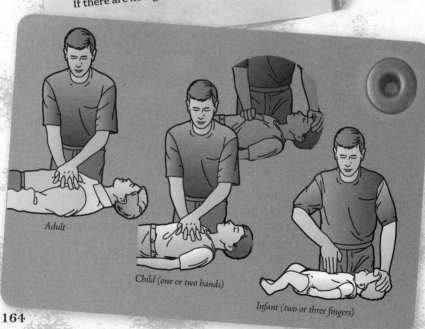

Adult

Child (one or two hands)

Infant (two or three fingers)

C Is for Circulation—Accidents that cause a person to stop breathing also can stop the heart, as can a heart attack and other medical conditions. When the heart is not pumping (circulating) blood through the body, the victim will not be breathing, moving, or making normal sounds. If you have delivered two rescue breaths and the person does not begin to breathe, immediately begin cardiopulmonary resuscitation (CPR).

Learning CPR requires instruction from a certified teacher. The American Red Cross, American Heart Association, and other organizations offer classes. Ask your Scout leaders to help you find training to learn this lifesaving skill.

While the techniques for CPR are different for adults, children, and infants, the cycle of 30 chest compressions followed by two rescue breaths applies to everyone.

D Is for Defibrillation—When someone is suffering a heart attack, a machine called a *defibrillator* can sometimes help the heart start beating regularly again. Most ambulances, hospitals, and emergency care facilities have defibrillators for trained medical personnel to use.

The *automated external defibrillator (AED)* can be used in emergencies by Scouts and other members of the public who have been trained in its use. Airports, shopping malls, and many other places where people gather have installed AEDs in much the same way that fire extinguishers are made available for quick access. Scouts can learn to use AEDs from trained instructors, often in combination with CPR training.

Find out where to get AED and CPR training at the *Handbook* Web site, *www.bsahandbook.org*.

Heart Attack

A heart attack happens when an artery that supplies blood to the heart is blocked. Heart attacks can damage or kill heart muscles and are a leading cause of death in the United States.

Learn to recognize the warning signals of a heart attack. Then be prepared to take prompt action by calling 911 or another local emergency-response number. In some cases, you may assist by responding to a heart attack victim's request for help in finding or opening medications. If you have the necessary training, perform CPR.

Common Warning Signals of Heart Attack

The warning signals of a heart attack include the following:

▶ Persistent, uncomfortable pressure, squeezing, fullness, or pain in the center of the chest behind the breastbone. The feeling may spread to the shoulders, arms, and neck. It might last several minutes or longer and may come and go. It is not always severe. (Sharp, stabbing twinges of pain usually are not signals of heart attack.)

▶ Unusual sweating. A person experiencing a heart attack may perspire even though a room is cool.

▶ Nausea. Stomach distress with an urge to vomit is an example of nausea that may occur in a person experiencing a heart attack.

▶ Shortness of breath.

▶ A feeling of weakness.

Women may experience different warning signals than do men. A woman might also have intermittent back, abdominal, and upper-body pain; unexplained fatigue; and dizziness. She might feel heaviness in the chest or a burning sensation rather than pain.

Should anyone complain of these symptoms, immediately call for medical help. Don't delay. Be ready to begin CPR if the heartbeat and breathing stop.

Severe Bleeding

A broken window. A car crash. A careless moment with a knife, an ax, or a power tool. Suddenly, blood is spurting from a nasty wound. Without quick first aid, a person suffering a severe cut might bleed to death in a matter of minutes.

First Aid for Severe Bleeding—Ask someone to summon help by calling 911 or another emergency number while you begin treatment.

Step 1—With a clean cloth or sterile dressing as a pad, use the palm of your hand to apply firm pressure directly over the wound. Use an elastic bandage, if you have one, to secure the pad tightly over the source of the bleeding.

Applying direct pressure on a wound will stop most bleeding.

Don't waste time. When clean material is not close by, use a neckerchief, shirt, or whatever else you can reach.

Step 2—After the bleeding stops, hold the pad in place with a sterile bandage (athletic wrap, strips torn from clean clothing, or something similar). Bind the pad firmly but not so tightly that it cuts off circulation.

Step 3—When the bandage is on an arm or a leg, check farther down the limb every few minutes for a pulse and for warmth, feeling, and color. If you can't feel a pulse and if the fingers or toes are numb, pale, or cold, the bandage might be too tight and should be loosened.

Step 4—If a pad becomes soaked with blood, don't remove it. Place a fresh pad over the first one and continue applying pressure.

The Boy Scouts of America Recommends

Approach safely, the third step of the first-aid method, is a reminder to protect yourself from injury and illness while you are providing first-aid treatment to others. This is especially important when blood or other bodily fluids are involved.

During first-aid emergencies, wear gloves and eye protection from a first-aid kit whenever possible to shield your hands and eyes. If gloves aren't available, use a bandage, a folded shirt, or other cloth pad—not your bare hands—to stop bleeding. A CPR breathing barrier can reduce the chances of infection while performing rescue breathing.

Use soap and water or a waterless cleanser to clean your hands and any other skin that might have been exposed to blood or bodily fluids while providing first-aid treatment. Bandages, clothing, or other items that have blood or bodily fluids on them should be stowed in a plastic bag for proper disposal.

Emergencies can happen anywhere. If you come upon an injured or ill person but have no first-aid supplies, use your best judgment in deciding what to do. Consider what you know about the health history of the person who needs help. Look around to see what you can use to provide good first-aid care while limiting risks to yourself.

Ingested Poisoning

Poisons can be swallowed or breathed in. Many chemicals can be absorbed into the skin. Overdoses of drugs also can be poisoning emergencies.

Among young children, poisoning is the most frequent cause of accidental death. They might swallow almost anything: fuels, battery acid, peeling wall paint, pills from a medicine cabinet, cosmetics, pesticides, cleaning products, and other household chemicals and poisons. If you see items in your home that could be dangerous to a child, store them in a safe place, out of children's reach.

> Some mushrooms, berries, and plant leaves are poisonous, too. Don't eat wild plants unless you are certain they will not harm you.

A person who has been poisoned may feel nauseated and suffer stomach pains. He or she may vomit, and there might be burns around the mouth. Breathing could be abnormal. If you suspect that someone has been poisoned, look for evidence. Spilled liquids and pill bottles are clues that medical professionals can use to identify a poisoning case and to carry out the correct treatment.

In any poisoning emergency, call:

- **Poison Control Center: 1-800-222-1222**
- **Emergency Information: 911**
- **Your community's emergency number**

First Aid for Swallowed Poisons

Step 1—Immediately take any poison containers to a telephone, call 1-800-222-1222 (the Poison Control Center), 911, or your local emergency response number, and follow the instructions you are given.

Step 2—Treat the victim for shock and monitor breathing. Do not give anything by mouth unless you are told to do so by medical professionals.

Step 3—Save any vomit in a bowl, cook pot, or plastic bag. It can help a doctor identify the poison and give the right treatment.

First Aid for Inhaled Poisons—Smoke, certain gases, and chemical fumes are poisonous. Inhaling them can cause a person to have trouble breathing and perhaps to lose consciousness. Left untreated, inhaled poisons can cause death.

Symptoms of inhaled poisoning include headache, dizziness, and nausea. Victims can lose consciousness without realizing they are in danger. To treat someone who has inhaled a poison:

1. Check the scene.

2. Approach safely. Make sure you protect yourself from inhaling the poison so you do not become another victim.

3. Move the victim to fresh air.

4. Get medical help.

5. Regularly check that the victim is still breathing and that the heart is beating.

6. If necessary, perform rescue breathing and CPR.

Preventing Carbon Monoxide Poisoning

The most common inhaled poison is carbon monoxide, a gas given off by gasoline engines, natural gas appliances, charcoal grills, furnaces, and fireplaces. To avoid carbon monoxide hazards, do not operate a car or lawn mower in a closed garage or shed. Don't cook indoors over wood or charcoal, and avoid using gas stoves, ovens, candles, or other flames in tents to stay warm. Carbon monoxide detectors installed in homes will sound a warning if carbon monoxide reaches dangerous levels.

Shock

When a person is injured or under great stress, the circulation system might not provide enough blood to all parts of the body. Known as *shock*, this life-threatening condition can cause organ failure and can be life-threatening. Someone suffering from shock may have some, all, or none of the following signals:

▶ Restlessness or irritability

▶ Weakness

▶ Confusion, fear, and dizziness

▶ Skin that is moist, clammy, cool, and pale

▶ A quick, weak pulse

▶ Shallow, rapid, and irregular breathing

▶ Nausea and vomiting

▶ Extreme thirst

Treat every accident victim for shock even if there are no signals. People who have been injured almost always experience some degree of shock, but they might not be affected right away. Prompt first aid might prevent shock from setting in.

First Aid for Shock—Never leave an accident victim alone unless you have no other choice—fear can hasten shock. In a calm voice, assure the victim that everything is being done to care for him or her. A person who appears to be unconscious might still be able to hear you, so keep letting the victim know that you are there.

Step 1—Call for help.

Step 2—Try to eliminate the causes of shock by treating "hurry cases"—check the airway and restore breathing and circulation; control bleeding; check for signals of poisoning; and treat wounds.

Step 3—Help the injured person lie down. If you don't suspect back, neck, or head injuries, or fractures in the hip or leg, raise the feet about 12 inches to move blood from the legs to the vital organs.

Step 4—Keep the victim warm with blankets, coats, or sleeping bags.

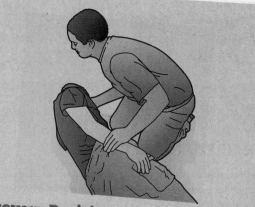

Recovery Position

Place a victim who is unconscious but breathing normally in the *recovery position*. This will help keep the airway open and prevent the person from choking on saliva, blood, or vomit.

Step 1—Extend the person's lower arm in line with his or her body.

Step 2—Support the head and neck as you grasp the victim's hip and shoulder. Then roll the person toward you so that he or she is lying on the side.

Step 3—Continue to check the person's breathing until medical help arrives.

Fire-Related Emergencies and Rescues

Should you find yourself in a burning building, get out by a safe route. Test the doorknob of a closed door by touching it. If the doorknob is cool, get close to the floor and put your shoulder against the door. Open the door carefully. Be ready to push it closed again if you discover heat or smoke on the other side.

If a doorknob is hot, do not open the door. Instead, seal the base of the door with clothing or towels to keep out smoke, which can damage the lungs if inhaled. Smoke rises, so stay close to the floor where the air will be fresher. Go to a window, open it, and signal for help. If a phone is available, call 911 or another emergency number.

Be very cautious about rescuing others from a smoke-filled room. A smoke-filled room is an extremely hazardous environment. Rushing into a smoky room or other dangerous scene to help someone will do no good if you also become a victim. When your safety will be threatened, wait until trained rescuers arrive.

If you do move an injured or unconscious person from a smoky room, do so as quickly as possible. A victim can be moved to safety with any of the rescuer assists described in this chapter. Avoid using a method that might make the victim's injuries worse.

OTHER FIRST-AID EMERGENCIES

The first-aid method used to address the most serious illnesses and injuries is a good place to start your treatment of other first-aid emergencies, too. Follow the steps and you'll know you've done all you can to help a person in need.

1. Check the scene.
2. Call for help.
3. Approach safely.
4. Provide urgent treatment.
5. Protect from further injury.
6. Treat every accident victim for shock.
7. Make a thorough examination.
8. Plan a course of action.

MOVING AN ILL OR INJURED PERSON

The decision to move an accident victim should be made carefully. In many cases, there will be emergency medical crews, fire department personnel, or others with special equipment and training who can transport an injured person. However, if someone is exposed to fire, smoke, water, electrical hazards, poisonous gases, dangerous weather conditions, or other immediate threats, the right decision could be to move that person to safety. You might also need to move the person in order to give proper first-aid care. Move the victim only as far as is necessary, and do not put yourself in danger.

Except in critical situations, do not attempt to move a person who is suffering from any of the following conditions:

▶ Shock

▶ Heart attack

▶ Head, neck, or back (spinal) injuries

▶ Frostbitten or burned feet

▶ Bone or joint injuries to the hips or legs

When an injured person must be moved, you may use one of several *assists* to move the victim. Choose the assist method you use carefully to avoid making the injuries worse and to prevent injury to yourself. Some of the following assists can be performed by a single Scout. Others require two or more rescuers. Practice the following assists so that you will know what to do during a real emergency.

Walking Assist—If the victim is conscious, has only minor injuries, and is able to move, you can safely help the person walk. Put one of the victim's arms around your neck. Place your other arm around the person's waist. When there are two of you to provide assistance, put one of the victim's arms around each rescuer's neck, then place your free arms around the victim's waist.

Walking assist

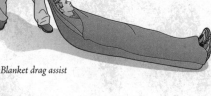

Blanket Drag Assist—To move a person to safety, roll him or her onto a blanket, coat, dining fly, or tablecloth and drag from behind the head.

Clothes Drag Assist—For short distances and to move a person who may have head, neck, or back injuries, use the clothes drag. Firmly grab the person's clothing behind the shoulder and neck area and pull headfirst.

Ankle Drag Assist—If a person must be moved out of a dangerous place, such as a smoky room, but is too large or too heavy to transport in any other way, drag him or her by both ankles.

Blanket drag assist

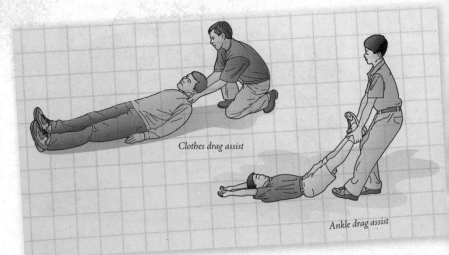

Clothes drag assist

Ankle drag assist

Pack-Strap Carry—The pack-strap carry is a way for a single first-aider to carry someone no larger than himself. Use this carry for emergency moves or after determining that a victim can be carried without making his or her injuries worse.

Pack-strap carry

Two-Handed Carry—
Use this method if the victim is conscious and not seriously injured. With one other rescuer, place your arms on each other's shoulders. Then link your free arms by grasping each other's wrists. Ask the injured person to sit on your linked arms. With the person sitting comfortably on your linked arms, move your other arms down from each other's shoulders to support the victim's back.

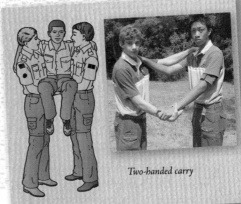

Two-handed carry

Four-Handed Seat—When no rescue equipment is available, the four-handed seat is the easiest two-rescuer carry. It is safe only if the victim is conscious and can hold on.

Four-handed seat

BEYOND THE BASICS

Emergency medical technicians in many American communities can reach an accident scene within minutes of being called. In the backcountry, a trained medical team could be delayed for hours or even a day or more. As first-aiders, you and others in your group might need to maintain the health and safety of injured or ill persons until help arrives. You might not have all the supplies you need and may have to think of ways to use what you have available to care for accident victims. For example, you might use a tent pole as a splint or tear a shirt into strips to use as bandages. You also will need to protect yourselves and others from weather and from further injury.

Completing the first-aid requirements for the Tenderfoot, Second Class, and First Class ranks will give you a basic understanding of how to use the first-aid method to evaluate an emergency situation wherever it occurs and to treat a number of injuries and illnesses.

Earning the First Aid merit badge will take you to the next level of knowledge. You also can learn a great deal by working on merit badges in Emergency Preparedness, Medicine, Safety, and Wilderness Survival. Advanced first-aid courses offered by the Boy Scouts of America, American Red Cross, American Heart Association, and other organizations will help you build your first-aid skills to respond to emergencies wherever you are.

The requirements and other resources for earning the First Aid merit badge are available on the *Handbook* Web site, *www.bsahandbook.org*.

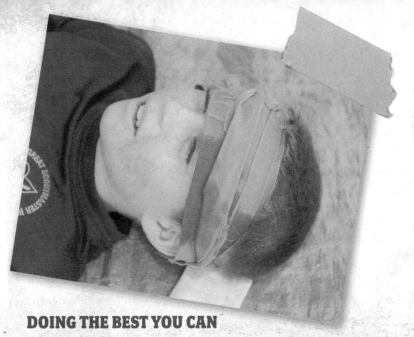

DOING THE BEST YOU CAN

Whenever you are faced with a first-aid emergency, use the skills you have to the best of your ability. Remember to watch out for your own safety as well as that of others in the area. Use the first-aid method to treat hurry cases, then put together a plan to get medical attention for injured or ill persons.

No one expects you to have the wisdom of a medical doctor. However, Scouting's history is filled with stories of Scouts who used their training to help others, sometimes even saving lives. Learn all the first aid you can and review it often. Perhaps one day you will be able to do just the right thing at a time when your actions make all the difference.

To read about Scout skills in action, go to the *Handbook* Web site, **www.bsahandbook.org.**

CHAPTER 5

Aquatics

"Swimming is certainly one of the greatest and best sports for all boys, but Scouts should train themselves specially to make their ability in swimming count for its usefulness."

—*Boy Scout Handbook*, 2nd ed., 1925

AQUATICS

"Come on in, the water's fine!" On a hot summer day, there may be nothing better than having fun in the water. Joining other Scouts for great times swimming in pools and lakes has always been a highlight of Boy Scout camps.

Become a swimmer and you'll be ready to learn how to steer small boats by trimming the sails and handling the rudder. Swimming skills also will prepare you for adventures in canoes, kayaks, rafts, and rowboats. Want to go snorkeling or waterskiing? Swimming is the key to those activities, too. If you want to see if you've got what it takes to go the distance, the BSA's Mile Swim Award sets a high standard for you to achieve.

Swimming is an important part of Scoutcraft—the building blocks of a young man. Being able to swim gives you confidence. It qualifies you to make the most of Scouting adventures in the water and on watercraft of all kinds. You will be able to take care of yourself if you ever fall out of a boat or tumble into a stream. With training in lifesaving, you also will be prepared to help someone who is struggling in the water.

IN THIS CHAPTER

▶ BSA Safe Swim Defense

▶ Learning to swim

▶ Basic strokes

▶ BSA swimmer test

▶ Floating

▶ BSA Safety Afloat

▶ Water rescues

▶ Aquatics opportunities

You can act as a leader, too, by doing your part to be sure that everyone stays safe while in and on the water. There might be opportunities for you to help teach younger Scouts the basics of swimming. With proper training, you can serve as a lifeguard during aquatic activities with your patrol and troop.

There are certain risks whenever you are in and on the water. To help manage those risks, you'll want to do things the right way. The BSA's Safe Swim Defense sets the rules for all Scout swimming.

For more information about aquatics achievements and awards in Scouting, see the *Handbook* Web site, *www.bsahandbook.org*.

BSA Safe Swim Defense*

1. **Qualified supervision.** An adult leader trained in Safe Swim Defense must supervise all swimming activities.

2. **Personal health review.** Each swimmer must provide a current and complete health history.

3. **Safe area.** The swimming area must be free of hazards.

4. **Response personnel (lifeguards).** Trained and properly equipped rescue personnel must be on duty whenever and wherever Scouts are swimming.

5. **Lookout.** A lookout appointed by the supervisor monitors the conduct of the swim from a position that gives a clear view of everyone.

6. **Ability groups.** Each participant is limited to the swimming area and activities that match his ability.

   • A *nonswimmer* is just learning.

   • A *beginner* can jump into deep water and swim 50 feet, changing directions at least once.

   • A *swimmer* can pass the BSA swimmer test.

7. **Buddy system.** Scouts never swim alone. Each Scout must stay close to a buddy who always knows where he is and what he is doing.

8. **Discipline.** Scouts know and respect the rules, and they always follow instructions from lifeguards and other adult leaders.

*For the complete statement of BSA Safe Swim Defense standards, see the Swimming merit badge pamphlet, Aquatics Supervision, or Guide to Safe Scouting.

 The full text of Safe Swim Defense, as well as more BSA aquatics policies, may be found at *www.bsahandbook.org*.

LEARNING TO SWIM

Most BSA local councils offer swimming classes during their summer camp programs. The American Red Cross, YMCA, and many other organizations also offer lessons. You might find opportunities to learn at a neighborhood pool, too. Your Scout leaders can help you find the instruction you need.

If you want to try out the basics of swimming, find a good swimmer to help you, and begin with floating. Wade into water that is waist deep. Hold your breath, bend down, and curl yourself into a ball. Clasp your arms around your knees. You should bob to the surface and float like a jellyfish.

Next, stand and turn to face the shore or the edge of the pool. Take a deep breath. Push off with your feet and plunge forward with your arms stretched in front of you. Glide across the water, then stand for a moment to get another breath. Push off and glide again.

Last, practice the way a swimmer breathes. Standing in waist-deep water, take a breath and put your face in the water. Slowly exhale through your nose and mouth. Repeat.

Floating

Gliding

Breathing

Swimming

For more on learning to swim, visit the *Handboook* Web site, www.bsahandbook.org.

SWIMMING STROKES

As you become comfortable with floating, gliding, and breathing like a swimmer, push off in waist-deep water and add the motions of different swimming strokes. The *front crawl, back crawl, sidestroke, breaststroke, trudgen,* and *elementary backstroke* are all good ways for a swimmer to move through the water.

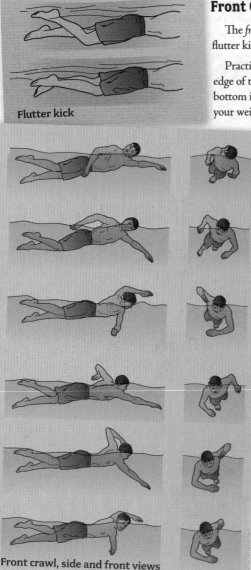

Flutter kick

Front crawl, side and front views

Front Crawl

The *front crawl* has three motions—the flutter kick, the arm stroke, and breathing.

Practice the *flutter kick* by holding the edge of the pool, resting your hands on the bottom in shallow water, or supporting your weight on a kickboard. Keep your legs straight as you kick, but not stiff. Use all of each leg, kicking from the hip and thigh, not just from the knee.

Try out the *arm stroke* while standing in waist-deep water. Bend forward so that your upper body is in a swimming position. Extend your right arm and sweep it down to your hip, bending your elbow so that you use both your hand and forearm to pull against the water. This part of the arm stroke is known as the *pull*. Next, raise your elbow and stretch your arm forward again—the *recovery* phase of the stroke. Alternate strokes with your left arm.

Push off into a glide and use the flutter kick and arm stroke together to move yourself through the water. Turn your head to the side and breathe when you need air.

Back Crawl

The *back crawl*, or racing backstroke, is a fast stroke that keeps your face above the water. The leg motion is the flutter kick. One arm pulls while the other recovers. Bring one arm out of the water near your hip and lift it above your head to slice back into the water. Roll slightly to that side, and bend your elbow to push water toward your feet. Alternate this stroking motion with your other arm. Keep your fingers together and your hands cupped.

Back crawl, side and front views

Sidestroke

A strong *scissors kick* powers the *sidestroke*. Breathing is easy because your face is always above the water. A long glide between strokes saves energy.

Begin by floating on your side. Draw your knees toward your chest. Next, spread your legs with your top leg moving forward, and then snap your legs together as if they were a pair of scissors. At the same time, thrust one arm forward and sweep the other through the water. Glide a moment, and then pull your forward arm down as you repeat the scissors kick.

Sidestroke, side and top views

Elementary Backstroke

The *elementary backstroke* is a stroke with a restful, energy-saving glide, which makes it ideal for long swims. Begin in a glide position by floating on your back with your arms at your sides and your legs straight. Begin the *whip kick* by bending your legs at the knees to drop your feet down. Slightly separate your legs, leading with your feet, and whip your lower legs back to the glide position. Extend your arms from your shoulders at the beginning of each kick, and then pull them down to your sides as though they were oars. Rest as you glide. Then repeat the stroke.

Elementary backstroke, side and top views

Breaststroke

The *breaststroke* is another restful stroke that is useful for long distances. It is a little like an elementary backstroke performed while you are on your belly, except that your legs and arms do not move together. Start in a glide position on your stomach with your arms in front of you and your legs together near the surface. Sweep your arms down to shoulder level as you raise your head to take a breath. Time your kick to provide power as you lower your head and extend your arms forward. Glide before the next pull and kick.

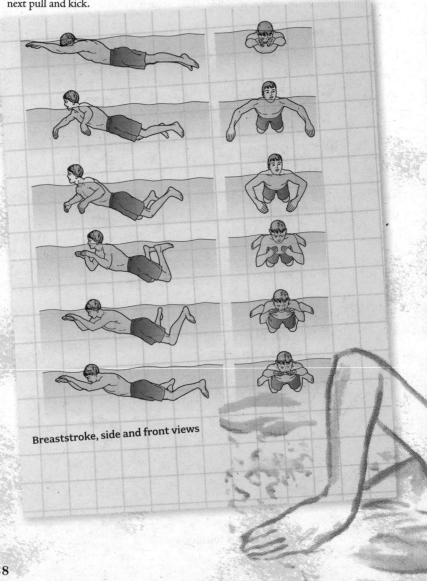

Breaststroke, side and front views

Trudgen

The *trudgen* stroke was named for English swimmer John Trudgen, who introduced it at a swimming competition in 1868. The trudgen combines the arm movements and breathing of the front crawl stroke with the scissors kick of the sidestroke. Perform the kick when your hip is turned upward as you are taking a breath and completing an arm pull. Allow your legs to relax and rest a moment while you power through the water with a stroke of your other arm.

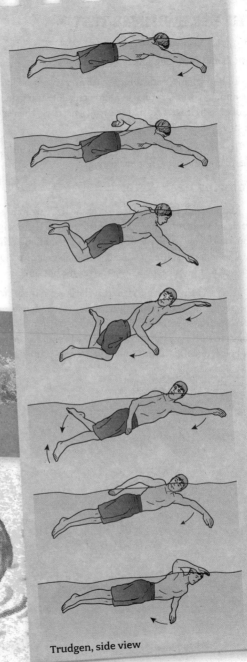

Trudgen, side view

189

THE BSA SWIMMER TEST

Passing the BSA swimmer test is a good way to know that you are prepared to take part in most Scouting aquatics activities.

To begin, jump feetfirst into water over your head in depth, level off, and begin swimming. Swim 75 yards in a strong manner using one or more of the following strokes: sidestroke, breaststroke, trudgen, crawl. Then swim 25 yards using an easy resting backstroke.

The 100 yards must be swum continuously and include at least one sharp turn. After completing the swim, rest by floating.

Entering Deep Water

Jumping into deep water is part of the BSA swimmer test. Jump feetfirst into deep water only when you have determined that the bottom is free of obstacles. Whenever you don't know the depth of the water or condition of the bottom, wade into the water or slide in feetfirst from a seated position. Never dive headfirst into deep water unless it is seven to 12 feet deep and you can see the bottom.

After you have made certain that the bottom is obstacle-free, stand at the edge of the pool or dock, bend slightly at the knees, and hop forward into the water. Once you get comfortable with that method of entry, try jumping farther out from the dock or poolside with your legs spread apart. Snap your legs together when you hit the water and push downward with your arms to keep your head above the surface.

3 feet maximum

Leaping entry (stride jump). Limit the height of the starting point to 3 feet above the water.

Stopping, Turning, and Resuming Swimming

To come to a halt while swimming, stop kicking and raise your head as you push down your arms. You'll find yourself upright in the water and able to look around. By sweeping your arms back and forth under the water and making an occasional scissors kick with your legs, you can tread water and keep your head above the surface. To turn, rotate your face and shoulders in the direction you want to go, then sweep your arms sideways to turn your body. Lean forward and kick with your legs to level off on the surface of the water. Then begin a swimming stroke to take you where you want to go.

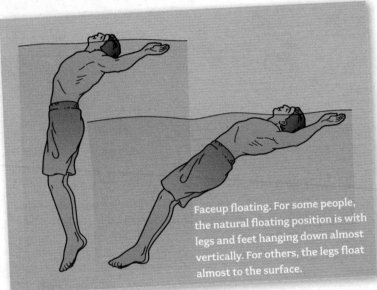

Faceup floating. For some people, the natural floating position is with legs and feet hanging down almost vertically. For others, the legs float almost to the surface.

FLOATING

Floating faceup is a good way to rest in deep, calm water. *Survival floating*—facedown floating—also is a good option, especially when the water is rough.

Practice faceup floating in chest-deep water. Start from a standing position. Take a deep breath and hold it. Bend your knees and lean gently backward, arching your back and stretching your arms above your shoulders. Relax and allow your body to settle into its natural floating position. Some people find that their legs hang down under the water in their natural floating position, while other people's legs and hips stay near the surface when they are in their natural floating position.

Survival Floating

If you are ever stranded in deep, warm water, survival floating is a way to stay alive until rescuers can reach you. Take a breath and relax facedown. Allow yourself to float with the back of your head near the surface. When you need air, push down with your hands and make one scissors kick to lift your mouth and nose above the water. Take a breath and then relax and float facedown again.

Survival floating

Using Clothing as a Life Jacket

If you fall into deep water far from shore, you can inflate your jeans or other pants to create a makeshift flotation device. Your inflated clothing will help you stay afloat until you are rescued or can make your way to safety.

While in the water, pull off your pants. Blow a puff of air into a pocket to inflate the pants so that they will float even if they slip out of your hands. Next, tie the pant legs together with a square knot near the cuffs. Close the fly, and you're ready to inflate your pants life jacket.

Step 1—Inflate a pocket.

Hold the pants waistband open just below the surface. Cup your hand and strike the water, following through so that air caught by your hand goes into the pants. Repeat until the pants are inflated.

Aquatics survival skills really do get put to good use in real life. Read about Scout lifesavers at the *Handbook* Web site, *www.bsahandbook.org*.

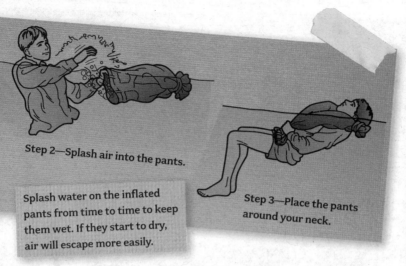

Step 2—Splash air into the pants.

Splash water on the inflated pants from time to time to keep them wet. If they start to dry, air will escape more easily.

Step 3—Place the pants around your neck.

Another way to inflate the pants is to place the pants behind your shoulders, hold the waistband open, and flip the pants overhead to trap air inside. When your pants life jacket needs more air, strike the water with your hand (as explained above) to reinflate the pants.

If the first two methods do not work for you, inflate the pants by blowing air into them from beneath. Be careful not to tire yourself or to hyperventilate.

Once you have filled your pants life jacket with air, use both hands to hold the waistband closed so that the air will not leak out. Slip your head between the legs of the pants, lie back, and float. Use a flutter kick or a whip kick to move toward safety.

If you're wearing a collared shirt made of cotton or another tightly woven material, it also can be used to help you stay afloat. Grip the shirt at the collar and trap air in back and shoulders. (This works best if your collar is buttoned and your back shirttail is tucked in.) Reinflate the shirt by opening the space between the second and third buttons and blowing air inside.

If you are wearing shorts, you can use them as a flotation device. Take off the shorts and inflate the pockets. Hold the shorts close to your chest while floating on your back.

SAFE TRIPS AFLOAT

Have you ever paddled toward a riverbank or lakeshore, ready to make camp during a long canoe trip with your Scout patrol? Have you hauled on the lines of a sailboat tacking into the wind or guided a kayak through the rapids and eddies of a fast-running stream? Do you smile when you think about rafting or waterskiing? Do you dream of someday riding a surfboard down the curling face of a powerful wave? Lots of terrific Scout adventures happen on the water. The BSA Safety Afloat guidelines help make sure that you and others stay safe during activities afloat.

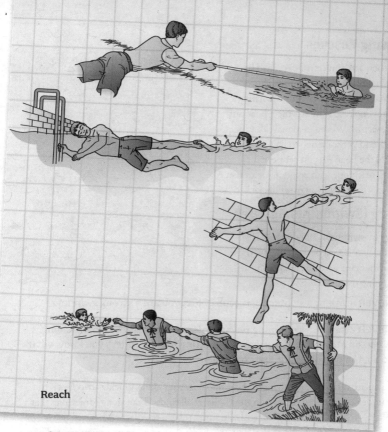

Reach

Reaching Rescues

Many water accidents happen close to shore. While staying on dry land or standing in shallow water, you might be able to reach a victim with your hand or foot, or with a pole, branch, canoe paddle, towel, deck chair, or whatever else is nearby.

Throwing Rescues

Is there a ring buoy on shore—or an air mattress, life jacket, picnic cooler, or other item that floats and can be thrown or shoved toward the victim? A floating object with a line attached to it is best, but either the object or the line can be used alone. Practice throwing a rope with a weight on it and without any weight. Remember to hold on to the other end.

Throw

197

Rowing Rescues

When a victim can't be rescued by reaching or throwing from the shore, you may be able to perform a reaching or throwing rescue by rowing a boat out to the victim. Wear a personal flotation device, and get someone to help you control the boat. As you get near the victim, reach out with a paddle or an oar, or throw the person an extra life jacket.

Row

Go

Going (Swimming) Rescues

Go by swimming only if there is no other way to save a person. Follow these rules whenever you are considering a swimming rescue.

▶ NEVER attempt a swimming rescue unless you are a strong swimmer.

▶ NEVER attempt a swimming rescue unless you are trained in lifesaving. A person struggling in the water is fighting for life. Unless you know what to do, the person might pull you under.

If you are trained in lifesaving and confident in your skills, quickly strip down to your underwear, keeping an eye on the victim at all times. Take along something that will float—a life jacket, an air mattress, an inner tube, a paddle, or whatever else is handy. Use the breaststroke so that you can watch the victim as you swim toward him or her, but stay beyond the victim's reach. Push the flotation device to the victim, then back off. Let the person grab the far side of the floating item you have brought. Wait until the victim becomes calm, even if that means that he or she loses consciousness. Then pull the person ashore.

Lifesaving

Becoming tangled with someone struggling in the water can lead to serious trouble for you and the victim. Don't put yourself in danger. If reaching and throwing aren't possible and you don't have the equipment to go with support, your best course of action could be to go for help. Only in rare situations will a swimming rescue be your only choice. Completing the Lifesaving merit badge will prepare you to use swimming rescue methods if they are ever needed.

Line Tender Rescue

The fourth point of Safe Swim Defense requires that troop swimming activities be protected by a rescue team ready to respond during a drowning situation. The Lifesaving merit badge and BSA Lifeguard training cover skills needed by such a rescue team. However, with a bit of practice, two strong swimmers can safely use the line tender procedure for troop swim protection.

Tie a bowline in the end of a rope to make a large loop. Then place the loop over the shoulder and under the opposite arm of the rescuer. If possible, the rescuer should take with him something that will float such as a ring buoy, seat cushion, or other flotation device. (On a backpacking trip, you may be able to use an inflatable or foam sleeping pad as a flotation device.)

As the rescuer swims toward the victim, his buddy (the *rope tender*) stays on shore to feed out the rope and prevent it from becoming tangled and to closely watch the rescuer and the struggling swimmer. The rescuer presents the floating device to the victim and, when the victim takes hold, signals for the rope tender to pull them to safety.

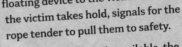

If no floating device is available, the rescuer can swim past the victim and then turn so that the line is pulled within the victim's grasp. The rescuer then signals for the tender to pull both of them to shore.

An unconscious person or someone who is injured might not be able to hold on to the rope. When that's the case, the rescuer can grasp the victim and hold the person's face out of the water while the rope tender pulls the rescuer and victim in.

 More on BSA Lifeguard training may be found on the *Handbook* Web site, www.bsahandbook.org.

AQUATICS OPPORTUNITIES

Swimming is much more than a fine way to spend a few hours on a hot afternoon. It is an important skill that will serve you well throughout your life. You'll be able to save yourself in a swimming or boating emergency. Lifesaving training can prepare you to help others.

Being able to swim also is the doorway to many great activities at lakes, rivers, and oceans. Scouting encourages you to continue building your skills by earning merit badges in Swimming, Lifesaving, Canoeing, Rowing, Motorboating, Whitewater, and Small-Boat Sailing. You also can find training and adventure as you complete the requirements for the BSA's special aquatics awards.

Swimming

Motorboating

LIFESAVIN

Water Sports

Whitewater

Canoeing

Rowing

Small-Boat Sailing

B·S·A LIFE GUARD

Requirements for all aquatics-related awards and merit badges may be found at *www.bsahandbook.org*.

"By Woodcraft I mean outdoor life in its broadest sense."

—Ernest Thompson Seton (1860–1946),
author, artist, and first Chief Scout
of the Boy Scouts of America

B oy Scouts have been exploring nature since the earliest days of the Boy Scouts of America. They've pitched their tents in forests, climbed hills, hiked prairies and coastlines, and traveled arid lands. The keels of their boats have cut through rivers and lakes, salt water and swamps. From city parks to wilderness, and from council camps to high-adventure bases, Scouts have enjoyed more than a century of challenge and discovery in the out-of-doors.

Scouting's founders believed that being in the open air is essential for growth and healthy development. Campcraft skills that boys and young men learn in the woods prepare them to take care of themselves and others under any conditions. Scoutcraft qualities thrive in the outdoors, too, as Scouts become physically and mentally stronger. They also develop into better leaders and more capable citizens.

In the outdoors, Scouts can build a lasting enjoyment and appreciation for the natural world. The earliest Scouters called this **Woodcraft**—the deep commitment to learning about and protecting nature.

Woodcraft continues to offer exciting ways for Scouts to learn about the environment and to better understand the complexity and importance of the natural world. Woodcraft expects those who use the outdoors to accept responsibility for taking care of it. The principles of Leave No Trace are guidelines for all Scouts and Scouters to follow. They explain ways that Scouting activities can be conducted without doing harm to the outdoor places Scouts enjoy.

Lastly, Woodcraft encourages Scouts to give back to the land by helping conserve, restore, and protect the environment. Good Turns, troop and patrol conservation projects, and Eagle Scout leadership service projects are all reminders of the commitment that millions of Scouts have made to care for our Earth.

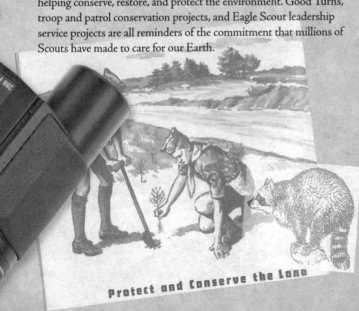

Protect and Conserve the Land

Nature

> "You'll have more fun on hikes or camping trips if you learn to do one important thing—live with nature instead of trying to change nature to fit your ideas. Think of yourself as a part of the world of nature, rather than as an observer apart from it somehow."
>
> —*Fieldbook*, 2nd ed., 1967

NATURE

"*Scouting* is two-thirds *outing*," goes an old Boy Scout saying. The outdoors is where Scouts want to be. The adventure of the Boy Scouts of America is strong in camp, on trails and waterways, and throughout America's forests, hill country, prairies, and mountains.

Sometimes you head outdoors for the fun of being with friends. You go to hike, to run and climb, to launch watercraft, and to swim. You go to test yourself and learn new skills. You go so that at the end of the day you can pitch your tent and sleep under the stars.

The outdoors is where you'll find the action of Scouting. It's where you can roam open country, find your way with a map and compass, and practice plenty of other Scouting skills. The promise of Scouting has room to unfold in the outdoors. Character, leadership, and good decision-making really do matter.

Your troop and patrol give you opportunities to see how the natural world affects all of us and to understand our impact on the land. Through Scouting, you can also increase your understanding of your responsibility to care for the environment and of ways to fulfill that responsibility.

Scouts have always done their best to take care of the world around them. It begins with the ninth point of the Scout Law—*A Scout is thrifty.* Part of being thrifty means that you protect and conserve natural resources. By following the principles of Leave No Trace, you can enjoy the outdoors in ways that do no harm. By taking part in service projects, you can give back to the land that gives so much to you.

IN THIS CHAPTER

▶ Ecosystems

▶ Understanding and identifying plants

▶ Identifying and observing wildlife

▶ Tracking and stalking

▶ Features of weather

▶ Stars and constellations

▶ Taking care of the environment

LEARNING ABOUT NATURE

A hawk soars above a mountain wilderness. Trees near your home sway in the wind. Ocean tides rise and fall. Birds, whales, and butterflies migrate thousands of miles around the globe.

The natural world is beautiful, complicated, and spectacular. It is huge, too, a place where redwood forests tower toward the sky and grasslands stretch to the horizon and beyond. Nature is present on a smaller scale as well—the eye of an insect, the nucleus of a cell, the secrets of an atom.

Nature sometimes makes itself known with the eruption of a volcano, the jolt of an earthquake, or the howl of a blizzard. Nature also moves very slowly. Continents drift a few inches every year. Over long periods of time, rivers carve canyons deep into solid rock. Animals gradually adjust their behavior to meet changes in where and how they live.

The relationships among plants, animals, and their surroundings are so complex that we can understand only some of the mysteries. Even so, you will discover much about nature if you open your eyes and your mind. Learn all you can about animals and plants. Investigate weather, geology, and the impact that people have on the environment. Find clues that lead you toward solving some of the inner workings of the natural world. Books and Web sites devoted to nature can help you understand much about the complex web of life going on all around you.

ECOSYSTEMS

The study of animals and plants and how they interact with each other and with nonliving parts of the environment such as weather, water, and sunlight is called *ecology*. It comes from the old Greek words *oikos*, meaning "house," and *-logy*, meaning "to study." Ecology is the study of the home we share with all other species.

Deserts, forests, oceans, mountain ranges, meadows—all these different areas on the planet have their own unique combinations of geology, weather, inhabitants, and much else that make each one special. These groupings of plants, animals, and their surroundings are called *ecosystems*. As you focus in on an individual ecosystem, you'll be astonished by the remarkable way in which everything fits together. Each species is important for the survival of others. Their survival also depends upon certain qualities of land, water, and space.

While no two places on the globe are alike, all share certain similarities that give us ways to compare one area with another and to help us make sense out of what we know of them. Scientists organize living things into groups with related characteristics. Two of the largest groups are *plants* and *animals*.

Learning about nature begins with enjoying it. Get outdoors, have fun, and begin noticing where you are and what is all around. Become curious about plants, animals, the shape of the land, and the feel of weather. Take time to actually *see* your surroundings, and you will find yourself learning new languages—the languages of the water, the prairies, the forests, and the peaks.

PLANTS

From grasses pushing through cracks in a city sidewalk to ancient forests covering a mountainside, plants are vital to our world. Plants help all animals because they release oxygen. All animals need oxygen to survive.

Plants protect the land, too. Their roots help keep soil from washing away. Leaves slow rainwater as it falls, giving it time to seep into the earth. Fallen trees, shrubs, and grasses enrich the soil as they decay.

Plants provide shelter and food for wildlife. A dead tree can be important to animals as a roosting site, a place to build nests, and a source of food.

People use plants in many ways, too. We eat fruits, vegetables, grains, and nuts. All come from plants. Lumber from trees goes into our buildings. Paper, medicines, and thousands of other products are possible only because of plants.

Trees provide shade in yards and city parks, offering us places close to home where we can relax and play. Forests are the perfect place to hike and camp. Roaming deep into a backcountry forest allows us to get far from roads, buildings, and crowds of people.

Covered with young vegetation and slowly decomposing on the forest floor, old trees act as "nurse logs" that help ensure the health of future generations of vegetation.

 For more information about plants, visit the *Handbook* Web site: www.bsahandbook.org.

Plant Power

Green chlorophyll in leaves draws energy from sunlight. A plant uses this energy to convert carbon dioxide from the air and water from the soil into sugars it can use for energy. The process is called *photosynthesis*—a combination of the words *photo* (meaning "light") and *synthesis* ("to make"). Photosynthesis also returns oxygen to the atmosphere.

Sun energy

Plant growth

Oxygen

Food from plants

Food from animals (and other products)

Animal food

Carbon oxide

Carbon dioxide

Plant food

Decaying matter

Soil nutrients

Photosynthesis

Trees

Trees are the biggest and the oldest living things on Earth. More than a thousand species grow in the United States, each different from all the rest. Some thrive in sunlight, others in shade. A few require fire for their seeds to open and take root. Certain trees grow very fast. Those living for hundreds of years gain their height and mass more slowly.

The two large groups of American trees are *conifer trees* and *broadleaf trees.*

Conifer Trees—Also known as *evergreens,* conifers have needle-like or scale-like leaves that usually stay on the trees for several years. Conifers include pines, firs, and spruces.

Broadleaf Trees—These trees have flat leaves that generally fall off at the end of the summer. Broadleaf trees include maples, oaks, ashes, beeches, and birches. Each autumn the leaves of many broadleaf trees turn yellow, red, orange, and brown. Those colors were in the leaves all summer, but were masked by the green of the chlorophyll. With the approach of colder weather, a tree's food production drops and so does the amount of chlorophyll in the leaves. The green fades and other colors show through.

Next, a layer of cells in a leaf stem cuts the tissues holding the leaf to its branch. The leaf falls to the ground where it decomposes, releasing nutrients into the soil so that they can be used again.

Broadleaf tree

Conifer tree

"Different sorts of trees look pretty much alike to many people; but by observing their different traits we can learn to know a large number of trees just as we have learned to know our friends. The natural history of trees can be learned only by keeping our eyes open, training ourselves to observe closely."

—*Handbook for Boys*, 2nd ed., 1914

Identifying Plants

Identifying trees and other plants in your community is a good way to become more aware of nature. Your troop leaders might know gardeners, botanists, or other plant experts who will enjoy sharing their knowledge with groups of Scouts. Land managers at public parks and forests may be able to show you how to recognize the shapes and sizes of different plants, the outlines of their leaves, and other clues that can lead to their identifications.

You can use Internet resources and books called *field guides* to help you learn to identify plants. Your Scout troop and your public and school libraries might have field guides you can borrow. Many field guides and plant identification Web sites also contain information about the important roles plants play in their surroundings.

A *plant key* is a plant-identifying tool that asks a series of questions that will lead you to the identity of a tree or plant. For example, suppose you have a leaf from a tree you would like to know more about. It looks like this:

You know it is a broadleaf tree because the leaf is not a needle, as you would find on a conifer. Going online or using a plant key in a book, you would find a series of simple questions. The answer to each one leads you along a certain pathway until you have discovered the identity of your leaf. Here's how the process could work for this leaf.

For more help identifying plants in the field, see the *Handbook* Web site: www.bsahandbook.org.

Is it a *simple leaf* or a *compound leaf*? A simple leaf is a single blade attached by its stem to a branch. A compound leaf is a number of leaflets connected to a central stem attached to the branch.

Simple

Compound

Your leaf looks like a simple leaf. Choosing the simple leaf choice leads to a second question.

Is the simple leaf *lobed* or *unlobed*? A lobed leaf has deep notches around its edge. An unlobed leaf does not.

Lobed

Unlobed

Your leaf is unlobed. The next question takes you closer to your goal.

Does your unlobed leaf have a *toothed edge* or an *untoothed edge*? A toothed leaf has an edge that looks a bit like a saw. An untoothed leaf has a smooth edge.

Smooth edge

Toothed edge

It has a toothed edge.

You're close to an answer now. The next questions will limit the leaf to certain kinds of trees.

Does the leaf have double teeth around the edge, and is the stem off-center? If so, it is probably a leaf from an elm tree.

If not, is the leaf oval shaped with small teeth along the edge and a stem that is centered? If so, then it is probably a leaf from a cherry tree.

If not, does the leaf have sharp, curving teeth and a smooth, shiny surface? If so, then it is probably a beech.

If not, is the leaf long and narrow? If so, then it is probably a willow.

If not, does the leaf have double teeth around the edge and a stem that is centered? Your leaf *does* have double teeth around the edge *and* a centered stem. This tells you it is from a birch tree.

The plant key might ask a few further questions so that you can decide on the type of birch you've found. It also will tell you about the area where the tree grows, what its bark looks like, and any uses of the wood and foliage.

Elm

Cherry

Beech

Willow

Birch

214

Identifying Native Plants 🏵️

Identify or show evidence of at least 10 kinds of native plants found in your community.

1. _____

2. _____

3. _____

4. _____

5. _____

6. _____

7. _____

8. _____

9. _____

10. _____

Showing Evidence of Plants

As you learn to identify trees and plants, you can gather evidence from them that helps you remember their characteristics. Three forms of evidence are digital leaf collections, pressed leaves, and leaf ink prints.

Digital Leaf Collections—With computer tools, you can create a database of your plant discoveries. In the field, you can take pictures of a leaf without removing it from a plant. Place a blank piece of paper flat behind the leaf and take a photo using a digital camera.

Photograph the tree the leaf came from and its surroundings, too. Take close-up shots of its bark and any nuts, cones, or fruits you find on the branches or on the ground.

Build a computer file featuring the image of the leaf, then add your photos of other evidence that helps identify the tree. Type in some information about the tree, and add links to Web sites that offer additional information about the plant.

As your digital leaf collection grows, you might post it on a Scout blog so that members of your patrol and troop can use it to learn about the plants of your area and then add leaf files of their own. You could also create an online leaf identification quiz that flashes clues on the screen—a leaf outline, a full tree, a photo of a tree's bark—and challenges Scouts to figure out what they are seeing.

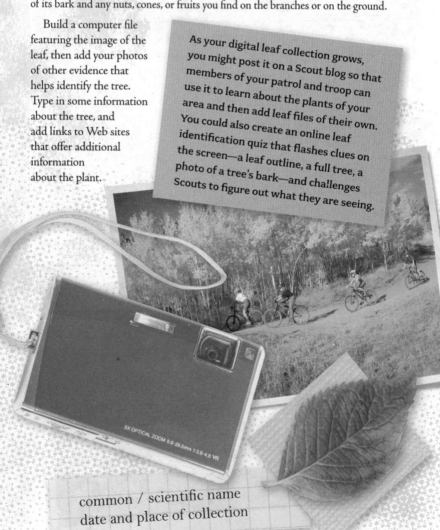

common / scientific name
date and place of collection

Pressed Leaves—Put each leaf you want to preserve between two sheets of newspaper, then lay the sheets on a table or other flat surface and place several heavy books on top. Give the leaves a few days to flatten and dry. Mount each one in a scrapbook along with the details of where and when you found it, the identity of the plant, and information about the plant it came from.

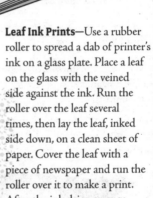

Leaf Ink Prints—Use a rubber roller to spread a dab of printer's ink on a glass plate. Place a leaf on the glass with the veined side against the ink. Run the roller over the leaf several times, then lay the leaf, inked side down, on a clean sheet of paper. Cover the leaf with a piece of newspaper and run the roller over it to make a print. After the ink dries, arrange the pages in a scrapbook.

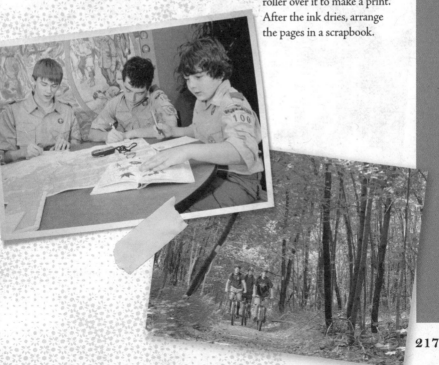

WILDLIFE

Scout hikes and campouts are good times to observe wild animals. You also can find plenty of evidence of animals in your neighborhood even if you live in the middle of a city. Try to figure out a little bit about how they live. What do they need to survive? How do they raise their young? What do they eat? Are they prey to other animals, or are they predators?

Just as trees can be divided into broadleaf trees and conifer trees, animals can be placed into two groups: *vertebrates* and *invertebrates*.

▶ **Vertebrates have backbones.**

▶ **Invertebrates are animals that do not have backbones.**

Vertebrates are further divided into five groups: fish, amphibians, reptiles, birds, and mammals.

Fish—Fish are cold-blooded, live in water, and breathe through gills. Their bodies are covered with scales.

Amphibians—Most frogs, toads, newts, salamanders, and other amphibians start life in the water as gilled aquatic larvae that have hatched from eggs. Adults breathe air through lungs and generally live on land.

Reptiles—Snakes, alligators, crocodiles, lizards, and turtles are all reptiles. They are cold-blooded, air-breathing animals that are covered with scales or bony plates. Some move on short legs. Others, like snakes, slither along on their bellies.

Birds—Birds are warm-blooded animals with wings and feathers. They hatch their young from eggs.

Mammals—Deer, bears, foxes, squirrels, and other mammals are warm-blooded vertebrates that have some kind of fur or hair. They nurse their babies with milk.

Invertebrates greatly outnumber the planet's vertebrates and can be divided into many more groups. The largest invertebrate group is made up of *arthropods*—insects, arachnids (such as spiders and scorpions), and crustaceans (such as crabs and shrimp). The *mollusk* group, second in size to the arthropods, includes snails, clams, oysters, mussels, and squid.

How to Find Evidence of Animals

Looking, listening, smelling, and *touching* are all ways you can gather evidence of animals in your neighborhood and in the backcountry.

Looking—Hawks in flight can see the movements of small animals far below. Owls see well enough in the dark to fly silently among the branches of trees. Human eyes are not as sharp as those of hawks and owls, but our eyes can still tell us plenty about our surroundings.

Slow down and give your eyes time to notice what is all around you. You might start by glancing quickly at a forest or a front yard, then carefully examining one tree. Try getting down on your hands and knees and inspecting a square foot of earth. Look for animal footprints, overturned stones, tufts of fur caught on twigs, or a feather on the ground. Be alert to movement in the brush, in the water, and in the sky. Use a magnifying glass or binoculars for even closer looks.

Scat

Droppings called *scat* are evidence of an animal's diet. Break scat apart with a stick. Remains of seeds, skins of berries, and bits of leaves suggest the animal is an *herbivore*—an animal that eats only plants. Small bones, fur, and feathers may appear in the scat of a *carnivore*—an animal that feeds on other animals. Mixed scat indicates an *omnivore*—an animal whose diet includes both animals and plants.

 Resources on the *Handbook* Web site, *www.bsahandbook.org*, can help you more easily identify wildlife in your area.

Listening—Sit quietly and you will discover that the outdoors is full of sounds. The buzz of insects and the croaking of frogs can be mating calls. Birds often use songs to claim their territory. The chatter of a squirrel and the slap of a beaver's tail might be warnings. Sometimes it is the absence of sound that is important. When birds suddenly stop singing, it could be because they have noticed a cat or other threat nearby, or maybe they've seen you.

Many animals have very good hearing. The ears of a deer are shaped like big scoops that can be turned in any direction to pick up faint, faraway sounds. You can increase your own hearing by cupping your hands behind your ears. Turning your head from side to side might help you pinpoint the location of a sound.

Smelling—A keen sense of smell is as important to some animals as hearing and seeing are to others. Ants lay down aroma trails that lead them back to their nests. Wolves sniff the wind for signs of prey. Elk are startled by the smell of predators nearing them. Mountain lions mark their territory with the scent of their urine.

Even though humans in the outdoors depend less on smell, your nose can still provide clues to what's going on. Notice the scents of flowers, trees, soil, and moss. A fresh stream smells different than a pond. The stench of an animal carcass may reveal its location.

Touching—A snake flicking out its tongue is picking up vibrations in the air. Nerves running along the bodies of fish alert them to changes in the water. With whiskers or feelers, moles and opossums rely upon touch more than upon their other senses. Even animals with sharp eyesight or finely tuned noses are aware of the feel of things around them.

You can use touch to better understand your surroundings, too. Feel the texture of leaves; some are rough, others smooth. Weigh stones in your hand. Wade in ponds. Crawl through tall grass. Roll in the snow. Imagine what it would feel like to live as different animals.

"Any boy who cares enough for the outdoors to be a scout is sure to want a good acquaintance with the birds. . . . Scouts whose eyes are sharp and ears are keen will find the study of birds a fascinating sport, which may prove to be the best fun that the woods provide."

—*Handbook for Boys*, 2nd ed., 1914

Birds

Birds are among the animals you are most likely to see around your home and during hikes and campouts. Many people make a hobby of studying birds, keeping lifetime lists of those they have seen. Watching birds can be a satisfying part of outdoor adventures and good practice for developing your powers of observation.

Scan the trees and take time to watch the birds that you notice. Binoculars can help you make out small details. Use a bird identification book for your area to discover the names of birds and to learn about their habits. The Internet is another good source of information for identifying birds and for learning about their habits and ranges. Your patrol can keep a notebook in which you list all the birds you see on your outings.

You might be able to attract birds by whistling. With a hunter's duck call or goose call, you can try bringing waterfowl close. An old stalking trick is to make a smacking sound by kissing the back of your hand. Birds recognizing the sound as a distress call may be drawn toward you.

As you observe birds, the *Six S's* can give you a quick way to gather clues that can lead to a bird's identification and help you solve some of the mysteries about how it lives.

Size—A hummingbird is just a few inches long and weighs only ounces. A turkey vulture weighs several pounds and has a wing span of three feet or more. When you see a bird, compare its size with those of birds you know. Is the new one larger than a sparrow? About the same size as a robin? Smaller than a crow? Can you think of ways the size of a bird might affect how it gathers food, makes its nests, and avoids predators?

Shape—A bird's shape helps it thrive in its environment. The powerful talons of eagles and owls allow them to grip their prey and lift it into the sky. The long, slender legs of the heron let it wade in waters where it can feed on small fish. The beaks of different species of finches have shapes that allow them to eat the kinds of seeds, berries, or other foods present in their environments.

The Six S's of Bird Identification

- ▶ Size
- ▶ Shape
- ▶ Shading
- ▶ Song
- ▶ Sweep
- ▶ Surroundings

Shading—Bright feathers help many birds attract mates. For others, drab colors act as camouflage so that the birds can blend into their backgrounds. The ptarmigan is a good example. Its brown feathers hide it during summers in mountain forests. When winter comes, the ptarmigan's feathers become as white as the snow.

Song—Birds use their songs to warn of danger, guard their territories, and find mates. Sometimes they sound as though they are singing for the sheer joy of making noise. When you know the songs of birds, you can identify them even without seeing them. A good way to learn bird songs is to hike with bird watchers who already know a few bird songs. They can teach you how the songs of each species differ from all others.

Sweep—Sweep refers to the movement a bird makes. Some hop across the ground or scurry along in a fast waddle. Others flit from tree to tree. Soaring birds catch updrafts of wind and hover without flapping their wings. Some water birds dive into cold mountain streams. Close observation of the sweep of a bird may lead to the most interesting part of bird watching—seeing how each has adapted to its surroundings.

Surroundings—From the Arctic to the equator and all the way to Antarctica, birds seem to be everywhere. Like all animals, a bird must be able to get the things it needs from its surroundings or it will die. It must find food, water, shelter, and a mate so it can breed and raise young. The first five S's (size, shape, shading, song, and sweep) are ways that birds have adapted to S number six—surroundings.

Bird Study

You can improve birds' surroundings by putting up birdhouses and bird feeders near your home. Bird feeders containing seed and suet are especially important in northern states when winter snows have covered other sources of food. The *Bird Study* merit badge pamphlet has plans for building birdhouses and feeding stations.

MERIT BADGE SERIES

BIRD STUDY

TRACKING

Every animal traveling on land leaves tracks: footprints, bent grass, broken twigs, chewed leaves, scat, rubbed bark, a shiny strip of slime. Following these and other clues can teach you much about the habits of animals. With a little luck, the tracks might lead you to the creatures themselves. Tracking is a skill you can master over time. Practice in your yard and in parks, fields, and forests. Here's how to get started.

Find Some Tracks to Follow

Winter snow can reveal a surprising number of tracks. During other seasons, try the soft soil near ponds and streams. In dry country, scan the dust for prints and look for pebbles and brush that have been disturbed.

Study a Single Track

Examine one footprint and fix its details in your mind. You might measure it and make a sketch of it, or take a digital photograph. These memory aids can help you stay with a trail even if other animals have crossed the tracks you are following.

Track Early or Late

Shadows cast in an animal's footprints early in the morning and late in the day make tracks easier to see.

Think Like the Animal

If you lose the trail, ask yourself where you would go if you were the animal and then look in that direction. Mark the last print with a stick so you can find it again. Explore all around it until you find more evidence of the animal's route.

For more track identification resources, visit the *Handbook* Web site: www.bsahandbook.org.

Generally, the front foot and the hind foot of the same mammal make different tracks. The size, shape, and number of toes are likely to be different. Like anything else, skill in reading tracks comes with practice.

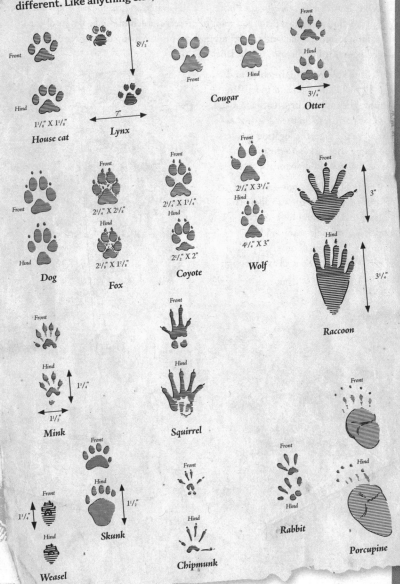

Front / Hind
1¼" X 1¼"
House cat

8½"
7"
Lynx

Front / Hind
Cougar

Front / Hind
3¼"
Otter

Front / Hind
Dog

Front
2½" X 2½"
Hind
2½" X 1⅞"
Fox

Front
2½" X 1¾"
Hind
2½" X 2"
Coyote

Front
2⅛" X 3¼"
Hind
4¼" X 3"
Wolf

Front
3"
Hind
3¾"
Raccoon

Front / Hind
1¼"
1½"
Mink

Front / Hind
Squirrel

Front / Hind
1½"
Skunk

Front
Hind
1¾"
Weasel

Front / Hind
Chipmunk

Front / Hind
Rabbit

Front / Hind
Porcupine

Collecting Tracks

Perhaps you have heard the Leave No Trace hiking slogan, "Take only photographs, leave only footprints." Here's a way you can bring home some footprints, too.

When out tracking, carry some plaster of paris, water, and cardboard strips with you. When you find an animal print you want to preserve, notch the ends of a cardboard strip, form it into a collar, and place it around the print. Mix up the plaster of paris according to the instructions on the label.

Pour the plaster into the collar and wait 10 to 20 minutes for it to harden. Remove the cast and brush off any dirt or other particles. On the back of the cast write the date, the location where you found the track, and the name of the animal you think made the track.

Casts of prints are fine souvenirs of your adventures. You can also press a cast into damp sand to re-create a track—a valuable study aid for improving the animal observing skills of everyone in your patrol and troop.

Plaster of paris is available at drug stores.

"A Scout walks through the woods with silent tread. . . . He sees tracks and signs which reveal to him the nature and habits of the creatures that made them. He knows how to stalk birds and animals and study them in their natural haunts. He sees much, but is little seen."

—*Boy Scout Handbook*, 2nd ed., circa 1925

STALKING

Getting close to animals without them knowing you are there is an ancient art. It allows you to find out what animals look like, where they go, and what they do. Stalking is an exciting challenge that will test your patience and skill. If you have a camera, stalking also may give you some great opportunities for photographing wildlife.

Stalking is a terrific mental exercise. To get close to wildlife, become a shadow. Become so much a part of your surroundings that you seem to disappear. Be patient and control your body, moving smoothly and silently.

Stalking and Leave No Trace

"Respect wildlife." That's one of the Leave No Trace principles Scouts use to care for the outdoors. Respect the boundaries of animals and their needs. Don't chase wild animals or touch nests or burrows. If you come upon a young animal, leave it alone. Its parents could be hiding nearby, waiting for you to leave. When you can quietly move close to an animal, you can just as quietly slip away without disturbing it.

Stalking by Waiting

Let animals come to you. Hide long enough near a well-used animal trail and there's a good chance you'll see them coming by. Take cover in the brush or in a blind, or climb into a tree and wait for wildlife to appear.

Much of the animal world is active after dark. On a night with a full moon, sit quietly at the edge of a meadow or near a lake or stream. You might hear and see lots of activity.

Stalking by Moving

To move closer to animals, make yourself invisible and silent. Hide behind trees, stumps, and clumps of grass. Keep near the ground and look around the sides of rocks and bushes, not over the top. Stay low as you cross hilltops and ridges so that your silhouette doesn't show against the sky.

Move only when animals are looking away. Freeze if they glance in your direction. Place your feet with care. Stepping on twigs or dry leaves might make enough noise to send wildlife running.

Many animals will be able to smell you from long distances. Try to stay downwind as you are stalking. When the wind is coming toward you, it won't carry your scent to an animal.

Identifying Wild Animals

Identify or show evidence of at least 10 kinds of wild animals (birds, mammals, reptiles, fish, amphibians) found in your community.

1. _____

2. _____

3. _____

4. _____

5. _____

6. _____

7. _____

8. _____

9. _____

10. _____

WEATHER

Checking weather reports is part of the planning you do before a Scout hike or campout. You'll have a better idea of what clothing to carry with you and what to expect when you reach the trail. Studying weather also can be a terrific way to understand the bigger picture of nature.

The atmosphere surrounding our planet extends about 60 miles from Earth's surface to the edge of space. Air over tropical regions rises as the sun heats it. Air above the Arctic and Antarctic cools and sinks, pulling the warm tropical air toward the North and South poles. The spinning of the planet swirls the air, too, keeping the atmosphere in motion. Moisture that rises from the surface into the sky forms clouds that can travel hundreds of miles before the moisture falls back to the surface as rain or snow.

Weather reports on television and on Web sites often include maps showing the movement of areas of low pressure and high pressure in the atmosphere. Regions experiencing high atmospheric pressure usually have stable weather. Where the pressure is low, though, winds will be pulled in. If those winds are carrying moisture, storms can occur.

For more information on finding weather reports and reading weather maps, visit the *Handbook* Web site: *www.bsahandbook.org.*

READING A WEATHER MAP

Take a look at a weather map and you might think you are seeing a topographic map with contour lines showing elevation. To map the weather, those lines are called *isobars*. Instead of elevation, they show the *barometric pressure* of an area—how dense the atmosphere is at a given moment. By studying pressure readings and noting how they are changing, meteorologists (scientists who study the atmosphere and weather) can put together a map that shows current weather conditions. The map can be used to predict the weather for the hours and days to come.

A *front* is the line between an area of high pressure and one of low pressure. A front passing through an area is a sign that the weather is about to change.

1. Blue indicates a *cold front* with cool or cold air moving in the direction of the points.

2. Red shows a *warm front*—warm or hot air moving in the direction of the half-circles.

3. If a cold front or a warm front stops moving, it becomes a *stationary front*. A weather map shows a stationary front with half-circles on one side of a line and triangles on the other.

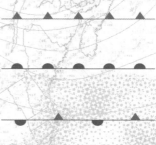

Clouds

Moisture rising into the air can form droplets and ice crystals that build into clouds. Clouds take three basic shapes. Meteorologists give each shape a Latin name:

▶ Streak clouds—*Cirrus*

▶ Layer clouds—*Stratus*

▶ Heap clouds—*Cumulus*

Nimbus describes any cloud from which precipitation might fall. A *nimbostratus* cloud, for example, is a layer-shaped cloud that could produce rain.

National Weather Radio

A 24-hour service of the National Oceanic and Atmospheric Administration, National Weather Radio airs constant weather updates. Keep your radio tuned in during bad weather so that you can hear forecasts, warnings, and other important information. To find the radio frequency to use in your area, see the *Boy Scout Handbook* Web site.

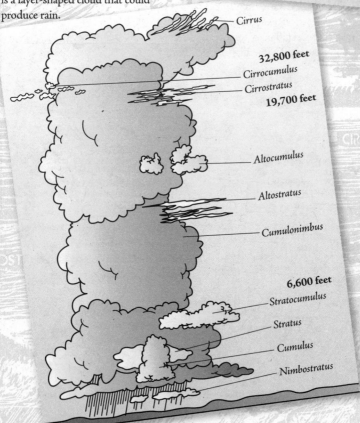

Cirrus

32,800 feet
Cirrocumulus
Cirrostratus
19,700 feet

Altocumulus

Altostratus

Cumulonimbus

6,600 feet
Stratocumulus

Stratus

Cumulus

Nimbostratus

Using Clouds to Predict Weather

The first sign of an approaching storm might be the appearance in a clear sky of high, feathery cirrus (streak) clouds. Over several hours or days, they will thicken and lower until the sun is hidden by a thin cirrostratus veil. A gray curtain of altostratus clouds comes next, followed by a moist blanket of dark stratus clouds rolling close to Earth. Finally, nimbostratus clouds, black and threatening, bring rain.

Not all clouds signal bad weather. Cirrus clouds not attached to one another are a sign that the weather will stay fair for a while. A "mackerel sky" formed by cirrocumulus clouds that look like fish scales usually promises fair weather, but might also bring unsettled conditions with brief showers.

Scout patrols eager to hike dry trails welcome the sight of white, fluffy cumulus clouds. On hot days, though, backcountry travelers should keep an eye on cumulus clouds that are swelling. Take cover if those clouds develop into dark cumulonimbus thunderheads, a source of violent storms.

Lightning

A bolt of lightning streaking through the sky is one of nature's most dramatic features. Here's how it happens.

The basic electrical charge of the Earth's surface is negative. Six or seven miles up, the atmosphere carries a positive charge. When the weather is clear, there is nothing between the ground and the sky to conduct electrons.

When a cumulonimbus cloud billows miles into the sky and becomes a *thunderhead*, the positive electrical charge in the top of the cloud can be drawn down into the cloud and sometimes all the way to the Earth's surface in the form of a lightning bolt. Traveling at 31,000 miles per second, lightning can heat a narrow pathway of air to temperatures higher than 45,000 degrees. The violent expansion and contraction of the air results in a clap of thunder.

The instability of electrical charges within a cloud is heightened by collisions of ice crystals and hail and by differences in air temperature at different altitudes. When the imbalance becomes great enough between negatively charged and positively charged areas of clouds or between a cloud and the ground, electrons (negatively charged subatomic particles) form a pathway called a leader and flood from one zone to the other, resulting in a lightning strike.

For more information on weather, visit the *Handbook* Web site, www.bsahandbook.org.

Tornadoes

Conditions that can form cumulonimbus clouds capable of producing lightning also might sometimes cause tornadoes. Usually occurring in the middle part of the United States, tornadoes can take shape when cold, dry air moving in one direction collides with warm, moist air going another way. Differences in the direction, speed, and temperature of the two air masses can cause a rotating weather system to form, which might develop into the rapidly spinning funnel cloud of a tornado.

Warning signs of a tornado include very dark clouds that sometimes have a greenish tint, heavy rain and hail, and a roaring sound. Meteorologists tracking storms broadcast warnings with information telling people in the path of a storm what they should do.

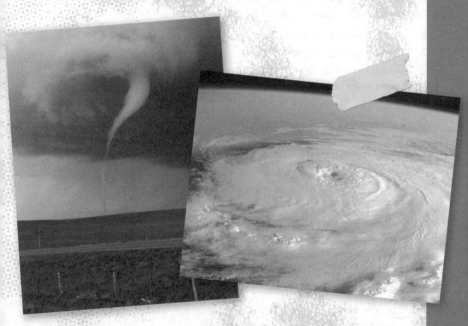

Hurricanes

Hurricanes develop out of deep low-pressure areas over warm ocean water. Under certain conditions, moisture rising into the sky generates energy that can cause a spinning storm to build into a hurricane. It may be hundreds of miles across and have winds of well over 100 miles per hour. Hurricanes that come ashore are extremely dangerous and can do tremendous damage. People in the path of a hurricane should follow the guidance of local and state officials to protect themselves.

OTHER WEATHER SIGNS

Through the ages, people have used sayings as a way of sharing weather lore. The weather sayings below are very old, but you might be surprised how often they accurately foretell the weather to come.

Fair-Weather Signs

Expect pleasant weather when you see some of these signs:

"Red sky at night, sailor's delight." The dust particles in the dry air of tomorrow's weather produce a glowing red sunset.

"Swallows flying way up high mean there's no rain in the sky." Swallows are birds that catch and eat flying insects. In the high pressure that comes with fair weather, insects may be carried aloft by air currents.

"If smoke goes high, no rain comes by." Campfire smoke rises straight up when there is no wind. Still air does not move moisture into an area.

"When the dew is on the grass, rain will never come to pass." Dew forms when water vapor in the air condenses into droplets on cool leaves and grass. This happens especially during the cool, clear nights that accompany good weather.

Stormy-Weather Signs

The following signs suggest bad weather is on the way:

"Red sky at morning, sailor take warning." Dry, dusty air moving toward the east causes the sun to appear reddish as it comes over the horizon. This could mean that moist air is pushing in from the west, bringing stormy weather with it.

"Swallows flying near the ground mean a storm will come around." The low air pressure that pulls in stormy weather causes insects to fly close to the ground on heavy, moist wings. Swallows follow.

"If smoke hangs low, watch out for a blow." Low air pressure also can prevent campfire smoke from rising very high.

"When grass is dry at morning light, look for rain before the night." On a cloudy night, grass might not cool enough for dew to form.

"Mackerel scales and mares' tails make lofty ships carry low sails." The "scales" and "tails" refer to cirrus cloud formations that warn of changing weather.

"All American boys know the Dipper or Great Bear. This is, perhaps, the most important star group in our sky, because of its size, peculiar form, and the fact that it never sets in our latitude, and last, that it always points out the Pole-star, and, for this reason, it is sometimes known as the Pointers."

—*Handbook for Boys*, 1st ed., 1911

STARS AND CONSTELLATIONS

One of the pleasures of camping is looking into the night sky. Away from the glow of a city, you can see thousands of stars. At first, they might seem to be a random scattering of brilliant points of light. Look more carefully, though, and you will notice that some stars are brighter than others. Night after night, they appear at almost the same places in the sky. There is an order to their location. By learning about that order, you will have a powerful skill for finding directions at night.

A *star chart* is a map of the heavens. The revolution of Earth around the sun allows us to see different parts of the sky during different seasons of the year. At 10 P.M., the summer sky overhead looks much different than the sky at the same hour in the middle of the winter. Choose a star chart that is set for the month that you want to use it. Soon you will be able to locate the constellations that can guide you as you travel at night and connect you with the long, colorful history of the pictures in the sky.

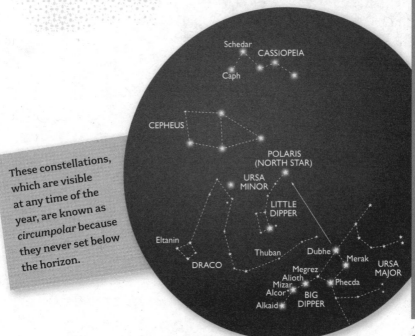

These constellations, which are visible at any time of the year, are known as circumpolar because they never set below the horizon.

239

The Constellations

For thousands of years, people watching the night sky have grouped stars together into pictures, or *constellations*. The custom might date back to times when ancient shepherds spent their nights under the open sky. They may have imagined that the patterns of stars suggested the shapes of kings and queens, warriors, maidens, animals, and monsters. Many of the constellations they named are still called that today.

You can find the same constellations in the sky over your camp. Read about them, and you will discover much about the history and mythology of people from the past who, like you, looked with wonder at the stars above.

Perhaps the best-known star grouping in the northern sky is the Big Dipper. It is part of a constellation called Ursa Major, or the Great Bear. It can be seen from most locations in the United States.

Look to the south during clear winter evenings and you'll see the constellation Orion, or the Hunter, spreading across the sky. The stars form the shape of a hunter. Three stars close together are his belt, and a string of fainter stars is the scabbard of his sword. A giant red star known as Betelgeuse is at one of Orion's shoulders, and Bellatrix marks his other shoulder. The blue-white star Rigel, one of the brightest in the sky, marks one of Orion's legs.

For more on stars, constellations, and the legends behind them, see the *Handbook* Web site: *www.bsahandbook.org*.

TAKING CARE OF THE ENVIRONMENT

The BSA encourages all Scouts to learn about nature and to do their part to care for the environment. Service projects for rank advancement and the Eagle Scout Award can help you learn to plan and complete good work that is of value to the Earth.

Merit badges are fine opportunities for exploring the natural world, too, and for learning about career possibilities in environmental fields. These merit badges are a few of the nature-related subjects you can explore.

▶ **Astronomy**

▶ **Bird Study**

▶ **Environmental Science**

▶ **Fish and Wildlife Management**

▶ **Forestry**

▶ **Geology**

▶ **Insect Study**

▶ **Mammal Study**

▶ **Nature**

▶ **Plant Science**

▶ **Reptile and Amphibian Study**

▶ **Soil and Water Conservation**

▶ **Weather**

Forestry

Nature

Plant Science

As a Scout, you will be recognized as a young person who enjoys the outdoors and as someone doing your part to care for the environment. A lifetime of service to the environment can begin now. Recycling, being thrifty in the use of natural resources, and following the principles of Leave No Trace while hiking and camping are a few of the ways each of us can help. Learning about nature and enjoying time in the outdoors can help you make choices that are good for Earth's health.

"The serious Scout will use his imagination, and his knowledge, in looking for conservation work to do. He will remember what he has learned—that one of the secrets of conservation is the web of life; that the other is careful study of all possible outcomes of his project, so that it will result in the greatest good for the largest number of people."

—*Handbook for Boys,* 4th ed., 1940

CHAPTER 7
Leave No Trace

> "A Scout is Thrifty. One of the most important ways in which you can show that you are thrifty is the way you go about protecting and conserving our country's natural resources—its soil and water, its woods and fields, its wildlife."
>
> —*Boy Scout Handbook*, 6th ed., 1959

LEAVE NO TRACE

In the early years of our nation, you could have camped almost anywhere. The population of the country was small. In fact, most of the land was wilderness. Towns, roads, and farms were few. There weren't yet many demands on the land. As the nation grew, its needs began to turn much of the land into farms and cities. Dams tamed rivers to provide electrical power. People cleared forests for lumber and to make room for crops.

The open country that remains today is home to a rich variety of animals and plants. It is the source of clean water for everyone to drink, and its vegetation freshens the air we breathe. When you want to camp and hike, you can visit parks, forests, and Scout camps across the nation. With that freedom comes a duty to care for the environment. That means enjoying the outdoors, learning from it, and then leaving it as you found it. Scouts do this by following the principles of Leave No Trace—guidelines for traveling and camping without leaving any signs you were there.

SCOUTING'S TRAIL TO LEAVE NO TRACE

For more than a century, the Boy Scouts of America has been a leader in teaching the conservation of natural resources. The 1910 edition of the *Boy Scout Handbook* included a Conservation merit badge. To earn that badge, Scouts had to learn the value of timberland, the causes of water pollution, what made a farm field suitable for growing crops, and which game animals could be found nearby.

Conservation *merit badge pamphlet, circa 1925*

Web resources are handy when your patrol or troop is looking for a place to camp or hike. Start with the National Park Service site, *www.nps.gov*.

William T.
Hornaday

IN THIS CHAPTER

▶ Scouting's trail to
Leave No Trace

▶ Using Leave No Trace

▶ Beyond Leave No Trace

William T. Hornaday, director of the New York Zoological Park and a strong supporter of Scouting, made a plea in the *Handbook's* second edition (1914) for Scouts to help preserve wildlife habitat. The Gold Award of the Permanent Wild Life Protection Fund (later renamed the William T. Hornaday Award) was created to recognize Scouts who were making special efforts to care for the environment.

In the decades that followed, *Handbooks* continued to encourage Scouts to see themselves as protectors of nature. In 1948, the BSA introduced the Outdoor Code— a conservation pledge that Scouts could use during all of their outdoor adventures.

Scouts continued to increase their skills and to make their way deeper into the backcountry. They were paddling, pedaling, and climbing farther than ever before. They were learning to feel at home in wilderness areas. As they understood more about the impact they could have, they increased their efforts to protect trails and campgrounds. *Handbooks* and merit badge pamphlets discussed minimum-impact camping, and the BSA encouraged the use of camp stoves in places where campfires might scar the land. Other groups were moving in the same direction as they encouraged people who liked going to the outdoors to help care for it, too.

In the early 1990s, a number of federal land-management agencies agreed that Leave No Trace would give everyone basic guidelines for using the outdoors responsibly and a common language for discussing the best ways to minimize our recreational impacts. Today, the principles of Leave No Trace are used throughout America. Scouting is proud to be a partner in this ongoing effort.

Outdoor Code

As an American, I will do my best to

Be clean in my outdoor manners,

Be careful with fire,

Be considerate in the outdoors,

and

Be conservation-minded.

Learn more about William T. Hornaday and the BSA's Hornaday Awards at http://www.scouting.org/Awards/hornadayawards.aspx.

Land Managers

Land managers are deeply involved in caring for America's open lands. Park rangers, forest supervisors, camp directors, urban recreation directors, and other officials set the standards expected of those visiting public and private areas. Most land managers know about Leave No Trace and can be terrific resources for helping Scouts understand how to protect the land while fully enjoying time in the outdoors. Many Scout troops and land managers have formed ongoing partnerships that encourage Scouts to help out with well-planned projects for restoring and preserving the environment.

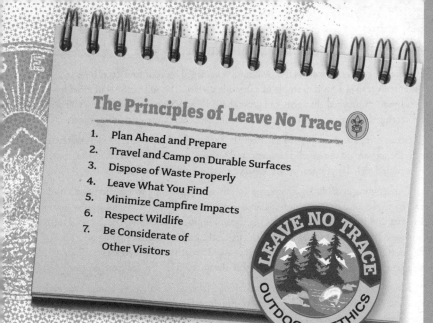

The Principles of Leave No Trace

1. Plan Ahead and Prepare
2. Travel and Camp on Durable Surfaces
3. Dispose of Waste Properly
4. Leave What You Find
5. Minimize Campfire Impacts
6. Respect Wildlife
7. Be Considerate of Other Visitors

USING LEAVE NO TRACE

Scouting's adventures cover a wide range of activities—from tenting at public campgrounds and BSA council camps to backpacking many miles through forests, deserts, and mountains.

Think about Leave No Trace wherever you hike, camp, or do any other outdoor activity, and do your best to follow its principles. Make them a guide for how you conduct yourself in the outdoors.

1. Plan Ahead and Prepare

Good leadership happens when you have a vision of what a successful adventure will look like. Plan the steps to put yourself and your patrol into that picture. Being ready for the challenges that might arise is such an important part of Scouting that *Be Prepared* is the Boy Scout motto! A lack of planning can lead to unintended damage to equipment and the land.

Planning and being prepared are important for protecting the outdoors, too. Plan ahead and you'll know what to expect wherever you are going. You can find out from land managers if there will be limits on the size of your group and what permission you might need to obtain. The land managers also might suggest other ways you can lessen your impact.

Visit Leave No Trace's Web site for more information on the principles: *http://www.lnt.org/programs/principles.php.*

2. Travel and Camp on Durable Surfaces

Durable surfaces are areas that will not be damaged by your footsteps, bicycles, or tents. A trail is a good example of a durable surface. The soil of the trail tread has become so compacted that little can grow there. By staying on existing trails, you are protecting the surrounding landscape and the plants and animals that live there.

Scout camps and many public parks and forests already have durable campsites laid out. If there are no designated camping areas, make your camp on sand, gravel, rock, compacted soil, dry grasses, or snow. All of these are durable surfaces.

Carelessness in choosing a campsite and hiking or pedaling where there is no trail can harm the land in several ways. Campers walking to and from cooking areas, water sources, and their tents can trample plant communities, pack down the soil, and form unwanted pathways. Hikers and cyclists using the edges of trails or going off a trail to get around a rutted or muddy stretch can widen pathways unnecessarily. Taking shortcuts, especially down hillsides, almost always leads to damage from erosion.

Pitch your tents well away from streams and lakes. This will allow animals to reach the water and will lessen your impact on shorelines. In addition, try to camp in the forest away from meadows and the trees at their edge. Deeper in the woods you will be sheltered from sun and wind, and your camp will blend into its surroundings. You are also less likely to beat down meadow grasses or to frighten away animals that use meadows as feeding grounds. Camping away from meadows is especially important in mountainous regions. Camping on top of fragile alpine meadow vegetation can cause it serious harm. Make your high-elevation camps in established campsites or on bare ground or snowfields.

Use good judgment if you are thinking about playing Capture the Flag or other wide games that are popular with many troops. Dry fields with tough vegetation could be perfect, while a damp meadow might be too fragile.

3. Dispose of Waste Properly

Getting rid of human waste outdoors requires special care. In campgrounds that have restrooms or outhouses, be sure to use them. Where there are no such facilities, follow the guidance of local land managers. They are likely to direct you to dig a cathole or a latrine.

Digging a Cathole—Find a private spot at least 200 feet (75 steps) from water, campsites, and trails. Dig a hole 6 to 8 inches deep (4 to 6 inches in more arid areas) with your heel, a stick, or a trowel. Relieve yourself, and then refill the cathole with the soil. Organisms in the topsoil will safely break down the waste. Replace pine needles, leaves, or other ground cover. Push a stick into the ground to warn against digging in the same place. Always use a hand sanitizer afterward, or wash your hands with camp soap and plenty of water.

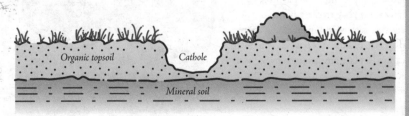

Organic topsoil   Cathole

Mineral soil

Often the best way to dispose of biodegradable toilet paper is to bury it completely. Where other methods are more appropriate, land managers can instruct your troop in the right methods. Don't burn toilet paper or anything else in a cathole or latrine, as sparks might spread into surrounding ground cover.

Making a Latrine—A patrol, troop, or other group camping in the same place more than a night or two can help reduce its impact by digging a latrine rather than making lots of catholes. For advice, check with land managers of the area where you will be camping.

To make a latrine, set aside any ground cover, then dig a shallow trench a foot wide, 3 to 4 feet long, and 6 to 8 inches deep. As with a cathole, go no deeper than the topsoil so that soil organisms will be able to break down the waste. Sprinkle a layer of soil in the trench after each use to help keep away flies and hold down odors. Return the remaining soil to the latrine when you break camp. Replace the ground cover you set aside.

Disposing of Dishwater—Strain food bits out of your dishwater and put them in your trash. Carry dishwater and rinse water away from your camp and at least 75 steps from any streams or lakes. Give the water a good fling to spread it over a wide area.

For long stays at one site, dig a sump hole at the edge of camp and at least 75 steps from streams, lakes, or other open water. The sump should be about a foot across and 2 feet deep. Use a sieve to catch food particles as you pour dishwater into a sump. Empty the particles into a trash bag to carry home, or consult with a land manager on proper disposal. Fill the sump when you break camp. Replace any ground cover.

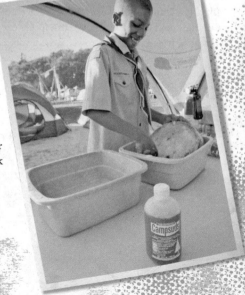

Keep Soap Away From Open Water

Any soap, even the biodegradable kind, can leave residue in water that might harm fish, plants, and other organisms in streams and lakes. Choose soap that is designed to be kind to the environment, then dispose of soapy water at least 200 feet (75 steps) away from bodies of water.

4. Leave What You Find

Among the joys of being outdoors is finding evidence of the natural world and of our past. Resist the temptation to collect antlers, petrified wood, unusual rocks, alpine flowers, and other natural souvenirs. Hikers coming after you will want to enjoy these items, too. Removing almost anything can change an environment in ways that might have a negative effect on wildlife and plant communities.

Leave a place in as good a condition as you found it by removing everything that you bring into an area. Don't leave structures or furniture at a campsite, and don't dig trenches. "Pack it in, pack it out" is good advice when it comes to food wrappers, cans, paper, and whatever else you have carried to camp or along a trail.

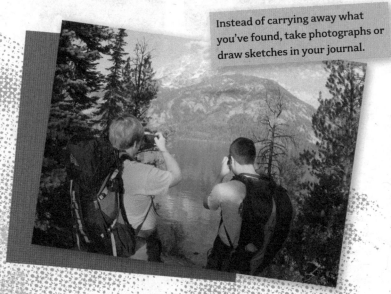

Instead of carrying away what you've found, take photographs or draw sketches in your journal.

Pioneering Projects

Using ropes and poles to lash together a bridge, signal tower, or other pioneering project can be great fun and a terrific learning experience. Choose your site carefully to avoid harming the environment. In most cases, you will build your projects at a designated place in a Scout camp or another location with a durable surface.

Lashing completed

Leave No Trace pioneering often means using staves, poles, and ropes provided by your troop or a BSA camp or council staff. After structures are taken apart, the materials can be stored for use by the next Scouts eager to practice their pioneering skills.

5. Minimize Campfire Impacts

Many Scouts use stoves rather than campfires on all their camping trips. Without a wood fire at the center of a camp, they often find that they are more aware of their surroundings and of the night sky. Stoves are clean, quick to heat water and cook food, and easy to light in any weather. Best of all, they leave no marks on the land.

Campfires have their place, too. A fire can warm you, dry your clothes, and provide a focal point for gathering with friends. Bright flames can lift your spirits on a rainy morning. At night, glowing embers can stir your imagination.

A good Scout knows how to build a fire, especially in an emergency. He also knows there are often reasons not to light one.

▶ Campfires can char the ground, blacken rocks, and sterilize soil. Vegetation might have a hard time growing where a fire has been.

▶ Fires consume branches, bark, and other organic material that would have provided shelter and food for animals and plants.

▶ Campfires must be closely watched to prevent them from spreading into surrounding grasses, brush, and trees.

Find out ahead of time if the area where you want to camp permits the use of fires. If you build one, use an existing fire ring and use wood no thicker than your wrist. Dispose of ashes properly. Even where fires are allowed, a lightweight stove can make it easier for you to camp without leaving a trace.

American bison

Snowy owl

The Scout Law reminds us that a Scout is kind. This advice applies to the treatment of animals and the environment as much as it does to people. A Scout is courteous, too, both at home and when he is in camp and on the trail.

6. Respect Wildlife

Among the great pleasures of outdoor adventure is sharing your surroundings with wildlife. When you are in the backcountry, you are visiting the creatures' homes. It is important to be a good guest.

Travel quietly and give animals enough space so that you don't disturb them. Avoid nesting sites, feeding areas, and other places critical to wildlife. Chasing or picking up wild animals causes them stress and can affect their ability to survive.

Many Scouts learn to track and stalk wildlife to study animals, photograph them, and learn about their habits. Do so with great care and respect. You are too close if an animal changes its activities because of your presence.

Butterfly

Cottontail

Black bear

Plan your trips so that you can protect your food from wildlife. This is especially important when you will share the woods with bears. Bears that find food in campsites might come back for more, and that can be dangerous for the animals and for campers. Keep your camp clean and hang your food from trees or store it in bearproof containers.

Visitor Registration ↑

Take Nothing
But Pictures;
Leave
Nothing But
Footprints

7. Be Considerate of Other Visitors

Scouts are not alone in wanting to go on outdoor adventures. You're likely to pass a few people on a hiking trail, or perhaps dozens. You could find yourself sharing a council camp with other BSA troops. In public parks and forests, your patrol might spend the night near campers who are not Boy Scouts.

Be considerate of everyone you meet along the way. They have come to the outdoors to enjoy nature, to hike, and to camp in the open air. Some want to get away from it all—including other people. Respect their privacy.

If you can, select campsites away from those of other campers. Trees, bushes, and the shape of the terrain can screen your camp from trails and neighboring campsites. Tents with muted colors that blend into the background will reduce the visual impact of your camp.

Leave portable music players at home and hold down noise in your troop and patrol. Keeping noise to a minimum will make it easier to appreciate the outdoors, and you will be less likely to disturb wildlife and other backcountry travelers.

Sometimes it might be appropriate to go with your adult leaders to introduce yourselves to nearby campers and let them know you are Scouts who follow the principles of Leave No Trace. Ask if there is anything you can do to help make the experience good for everyone.

BEYOND LEAVE NO TRACE

Leave No Trace is a common-sense approach to caring for the environment. It is just the beginning of outdoor explorations that will enrich your life.

Many merit badges are designed to deepen your understanding of nature, beginning with the Nature merit badge. Working toward earning other nature-related merit badges, such as the Backpacking, Bird Study, Camping, Environmental Science, Geology, Hiking, Insect Study, Mammal Study, and Weather merit badges, can expand your knowledge for every adventure.

You can earn the William T. Hornaday Award—just as Scouts did decades ago—for distinguished service to the conservation of natural resources. Service projects that protect and restore natural areas are good ways for Scouts to give back to the land.

Earning merit badges and other awards is a tangible way to know you've made a difference to the environment, but the real prize comes from knowing that your practice of Leave No Trace has quite possibly saved that land for generations of Scouts who will come after you.

William T. Hornaday
silver medal

"A thing is right when it tends to preserve the integrity, stability, and beauty of the biotic community. It is wrong when it tends otherwise."

—Aldo Leopold (1887–1948), U.S. Forest Service land manager and professor of ecology. Leopold's writings helped lay the groundwork for people to make ethical decisions about using and caring for the environment.

Requirements for all merit badges can be found at *http://www.scouting. org/BoyScouts/AdvancementandAwards/MeritBadges.aspx*. You can also find information on the Leave No Trace Achievement Award on the *Handbook* Web site: *www.bsahandbook.org*.

"Campcraft is the how-to-do-it of good camping. The Boy Scout learns Campcraft along with many other useful things in the most interesting way. In fact, Campcraft features are so prominent that no Scout can reach First Class without being well on the way in the fundamentals of safe, efficient, and enjoyable out-of-door living."

—*Boy Scout Handbook*, 1940

The *Boy Scout Handbook* gives you basic campcraft skills—enough to camp and hike well and to apply the principles of Leave No Trace. That's only the beginning of what you can achieve. Build on the foundation of Scoutcraft, woodcraft, and campcraft, and you will find yourself ready for a lifetime of adventures of increasing distance, duration, and challenge.

Scoutcraft helps a young man become a better leader, make good decisions, serve his community and nation, and explore the world around him.

Woodcraft guides Scouts toward a greater understanding and appreciation of nature and a commitment to care for the land.

Campcraft is the rich storehouse of information that Scouts can draw upon to hike, camp, cook, navigate, and use modern and traditional tools. Combined with Scoutcraft and woodcraft, Campcraft prepares Scouts to take care of themselves in the outdoors while they take care of the outdoors, too.

The skills of campcraft have evolved over Scouting's first century. Guided by the principles of Leave No Trace, today's Scouts know much more about ways to protect the environment wherever they travel and roll out their sleeping bags. Modern backpacking stoves have freed them to camp in places where a traditional fire might have scarred the land. More rugged clothing and more lightweight gear are extending the range of Scouts in the field.

Understanding how to use and care for a pocketknife, a saw, and an ax—and knowing when *not* to use them—have always been important Scouting skills. Lashing together bridges, signal towers, and other pioneering structures links boys today with Scouting through the decades. Kindling a blaze in a campfire ring or a family fireplace is a terrific skill for a young man to learn. Being able to light a fire without using matches on a cold, rainy day in the woods is a mark of an expert outdoorsman.

Campcraft is about being smart in planning your adventures, preparing for them, and conducting yourself once you are on your way. Using campcraft skills wisely can make every outdoor adventure better. Learning campcraft skills will challenge you and build your confidence—and one day it might even save your life.

CHAPTER 8
Hiking

"To hike over hills and through deep valleys, under big trees and along murmuring streams is one of life's real pleasures."

—*Boy Scout Handbook*, 1939

HIKING

One of the best sights in Scouting is the beginning of an open trail. Lace up your boots, swing your pack onto your back, and set off toward adventure. Leave roads and automobiles behind—and sometimes the towns and cities, too. Go without mobile phones, electronic games, and music players. What lies ahead are possibilities, discoveries, and a closeness with nature that you earn one footstep at a time.

Hiking has always been among the Boy Scouts of America's great adventures. On trails, across open country, and along city streets, traveling by foot is a terrific away to get out with your friends and see the world.

Every season is special when you are hiking, and so is every place you go. Roam the backcountry with a map and compass to guide you. Walk through urban parks and neighborhoods. Follow a pathway to the summit of a mountain or along the banks of a river. Everywhere you hike will offer much to learn and enjoy as you unlock some of the secrets of wildlife, plant life, and the land.

It might rain. It might even snow. Your route might be rocky and steep. There could be times when you are weary to the bone. But overcoming hardships can be part of hiking, too.

IN THIS CHAPTER

- ▶ The Scout Basic Essentials
- ▶ Food and water for a hike
- ▶ Making a trip plan
- ▶ Appropriate clothing
- ▶ Leave No Trace hiking
- ▶ Pace
- ▶ Trail manners
- ▶ Cross-country hiking
- ▶ Hiking and weather safety
- ▶ Staying found

The skills you practice on even the shortest hike can prepare you for longer journeys.

- ▶ Clothing and rain gear for hiking are the same you'll need for camping and backpacking.

- ▶ The Scout Basic Essentials are items to take whenever you go to the backcountry.

- ▶ The Leave No Trace principles you follow to protect the trails you hike will guide you during cross-country travel and will help you care for campsites.

- ▶ A trip plan is important for every journey—from an afternoon hike to a wilderness trek.

THE SCOUT BASIC ESSENTIALS

The Scout Basic Essentials can make every outdoor adventure even better. In an emergency, they can help you get out of a jam.

The Scout Basic Essentials

- [ ] Pocketknife
- [ ] First-aid kit
- [ ] Extra clothing
- [ ] Rain gear
- [ ] Water bottle
- [ ] Flashlight
- [ ] Trail food
- [ ] Matches and fire starters
- [ ] Sun protection
- [ ] Map and compass

Insect repellent, a whistle, and other items also might be considered essentials, depending on your destination, the length of your trip, and the season.

Pocketknife

A pocketknife could be the most useful tool you can own. Keep yours clean, sharp, and secure.

First-Aid Kit

Your patrol leader or troop leader will bring a group first-aid kit on most Scout trips. In addition, you can carry a few supplies to treat blisters, small cuts, and other minor injuries.

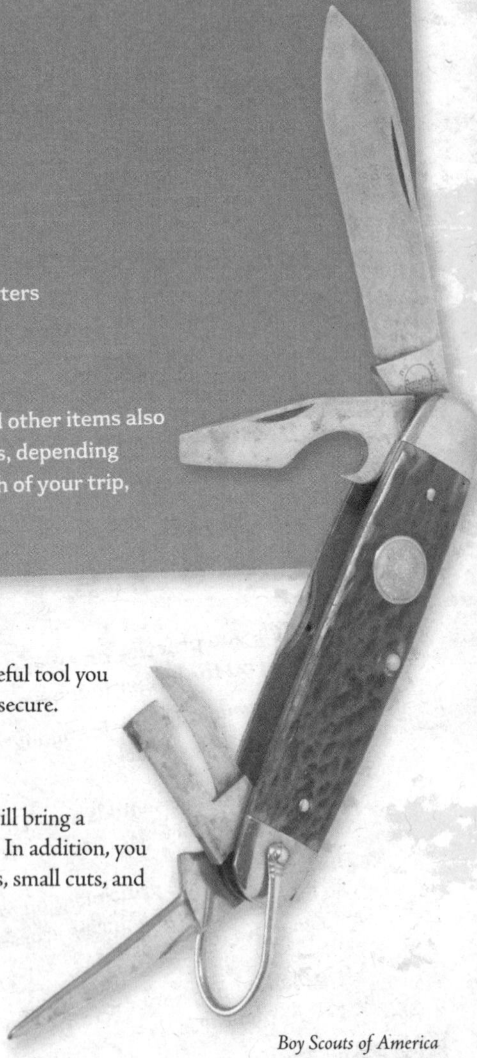

Boy Scouts of America pocketknife, circa 1946

Extra Clothing

Layers of clothing allow you to adjust what you wear to match the weather. During an afternoon hike, a jacket might provide all the extra warmth you need. Bring additional clothing on camping trips to meet changes in temperature during the days and nights you're on the trail.

Rain Gear

A poncho or a rain parka can protect you from light showers and heavy storms.

Water Bottle

Drinking enough water is important for your health during any outdoor activity. Always take along at least a 1-quart bottle filled with water. On hot days, in arid regions, and at high elevations, carry two bottles or more.

Flashlight

A flashlight casts a strong beam with just a couple of AA batteries, and it doesn't weigh much. Reverse the batteries during the day or put tape over the switch to prevent the light from accidentally turning on in your pack and draining the power.

LED flashlights use light-emitting diode technology to produce plenty of light. They weigh just a few ounces and have a long battery life. Consider using an LED headlamp to free your hands for camp tasks after dark.

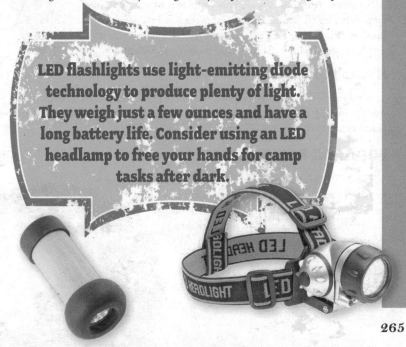

Trail Food

A small bag of granola, some raisins and nuts, or a couple of energy bars can give you a boost when you get hungry on the trail. High-energy foods you can snack on are especially important if you are out longer than you had expected.

Matches and Fire Starters

With strike-anywhere matches or a butane lighter, you can light a stove or kindle a fire in any weather. Protect matches and other fire starters from moisture by storing them in a self-sealing plastic bag or canister.

Sun Protection

Exposure to the sun's rays can be harmful to your skin, especially for people with fair complexions. Guard your skin by applying a good sunscreen (SPF 15 or greater) and wearing a broad-brimmed hat, sunglasses, and lip balm that contains sunscreen ingredients.

Map and Compass

A map and a compass can show you the way in unfamiliar areas. Of course, they won't be much good unless you know how to use them! Learn the basics and then enjoy practicing with a compass and a map when you are in the field.

FOOD FOR A HIKE

The most important meal for hiking might be the breakfast you eat before you hit the trail. In camp and at home, a hearty breakfast helps start the day right. If you'll be out much of the day, carry a lunch in your pack. Make a couple of sandwiches and take along some fruit, nuts, and raisins. You might also carry some crackers, peanut butter and jelly, jerky, or cheese.

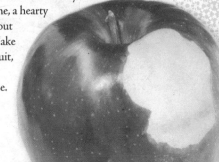

SAFE DRINKING WATER

Whether in cold or warm weather, drink at least 2 quarts of fluid each day. That's about 8 cups. When you're drinking enough water, your urine will remain clear. Fill your water bottle with fresh tap water before you set out on a hike and drink from it often—not just when you feel thirsty. In hot weather, you may need to carry several containers of water.

Water you bring from home or take from faucets and drinking fountains in campgrounds and Scout camps has usually been tested by public health officials. It is almost always safe to use. Water from streams, lakes, and springs may contain bacteria, viruses, and parasites too small for you to see. Treat any water that does not come from a tested source.

How to Treat Drinking Water

Three ways to make water safe for drinking are boiling, filtering, and treating it with tablets.

Boiling—Bringing water to a rolling boil for a full minute will kill most organisms.

Filtering—Water treatment filters made for hikers and campers are effective and easy to use. Some pump water through pores small enough to strain out bacteria and parasites. Others contain chemicals or carbon that help make the water safe to drink. Follow the instructions that come with the filter you plan to use.

Treating—Water treatment tablets are sold in small bottles and in packets. To treat water, follow the instructions on the packaging. Most treatment tablets call for you to drop one or two tablets into a quart of water and then wait 30 minutes before drinking it. Water treatment tablets can lose their strength over time, so check the expiration date on the label. Use only fresh tablets.

MAKING A TRIP PLAN

Writing a trip plan encourages you to think through your preparations for a hike, a campout, or any other outdoor activity. Give copies of your plan to your Scoutmaster, parents, and other responsible adults. Your plan will fill them in on what you hope to do and when you expect to return.

Organizing your ideas well enough to put them down on paper is good writing practice, too. Keeping a journal of the adventure while it is happening, then writing a record of the trip when you get home, is another excellent idea. A trip plan can also be a leadership tool for helping you explain your vision of what a successful trip will look like and then figuring out the steps to make it happen.

Develop a trip plan by writing answers to the five W's—where, when, who, why, and what.

▶ **WHERE are you going and how will you get there? Decide on your destination and the route you will use to reach it and to return. For backcountry trips, include a copy of a map with your route marked in pencil.**

▶ **WHEN will you go and return? If you are not back close to the time you listed on your trip plan, Scout leaders and your family can take steps to locate you and, if necessary, provide assistance.**

▶ **WHO is going with you? List the names of your hiking partners and adult leaders. If you need a ride to or from a trail, write down who will be driving.**

▶ **WHY are you going? To fish in a lake? Climb a peak? Photograph wildlife? Explore an island? Write a sentence or two about the purpose of your journey.**

▶ **WHAT are you taking? Always carry the Scout Basic Essentials. If you will be camping, you will need additional food, gear, clothing, and shelter.**

Add one more item to the list:

▶ **HOW you will respect the land by using the principles of Leave No Trace?**

Hiking Trip Plan

Name of this trip: _____

WHERE are we going and how will we get there? _____
_____
_____

WHEN will we go and return? _____
_____
_____

WHO is going with us? _____

    Adult leaders: _____
_____
_____

    Patrol members: _____
_____
_____

WHY are we going? (Write a sentence or two about the purpose of the hiking trip.) _____
_____
_____

WHAT do we need to take with us? _____
_____
_____

HOW will we respect the environment by using the principles of Leave No Trace? _____
_____

CLOTHING FOR OUTDOOR ADVENTURES

Dress for the outdoors by wearing layers so that you can adjust your clothing to match changing weather conditions. Imagine setting out on a snowy trail. The sky is clear and there is no wind. You're wearing a wool shirt and a sweater. Your gloves and stocking hat feel just right for the weather.

Hiking burns energy, and soon you are too warm. You stop for a moment to peel off your sweater and gloves and stuff them into your pack. As the miles pass, clouds fill the sky and the air becomes colder. You put your gloves and sweater back on. If the wind begins to blow, you can take a parka out of your pack and pull it on, too.

Most of the clothes you use for hiking are the same as those you'll wear when you go camping. If you are carrying all your gear in a backpack, make good clothing choices so you will have everything you need but won't be carrying unnecessary clothing that weighs down your pack.

Choosing Appropriate Fabrics

Outdoor clothing may be made of wool, cotton, or synthetics. Each type of fabric has its advantages.

Wool—Wool can keep you warm even when it is damp with rain. Some people find that wool feels scratchy against their skin. Wearing long underwear or a T-shirt beneath wool garments can help lower the itch factor.

Cotton—Cotton is fine for warm, dry weather. Once wet, though, cotton will not keep you warm. This can make it dangerous to wear on trips when conditions turn chilly, rainy, or snowy.

Synthetics—Many synthetic fabrics offer the comfort of cotton and the warmth of wool. Clothing made of human-made fibers such as polypropylene or polar fleece can insulate you even if it gets wet. Long underwear, sweaters, vests, parkas, gloves, hats, and activity shirts are often made of synthetic fabrics.

Warm-Weather Clothing Checklist for Outdoor Adventures

- [ ] Long-sleeved shirt
- [ ] T-shirt
- [ ] Hiking shorts
- [ ] Long pants
- [ ] Sweater or warm jacket*
- [ ] Hiking boots or sturdy shoes
- [ ] Extra socks
- [ ] Hat with a brim for shade
- [ ] Bandanna
- [ ] Rain gear
- [ ] Extra underwear (for longer trips)

Cold-Weather Clothing Checklist for Outdoor Adventures

☐ Long-sleeved shirt
☐ Warm shirt*
☐ Long pants*
☐ Sweater*
☐ Long underwear*
☐ Hiking boots or sturdy shoes
☐ Extra socks
☐ Insulated parka or coat with hood
☐ Warm hat*
☐ Gloves*
☐ Rain gear
☐ Extra underwear (for longer trips)

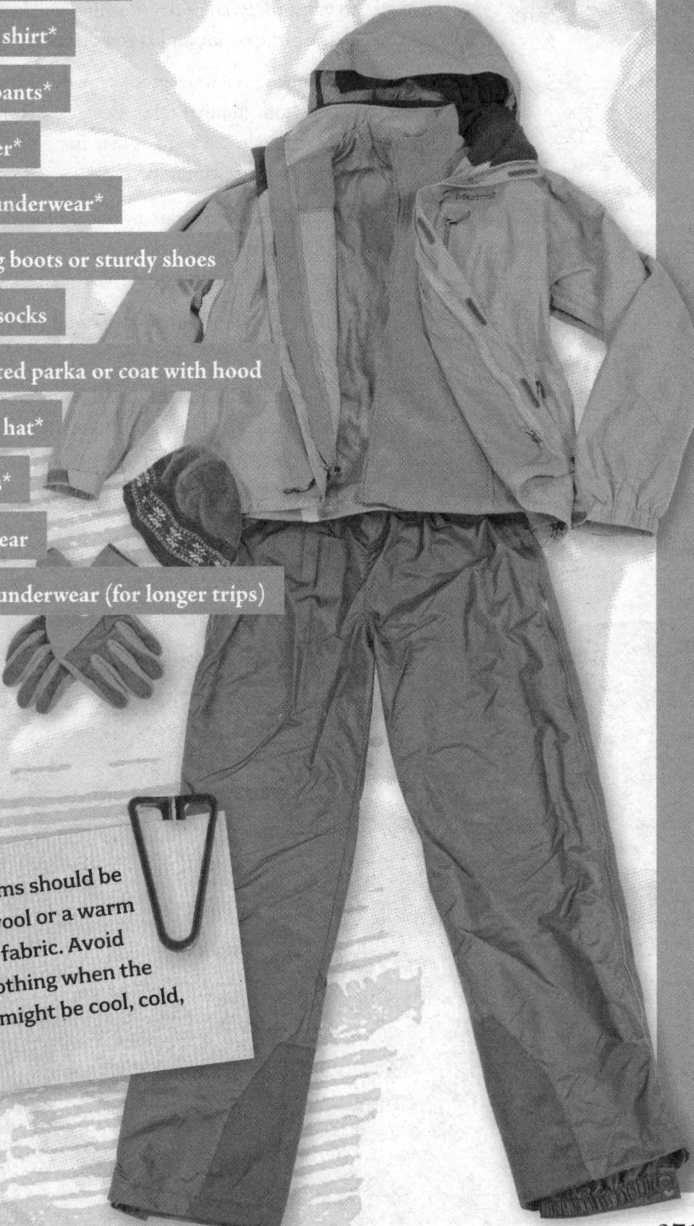

*These items should be made of wool or a warm synthetic fabric. Avoid cotton clothing when the weather might be cool, cold, or wet.

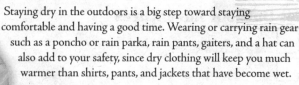

Rain Gear

Staying dry in the outdoors is a big step toward staying comfortable and having a good time. Wearing or carrying rain gear such as a poncho or rain parka, rain pants, gaiters, and a hat can also add to your safety, since dry clothing will keep you much warmer than shirts, pants, and jackets that have become wet.

Poncho—A poncho is a waterproof cape that can protect you and your gear from summer rains. Because a poncho is loose-fitting and can flap in the wind, it may not be the best choice for severe weather and for winter travel.

Rain Parka—A rain parka is a long jacket that repels rain, sleet, and snow. It should have a hood that you can pull over your head.

Rain Pants—Rain pants extend the protection of a poncho or parka down to your ankles.

Gaiters—Gaiters can shield your feet and lower legs from rain. During winter hikes, they'll help keep snow out of your boots.

Hat—A broad-brimmed hat protects your face from sun and from storms. If you wear eyeglasses, the brim of a hat can keep them clear when it's raining.

Fabrics That Breathe and Fabrics That Don't

Rain gear may be made of breathable fabric or nonbreathable fabric. There are pros and cons to both.

Breathable—Breathable fabrics repel rain and also let body moisture escape—the ideal combination for rain gear. The drawback is that these garments can be expensive.

Nonbreathable—Many ponchos, parkas, rain pants, and gaiters are made of coated nylon and plastic. This nonbreathable gear is waterproof and often inexpensive. The disadvantage of nonbreathable rain gear is that moisture given off by your body may be trapped inside, causing you feel to damp and chilled.

Footgear

If your feet feel good, chances are you'll have a great time hiking. Taking care of your feet begins with choosing what to wear. Almost any shoes are fine for short walks over easy ground. For longer hikes in good weather, lightweight boots usually work well.

Leather shoes and boots were once the only choices for Scouts. Leather hiking boots are still popular today and can give your feet and ankles plenty of protection and support. They will also keep snow and rain from soaking your socks. They are a good choice if you will be hiking and backpacking on rugged trails. Choose carefully when selecting leather boots, though. Stiff boots for mountaineering or serious winter travel can be quite heavy and are better suited for more experienced hikers.

Many styles of modern outdoor footwear are made of nylon mesh and other manufactured materials. Most of these boots are lightweight and sturdy. They could be just what you need for the trail.

The footwear you choose must fit well. If you shop for a new pair of boots or hiking shoes, try them on while wearing the same socks you will use on the trail. Your heels should not slip much when you walk, and your toes should have a little wiggle room. Before using your new hiking shoes or boots on a hike, wear them around home for a few days until they adjust to the shape of your feet.

Caring for Hiking Boots

Hiking boots will last a long time if you take care of them. When you get home from a trip, remove mud or soil from your boots with a stiff brush or by hosing them off. Allow them to dry at room temperature. (High heat can melt nylon and harm leather, so don't put your boots too close to a fire.) Treat leather with a boot dressing meant for outdoor footwear. Oils and waxes in the dressing will keep leather flexible and help the boots repel water.

Camp Shoes

Many campers and backpackers carry a pair of lightweight shoes in their packs so that they can get out of their boots at the end of the day. Choose closed-toe shoes that will help protect you from injury. A pair of running shoes might be just right. Water shoes can work well, too, if they are also comfortable for walking about on dry land. Your extra shoes will come in handy when you need to wade across a stream. Take off your hiking boots and socks and change into your extra shoes to cross the water.

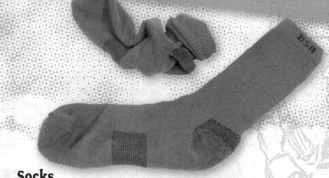

Socks

Hiking socks made of wool or a wool-nylon blend will help cushion your feet as you walk. Try wearing a pair of thin, synthetic-blend socks underneath your hiking socks. The inner socks will slide against the heavier outer socks and wick moisture from the skin. This will reduce friction and your chances of getting blisters. Carry spare socks on your hikes. If your feet get tired, change into fresh socks and hang the damp ones on your pack to dry.

Hiking Sticks and Trekking Poles

Baden-Powell's first drawing of a Boy Scout shows a young man with a hiking stick in his hand. Try one yourself, and you may find that it helps the miles glide by.

Use a hiking stick to push back branches and to poke behind rocks. When you wade a stream, a hiking stick will give you extra stability.

You can keep count of your adventures by whittling a notch on your hiking stick for every five miles you walk. Somewhere else on the stick, cut a notch for each night you camp out with your patrol and troop.

Trekking poles are a lot like ski poles. They can improve your balance and lessen the strain on your knees. Adjustable trekking poles can be made shorter or longer to match your height. Those with rubber tips might have less impact on the edges of trails.

LEAVE NO TRACE HIKING

Hiking so that you leave no trace shows that you care about the environment and know how to travel through it wisely. Following a trail is usually the best way to reach the places you want to go. Don't cut switchbacks or take other shortcuts. By staying on pathways you can avoid trampling and harming plants, and you will be less likely to get lost if your feet are on a trail.

Areas of some parks and forests are managed as wilderness. Regulations protecting them might limit group size, forbid campfires, and restrict other activities. Learn what the rules are before you start a hike, and then obey them.

A Scout group on a hike or a campout will often be out of sight of anyone else. Following guidelines designed to protect the land is a matter of ethical decision-making—doing the right thing even when no one is watching. Outdoor adventures can also be opportunities for Good Turns. Keep trails and campsites clean by picking up any litter you see—even if it isn't your own. Find out if your patrol or troop can help land managers repair and maintain the hiking trails you enjoy using.

PACE

Hike at a pace that is comfortable for the slowest member of your patrol. Though you may feel that you could race along forever, the safety and good fellowship of the whole group is more important than speed. The journey really is as important as reaching your destination.

When you're stopping often to look at plants, animals, and scenery, you may not need rest breaks. If you are pushing steadily along the trail, though, a five-minute break every half hour is a good idea. It will give everyone a chance to adjust clothing, check feet for signs of blisters, drink some water, and have a bite of food.

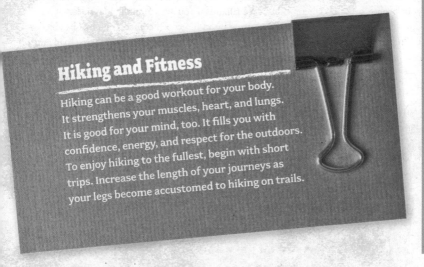

Hiking and Fitness

Hiking can be a good workout for your body. It strengthens your muscles, heart, and lungs. It is good for your mind, too. It fills you with confidence, energy, and respect for the outdoors. To enjoy hiking to the fullest, begin with short trips. Increase the length of your journeys as your legs become accustomed to hiking on trails.

TRAIL MANNERS

A Scout is courteous. That's as true on the trail as when you are in your hometown. Travel single file on most trails, leaving space between you and the Scout ahead of you. You can see where you are going, and you won't run into him if he suddenly stops. Step to the side of the trail when you meet other hikers and allow them to pass.

Many trails are open to cyclists as well as hikers. If you are riding a bike, limit your impact on the land by staying on trails. Keep your speed under control, both for your own safety and that of hikers and other cyclists. As a hiker, be alert for cyclists approaching from ahead of you and from behind.

People enjoying trails sometimes bring dogs with them. If the pets are on leashes, they will be close to their owners. Dogs sometimes run free, though, and you might suddenly come face to face with one. Don't approach a dog you don't know or reach your hand toward the animal. Speak calmly to a dog while you wait for it to pass or for its owner to arrive.

If you encounter people on horseback, stop where you are and ask the riders what you should do. They will probably suggest that you go a few paces downhill from the trail and stand quietly while the animals pass.

CROSS-COUNTRY HIKING

Cross-country hiking allows you to get away from everything, including trails. Before setting out, decide whether leaving the trail is a good idea. Where vegetation is fragile (as it often is in wet meadows, some desert areas, and high mountain tundra), stay on pathways. Even where ground cover is more durable, avoid walking on vegetation. Try to stay on bare ground, rocks, and snow whenever you can.

Away from a trail, footing can be uncertain. Brush and rugged terrain might slow your progress. Watch where you put your hands if you are scrambling on rocks—you don't want to get bitten by a snake or stung by an insect. Of course, you must be able to find your way and keep track of where you are. You will likely need to use a map and compass or a GPS receiver.

By writing a good trip
plan and studying your map before you
start a cross-country hike, you shouldn't be surprised by rivers,
cliffs, and other barriers. If you do run into obstacles that you aren't sure you can
navigate safely, detour around them or go back the way you came.

Staying with your patrol is as important in cross-country hiking as for any other
outdoor adventure. Leaders of your patrol and troop will often encourage you to use
the buddy system on hikes. Hiking with a buddy helps you stay alert to each other's
safety. Your buddy can watch out for you while you keep track of him.

HIKING SAFETY

Whether you're cross-country hiking or hiking on trails, you should always watch
where you place your feet to avoid slipping or twisting an ankle. Use bridges to cross
streams. Wade through water only if there is no other way to go and only if the
water is shallow and the current is slow. Release the hip belt of your backpack before
crossing a stream.

If you come across areas that appear to be dangerous, make a detour or go back
the way you came. Your safety is always much more important than reaching the
destination of a hike.

Hiking on Highways and Roads

Any time you hike next to a highway or road without a sidewalk, stay in
single file on the left side facing the traffic. If you must walk alongside a road
at night, make yourself visible by wearing light-colored clothing or tying
strips of white cloth or reflective ribbon around your right arm and leg. Use a
flashlight to brighten your way and to alert drivers that you are there.

Never hitchhike. It can be dangerous, it may be illegal, and it spoils the
spirit of a hike.

STORMY WEATHER

Checking weather forecasts before setting out on any outdoor adventure can help you decide what clothing, shelter, and gear you will need. You can find forecasts in daily newspapers, on radio and television newscasts, and by checking weather sites online.

You'll want to be prepared for the worst conditions that might develop. This can mean bringing extra clothing if the weather will be cold and additional water if you'll be traveling while it is hot and dry. When you see that bad weather is coming your way, you might want to postpone a trip and set off later when conditions are less challenging. The swiftness of certain violent weather patterns might require quick action. Severe storms that produce lightning and tornadoes are a clear danger.

Lightning

Open water, mountaintops, the crests of ridges, large meadows, and tall or solitary trees can be dangerous places during lightning storms. If you are on water when a storm threatens, quickly head to shore. Plan to be off of mountain peaks and other exposed locations before afternoon, when thunderstorms are more likely to occur. If you are caught in a dangerous area on a trail, quickly hike down to a lower elevation. A dense forest offers the greatest protection. Stay clear of shallow caves and overhanging cliffs—ground currents might arc across them. Avoid bodies of water and metal fences, too, and anything else that might conduct electricity. In a tent, stay as far as you can from metal tent poles.

100 feet

If a lightning storm catches your group in the open, spread out so that people are at least 100 feet from one another. Further limit your risk by crouching low with only the soles of your shoes touching the ground, and take off your hat if it has any metal parts. You can also use your sleeping pad for insulation by folding it and crouching upon it.

Portable weather radios can keep you up-to-date on developing conditions.

Persons struck by lightning may suffer serious burns. Their hearts and breathing might stop, too. Call for medical help and then treat them by checking their circulation and respiration. Perform CPR, if necessary. Once circulation and breathing have been restored, provide first aid for burns or other injuries. Treat for shock, and keep a close watch on their condition until they are under medical care.

Tornadoes

When weather conditions occur that may cause tornadoes to form, the National Weather Service and other organizations issue a *tornado watch* that asks people to be ready to take action in case a tornado develops. A *tornado warning* is broadcast when a tornado has been sighted.

When you hear a tornado warning, take immediate action to protect yourself and those with you.

▶ If you are outside in a place far from shelter: Lie down somewhere that is below ground level or at least flat. A ditch might be the closest place to go. Use your arms to protect your head from flying debris. Avoid taking shelter beneath a bridge—it is not a safe place during a tornado.

▶ If you are in a house, school, or other building: Go to the established storm shelter area and stay there. The area might be a room such as a storm cellar or a basement. If there is no storm shelter area, go to the ground floor and move to the center of the building away from windows and doors. Leave windows closed. Crawl under a heavy table or desk and shield your head with your arms.

▶ If you are in a mobile home, trailer, or car: Get away from them. None of these places is safe in a tornado. Find shelter in a sturdy building or take cover in a ditch or other low area.

For more information on staying safe in hazardous weather, visit the *Handbook* Web site: *www.bsahandbook.org.*

STAYING FOUND

"Were you ever lost?" someone once asked Daniel Boone.

"No," he replied, "but once I was confused for about five days over where I was."

The best way not to get lost is to know at all times where you are. Before you leave home, mark the route of your hike on a map. Then study the map to become familiar with the countryside. Where is your destination? What landmarks should you be able to see as you are walking?

Pay attention while you are on the trail. Notice the direction you are going. Watch for hills, streams, valleys, buildings, and other landscape features. Use a map and compass or a GPS receiver to keep track of your location.

Be sure to look back often and get a good look at the way you have come. You will see your route as it will appear upon your return, which can help you find your way home.

What to Do When Lost

One day you might accidentally wander off a trail and be unsure how to find it again. Perhaps you will take a wrong turn and not know which way to go. If you think you are lost, stop where you are and follow the four steps that spell STOP.

Stay calm

Think

Observe

Plan

Stay Calm—Sit down and have some water and something to eat. If you are cold, put on a jacket or sweater. Breathe slowly and relax.

Think—Try to remember how you got where you are. If you have a map, open it and see what you can learn from the symbols and contour lines.

Observe—Look for your footprints in soft ground or snow. Notice any landmarks that can be clues to your location. Listen for sounds of other Scouts.

Plan—If you are convinced that you know which way to go to get back on track, move carefully. Use a compass to set a bearing in the direction of your destination. Then clearly mark the way you are going with broken branches, piles of stones, or whatever else is handy in case you need to find your way back. However, if you don't have a clear idea where you are, stay where you are. People will start looking for you as soon as someone realizes you are missing.

Help searchers find you with any signal repeated three times. For instance, you might give three shouts or three blasts on a whistle. A smoky fire in the daytime and a bright fire at night might also attract attention. Toss grass or green leaves on the flames to create additional smoke. Spread your rain gear, sleeping bag, and bright-colored equipment in the open to catch the eye of a rescue pilot, or flash a mirror in the direction of aircraft.

Pitch a tent if you have one, or find shelter against a rock or under a tree. Hang a T-shirt or something else on a branch above you to get the attention of searchers even if you have fallen asleep.

Be careful with fire even in emergencies. Take the time to build the fire correctly so that it does not spread. Never leave a fire unattended.

Use your Scout Basic Essentials and whatever else you have with you to stay warm and dry. In addition to serving as a signal to rescuers, a campfire can offer warmth and lift your spirits. Collect enough wood before dark to last through the night.

Finally, try not to worry too much. You can survive for several days without water and for several weeks without food. Stay where you are. You will be found.

"The worst thing you can do is to get frightened. The truly dangerous enemy is not the cold or the hunger, so much as the fear. It robs the wanderer of his judgment and of his limb power.... Keep cool and all will be well.... Use what you have, where you are, right now."

—Ernest Thompson Seton, 1906

CHAPTER 9
Camping

> "The man who goes afoot, prepared to camp anywhere and in any weather, is the most independent fellow on earth."
>
> —Horace Kephart, *Camping and Woodcraft*, 1906
> (An early friend of Scouting, Kephart encouraged
> thousands of people to enjoy the outdoors.)

CAMPING

Your patrol pitches its tents under the trees of a quiet forest or on a hillside overlooking a lake or a rushing mountain stream. It could be a hot summer day or a frosty winter afternoon with drifts of snow all around. The laughter of good friends drifts through camp as you work together to set up a dining fly and light your stoves to cook an evening meal.

You talk excitedly about what you might do for the next few days as you make the outdoors your home. Maybe you'll go fishing. Perhaps you'll build snow shelters or follow the tracks of wildlife. If you climb to the top of a mountain or set off across the lake in your canoes, you'll get some practice using maps and compasses.

The warm days and nights of summer are perfect for camping. In many parts of the country, winter snows can turn a familiar landscape into a frosty wilderness perfect for overnight trips that could include snowshoeing, skiing, building snow caves, and tracking animals.

Scenes like those are unfolding for Scouts all across America today. They could have happened any time in Scouting's first hundred years, too. Like millions of boys before you, a big reason you've joined a Boy Scout troop is to go camping. You want to go. You need to go. You know that while you are camping you are going to have some of the best times of your life.

Adventure, fun, discovery, and teamwork—that's Scout camping. You and your patrol will work together as a team to make good things happen. You can use your Scouting campcraft skills to handle conditions in all seasons and in any weather. The leadership you're practicing as a Scout will help you and your patrol make wise decisions to meet the challenges of living outdoors. Being surrounded by nature always helps you understand more about the environment and appreciate the wildlife, vegetation, and land. As you learn to handle yourself in the outdoors, you're discovering how to care for the environment, too.

IN THIS CHAPTER

▶ **Overnight camping**

▶ **Scout camps**

▶ **Planning a camping trip**

▶ **Choosing a backpack**

▶ **Choosing a campsite**

▶ **Choosing a tent**

▶ **Making your bed outdoors**

▶ **Keeping clean**

▶ **Protecting camp food**

▶ **Beyond campouts**

Perhaps you've already gone with your troop to a campsite near a road and settled in for a night or two. You may have set off with a small group of Scouts backpacking many miles along a trail and pitched your tents in a different campsite each evening.

You can broaden the range of your camping adventures by setting out on journeys with canoes, on bicycles, or with pack horses, mules, and burros. Imagine stowing your gear in a canoe, a raft, or kayak and paddling down a river for several days or through a string of lakes. When you and your buddies load your camping equipment onto your bicycles, the back roads and bike trails of America will be yours to explore.

Each time you go camping, you will be building your ability to live well in the outdoors. You'll have the experience to go farther, stay out longer, and find more ways to make "outing" a big part of "Scouting."

OVERNIGHT CAMPING

Many campgrounds can be reached by car or by hiking a short distance from a road. Even if you aren't going very far from home, you should choose and pack your clothing and gear with care. You'll be carrying just what you need and nothing that you won't use. That's good practice for bigger journeys to come. Overnight camping trips also are a great time to learn all about putting up tents and dining flies, cooking meals, sharing camp chores with your patrol, and practicing many other skills of outdoor leadership and living.

When you will be traveling to a campsite by car, you can consider bringing fresh foods in an ice chest or cooler and canned goods that would be too heavy for carrying in a pack. With one or two camping stoves, your patrol can prepare terrific meals. Try baking golden-brown biscuits and a tasty peach cobbler in a cast-iron Dutch oven, or fix a delicious breakfast of pancakes, bacon, and eggs on a griddle.

SCOUT CAMPS

For many troops, a week at a BSA council camp is one of the high points of the year. Hikes, camping trips, and other troop adventures prepare patrols to make the most of their council camp time. Days will be full as you and your patrol take part in everything from swimming and hiking to nature study. You'll practice first aid and complete some of the requirements for Scouting's ranks and merit badges. Some Scout camps can be used by troops for campouts at other times of the year, too.

BSA district and council camporees bring troops together to camp for a weekend or more. National Scout jamborees and world Scout jamborees encourage Scouts and adult leaders from many backgrounds to gather in the spirit of Scouting. The high-adventure bases of the Boy Scouts of America are destinations you can aim for in years to come.

Camping well builds on skills you began learning as soon as you became a Scout. Going on great camping trips is an adventure you can enjoy throughout your life.

Find a high-adventure camp online at *www.scouting.org*.

CHAPTER 9

PLANNING A CAMPING TRIP

In 1803, explorers Meriwether Lewis and William Clark set off on a three-year journey across the unmapped American West. Camping all the way, they got the food they needed by hunting and by trading with American Indians. They packed everything else with them—tools, blankets, medicine, pots, and pans.

Planning gear, clothing, and food is important for your camping trips, too. Take just what you need, and like those explorers of old you can focus on the adventure unfolding all around you and not on the weight in your pack.

Making a Camping Trip Plan

The "Hiking" chapter introduced ways to plan for a hike by asking Where, When, Who, Why, What, and How. Answer the same six questions as your patrol gets ready for a camping trip, and you'll be prepared for whatever you meet along the way. Make photocopies of the Camping Trip Plan form on the next page and fill one out before every outdoor overnight adventure. It will guide you in making good decisions before setting out on a camping trip. File a copy in a patrol notebook, and you'll have a good record of your adventures, too.

See the BSA *Fieldbook* for instructions on creating an emergency response plan, which will be instrumental in the event of bad weather, injury, or illness.

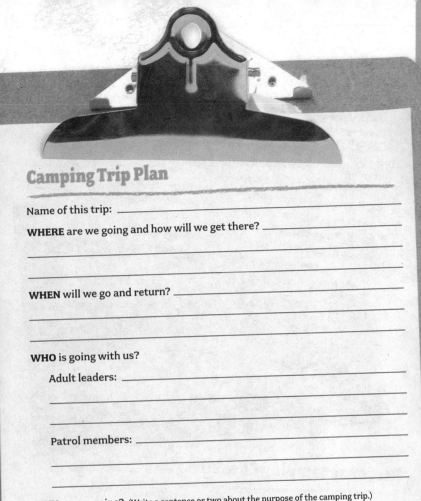

Camping Trip Plan

Name of this trip: _____

WHERE are we going and how will we get there? _____
_____
_____

WHEN will we go and return? _____
_____
_____

WHO is going with us?

    Adult leaders: _____
_____
_____

    Patrol members: _____
_____
_____

WHY are we going? (Write a sentence or two about the purpose of the camping trip.)
_____
_____

WHAT do we need and what are we taking?
(Attach a copy of your Camping Checklists and a copy of your menus/food list.)

HOW will we respect the environment by using the principles of Leave No Trace?
_____
_____

Lastly, check with those in charge of your destination for regulations you'll
need to follow on matters including group size, campfire regulations and
restrictions, and permits your troop or patrol must have.

Group Size

Managers of many campgrounds, forests, and parks place limits on the number of people who can travel and camp together. This lessens the impact on the land and on the experience of others who might be hiking and camping there, too. For these reasons, you should respect rules on group size. If no more than eight people are to be in a group, this doesn't mean a troop of 24 can travel in three patrols and then use the same campsite. Ethical decision-making shines through as you do what is right even when no one is watching.

Personal Camping Checklist

Use this checklist every time you go on a Scout outdoor trip.

Carry:

☐ The Scout Basic Essentials

Wear and Carry:

☐ Clothing appropriate for the season and the weather

Include:

☐ Food for the trip

☐ Personal camping gear:
   ☐ Backpack with rain cover

□ **Sleeping gear:**
　□ Sleeping bag
　□ Sleeping pad
　□ Ground cloth

□ **Eating kit:**
　□ Spoon
　□ Plate
　□ Bowl
　□ Cup

□ **Cleanup kit:**
　□ Soap
　□ Toothbrush
　□ Toothpaste
　□ Dental floss
　□ Comb
　□ Small towel

□ **Optional personal items:**
　□ Watch
　□ Camera
　□ Pencil or pen
　□ Small notebook
　□ Swimsuit

□ **Fishing pole and gear**

□ **Other gear for specific activities**

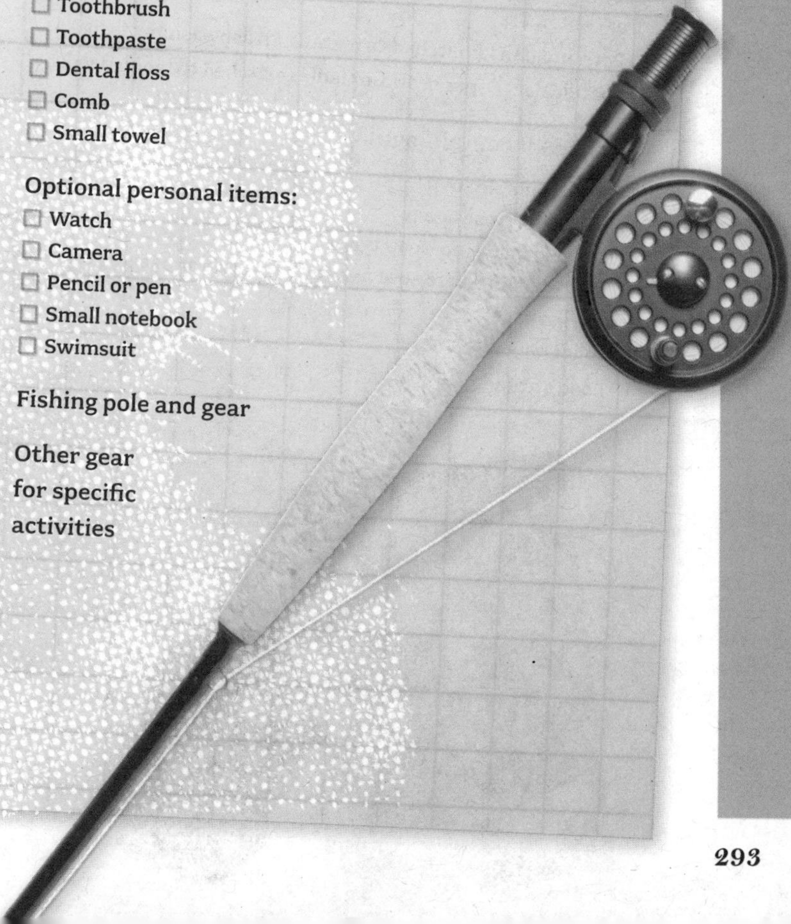

Group Camping Gear Checklist

The equipment you'll share with other Scouts can be divided up so each of you carries about the same amount of weight.

- [ ] Tents, ground cloths, and stakes
- [ ] Dining fly and stakes
- [ ] 50-foot nylon cord
- [ ] Cook kit containing:
  - [ ] Stove(s) and fuel
  - [ ] Matches and/or butane lighters (in resealable plastic bags or containers)
  - [ ] Pots and pans (matched to menu and dishwashing needs)
  - [ ] Spatula, large spoon, and/or ladle (matched to menu needs)

- [ ] Cleanup kit containing:
  - [ ] Biodegradable soap
  - [ ] Sanitizing rinse agent
  - [ ] Scouring pads (no-soap type)
  - [ ] Trash can liners (for use as bear bags and for packing out litter and garbage)
  - [ ] Toilet paper
  - [ ] Food strainer

☐ **Repair kit containing:**

☐ Thread
☐ Needles
☐ Safety pins

☐ **Group extras you may want to take:**

☐ Hot pot tongs
☐ Plastic, collapsible water container
  (1 or 2½ gallon)
☐ Water-treatment filter or tablets
☐ Two 4-by-4-foot plastic sheets for food
  preparation surfaces
☐ Spade
☐ Grill
☐ Patrol flag
☐ Small American flag
☐ Two 50-foot ropes and bear bags
☐ Patrol first-aid kit

☐ **Other gear for
specific activities**

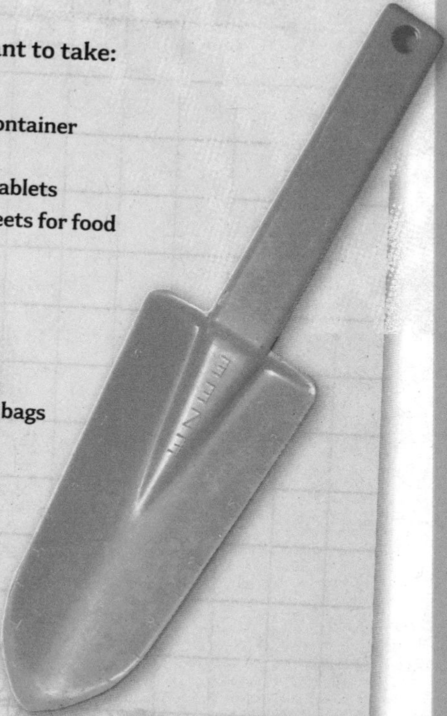

Planning Patrol Menus

Putting together a menu and turning it into a food checklist is an important part of getting ready for every camping trip. You'll also need to figure out which pots, pans, and utensils to bring.

Food for Trip/Day 2

Breakfast
○ oatmeal packets
○ hot chocolate mix

Trail Snack
○ gorp & dried apple slices

Trail Lunch
tuna pouch
crackers
dried mixed fruit
powdered drink mix

Camp Supper
chicken w/noodles (add water
& dehydrated peas to pouches)
powdered milk
s'mores

forget extra water bottles
water filters.

ROSTER

	FUEL/WATER	COOKING	CLEAN-UP
			Mark S. Mark D.
		Mike Jal	Mike Jal
	Rod Cal	Rod Cal	Paul Cal
FRI	Mark S. Mark D.	Mark S. Mark D.	Mark S. Mark D.
SAT	Mike Jal	Mike Jal	Mike Jal
SUN	Paul	Paul	Paul

CHOOSING A BACKPACK

For most camping trips you can carry your gear, clothing, and food in a backpack. Your pack should be comfortable for a short hike to a campground or a long day on the trail.

Nearly all backpacks have an external metal frame or a stiff internal frame. A hip belt shifts much of the weight of a pack from your shoulders to the strong muscles of your legs. Outside pockets on many packs are ideal for storing water bottles, maps, and other items you might want to reach quickly.

Shop for packs at stores with salespeople who know how to match you with the right pack for your height, experience, and the kinds of adventures you are planning. If your troop has packs you can borrow, try out different styles and sizes. Adjust the straps and hip belts for a good fit.

External-frame pack with hip belt

Internal-frame pack with hip belt

Packing Up

Sort your personal gear and clothing into nylon stuff sacks or a few resealable plastic bags (1-gallon size). Stuff sacks and plastic bags will help keep everything dry and organized inside your pack. The bags can be reused on future camping trips. Along with your personal gear, expect to carry some of your patrol's equipment and food, too. Your share might include a pot, the dining fly and poles, a camp stove, and ingredients for a breakfast.

Place softer items in your pack so that they will cushion your back. Keep your rain gear, flashlight, first aid kit, water bottle, map, and compass near the top of the pack or in outside pockets where they will be easy to reach.

Stuff your sleeping bag into its storage sack, then put it inside your pack if there is room. If not, then tuck it under the pack's top flap or strap it to the frame.

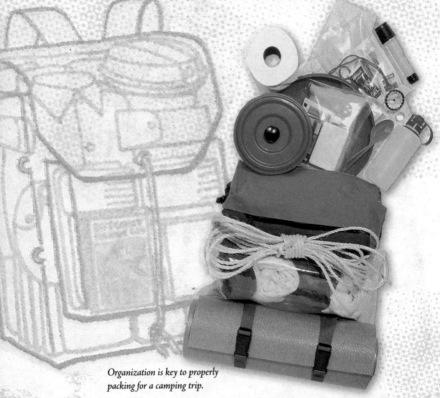

Organization is key to properly packing for a camping trip.

A rain cover will shield your pack when bad weather catches you on the trail. Put the cover over your pack in camp to protect it from nighttime rains and morning dew.

Cook pot too big to fit inside your pack? Try sliding it over one end of your sleeping bag before strapping the bag to the pack frame.

Before There Were Backpacks, There Were Bedrolls

In the BSA's early years, many Scouts made bedroll packs by rolling their equipment and supplies inside their blankets. They bent the loaded blankets into a horseshoe shape, tied the ends together, then slung the bundle over one shoulder. Bedroll packs weren't roomy or as easy to carry as today's backpacks, but for Scouts eager for outdoor adventures, they got the job done.

CHOOSING A CAMPSITE

A good campsite offers plenty to see and do. It is also easy on the land. Use established campsites whenever you can, or camp on durable surfaces, that is, surfaces that will not be harmed by your tents and footsteps. Campsites that work are found, not made. If you must move a log, a few rocks, or anything else as you pitch your tents, return everything to its original location before you leave. In addition, keep the following information in mind as you decide where to spend the night.

Safety

Pitch tents away from dead trees or trees with limbs that might fall in a storm, and stay out of gullies that could fill during a flash flood. Avoid lone trees, the tops of hills and mountains, high ridges, and other possible targets of lightning. Camp away from game trails, especially in bear country.

Size

A campsite must be large enough for your patrol to set up its tents and cook its meals. When hanging food to protect it from animals, choose trees that are well away from where you will be sleeping.

Water

Each Scout in your patrol will need several gallons of water every day for drinking, cooking, and cleanup. Treat water you take from streams, rivers, lakes, and springs. In dry regions, you might need to carry all your water to camp. That's information you will want to find out when you put together your Camping Trip Plan.

Stoves and Campfires

Where fires are permitted, appropriate, and desired, look for a campsite with an existing fire ring. Consider bringing kindling and firewood from home if your campsite can be reached by car. Where fires are not allowed, where wood is scarce, or when you want to prepare your meals quickly, plan on using a camp stove to heat your water and cook your food.

Privacy

A Scout is courteous. Respect others by selecting campsites away from theirs. Trees, bushes, and the shape of the land can screen your camp from trails and neighboring campsites. Keep noise down so that you won't disturb nearby campers, and respect quiet hours at public campgrounds and Scout camps.

Permission

Well ahead of the date of a camping trip, contact rangers or other managers of public parks and forests to let them know you are coming. They can issue the permits you need and suggest how you can fully enjoy your campout. Get permission from owners of private property, too, before camping on their land.

Download the required tour permits from the *Handbook* Web site: *www.bsahandbook.org.*

CHOOSING A TENT

Most Scout tents have the shape of an A-frame or a dome and are roomy enough for two, three, or four people. Many are made of nylon that allows moisture from your breath to escape rather than being trapped inside the tent and making it feel damp and clammy. A waterproof nylon rain fly that fits over the body of a tent sheds rain, snow, and wind.

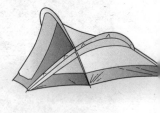

Tents also have metal or plastic stakes. Lightweight tent poles come apart to fit neatly into your pack. To divide up the weight, one Scout can carry the tent body while another takes the rain fly, poles, and stakes.

How to Pitch a Tent

Choose a fairly level spot on a durable surface. If there are pine needles, leaves, or other cover, don't rake them away. They can lighten your impact on the land by protecting the soil from erosion.

Spread out a ground cloth and unfold your tent on top of it. Assemble the poles and put them in place to give the tent its shape. Pull out the corners of the floor and stake them to the ground, then use taut-line hitches to tie any guy lines around stakes you've pushed into the soil.

The ground cloth will protect your tent floor from moisture. It should be just a little smaller than the size of your tent's floor. If your ground cloth is larger, tuck the edges under so that the cloth won't catch rainwater and cause it to flow under your tent. Finish pitching the tent by putting the rain fly over it and securing the fly in place.

Let your tent dry in the morning and shake out any leaves or other debris as you take it down. If you must pack a wet tent, prevent mildew by setting the tent up again at the end of a trip or hanging it on a line to dry before it goes into storage.

No Fires in Tents!

No tent is fireproof. Never use candles, matches, stoves, heaters, or lanterns in or near tents—*flashlights only!*

TARPS

A tarp is a large waterproof sheet often used on Scout trips as a dining fly to protect the kitchen area from sun and rain. When the weather is fair and the bugs aren't bad, tarps also make fine sleeping shelters that are usually lighter to carry than tents.

Some tarps have metal rings called grommets spaced along the edges so that you can tie on guy lines—lengths of nylon cord—with bowline knots. If there are no grommets, you can still attach lines to a tarp. Start with several smooth stones about the size of golf balls. Form a loop by tying a double half hitch in the end of a piece of cord, or make the loops for a clove hitch. Hold a stone under the corner of the sheet, then work the knot over the tarp fabric and the stone and draw the knot tight.

There are dozens of ways to set up a tarp, and you can have a good time experimenting with different possibilities. For starters, try tying a cord between two trees with taut-line hitches and tightening it so the cord is about 6 feet above the ground. Drape the tarp over the rope, pull out the corners, and use taut-line hitches to tie the guy lines at the corners of the tarp to stakes pushed into the soil or to nearby trees. Set the tarp closer to the ground if you want to sleep under it. Lowering the edges can give you protection from the wind.

A Homemade Tarp or Ground Cloth

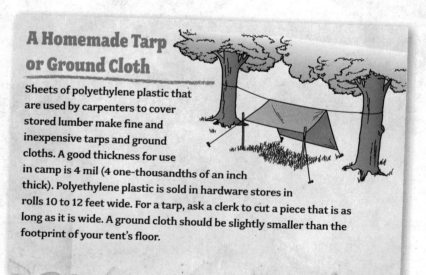

Sheets of polyethylene plastic that are used by carpenters to cover stored lumber make fine and inexpensive tarps and ground cloths. A good thickness for use in camp is 4 mil (4 one-thousandths of an inch thick). Polyethylene plastic is sold in hardware stores in rolls 10 to 12 feet wide. For a tarp, ask a clerk to cut a piece that is as long as it is wide. A ground cloth should be slightly smaller than the footprint of your tent's floor.

MAKING YOUR BED OUTDOORS

When you sleep at home, a mattress beneath you and blankets on top trap your body heat and keep you warm. A sleeping bag and a pad are a bed you can carry with you anywhere. They are easy to pack and to use. Most sleeping bags fit closely around your body and will keep you warmer and more comfortable outdoors than blankets.

Sleeping Bag

The cloth part of a sleeping bag is called the shell. Inside the shell is fill material made of synthetic fibers or the down and feathers of ducks and geese. Air pockets in the fill trap your body heat and hold it close to you. If your bag has a hood, you can pull the drawstring snug around your face for more warmth.

Sleeping Pad

Increase your comfort and warmth with a sleeping pad—a piece of closed-cell foam or other material that will give you a softer surface on which to spend the night. A pad can also prevent cold ground from drawing away your body heat.

Ground Cloth

Your ground cloth—a plastic sheet cut or folded to the size of your sleeping bag or tent floor—will keep moisture away from your bedding.

To sleep beneath the open sky in good weather, find a fairly level place to lay out your ground cloth. Don't rake away leaves or other ground cover that can cushion your bed and reduce your mark on the land.

Put your sleeping pad on top of the ground cloth, then arrange your sleeping bag on the pad. It's a good idea to leave your bag in its stuff sack until you are ready to sleep so that it won't be dampened by dew. You can make a pillow by putting some of your extra clothing inside the sleeping bag's stuff sack or inside a sweater.

Making your bed inside a tent is much the same as setting it up in the open. You won't need a ground cloth under your sleeping pad. There should already be one under the tent floor.

When you crawl into bed, keep your shoes or hiking boots close. Drop your watch, glasses, and other small items into one of them. Put your flashlight into the other so you can find it in the dark. Have a water bottle nearby, too, in case you wake up thirsty. Small creatures sometimes creep inside shoes or boots in search of shelter and warmth, so always shake out your footwear in the morning.

You will probably stay warmer inside of a tent when the door is zipped closed to block the wind. Wearing a stocking hat to bed also will help you keep warm. If you still feel chilly, pull on a warm, dry shirt during the night. Add a sweater, extra socks, or dry gloves if you still don't feel warm enough. Finally, don't go to bed hungry. Your body can produce plenty of heat if it has the calories to burn. Keep food out of your tent, though, so it won't attract animals.

KEEPING CLEAN

Staying healthy is a key to successful camping trips. The most important way to prevent sickness while you are outdoors is to use a hand cleanser or wash your hands with soap and water before touching food and after trips to an outhouse, cathole, or latrine.

> Three important things you can do to keep yourself and others healthy in the backcountry:
>
> Wash your hands. Wash your hands. Wash your hands.
>
> —*Fieldbook*, 2004

On overnight campouts, you'll also want to brush and floss your teeth before bed and in the morning. Take a shower or a bath when you get home. During longer adventures, you and those around you will be happier if you can bathe once in a while. Doing it the right way will prevent any harm to the environment.

Fill two cook pots or buckets with water and carry them at least 200 feet (75 steps) from any stream, lake, or spring. Use one container of water for washing yourself and use water from the other for rinsing away the soap. Scatter the remaining water when you are done. A little soap goes a long way outdoors. A small plastic bottle of biodegradable soap is ideal. Store the bottle in a plastic bag in case it leaks.

PROTECTING CAMP FOOD

Proper storage of food at campsites will prevent mice, squirrels, raccoons, or other small creatures from getting into your meal ingredients and spoiling them. It's also essential that you store your food out of the reach of larger animals. For example, if bears discover that they can get into your food supplies, they could be tempted to visit the campground later in search of more. This can be dangerous for you and future campers, and for bears that might have to be moved or destroyed to keep them away from humans.

As your troop plans a trip, find out from those who manage the areas where you will camp how you should store your food. Your storage method can be as simple as locking your food in the trunk of your vehicle during campouts near roads or using animalproof storage boxes located close to campsites. For travels in areas where there may be bears, the following tips will help you prepare a camping trip so that if bears do come by, they will find nothing of interest in your campsite and will move on.

To bearproof your camp, you will need nylon cord and stuff sacks for hanging your food from tree branches. Be certain to bring these items with you.

Pitch your tents away from your camp cooking area (200 feet or more is ideal) and have nothing in the tents except sleeping bags and pads, flashlights, and perhaps a book or two.

Clean up crumbs and bits of spilled food and put it all in with your trash. Wash and rinse cook pots, plates, and utensils after meals.

The clothing you wear during the day can pick up odors from food, sunscreen, and other items that might attract bears. Before going to bed in bear country, you can change into clothes that you keep in your pack just for sleeping. A clean T-shirt and long underwear pants could be just right. Store your day clothes along with your other equipment under a rain fly near the cook area.

At night and whenever you will be gone from your camp, protect your food and other smellables by hanging them in bear bags or stowing them in bear boxes away from the area where you pitch your tents.

EcoGuard™
Insect Repellent
DEET-FREE Lotion
Laboratory Proven Effective

2 FL. OZ. (60 mL)

Smellables

Smellables include all meal ingredients and leftover food, garbage, soap, shampoo, deodorant, lotions, toothbrushes and toothpaste, sunscreen, lip balm, insect repellent, first-aid kits, and anything else with an odor that might attract animals.

Bear Bags

Putting smellables into a bag or stuff sack and hanging it from a tree is a good way to protect your provisions and to keep any bears that might come near your camp from causing trouble. Bear bags will also keep your food away from chipmunks, raccoons, and other wildlife.

While there is still plenty of daylight, find a tree with a sturdy horizontal branch about 20 feet above the ground. Toss one end of a 50-foot length of nylon cord over the branch so that the cord is at least 6 feet from the trunk of the tree.

Stash your smellables in a sturdy bag or stuff sack, then twist the bag closed and secure it to one end of the cord with a clove hitch. Pull the other end of the cord to raise the bag until it is at least 12 feet off the ground and 6 feet from the tree trunk. This will place the bag beyond the reach of any bears that might stand beneath it, climb the tree, or go out onto the branch. Tie the free end of the cord to a tree.

Another bear-bag method requires two 50-foot cords. Toss the end of one cord over a high branch. Throw the end of the other cord over a branch of equal height on a second tree with a trunk at least a dozen feet away from the first. Tie one end of each cord to the bear bag. Haul on the free ends of the cords to hoist the bag to a height of at least 12 feet, centering the bag between the trees. Tie off the cords.

Many campsites in Scout camps and public parks and forests are equipped with a horizontal cable or pole set overhead between two trees. Throw a line over the center of the cable or pole, then use it to hoist bear bags out of the reach of animals.

BEYOND CAMPOUTS

From your first troop outdoor activities to great high-adventure journeys, a trail of terrific camping trips will mark your Scouting progress. Become an experienced camper and you will be ready for all that Scouting has to offer. You'll also realize that the best way to learn how to camp well is to camp a lot.

Scouting will encourage you to keep expanding the range of your camping trips and to use camping as a way to open other BSA opportunities. You'll soon discover that the camping trips you are enjoying also are helping you complete many of the requirements for the ranks of Scouting. Cooking over stoves and campfires; navigating with a map, compass, and GPS receiver; identifying plants and wildlife; and using woods tools are just a few of the outdoor skills that will lead you along the trail from Tenderfoot to First Class.

Camping also can be part of what you learn as you work on merit badges such as Backpacking, Canoeing, Cycling, Whitewater, Wilderness Survival, and of course, Camping. The 50-Miler Award is another way your camping successes could be recognized.

Pack It In, Pack It Out

Whatever you take to camp must be carried home. Don't leave anything behind—litter, cans, leftover food, or camp projects. Do not throw trash into lakes and streams or bury it in the woods. Making sure that a campsite is in better shape than you found it will help you reach the goal of Leave No Trace camping.

A camping trip also is a perfect time to put Scout spirit into action as you use the patrol method to plan a trip, travel to the campsite, set up your tents and kitchen area, prepare meals, and then clean up afterward.

For a hundred years, Scouts have been setting out to camp under the open sky. The sky is still there, and so are many terrific outdoor destinations for your patrol to pitch its tents and for you to make the outdoors your home. Learn to camp responsibly and well and you will soon agree with what those before you have always known—that camping is Scouting at its very best.

A Scout Is Reverent

Scout Vespers

Tune: "O Tannenbaum"

Softly falls the light of day,
While our campfire fades away.
Silently each Scout should ask:
"Have I done my daily task?
Have I kept my honor bright?
Can I guiltless sleep tonight?
Have I done and have I dared
Everything to be prepared?"

Taps

Day is done, gone the sun,
From the lake, from the hills,
    from the sky;
All is well, safely rest, God is nigh.

See the *Handbook* Web site, *www.bsahandbook.org*, for more campfire songs.

Cooking

> "Anyone who has spent much time in the outdoors knows that eating is one of adventuring's greatest pleasures."
>
> —*Fieldbook*, 1984

COOKING

Bacon and eggs sizzling at dawn over a backpacking stove. Fresh fruit, nuts, and raisins for a midday snack. A Dutch oven full of biscuits browning over charcoal at the end of a busy day of rafting. Food in the outdoors powers you through days packed with action. It helps you stay warm at night. When the sky turns stormy or you are tired, a hearty meal can cheer you up and energize your Scout patrol.

On a day hike, you can carry your lunch, some energy food, and plenty of fluids. For longer adventures, prepare meals by cooking over a camp stove or open fire. You'll have fun, too, as you work together with others in your patrol to fix meals that are delicious, healthy, and filling.

Knowing how to cook is for more than just camping trips. It is a life skill that can give you independence in the years to come and a lot of pleasure preparing good meals for yourself and for others.

A great way to practice cooking is by helping prepare family meals at home. Following recipes in your own kitchen and judging when a dish is done is terrific preparation for becoming a good chef on the trail.

Whether the ingredients are fresh foods for an evening cookout or dried menu items carried on a long backpacking journey, some basic steps, a few spices, and the willingness to try something new can result in camp feasts you'll remember as much as the adventure itself.

Tasty dinners, nutritious lunches, and hearty breakfasts that get the day off to a roaring start—there's nothing better than good meals in the outdoors, especially when you have cooked them yourself.

314

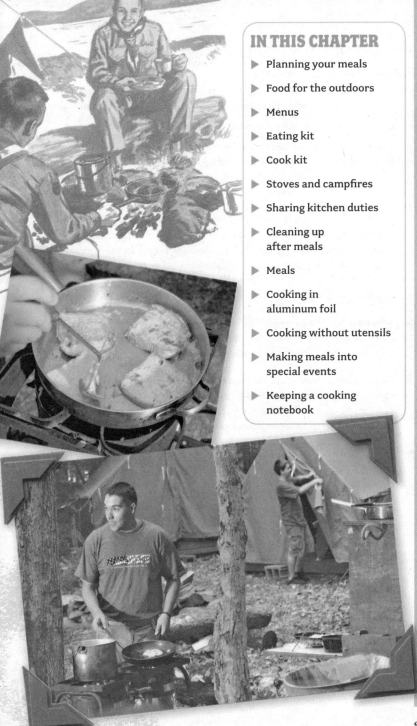

IN THIS CHAPTER

▶ Planning your meals

▶ Food for the outdoors

▶ Menus

▶ Eating kit

▶ Cook kit

▶ Stoves and campfires

▶ Sharing kitchen duties

▶ Cleaning up
   after meals

▶ Meals

▶ Cooking in
   aluminum foil

▶ Cooking without utensils

▶ Making meals into
   special events

▶ Keeping a cooking
   notebook

PLANNING YOUR MEALS

With good planning, you can take enough food on a trip so that everyone in your patrol eats well and there aren't many leftovers. You'll also know which pots, pans, and utensils to carry, and whether you'll be cooking over a camp stove or a campfire.

Begin making your plans by answering the following questions:

▶ **How many Scouts are going on the trip, and how long will we be away from home?** Decide on the number of meals you will need and who will be eating together. A patrol is often just the right size for organizing the food and cooking gear for a hike or camping trip.

▶ **Are there any special food needs? Discuss special food needs with patrol members.** Vegetarians don't eat meat but have plenty of other options for good nutrition. Some religious groups avoid certain foods. Scouts with allergies to dairy products, peanuts, or other foods should share that information with troop leaders so that their food needs can be addressed. Parents and guardians can help plan safe menus and guide troop leaders with information on how to treat food allergy reactions.

▶ **What are we going to do?** For days full of activities, choose recipes that won't take long to prepare. If you'll have time to make cooking a high point of a campout, take ingredients to put together meals that are special.

▶ **How will we reach camp?** Backpackers can keep their loads lighter by planning simple menus of nonperishable ingredients. When you will be traveling to the campsite by car, you can bring along griddles, fresh and canned foods, and even charcoal briquettes for a tasty Dutch oven meal.

▶ **What weather do we expect?** Winter menus should contain more fats and carbohydrates. Your body burns these substances to help you keep warm. Include mixes for soups and hot drinks to warm you up. Summer meals can be lighter. In summer and winter, your menus should include plenty of fluids.

 Information on meeting special dietary needs can be found on the *Handbook* **Web site:** *www.bsahandbook.org.*

FOOD FOR THE OUTDOORS

Scouts have been cooking outdoors for a hundred years, but in the early days they had fewer choices about what to prepare. The 1911 *Boy Scout Handbook* suggested a daily menu of pancakes, eggs, bacon, potatoes, bread, and fruit. A special treat was a recipe for Canned Salmon on Toast. The instructions began, "Dip slices of stale bread into smoking hot lard."

The variety of food that today's Scouts can carry on camping trips is much broader. With all the possibilities, there won't be much need to fry stale bread in lard. Here are some meal ingredients you can choose for the outdoors.

Fresh—Fresh foods have the most flavor and nutrition of any menu items. They also might be the heaviest. Some, such as fresh meats, must be kept cool until you are ready to cook them. Carrots, apples, and certain cheeses will last longer, though most fresh foods are best used on short trips or while car camping rather than during longer backcountry adventures.

Nonperishable—Pasta, beans, oatmeal, rice, flour, grains, and other foods that won't spoil are ideal for short-term and long-term camping. Stored in plastic bags, they can be stowed in a backpack or the duffel bags of canoes and rafts.

Dried/Dehydrated—Much of the weight of many foods is water. *Dehydrated* food has most of the water removed from it, so it is very lightweight and just right for campers. Most grocery stores carry dried milk and cocoa, potato flakes, soup mixes, and many other dried or dehydrated foods. Some camping stores sell complete camp meals that require only the addition of boiling water.

Canned—Many foods can be purchased in cans. Canned food is heavy to carry, and you'll need to take home the empty containers for recycling or proper disposal. That's not a problem when you are driving to a campsite. Sometimes an ingredient such as a can of peaches for a special dessert might be worth the effort it takes to carry it to your trail camp.

Convenience—Every supermarket has dozens of convenience foods that are ready to eat or quick to prepare. Those you might want to try are pasta sauce mixes, biscuit and pancake mixes, jerky, and energy bars.

MENUS

Once you know how many meals you will need, write down what you want to prepare and eat for each of those meals. The recipes in this chapter will give you some ideas.

List every ingredient for each dish. Use the Size of Servings Chart that follows to determine the amounts you will need for the number of people who will be eating together. Don't forget seasonings and other items you might need such as cooking oil, honey or sugar, salt and pepper, and other spices.

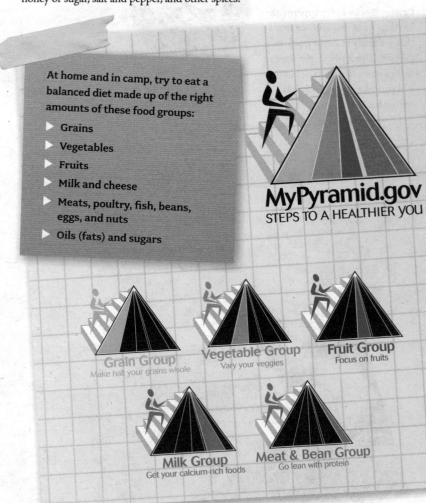

At home and in camp, try to eat a balanced diet made up of the right amounts of these food groups:

▶ Grains

▶ Vegetables

▶ Fruits

▶ Milk and cheese

▶ Meats, poultry, fish, beans, eggs, and nuts

▶ Oils (fats) and sugars

MyPyramid.gov
STEPS TO A HEALTHIER YOU

Grain Group
Make half your grains whole

Vegetable Group
Vary your veggies

Fruit Group
Focus on fruits

Milk Group
Get your calcium-rich foods

Meat & Bean Group
Go lean with protein

 For more information on the food pyramid, see the *Handbook* Web site: *www.bsahandbook.org.*

Size of Servings Chart ⚜

The "amount for one serving" is an approximate guideline for use when planning menus. For example, when your patrol is planning a spaghetti dinner, you will need about 3 ounces of pasta per Scout. If there are eight Scouts in your patrol, then:

8 Scouts x 3 ounces = 24 ounces of spaghetti

Check the weights on packages of spaghetti and put together the amount you'll want to take to your camp.

Grains (Bread, Flour, and Pasta)	Amount for one serving
Bread	2 to 4 slices
Brown rice	1/2 cup uncooked
Cold cereals	2 ounces
Cookies	2 ounces
Hot cereals (oatmeal)	2 ounces
Instant rice	1 1/2 ounces
Macaroni	3 ounces
Noodles	3 ounces
Pancake mix	3 ounces
Pudding mix	1 1/2 ounces
Ramen-style noodles	1 packet (3 ounces)
Spaghetti	3 ounces
White rice	1/2 cup uncooked

Vegetables and Fruits	Amount for one serving
Apples	1
Cabbage, fresh	1/4 head
Carrots, fresh	1
Corn, fresh	1 ear
Fruit, canned	5 to 6 ounces
Fruit, dried	2 ounces
Fruit, fresh	1 to 2 pieces
Juice	1 cup
Onions, fresh	1 medium
Oranges	1
Potatoes, dehydrated	2 ounces

Potatoes, fresh	2 medium
Soup mix	1 individual packet
Soup, condensed	1 to 2 servings per 15-ounce can
Tomatoes	1
Vegetables, canned	4 ounces
Vegetables, dehydrated	1/2 ounce

Milk and Cheese	Amount for one serving
Cheese	2 ounces
Cocoa, instant	1 individual packet
Milk, fresh	1 pint (2 cups)
Milk, powdered	2 ounces

Meats, Poultry, Fish, Beans, Eggs, Nuts	Amount for one serving
Bacon	2 ounces (3 to 4 slices)
Beef, canned	3 ounces
Chicken, canned	3 ounces
Chicken, fresh	12 ounces
Eggs, dried	1/2 ounce
Eggs, fresh	2
Fish, canned	3 ounces
Ham, precooked	3 ounces
Hamburger	4 ounces (1 patty)
Hot dogs	4 ounces (2 hot dogs)
Nuts	2 ounces
Pork chops	4 ounces
Steak	6 to 8 ounces
Stew meat	4 ounces

Drink plenty of water each day, in cold weather as well as warm. Bring your water from home or get it from public supplies. Water taken from springs, lakes, or streams must be treated before you drink it by boiling it, adding water-treatment tablets, or using a filter.

Use spices lightly. You can always add more, but you can't remove a spice if you use too much.

Spice Kit

Spices bring out the flavor of your cooking. Useful spices for camp cooking include salt, pepper, chili powder, thyme, oregano, garlic flakes, bay leaves, and cinnamon. Carry spices in small, self-sealing plastic bags, then stow all the containers in a stuff sack.

Miscellaneous Items

Other items you might need for preparing meals include condiments such as ketchup, mustard, relish, and salad dressing; baking ingredients such as flour honey, sugar, and butter or margarine; and spreads and toppings such as jam, jelly, peanut butter, and maple syrup.

Cost Per Person

Take your shopping list to a grocery store and write down the prices of the ingredients you plan to buy. Figure out each Scout's share by adding up the costs and then dividing the sum by the number of Scouts going on the outing.

Repackaging Your Food

Many foods are sold in cardboard or plastic containers. Reduce the weight and bulkiness of the items by getting rid of extra packaging before you leave home. Measure only as much of each ingredient as you will need for one meal and put it in a plastic bag. Write the name and amount of the ingredient on a label and tape it to the bag.

Place the repackaged ingredients for each meal in a larger bag. Include the recipes, too. Pull out the bag when you reach camp and you'll have all the ingredients and instructions together for a meal.

EATING KIT

A spoon and a lightweight unbreakable plate and bowl are all you will need for eating most outdoor meals. An insulated plastic mug will keep drinks and soup warm.

If you reach camp and discover you've forgotten to bring eating utensils, try whittling a spoon from a piece of wood, or remove the bark from a couple of slender, foot-long sticks and use them as chopsticks.

A plastic flying disk makes a fine plate for camping trips. After it has been washed, you can use it for patrol games.

COOK KIT

An important part of menu planning is figuring out which pots, pans, and utensils you will need for cooking and serving your food. By taking only the kitchen gear you will use, you can keep your load lighter and help keep your camp free of clutter.

Many troops have cook kits made for camping. The handles of frying pans can be removed, and the pots will nest together for easy packing. You also can find cooking gear at garage sales and surplus stores.

Your cook kit should include hot-pot tongs or gloves so that you can lift pots and pans off a stove or fire without burning your hands.

Pots and pans used over campfires will get blackened by soot. Some Scouts scrub off the soot after every use. Others make sure the insides of their pots and pans are washed clean but don't worry too much about removing every bit of black from the outside. Stowing a pot or pan in a nylon stuff sack as you are breaking camp will keep any remaining soot from rubbing off in your pack.

STOVES AND CAMPFIRES

Many Scouts use stoves on all their camping trips. Stoves are clean, quick to heat water and cook food, and easy to light in any weather. They leave no marks on the land. A stove in your pack can make it easier for you to camp without leaving a trace.

Before cooking over a campfire, smear a film of liquid biodegradable soap on the outside of your pots. This will help soot wash off more easily.

Grilling and Dutch oven cooking are two other ways of preparing food in the backcountry. Bring charcoal and a means to protect the ground for a fast, consistent heat and tasty meal. Campfires can be used as well if you don't have a stove.

Lighting a fire brings with it the responsibility to protect the environment. The principles of Leave No Trace will guide you in deciding whether a fire is appropriate and then building it in a way that minimizes its impact. Find out ahead of time if fires are allowed in the camping area you will be using. Even where fires are permitted, a lightweight stove is often a better choice.

SHARING KITCHEN DUTIES

There might be times when you prepare a meal by yourself in the outdoors. Often, though, you can share the joy and the work of camp cooking with another Scout or with everyone in your patrol.

Cooking With a Buddy

When there are two of you, both you and your buddy can pitch in and help with all the cooking and cleanup. For example, one of you can act as cook while the other cares for the stove, brings in water, and washes the pots. Switch responsibilities next time so that each of you has a chance to do everything.

 For more guidelines on safely using camp stoves and campfires, see the *Handbook* Web site: *www.bsahandbook.org.*

Cooking With a Patrol

Write down a duty roster. Two of you can cook, two more can fuel and light the stoves or build and manage a campfire, and the others can get things ready for dishwashing and organize the cleanup.

On overnight campouts, each Scout can have the same responsibility for all the meals and then move to a new spot on the chart for the next outing. During adventures lasting a few days or more, Scouts can change places on the chart each morning. Everyone pitches in to store extra food and keep it out of reach of animals.

> "A Patrol cooking its own meals is playing one of the most fascinating games in Scouting."
>
> —*Handbook for Boys*, 1948

Sample Duty Roster

Day	Cooks	Fire and Water	Cleanup
Friday	Nick Rory	Tony Carlos	William Raj
Saturday	William Raj	Nick Rory	Tony Carlos
Sunday	Tony Carlos	William Raj	Nick Rory

Be Food-Safe

Keeping a clean kitchen in camp and at home helps everyone stay healthy. The U.S. Department of Agriculture suggests four steps to be food-safe—*clean, separate, cook, chill.*

Clean: Wash your hands, cooking utensils, and food preparation surfaces often.

Separate: Keep raw meat separate from other foods. If you use a cutting board to prepare raw meat, wash the board and utensils before other foods touch them. Wash containers and plates that have touched raw meat before using them to hold meat that has been cooked.

Cook: Cook foods thoroughly.

Chill: Refrigerate leftovers right away. (In campsites without coolers or other ways to protect cooked foods, plan the sizes of meals so there won't be many leftovers.)

CLEANING UP AFTER MEALS

Whether you cook with a stove or over an open fire, put on a pot of water before you serve a meal. You'll have hot water for cleanup by the time you finish eating.

Begin cleanup by setting out three pots:

1. Wash pot—Contains hot water with a few drops of biodegradable soap

2. Hot-rinse pot—Clear, hot water

3. Cold-rinse pot—Cold water with a sanitizing tablet or a few drops of bleach to kill bacteria

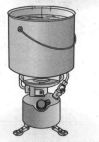

Each Scout can wash and rinse his own plate, cup, and spoon. If everyone also does one pot, pan, or cooking utensil, the work will be finished in no time at all. Use hot-pot tongs to dip plates and spoons in the hot rinse. Lay clean dishes, pots, and utensils on a plastic ground sheet or hang them in a mesh dish hammock and let them air dry.

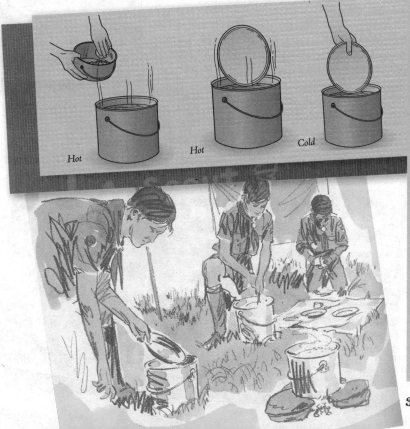

Hot   Hot   Cold

Dealing With Leftovers

Carry food scraps home in a sealed trash bag. Don't bury leftover food or scatter it in the woods. Animals will almost always find it, and it is not healthy for them to eat your leftover food. Food scraps can also draw animals close to campsites, where they may lose their fear of humans. That can be dangerous for them and for you.

Wash empty jars and cans and carry them home for recycling. Save space by cutting out the ends and then flattening cans.

Getting Rid of Dishwater

During campouts lasting just a couple of days, use a sieve or piece of window screen to strain any food bits out of your wash water, then put them in your trash. Carry wash water and rinse water away from camp and at least 75 steps from any streams or lakes. Give it a good fling to spread it over a wide area.

For longer stays at one site, check with the local land manager for preferred ways to dispose of dishwater. One way is to dig a *sump hole* at the edge of camp and at least 75 steps from streams, lakes, or other open water. It should be about a foot across and 2 feet deep. Pour dishwater into the sump through a sieve or piece of window screen to catch food particles and shake them into a trash bag. Fill the sump hole when you break camp and replace any ground cover.

Keep Soap and Detergent Away From Open Water

Many soaps, detergents, and shampoos contain chemicals that encourage algae to grow. Algae can crowd out native plants, making it harder for fish and other animals to survive. Soap and detergent might also leave an oily film in the water that can harm tiny water animals.

Food Storage

Plan how you will store food while you are in the backcountry. Fresh meats, dairy products, and other perishable items can be kept chilled by stowing them with chunks of ice in an insulated cooler. Other foods won't need to stay cold but could require protection from mice, raccoons, and even bears.

If your camp will be near a cabin or other building that is safe from animals, you might be able to store your food inside. The trunk of a car is another possibility. Some campgrounds have metal boxes where you can leave your food and know it is protected from wildlife and weather. You also can keep food out of reach of animals by hanging it from a tree.

MEALS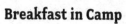

The best part of planning the menu for a backpacking trip, campout, or evening meal is deciding what to fix and serve. The sky's the limit on what you can do with nutritious ingredients. Here are some suggestions to get you started.

Breakfast in Camp

Get your day off to a strong start with a stick-to-your-ribs breakfast. Here are some suggestions.

Fruit

Fresh Fruit—Apples, oranges, bananas, peaches, melons, and berries can all be tasty additions to camp menus.

Dried Fruit—Raisins, banana chips, apple chips, and dried peaches, apricots, and mangos are delicious just as they are, or you can soak them overnight or cook them with hot cereal.

Canned Fruit—Many kinds of fruit are available in small and medium-sized cans. Plan on about 6 ounces per serving.

Cereal

Hot cereal tastes great on chilly mornings. In the summer, you might want cold cereal or granola with milk. Avoid flakes and other kinds of cereal that could get crushed in your pack.

Oatmeal—For each serving, bring 1 cup of water to a boil. Add a pinch of salt. For extra flavor, drop raisins or chopped fruit into the boiling water. Stir in 1/2 cup of rolled oats. Put the lid on the pot and cook until ready. Serve oatmeal with milk, brown sugar, butter, cinnamon, or a spoonful of jam.

Granola—Made of toasted oats, granola is terrific for outdoor breakfasts when you don't want to cook. Many brands of granola also contain nuts, raisins, dried fruit, and other good things. Try a bowl of granola with milk. By itself, granola is a tasty trail snack.

Eggs

Boiled Eggs—Use a spoon to gently lower eggs into boiling water. Cook eggs 5 minutes for soft-boiled or 10 minutes for hard-boiled.

Fried Eggs—Heat a teaspoon of butter, margarine, or cooking oil in a pan. Crack in two eggs and fry over low heat until the white becomes firm. Flip them if you like your eggs over easy, or serve them sunny-side up.

Scrambled Eggs—Beat two eggs in a bowl. Add a tablespoon of milk if you have it and a pinch of salt and pepper. Heat butter, margarine, or cooking oil in a pan, then pour in the eggs and cook over low heat. Stir occasionally, scraping the bottom of the pan with a spatula. For variety, add chopped onions, tomatoes, green peppers, mushrooms, or shredded cheese to the eggs before you cook them.

Bacon and Ham

Fried Bacon—Put bacon slices in a pan and cook over low heat, turning them once.

Fried Ham—Heat a little cooking oil, butter, or margarine in a pan. Put in slices of precooked ham and fry over low heat until the meat is lightly browned. Turn and fry the other side.

Pancake Mix

You can make your own pancake mix before leaving home by combining 1/2 cup white flour, 1/2 teaspoon baking powder, a pinch of salt, and 1/2 teaspoon sugar. Carry it in a self-sealing plastic bag. In camp, prepare the batter by stirring in one egg, 2 tablespoons of cooking oil, and 1/4 to 1/2 cup of milk. Some premade pancake mixes require only water and may be more practical for your troop outing.

Pancakes

Flapjacks are a treat on mornings when you aren't in a hurry to break camp. Follow the instructions on a box of pancake mix. Add fresh berries, chopped fruit, or nuts to the batter, if you have them. Pancakes are best cooked on a griddle or in a heavy frying pan.

Heat the pan or griddle and grease it with a little cooking oil, butter, or margarine. Pour in just enough batter to form each cake and fry over low heat. When the edges begin to brown and bubbles break in the center of the cake, turn it and fry the other side. Serve with butter, syrup, or jam.

French Toast—Beat together two eggs, a pinch of salt, and 1/2 cup of milk. Add a pinch of cinnamon if you have it. This should make enough batter for three to four slices of French toast. Dip a slice of bread in the egg mix, coating both sides. Then fry the bread as if it were a pancake. Serve with butter, syrup, or jam.

Breakfast Drinks

Milk, cocoa, and fruit juices all go well with breakfast. Use fresh drinks, dried milk, cocoa mixes, or fruit juice powder.

See the *Handbook* Web site, *www.bsahandbook.org*, for more recipes and camp meal ideas.

Lunch

By the middle of the day in camp or on the trail, you'll be ready to rest and refuel. You can put together your lunch right after breakfast and pack it along so it's ready to eat wherever you are. When you will be near the camp kitchen, though, you might want to cook a hot meal, especially if the weather is rainy or cold.

Sandwiches

An easy way to serve sandwiches is to lay out the bread and fillings on a sheet of plastic. Ask each Scout to wash his hands and then build his own sandwich. Choose from peanut butter and jelly, cheese, luncheon meats, canned tuna or salmon, sardines, sliced tomatoes, hard-boiled eggs, pickles, and lettuce. Round out the meal with milk, a piece of fruit, and a few cookies.

Hot Dishes

A cup of soup will warm you on a chilly day. Follow the instructions on the label to make it from a can or a mix. Try toasting a cheese sandwich by frying it on both sides in a little butter or margarine. If you have fresh foods, light a stove and fry a hamburger or boil some hot dogs.

Backpacker's Lunch

On longer trips or when you aren't able to carry fresh foods, you can take along a lunch of crackers, jelly or jam, hard cheese and salami, summer sausage, fruit, and small cans or foil pouches of chicken or tuna. Add powdered drink mix and a dessert for a lightweight meal that's full of nourishment.

Supper

A one-pot stew is a satisfying evening meal that is easy to prepare. You also can fix a main dish with meat, chicken, or fish, and some vegetables. Bake some biscuits, add a dessert, and something to drink to complete a memorable feast.

Handling Meat and Fish Safely

Beef, chicken, fish, and other meats can be the centerpiece of many camp meals. To keep meat fresh, it should be kept chilled in camp, for example, by storing it in an insulated cooler that also holds ice.

Wash your hands with soap and water before and after handling meat, and wash cutting boards, knives, plates, and any other kitchen items that have been touched by raw meat products before using them with cooked meats and other foods.

Cooking Red Meat

Grilling—Use a grill holding charcoal briquettes, or let a campfire burn into a bed of coals. Place a wire grill so that it is 4 to 6 inches above the coals and lay the meat on the grill. Cook hamburgers 3 to 4 minutes on each side until the pink color is gone from the inside. A 1-inch-thick steak needs about 5 to 10 minutes on a side, depending on the heat of the coals. Cut into the center to see if the meat is done the way you like it.

Frying—Heat a spoonful of cooking oil in a frying pan. Add your hamburger patties, pork chops, or steak, and fry over coals or a stove until done. Pork must always be thoroughly cooked.

Stew—For each serving, use 1/4 pound of beef cut into cubes. Rub flour into the cubes or shake them in a paper bag with a small amount of flour. Place the meat in a pot with a few spoonfuls of cooking oil, and fry until brown. Then add enough water to cover the meat, put a lid on the pot, and simmer for 30 minutes. Add a chopped onion, carrot, and potato, and simmer 30 minutes more. Season with salt and pepper.

Cooking Chicken

Frying—Roll chicken pieces in flour or shake them in a paper bag with a small amount of flour. Place the chicken in a pan and fry it in a few tablespoons of cooking oil until golden brown. Add 1/2 cup of water, cover the pan with a lid, and steam over low heat for about 20 minutes more.

Broiling—Lay pieces of chicken on a wire grill. Cook over coals for about 15 minutes on each side. Keep the chicken moist as it broils by brushing it with butter, margarine, or barbecue sauce.

Cooking Fish

When you've had some luck with your fishing pole, there are plenty of ways to turn your catch into dinner. First, clean each fish by slitting open the belly and pulling out the guts. If you want to remove the scales, scrape the skin with a knife from the tail toward the head. Rinse the fish with water inside and out. (Check with local land managers ahead of time for the best ways to dispose of fish guts. There might be fish-cleaning stations they will want you to use, or they could ask you to toss the guts into deep water or pack them out of the backcountry with the rest of your trash.)

Frying Fish—Roll each fish in flour or cornmeal. Heat a few tablespoons of cooking oil in a frying pan or on a griddle. Carefully place the fish in the hot oil and fry until golden brown, turning the fish once. Keep your eye on the fish. It won't take long to cook.

Grilling Fish—Using a grill placed over coals is a perfect way to prepare fish. While it is still cool, brush the grill with cooking oil. Lightly brush the outside of the fish with oil, too, and place it on the grill. Let the fish cook a couple of minutes, then turn it once. You'll know it is done when the meat is flaky and no longer shiny. Avoid overcooking fish.

Vegetables

Fresh and Canned Vegetables—Many fresh vegetables can be washed and eaten raw for maximum nutritional value. To cook vegetables, cover with water and simmer over low heat until done. Corn on the cob cooks in about 6 to 10 minutes, while fresh carrots, peas, and green beans can take longer. Most canned vegetables are already cooked. Pour them into a pan and heat them in their own liquid.

Boiled and Mashed Potatoes—Wash potatoes and peel them, or leave the skins on for the vitamins and minerals they contain. Cut the potatoes into 1-inch cubes and boil gently in a pot of water for about 20 minutes. Test a cube with a fork. The potatoes are done when the fork goes in easily. Drain, season the potatoes with salt and pepper, and serve with a little butter or margarine. If you wish, you can mash the cubes with a fork.

Fried Potatoes—Boil several whole potatoes and let them cool. Slice the potatoes and fry in hot oil until they are brown. For extra flavor, chop up an onion and fry it along with the potatoes. Season with salt and pepper.

Quick One-Pot Stew

It's hard to beat a one-pot stew for speedy outdoor dining. With a few ingredients and a little imagination, you can make dozens of different versions. Just combine one item from each of the following lists. All amounts are for one serving.

3 to 4 oz. cooked:	Add a 3- to 4-oz. can or foil packet:	Add 1 packet:	Add:
Spaghetti	Canned tuna	Gravy mix	Cooked vegetables
Macaroni	Canned chicken	or	Chopped cheese
Noodles		4 to 8 oz.:	Chopped nuts
Ramen noodles		Spaghetti sauce	
Rice		Stroganoff sauce	
		Tomato sauce	

Serve vegetables separately from the stew, or drain and stir them right into the pot. Season to taste. Add a beverage and a dessert to round out the meal.

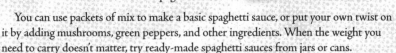

Pasta and Rice

Spaghetti—Bring a large pot of water to a boil. Add a tablespoon of cooking oil, butter, or margarine if you have it, then drop in 4 ounces of spaghetti for each person. Boil for 5 to 10 minutes until tender. Drain and serve with spaghetti sauce.

You can use packets of mix to make a basic spaghetti sauce, or put your own twist on it by adding mushrooms, green peppers, and other ingredients. When the weight you need to carry doesn't matter, try ready-made spaghetti sauces from jars or cans.

Macaroni and Cheese—For each serving, stir 4 ounces of macaroni into a pot of boiling water. Boil for 10 to 15 minutes until done, then drain the water. Stir into the cooked macaroni 2 ounces of cut-up cheese, 1 teaspoon of powdered milk, and 1 tablespoon of margarine or butter.

Rice—Both white and brown rice are rich in minerals and fiber. For one serving, pour 1/2 cup of raw rice and 1 cup of cold water into a pot. Cover with a lid and bring to a boil. Let it simmer until done—about 10 minutes for white rice, 30 minutes or more for brown rice. There's no need to stir rice while it is cooking.

Ramen Noodles—Ramen-style noodles come in a 3-ounce package just right for a single serving. Before you open the package, crush the noodles into small pieces. Tear open the wrapper and pour the noodles into 1 1/2 cups boiling water. Remove from heat and let stand a few minutes until done. If you wish, stir in the flavor packet that comes with the noodles and add canned tuna or chicken, canned vegetables, and other ingredients to make a hearty soup.

Bread

Bread is good to serve in camp alongside dinnertime stews and soups. It's also a great addition to all other meals. You can bring bread or crackers from home or bake bread in camp. Fresh biscuits are hard to beat.

Homemade Biscuit Mix

Prepare your own biscuit mix at home by stirring together:

☐ 1 cup flour

☐ 1 teaspoon baking powder

☐ 1/4 teaspoon salt

When you're ready to make biscuits, add 2 tablespoons of cooking oil and just enough water or milk to keep the dough together but not too sticky.

Biscuits—Follow the package instructions for preparing premixed biscuit flour. Shape the dough into biscuits about 1/2-inch thick. Place them on a greased pan and bake for 10 to 15 minutes in a stovetop oven or Dutch oven. Test the biscuits for doneness by pushing a matchstick or wood shaving into a biscuit. The biscuits are done when the wood comes out clean.

Dutch Ovens

A Dutch oven is a heavy iron or aluminum pot that's perfect for baking bread, cobblers, and pies as well as for cooking stews and beans. An iron Dutch oven must be seasoned before its first use and whenever it has been scrubbed with soap and water.

Season an oven by heating it over a fire and then putting in several tablespoons of cooking oil. Spread the oil all over the inside of the oven with a paper towel and let the oven cool. The metal will be protected from rust, and foods you prepare are less likely to stick. Soap strips away the grease, so it is often best to wash out a Dutch oven with hot water that contains no soap.

Dutch-Oven Biscuits.—Mix enough dough for eight biscuits. Use a shovel to move a scoop of coals onto a fire-safe surface, then place the empty oven on them and let it warm. Arrange the raw biscuits in the oven. Cover with the lid, then shovel coals on top—three times as many coals on the lid as underneath the oven. Check in about 10 minutes. The biscuits will be ready when they are golden brown. Gloves and hot-pot tongs will make it easier to handle a hot oven.

Stovetop Oven Bread—Ovens for use with backpacking stoves are available at camping supply stores. Use them as you would an oven at home, keeping your stove flame low to allow for gentle baking.

Frying Pan Bread—Almost any bread or biscuit recipe can be cooked in a frying pan greased with a few tablespoons of cooking oil. Flatten the dough into a large pancake, put it in the oiled pan, and fry it over the fire. A lid will hold in the heat. Turn the bread with a spatula to allow both sides to brown. The trick is to cook the dough slowly enough for the center to become done before the crust is too brown.

Dumplings—Drop spoonfuls of biscuit dough on top of a one-pot stew when the stew has about 10 minutes left to cook. Cover and let the stew simmer. Steam from the stew will turn the dough into mouth-watering dumplings.

Desserts

Fruit or cookies finish a meal nicely. Pudding is another tasty choice. Pudding mixes come in many flavors, and instant pudding requires no cooking. Cobbler, brownies, and other baked desserts are always great in camp.

Ranger Cobbler

A traditional Scout dessert is peach cobbler baked in a Dutch oven. Here's the recipe.

Ingredients:

- ☐ 2 large (28 ounces) cans of peaches
- ☐ 2 cups of dry biscuit mix
- ☐ 1/2 cup sugar
- ☐ 1 teaspoon cinnamon

Heat a Dutch oven over a good bed of charcoal. Pour the juice from one can of peaches into the oven. Use the juice from the other can in place of water to mix up the biscuit dough. Put the peaches from both cans into the oven. Add the sugar and cinnamon and bring to a boil.

Drop spoonfuls of biscuit dough onto the hot peach mixture in the same way you would make dumplings. Put the lid on the Dutch oven and move it onto a small shovelful of charcoal. Scoop three times as many coals onto the lid of the oven and let the cobbler bake about 20 minutes until the biscuit topping is golden brown.

COOKING IN ALUMINUM FOIL

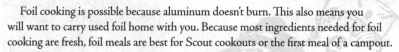

Want to leave the pots and pans at home? Then give aluminum-foil cooking a try. Wrap food in a piece of heavy-duty foil and fold over the edges to make a packet from which liquids and steam can't escape. Place the foil packet on a bed of coals and turn it at least once while it cooks. When you unwrap your dinner, you can eat it right out of the foil.

Foil cooking is possible because aluminum doesn't burn. This also means you will want to carry used foil home with you. Because most ingredients needed for foil cooking are fresh, foil meals are best for Scout cookouts or the first meal of a campout.

Hamburger—Shape 4 ounces of hamburger into a patty. Cut a medium potato and a carrot into thin strips. Peel and slice a small onion. Arrange all the ingredients on a square of heavy-duty foil and sprinkle lightly with salt and pepper. Close the foil and lay the package on the coals. Cook for about 7 to 8 minutes, then turn it over and let it cook for another 7 to 8 minutes.

Stew—Cut 4 ounces of beef into cubes. Thinly slice a potato, carrot, and small onion. Place all the ingredients on a heavy-duty piece of foil and sprinkle with salt and pepper. Add several tablespoons of water and fold the foil to form a packet. Cook on the coals for about 20 minutes, turning it at least once.

Chicken—Smear chicken pieces with butter or margarine. Salt lightly and wrap each piece in a separate sheet of heavy-duty foil. Place the packets on the coals and cook for about 20 minutes, turning them several times.

Potato—Pierce the skin of a potato in several places with a fork or your pocketknife, then wrap the potato in foil. Bury it in the coals for 15 minutes or more.

Corn on the Cob—Dab butter or margarine on an ear of corn, wrap it in foil, and roast on the coals for 10 minutes. Turn it several times while it is cooking.

Baked Fish—Wrap fresh fish in heavy-duty foil by itself or along with some chopped onion and lemon slices. Bake on the coals about 3 to 5 minutes per side for a small fish. Allow 10 minutes or more on each side for a large fish.

Fruit—Cut the core out of an apple and replace it with a pat of butter, a few raisins, some cinnamon, and a teaspoon of brown sugar. Wrap in foil and bake in the coals for 30 minutes.

COOKING WITHOUT UTENSILS

The secret to cooking a meal without pots, pans, or aluminum foil is a bed of hot coals.

Roast Potatoes—Coat each potato with a thick layer of mud and bury it in the coals. Bake 30 to 40 minutes. The mud will become caked and hard, but the potato inside should come out just right.

Kabob—Slide a 1-inch cube of beef or chicken onto a bamboo skewer. Alternate whole mushrooms, chunks of tomato, onion, green pepper, pineapple, or slices of zucchini. Broil the kabobs a few inches above the coals for 10 to 15 minutes, turning often.

Fish—Run a bamboo skewer into the flesh along the length of a small trout's spine. Another option is to tie the fish to the stick with several wraps of string. Hold the fish over the coals and cook a few minutes. Fins and skin will pull off, leaving the tender meat beneath.

Bread Twist—Roll stiff biscuit dough into the shape of a long sausage. Twist the dough around a clean, wooden broom handle. Lean the handle over a bed of coals and turn occasionally until the baking is done.

Bread Cup—Instead of twisting the dough, mold it onto the end of the handle, then bake it over the coals. When it is done, slip it off the handle and you'll have a bread cup you can stuff with sandwich fillings or stew.

Roasted Corn. Open the husks and remove the silks. Replace the husks, dip the ears in water, and place them on the coals. Roast for 8 to 10 minutes, turning them as they cook.

MAKING MEALS SPECIAL EVENTS

Mealtime is a terrific opportunity for you to sit down with your patrol and enjoy good food and the fellowship of Scouting. Even a simple meal can be turned into a special moment.

Take a minute or two before you eat to share your thanks for the food you have been given, the experiences you are having, and the fun of being with friends. The grace used at Philmont Scout Ranch is one way of expressing that gratitude.

Philmont Grace

For food

For raiment

For life

For opportunity

For friendship and fellowship

We thank Thee, oh Lord.

High Adventure *(1957), by Norman Rockwell*

KEEPING A COOKING NOTEBOOOK

Write your food lists and recipes in a notebook each time you get ready for a campout. At the end of a trip make notes about what worked well and what didn't. Perhaps you needed a larger frying pan or more oatmeal, or maybe you brought too much cocoa. As you plan your next adventure, your notebook will remind you of changes you want to make.

Continue to try different recipes, too. Earning the Cooking merit badge is a great goal to set as your skills increase. Your biggest reward will be the smiles on the faces of your patrol every time you sit down to a delicious outdoor meal that you've cooked yourselves.

MERIT BADGE SERIES

COOKING

BOY SCOUTS OF AMERICA

Navigation

"As a camper and hiker, there is one piece of your equipment you should know, and know well—your compass. With your compass, you can follow trail maps, or lay out plots of land. You will have little excuse for being lost in any kind of country, if you can use your compass correctly."

—*Handbook for Boys*, 1949

NAVIGATION

Scouts on a high-adventure canoe trip match symbols on a map with landmarks on the shore and paddle toward their next portage trail. Patrol members on a prairie campout use a star chart to learn the names of constellations sparkling in the clear night sky. With maps and compasses, Scouts on orienteering courses race through the woods, completing challenges that test their physical abilities and navigation skills. Handheld Global Positioning System receivers guide Scouts to their next geocaches as they take part in high-tech games of hide and seek.

Navigation—the art of finding your way—is important for every Scout to learn. Much of navigating involves paying attention to your surroundings and making good decisions. With a compass and a map, you'll have the tools to chart routes through the deepest wilderness. A GPS receiver will add even more power to your ability to figure out where you are, where you want to go, and the best ways to get there.

MEASURING

Navigation begins with understanding the shape and size of the world around you. For quick estimates, nothing beats the measuring tool you have with you all the time—yourself.

Navigation is problem-solving at its best. It is a set of skills you can use to find your way in cities, to reach camp, and to plot out high-adventure treks on foot and afloat.

IN THIS CHAPTER

▶ Measuring

▶ Tools of navigation

▶ How to use a compass

▶ Using maps and compasses on hikes, bike trips, and other Scout adventures

▶ Global Positioning System (GPS) receivers

▶ Finding directions using the stars, the sun, and the moon

▶ Compass game

▶ Orienteering courses

▶ Navigating your way forward

Tomorrow's Leader (1959),
by Norman Rockwell

Use a ruler or yardstick to determine the following measurements. With these numbers in mind, you can use your arms, hands, and feet to figure out the sizes of everything from the diameter of a tree to the length of the next fish you catch.

Arm span _____   Finger length _____

Arm reach _____   Foot length _____

Hand span _____   Height _____

"In judging distances, the Scout should know and use his height, his reach, his finger length, his pace, etc. These serve as units for him."

—*Handbook for Boys*, 1927

Measuring Distances

If you know the length of your footsteps, you can measure distances just by walking. Here's a way to learn how far you go with each step.

Step 1—With a tape measure, mark a 100-foot course on the ground. (A distance of 100 feet on a football field begins at the goal line and goes to 1 foot past the 33-yard hash mark.)

Step 2—Walk at your normal pace from one end of the course to the other. Count your steps as you go.

Step 3—Divide the total number of steps into 100, and you'll know the length in feet of one step.

For example, if you used 50 steps to go 100 feet, the length of each step you take is 2 feet. If it took you 40 steps, figure a length of about 2.5 feet per step. If 33 steps got you close, your stride is about 3 feet, or 1 yard, per step.

Some Scouts find that measuring distances is easier when they count every step along the way. That's called a *stride*. Others have better luck counting each time their right foot touches the ground. That's a *pace*. A pace is twice the length of a stride.

To measure distances, count your steps as you walk. Multiply the total number of steps by the length of your stride and you'll know how far you have gone.

Measuring Heights

Scouts through the decades have used simple, reliable ways to measure the heights of trees and to estimate the elevations of towers, waterfalls, cliffs, buildings, and walls. Now you can do that, too.

Stick Method

Step 1—Have a friend whose height you know stand next to a tree you want to measure. Step back and hold a straight stick upright at arm's length in front of you.

Step 2—With one eye closed, sight over the stick so that the top of it appears to touch the top of your friend's head. Place your thumbnail on the stick where it seems to touch the base of the tree.

Step 3—Now move the stick up to see how many times this measurement goes into the height of the tree. Multiply that number by your friend's height and you will know the approximate height of the tree. For example, if your friend is 5 feet tall and his height goes into the tree six times, the tree is about 30 feet tall.

Felling Method

To use the felling method of measurement, back away from the object you want to measure—a flagpole, for example.

Step 1—Hold a stick upright at arm's length. Adjust the stick so that its tip appears to touch the top of the flagpole while your thumb seems to be at its base.

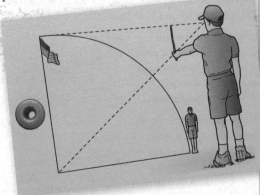

Step 2—Swing the stick 90 degrees to a horizontal position, tracing the same arc as if the flagpole had fallen sideways to the ground.

Step 3—Keep your thumb in line with the base of the pole and notice where the tip of the stick appears to touch the ground. Have a friend stand on that spot. Measure the distance from the point where your friend is standing to the base of the flagpole, and you'll know the flagpole's height. (This is a good problem to solve by using the length of your step as a measuring tool.)

Measuring Widths

Imagine that you need to figure out the width of a stream. There is no bridge and you can't wade or swim across. What will you do? You could use the salute method, the stick method, or the compass method to find the stream's width.

Salute Method

Step 1—Stand on the shore and hold your hand to your forehead in a salute. Move your hand down until the front edge of it seems to touch the opposite shore.

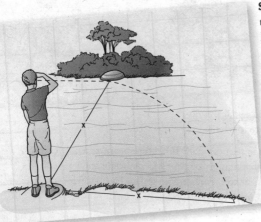

Step 2—Without changing the position of your head or hand, make a quarter turn or more. Notice the place that your hand seems to touch the ground on your side of the stream. Measure the distance from where you are standing to that point, and you will know the stream's width.

Stick Method

Step 1—Locate a rock or some other object on the far side of the stream (*A*).

Step 2—Place a stick on this side opposite the rock (*B*).

Step 3—Walk along the shore at right angles to *AB*. Take any number of steps (50, for example), and place another stick there (*C*).

Step 4—Continue walking along the shore in the same direction for as many steps as before (in this case, 50 more). Put a stick there (*D*).

Step 5—Finally, walk away from the stream at right angles to *DB*. When you can sight a straight line over stick *C* to the rock on the far side, stop and mark your spot (*E*).

Step 6—Measure *DE* to get the width of the stream.

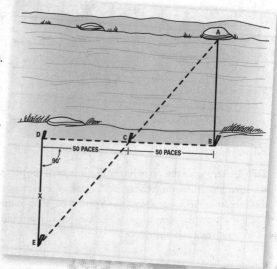

Compass Method—If you know how to use a compass, you can use it as a tool for measuring widths, such as the distance across a stream.

Step 1—While standing on one side of a river (*B*), locate a rock or other object directly opposite you on the far shore (*A*).

Step 2—Take a bearing by pointing the direction-of-travel arrow of your compass at the rock and turning the compass housing until the needle lies over the orienting arrow. Read the degrees (in this case, 120 degrees).

Step 3—Add 45 degrees (120 + 45 = 165). Set your compass at the new reading (in this case, 165 degrees).

Step 4—Walk along the shore, pointing the direction-of-travel arrow toward the rock. When the compass needle again lies over the orienting arrow, stop and mark your spot (*C*). Distance *CB* is the same as the width of the river.

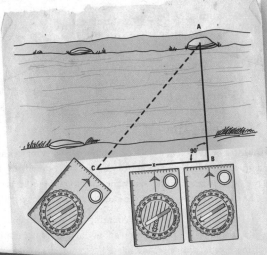

Time and Weather

Counting seconds during a thunderstorm can tell you how far away lightning strikes are occurring and whether the storm is coming toward you or is drifting away. You can use the speed of sound to estimate the distance of a storm from you. Sound moves through the air at a speed of approximately 770 feet per second, or about a mile every 7 seconds. When you see a flash of lightning, start counting by thousands until you hear the thunder. If you've reached a number higher than one-thousand-seven, you'll know the lightning bolt was more than a mile away. Less than one-thousand-seven means the lightning was closer.

Measuring Time

Most of us look at a clock or watch when we want to know the time or how long something will take to complete. You can also estimate the time of day by noticing where the sun is in the sky. Obviously, the day has just started as the sun rises in the morning. The sun is directly overhead at midday, and when it sets, night is about to begin.

To estimate shorter times, counting "one-thousand-one, one-thousand-two, one-thousand-three . . ." will give you about one second per number. Practice counting by using a watch with a second hand. Pace yourself so that when you count to one-thousand-thirty, about 30 seconds will have passed.

Measuring Level

When you're lashing together a signal tower, you'll want the cross pieces supporting the platform to be level. A clear plastic water bottle half full of water makes a good measuring tool. Lay it on its side on one of the cross pieces and check to see if the water inside is level. If it is, then the crosspiece under it is level, too.

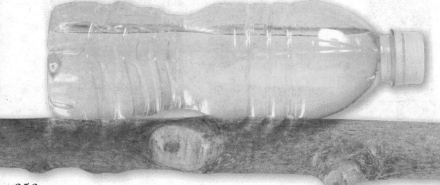

TOOLS OF NAVIGATION

"Probably the best thing to do is not to get lost."

—*Boy Scout Handbook*, 1940

Many Scout hikes will lead along trails you know well. Sometimes you'll want to take off for places you've never visited before. Wherever you go, you can find your way with the help of the tools of navigation—maps, compasses, and GPS receivers.

Maps

The United States Geological Survey has developed useful maps for outdoor adventures. They are called topographic maps—from the Greek words *topos* ("place") and *graphein* ("to write"). Because they enclose a four-sided area, topographic maps are also known as quadrangle maps.

Sporting goods shops and camping stores often sell topographic maps of nearby recreation areas. With your parent's permission, you can download topographic maps of just the area you need that highlight exactly the features that will be useful when you are in the field.

What Map Symbols Mean

From an airplane, you can look down and see roads, rivers, forests, cities, and towns. A map is like a painting of that land. Since mapmakers can't include every detail, they choose information they hope will be valuable to anyone using the map. Some of the most important data are represented by symbols located in the *map key* in a map's margins.

Directions—*North* is toward the top of most maps. The bottom is *south*; the left side is *west*; and the right side is *east*. A map will often have a *true north* arrow in its margin and an arrow showing the direction of *magnetic north*.

Distances—*Bar scales* can be used for measuring feet, meters, and miles on a map.

Scale—The *scale of a map* compares the size of the map with the size of the area it represents. A map scale of *1-to-24,000* (shown in the margin as 1:24,000) means 1 unit of distance on that map (an inch, for example) equals 24,000 units of that distance on the ground (24,000 inches, in this example. Thus, 1 inch equals 2,000 feet.)

Date—A map's *date* tells when it was drawn or last updated. An older map will not show new buildings, roads, trails, or other recent changes on the land.

Open pit, mine	⚒
Index contour	
Intermediate contour	
Levee (with road)	
Boundary	
Power line	
Telephone line	
Railroad	
Hard surface roads	
Improved road	
Unimproved road	
Trail	
Bridge	
Footbridge	
Perennial streams	
Water well, spring	
Lake	
Marsh (swamp)	
Buildings (dwelling)	
School, church, cemetery	
Buildings (barn, etc.)	
Sand area	
Woods	
Orchard	
Scrub	

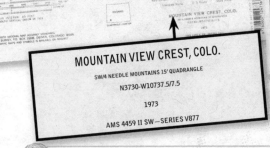

MOUNTAIN VIEW CREST, COLO.

SW/4 NEEDLE MOUNTAINS 15' QUADRANGLE

N3730-W10737.5/7.5

1973

AMS 4459 II SW—SERIES V877

For more information on map symbols, visit the *Handbook* Web site: www.bsahandbook.org.

Colors—The colors used on a USGS map also are meaningful.

Green indicates heavy vegetation such as forests, woodlands, or orchards.

White is used to show areas that are mostly clear of trees such as fields, meadows, rocky slopes, and other open country.

Blue means water. A patch of blue is usually a pond or a lake. A blue band is a river, and a blue line is a stream. If the line is broken, the stream it represents doesn't flow all the time. Marshes and swamps are drawn with broken blue lines and tufts of grass. The names of all water features are in *italics*.

Black ink is used to show anything that is the work of humans. Rail lines, bridges, boundaries, and the names of landmarks are printed in black. Roads are shown as parallel black lines. The lines are solid for paved and gravel roads. A broken line is a dirt road. A single broken line is a hiking trail. Black squares and rectangles are buildings; those that are completely black are inhabited buildings such as houses and schools. Black just around the sides of buildings indicates barns, sheds, and other outbuildings.

Brown is the color used for *contour lines*. Maps are flat, but the areas they represent may be full of hills, valleys, mountains, and plains. Mapmakers use contour lines to show the shape of the land.

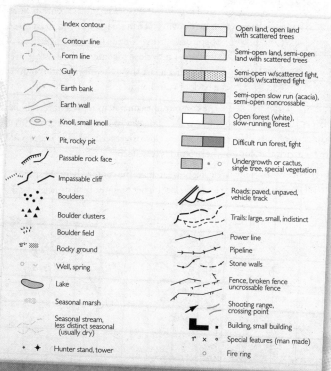

Contour Lines

Here's a good way to understand contour lines.

Make a fist with one hand. Your fist has contours of *length*, *width*, and *height*, just as the land does.

Holding your fist steady, draw a level circle around your highest knuckle (washable ink will be easy to remove). Draw a second circle just below that one. Start a third line a little lower. Notice that to stay on the level, the pen may trace around another knuckle before the third circle is closed.

Continue to draw level circles, each one the same distance beneath the last. The lines will wander in and out of the valleys between your fingers, over the broad slope on the back of your hand, and across the steep cliffs above your thumb.

After all the lines are drawn, spread your hand flat. Now, like a map, your hand has only *width* and *length*. But by looking at the contour lines you have drawn, you can imagine *height*, too, and see the shape of your fist. Small circles show the tops of your knuckles. Lines close together indicate steep areas. Lines farther apart show the more gentle contour of the back of your hand.

The contour lines on a map represent terrain in the same way. Every point on a contour line is the same elevation above sea level. Small circles are the tops of hills. Where the lines are close together, a hillside is steep. Where the lines are far apart, the slope of the ground is less steep.

A note in the map's margin will tell you how far apart the contour lines are spaced. *Contour Interval 50 Feet* means each line is 50 feet higher or lower than its neighboring lines.

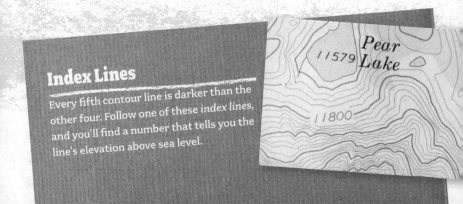

Index Lines

Every fifth contour line is darker than the other four. Follow one of these *index lines*, and you'll find a number that tells you the line's elevation above sea level.

Longitude and Latitude

The longest black lines on a map are lines of longitude and latitude. They form a grid around the globe that can be used to locate any spot on Earth. GPS systems use them as well to mark locations and set out *waypoints* leading toward a destination.

Longitude

To begin understanding longitude and latitude, look at a peeled orange. Notice how the segments of the orange fit together. The lines between the segments all touch at the top of the orange and again at the bottom.

Choose one of the orange segment lines and call it *zero*. From there, you can number the other lines around the orange—1, 2, 3, 4, and so on. This will tell you how many segment lines you are away from the *zero* segment line.

Latitude

On a globe of Earth, mapmakers have drawn lines that are similar to the lines separating the segments of your peeled orange. These are *meridians* (lines) *of longitude*. They *converge* (come together) at the North Pole (the top of the globe) and at the South Pole (the bottom of the globe).

Latitude and longitude

Just as there are 360 degrees in a circle, there are 360 degrees of longitude. The meridian of longitude marked *zero* is the one that passes through the Royal Observatory at Greenwich, England. It also is called the *prime meridian*. On a map of the world, the meridians of longitude will tell you how far you are from the prime meridian. New York City is about 74 degrees west of the prime meridian. Seattle is 122 degrees of longitude west of the prime meridian.

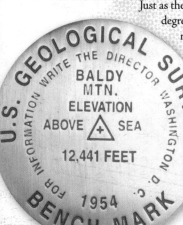

USGS benchmark for Baldy Mountain at Philmont Scout Ranch. Benchmarks are set in the field to give surveyors a stationary reference point.

Go back to the peeled orange and imagine drawing a line around the center of it, crossing all the segments at an equal distance from the top and the bottom. That line is the *equator* of the orange. Earth's equator is an imaginary line that is equally far from the North Pole and the South Pole. (*Equator* comes from the word *equal*.) The equator also serves as *zero degrees latitude*. Lines drawn parallel to it are numbered to the poles. The North Pole is 90 degrees of latitude north of the equator. The South Pole is 90 degrees south.

Meridians of longitude are numbered both west and east from the prime meridian, meeting on the far side of the globe in the Pacific Ocean at 180 degrees longitude (a meridian that also serves as the international date line).

Degrees, Minutes, and Seconds

To show detailed locations, each *degree* of longitude and latitude is divided into 60 *minutes*, and each minute of longitude and latitude is divided into 60 *seconds*.

A position on the globe is stated latitude first, followed by longitude. For example, the coordinates of latitude and longitude for the summit of Baldy Mountain, the highest point on Philmont Scout Ranch in New Mexico, are:

36°37'45" N, 105°12'48" W

That means that hikers standing on top of Baldy are 36 degrees, 37 minutes, 45 seconds north of the equator, and 105 degrees, 12 minutes, 48 seconds west of the prime meridian (the meridian of longitude passing through Greenwich, England).

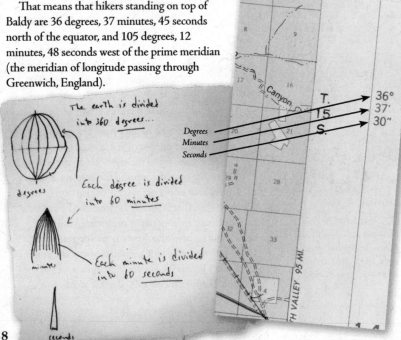

The earth is divided into 360 degrees...

degrees

Each degree is divided into 60 minutes

minutes

Each minute is divided into 60 seconds

seconds

Degrees
Minutes
Seconds

36°
37'
30"

UTM System

Another grid used for identifying locations is the Universal Transverse Mercator system. The UTM system is especially useful with Global Positioning System receivers. It divides the globe in much the same way as longitude and latitude, but uses meters for measurements rather than degrees, minutes, and seconds. Many maps show the UTM grid in great detail.

UTM *zones* extend from the North Pole to the South Pole. Each of the 60 zones covers 6 degrees of longitude and are numbered from west to east beginning at the international date line (180 degrees longitude).

Like lines of latitude, the east-west lines of a UTM grid are parallel to the equator. Their distance above or below the equator is given in kilometers and meters.

In the margin of a map with a UTM grid, you will find the number of the zone that includes that map. You'll also see several sets of UTM numbers.

▶ The numbers along the left and right margins show a location's distance in meters from the nearest UTM north-south meridian. This measurement is called easting.

▶ The numbers across the top and bottom margins show the distance in meters north of the equator. This reading is called northing.

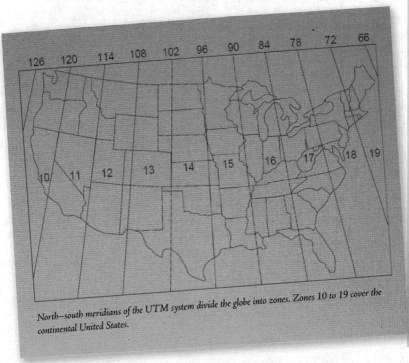

North–south meridians of the UTM system divide the globe into zones. Zones 10 to 19 cover the continental United States.

The top of Baldy Mountain at Philmont Scout Ranch has these UTM coordinates:

Zone 13   480929E, 4053843N

▶ Baldy Mountain is located in Zone 13.

▶ 480929E indicates that the easting of the summit is 480 kilometers and 929 meters in relation to the Zone 13 meridian.

▶ 4053843N means the Baldy summit is 4,053 kilometers and 843 meters north of the equator.

Most GPS receivers can accept data either in longitude and latitude format or as UTM coordinates. Simply enter longitude and latitude numbers or a set of UTM coordinates—those for Baldy Mountain, for example—and the GPS receiver will give you the direction of travel and the distance you must go to reach that destination.

Likewise, asking a GPS receiver to show your present location will bring up the numbers of UTM coordinates or of longitude and latitude that can then be located on a map to show you exactly where you are.

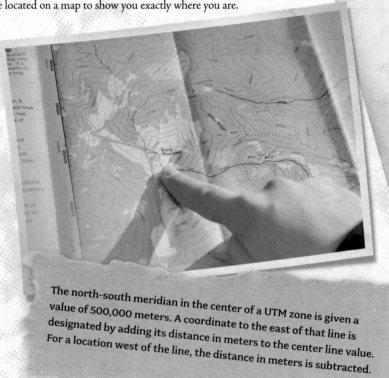

The north-south meridian in the center of a UTM zone is given a value of 500,000 meters. A coordinate to the east of that line is designated by adding its distance in meters to the center line value. For a location west of the line, the distance in meters is subtracted.

HOW TO USE A COMPASS

Compasses appeared in China about a thousand years ago and in Europe a few hundred years later. Travelers noticed that a magnetized needle floating on a chip of wood always swung around to point north. Many people thought the needle moved by magic.

Today we know that Earth's rotation causes its axis to act as a huge magnet. A pole of that global magnet is in northern Canada, and one end of every compass needle is drawn toward it. That end of the needle is usually painted red or stamped with the letter N, for *north*.

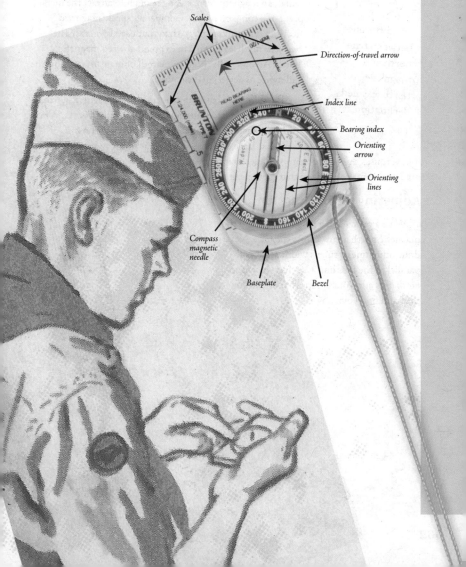

Scales

Direction-of-travel arrow

Index line

Bearing index

Orienting arrow

Orienting lines

Compass magnetic needle

Baseplate

Bezel

Two Norths

The maps you are most likely to use on Scout adventures are drawn with their tops aimed exactly at the North Pole, or true north. You could say that maps are made to speak the language of "true north." A map's *true north arrow* points toward the North Pole.

Compass needles, however, do not point true north. Instead, they are pulled toward *magnetic north*, an area more than a thousand miles away from the North Pole that radiates a magnetic force strong enough to attract the metal point of a compass needle. Compasses speak "magnetic north," a different language than that used by maps. The *magnetic north arrow* on a map points toward magnetic north. Arrows in the bottom margin of many maps show the difference as *degrees of declination*.

The difference between true north and magnetic north is called *declination*. Declination is measured in degrees. When you use a map and compass together, declination can cause large errors as you take bearings and try to follow routes. Avoid problems with declination by making adjustments to your map or to your compass so that they speak the same language.

> 14 degrees
>
> True north Magnetic north
>
> **The difference between true north and magnetic north is called declination.**

Adjusting for Declination

With a pencil and a long ruler, extend the magnetic north arrow across the map. Next, draw other lines a ruler's width apart and parallel to the first line. Use these *magnetic north lines* and your compass to orient the map and find your way.

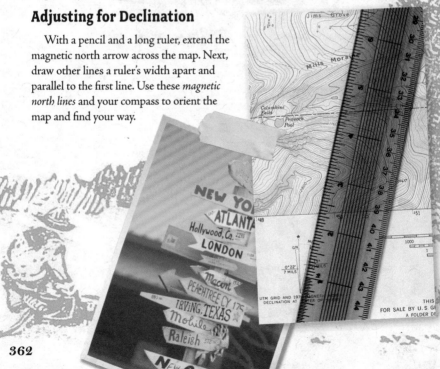

Drawing magnetic north lines across a map is one of several ways for dealing with declination so that a map and compass can be used together. You also may use methods involving adding or subtracting the declination from compass bearings, depending on the type of map you use. These methods may provide more accuracy, but they can be more difficult to learn.

Another solution is to use a compass that can be adjusted so that its readings are aligned with true north rather than magnetic north. Once the adjustment has been made, the compass uses as its reference any true north lines on a map (map borders, lines of longitude, township boundaries, etc.). You can ignore any magnetic north map lines.

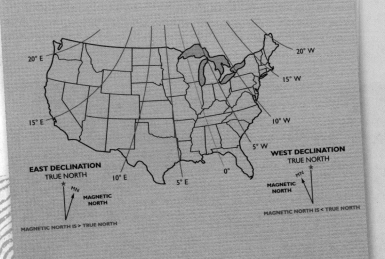

When using a compass that has been adjusted for declination, put the edge of the compass baseplate along any true north line, including the north-south borders of the map.)

For more information about declination, visit the *Handbook* Web site: www.bsahandbook.org.

How to Orient a Map

Hundreds of years ago, European explorers were trying to reach regions of East Asia that they called the Orient. Many of their maps had the Orient at the top. Today, most maps are drawn with north at the top, but the act of turning a map to match the landscape is still called *orienting*.

Here are two ways to orient a map:

▶ Look around for landmarks such as buildings, a bridge, or perhaps the top of a hill. On your map, find the symbols for those features. Turn the map until the symbols line up with the landscape features they represent.

▶ If you have a compass, rotate the compass housing until N (360 degrees) touches the direction-of-travel arrow. Place the edge of the compass baseplate alongside any magnetic north line on the map or along the magnetic north arrow in the map's margin. Turn the map and compass as a unit until the compass needle lies directly over the orienting arrow in the compass housing.

USING MAPS AND COMPASSES ON HIKES, BIKE TRIPS, AND OTHER SCOUT ADVENTURES

Orienting a map so that it matches the terrain can give you the guidance you need to travel over long distances. Stop often to orient the map again and double-check your position.

When you are in areas that are new to you or when going cross-country, a couple of other map and compass skills can show you the way.

Following a Route Drawn on a Map

Step 1—On the map, place the edge of your compass along your planned route. Find the symbols on your map for your current location and for the place you want to reach. Lay your compass on the map with the edge of the compass baseplate touching those two symbols. Be sure the *direction-of-travel arrow* is pointing in the direction you plan to go. (If the symbols are far apart, connect them with a ruler, pencil a straight line between them, then place the compass baseplate along that line.)

Step 2—On the compass, set the bearing. Hold the baseplate firmly on the map. Ignore the magnetic needle and turn the compass housing until the meridian lines are parallel with any magnetic north line drawn on your map—probably an extension of the magnetic north arrow in the margin. The *N* on the compass housing should point toward the top of the map.

Step 3—In the field, follow the compass bearing. Hold your compass in front of you with the direction-of-travel arrow pointing straight ahead. Turn your entire body until the magnetic needle covers the orienting arrow on the floor of the compass housing (the north end of the needle should be toward north on the housing). The direction-of-travel arrow will point toward your destination.

If there is a trail or a road that leads in the direction you want to go, follow that route. When going cross-country, pick a tree, rock, or something else in line with the direction-of-travel arrow and walk to it. Take another compass bearing and head toward the next landmark along your route. Repeat, walking from one point to another until you reach your destination.

Identifying Landmarks

If you can locate where you are on the map, you can identify the mountains, lakes, buildings, and other landmarks that you see.

Step 1—Take a bearing on the landmark. Holding the compass in your hand, aim the direction-of-travel arrow at the landmark you want to identify. Turn the compass housing until the magnetic needle lines up over the orienting arrow. The north end of the needle should be pointing at *N* on the compass housing.

Step 2—Locate your position on the map. Find the map symbol that represents the place where you are standing.

Step 3—Identify the landmark. Place your compass on the map with one edge of the baseplate touching the symbol for your location. Move the entire compass until the meridian lines in the housing are parallel with any magnetic north line drawn on the map. The *N* on the compass housing should be pointed toward the top of the map. Draw a line along the edge of the baseplate starting at your location and going in the direction of travel. Look at the symbols under that line. One of them should represent the landmark you want to identify.

GLOBAL POSITIONING SYSTEM (GPS) RECEIVERS

A Global Positioning System receiver is an electronic tool that uses satellite signals to calculate its location anywhere on Earth. With it you can determine your current position and speed, the distance traveled, and the direction in which you are going. A GPS unit also will estimate your elevation above sea level. By recording where you have traveled, you can retrace your steps and find your way home. Some GPS units can be programmed with topographic maps showing your route and providing constant updates of your progress.

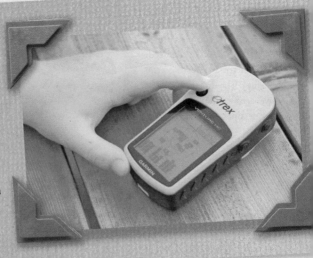

A GPS receiver is not a substitute for developing skill with maps and compasses. A GPS unit with dead batteries is no more useful for helping you find your way than is a rock you pick up on the trail.

Waypoints

A *waypoint* is a location recorded in a GPS receiver. Allow the GPS unit to find its current location, then save that location as a waypoint. Waypoints are handy when you are boating and want to mark a great fishing hole in a lake, when you want to remember how to return to a good campsite, or when you are documenting the locations of environmental service projects in the backcountry.

Waypoints also are extremely useful as you set out on a journey and as you are coming home.

▶ Pencil your route on a topographic map. Mark a number of waypoints—trail intersections, stream crossings, etc. Determine the longitude and latitude or UTM coordinates of the waypoints and enter those numbers into your GPS receiver. Bring up the waypoints on the GPS screen as you travel. They will guide you along your route by telling you how far and in which direction you must go to reach each waypoint.

▶ During a trip, stop at recognizable landmarks (a big tree, a cabin, a bridge) and use your GPS receiver to determine your location. Program that spot into the GPS waypoint memory. On your return journey, those GPS waypoints will provide guidance so you can find your way even if visibility is poor or you can't remember where you should go.

Geocaching

The sport of *geocaching* is a great patrol adventure. Troop members and staffs of Scout camps can prepare an area by hiding items in the field and using GPS receivers to note their exact locations. You can then set off on a scavenger hunt by following the coordinates to locate whatever has been hidden.

Geocaching is also an enjoyable public activity. Web sites list the GPS coordinates of caches hidden in city parks and other open spaces across America—simply enter a zip code and coordinates for nearby geocaches will appear. Many of the caches are small containers with a few trinkets and a notebook. Those who succeed in finding a cache are invited to take a trinket and leave one of their own. After writing their names in the notebook, geocachers return a cache to its hiding place and go in search of another.

For more information about geocaching and using GPS, visit the *Handbook* Web site: *www.bsahandbook.org.*

FINDING DIRECTIONS USING THE STARS

Maps, compasses, and GPS receivers are useful, but for thousands of years travelers have managed to find their way with no navigation instruments at all. The stars were their guides, and they used them to explore the world.

People have long imagined that groups of stars formed the shapes of warriors, animals, maidens, and monsters. Many of the names they gave these constellations are still with us today. You can use a *star chart*—a map of the night sky—to find the constellations.

With the stars to guide them, sailors of old crossed the seas, and explorers made their way to distant lands. You can use the stars to find directions at night, too.

North Star Method

Ursa Major is the ancient name for a constellation known as the Great Bear. The Big Dipper forms part of the Great Bear. Four bright stars form the Big Dipper's bowl, and three more make up the handle.

To find the North Star (also known as *Polaris*), train your eyes on the *pointer stars* of the Big Dipper—the two stars farthest from the Dipper's handle. Extend an imaginary line through them. The North Star is on that line at a distance of about five times the span between the two pointers. Earth's North Pole lies directly under the North Star.

Push a 2-foot-long stick into the ground. Hold a shorter stick in such a way that when you sight over the tips of both sticks, you see the North Star. A straight line scratched between the sticks is a true north–south line.

> Look closely and you might see that the middle star in the Big Dipper's handle is really two stars, Mizar and Alcor. Some American Indians thought of the larger star as a horse, the smaller as a rider.

Northern sky

Constellation Method

As you become familiar with the constellations, their locations will suggest directions. Scorpio, for example, fills the southern sky in the summer. Orion rises in the southeast on winter evenings. The Northern Crown, which is shaped like a horseshoe, opens toward the north. Cassiopeia circles the North Star opposite the Big Dipper.

For more information on finding your way at night, visit the *Handbook* Web site: *www.bsahandbook.org.*

FINDING DIRECTIONS USING THE SUN

The sun rises over the eastern horizon and sets in the west. At other times of the day, use the sun to find directions using the watch method, shadow-stick method, or equal-length shadow method.

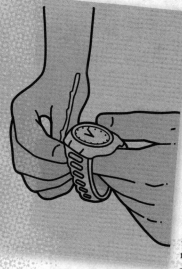

Watch Method

Hold your watch level. Place a short, straight twig upright against the edge of the watch at the point of the hour hand. (If you're wearing a digital watch, note the hour, imagine where an hour hand would be pointing if the watch had one, and place the twig accordingly.) Turn the watch until the shadow of the twig falls along the hour hand's position—that is, until the hour hand points toward the sun.

Notice the angle formed between the numeral 12 (or the top of a digital watch) and the shadow lying on the real or imaginary hour hand. A line from the center of the watch that divides that angle in half will point south. (Note: This method requires standard time. If your watch is on daylight-savings time, turn it back one hour.)

Shadow-Stick Method

Push a short, straight stick into the ground. Angle it toward the sun so that the stick makes no shadow. Then wait until it casts a shadow at least 6 inches long. The shadow will be pointing east from the stick. A line at right angles across the shadow will be north–south.

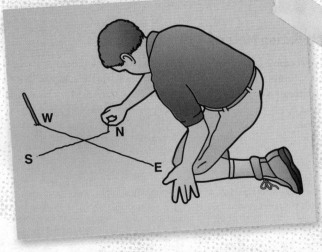

FINDING DIRECTIONS USING THE MOON

The moon comes up in the east and goes down in the west, as does the sun. The shadow-stick method for use with the sun will work just as well on nights when the moon is bright enough to cause shadows to form.

Equal-Length Shadow Method

In the morning, push a straight 3-foot-long stick upright into the ground. Tie a string around the base of the stick with a bowline. Next, extend the string to the end of the stick's shadow. Tie a peg to the string at that point and use it to scratch a circle on the ground around the stick. Push the peg into the ground where the tip of the stick's shadow touches the circle.

In the afternoon, place another peg where the tip of the shadow again touches the circle. A straight line drawn between the pegs is a west–east line, with west at the morning peg. A line drawn at right angles across the west–east line will be north–south.

"When you are acting as scout to find the way for a party you should move ahead of them and fix your whole attention on what you are doing, because you have to go by the very smallest signs, and if you get talking and thinking of other things you are very apt to miss them."

—Robert Baden-Powell, *Scouting for Boys*, 1917

COMPASS GAME

Try the following challenge to refresh your memory and test your skill with using a compass and making measurements.

Step 1—Push a stick into the ground beside your foot. Turn the housing on your compass to any bearing (15 degrees, for example). Orient the compass and sight along the direction-of-travel arrow to a landmark. Walk 50 steps toward it.

Step 2—Add 120 degrees to your first bearing, and set your compass again (in this example, 120 degrees plus 15 degrees equals 135 degrees). Take a second bearing and walk 50 steps on the new heading.

Step 3—Finally, add 120 degrees to the second compass setting (120 degrees plus 135 degrees equals 255 degrees) and adjust the compass housing. Take a final bearing and walk 50 steps.

If your bearings have been accurate and your steps all the same length, you should be standing near the stick where you started.

ORIENTEERING COURSES

Some troops set up orienteering courses for patrols to practice and enjoy map and compass skills. Many Scouts also sharpen their orienteering abilities in open country, using their maps, compasses, and GPS receivers to reach destinations chosen by troop leaders.

Whether going cross-country or traveling in an area you know well, an orienteering course offers several challenges:

▶ You will be given a map marked with five or six destinations called *control points.* Orient the map and determine the direction of the first control point, then follow the features and landmarks on the map to make your way toward it.

▶ Upon reaching the control point, you will find a marker (a brightly colored card or a flag hanging from a branch, for example) or a landmark/waypoint (a road intersection, a stream, a hilltop, etc.).

▶ After making a note of the landmark or punching your control card to prove you were there, orient your map again and set out for the next destination on the course.

Orienteering can be an exciting sport for everyone in a patrol or troop. Teams of Scouts work together to complete the course quickly and accurately, combining their map and compass abilities with route finding, observation, and physical fitness.

For more information on orienteering, including requirements for the Orienteering merit badge, visit the *Handbook* Web site: *www.bsahandbook.org.*

"The quickest and most interesting way to learn to read and use a map is by taking a map with you on a hike. Starting from a definite and readily identified point, such as a cross roads or a bridge, follow closely on the map the route traveled."

—*Handbook for Boys*, 1927

Using Your Orienteering Skills on Scout Adventures

In addition to the fun you can have, knowing how to use a map and compass will make your outdoor adventures better. An orienteering hike might use a topographic map like the one shown above.

Let's say you want to hike from Log Chapel to the road intersection at 179. Study the map and figure out your route before you begin hiking. Here are three possibilities.

1.   Stay on quiet roads to Meadow Knoll Cemetery, and then turn north toward intersection 179. Avoid most of the roads by walking south of the chapel until you reach a stream, then turn left and follow the stream bank in an easterly direction. From the point where it spills into a second stream, you may be able to see your destination. If not, place your compass on your map, determine the correct bearing to reach intersection 179, then let the compass lead you the rest of the way.

2. Another route can take you over the tops of the hills in the center of the map. To stay on course, you may need to take compass bearings from your starting point to the top of the first hill and then from one summit to the next.

3. For a *beeline hike*, use the map and compass to figure out the bearing for a straight line from Log Chapel to intersection 179. Follow that bearing as carefully as you can and see how close you come to your goal.

Want to figure out how far you will hike? Try this method. Put one end of a piece of string on the map at your starting point—in this case, the Log Chapel. Lay out the string so that it rests on top of your entire route. Pinch the string where it touches your destination (intersection 179) and pick it up. Stretch the string on the bar scale at the bottom of the map and measure it up to the point where you are pinching it. That's the length of your hike.

NAVIGATING YOUR WAY FORWARD

Teaching navigation skills to others is a fine way to share the lore of Scouting and to improve your own mastery of maps, compasses, and GPS receivers. Earning the Orienteering merit badge is another great way to improve your navigation skills.

You'll also find that the tools of navigation come in handy whenever you are leading your patrol and troop during outdoor adventures. If you know how to navigate, wilderness travel becomes possible. That's also true of sailing adventures, rafting trips, long-distance bicycling, and much more. Understanding ways to use a GPS receiver opens the fun and satisfaction of geocaching.

Scouting's navigation skills can lead to some of the BSA's greatest adventures. Being able to use a map is a life skill that will be important wherever you go. With a compass and perhaps a GPS receiver, too, you can be ready to find your way almost anywhere on the globe.

CHAPTER 12
Tools

TOOLS

By now you're having a great time hiking and camping with your patrol and learning to take care of yourself in the outdoors. Scouting is helping you develop skills for solving problems when your only tools are what you can carry in your pockets and your pack. That's almost always enough, especially if you have been tying knots, using a pocketknife, cooking over a backpacking stove, and practicing with the other outdoor tools so that you are ready to use them anywhere and in any weather.

The tools of Scouting are a link to Boy Scouts of the past. Use ropes and lashings to build a bridge or a signal tower, and you'll be practicing skills that Scouts have used for more

IN THIS CHAPTER

▶ Whipping and fusing rope ends

▶ Tying knots

▶ Lashings

▶ Using and caring for pocketknives, saws, and axes

▶ Building, lighting, and managing campfires

▶ Camp stoves

than a hundred years. Sharpen your pocketknife and an ax, and your woods tools will always be ready. Learn how Scouts of old could light a campfire without using matches and how today's Scouts use camping stoves. You'll be preparing yourself for anything you might face during days and nights in the backcountry, and you'll be ready at home and in your community during storms and other emergencies.

Knowing how to use tools well—and when not to use them—are marks of a good Scout. Skill with tools will help you and your patrol accomplish all you set out to do. Ethical decision making is part of it, too. Deciding when and where to build a campfire or a pioneering project, for example, are important choices to make, both for you and for the environment.

Learning about knots, lashings, woods tools, stoves, and campfires is time well spent. You never know when they will come in handy, but when the time is right, you'll be glad that you have the right tools with you and the knowledge to use them.

For more on making rope, the types of rope, and uses for rope, see the *Handbook* Web site, *www.bsahandbook.org.*

HOW TO WHIP OR FUSE THE ENDS OF A ROPE

Handling rope and tying knots is a good place to begin exploring the uses of tools for the outdoors. You've already tied the square knot as a step in joining the Boy Scouts of America. Learn half a dozen more knots, and you'll know the right way to tie rope and cord for just about any need.

Rope has been made for centuries by twisting together the stringy fibers of plants such as sisal, manila, and hemp. Many ropes are still made this way. More recent rope-making techniques involve winding and weaving together strands of nylon, plastic, or other modern materials. The twists or weaves at the ends of a rope can sometimes loosen and begin coming apart. For a quick fix, you can wrap the ends with duct tape. However, the permanent way to protect ropes from unraveling is by *whipping* or *fusing*.

Whipping

To whip the end of a rope, use your pocketknife to cut away any of the rope that has already unraveled. Next, form a loop in a 2-foot-long piece of strong string and lay the loop along one end of the rope. Tightly wrap, or *whip*, the string around the rope, working your way toward the loop formed in the string. When the whipping is at least as wide as the rope is thick, tuck the end of the string through the loop, then pull hard on the free ends to tighten the string and secure the wrapping. Trim away the extra string, then whip the rope's other end.

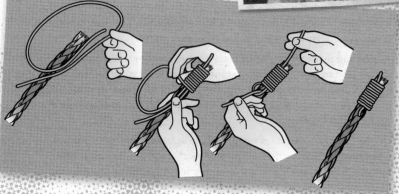

 To see a video of fusing and whipping rope, visit the *Handbook* Web site, www.bsahandbook.org.

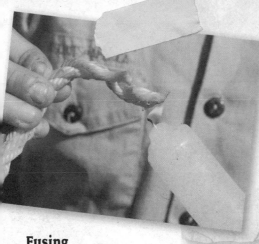

Do not try to fuse ropes made of manila, sisal, hemp, or other natural fibers. They will burn rather than melt.

Fusing

Fusing is a technique that you can use with rope and cord made of plastic or nylon. This method uses heat to melt (fuse) the fibers, forming a permanent bond that will prevent unraveling. Start by cutting the frayed part of the rope. Then, working in a well-ventilated area, hold the rope end a few inches above a lighted match or candle to fuse the strands together. Do not touch a newly fused rope end until it has cooled—melted rope will be hot and sticky. Remember to fuse both ends of the rope.

Coiling a Rope or Cord

Neatly coiling cords and ropes makes them easy to carry and store. It also keeps them from tangling when they are not in use. To coil a cord or rope, hold an end with one hand, and use your other hand to form neat coils in the rope or cord. Wrap the last few feet of the other end of the line around all the coils. Pass a bend of the line through the center of the coils and run the end of the line through the bend. Pull the end to tighten the bend around the coils.

"To tie a knot seems to be a simple thing, and yet there are right ways and wrong ways of doing it, and Scouts ought to know the right way."

—Robert Baden-Powell, *Scouting for Boys*, 1915

KNOTS

Knots have thousands of uses. On camping trips, they'll hold gear on your pack, secure tents and dining flies, and prevent canoes and boats from drifting away. If an accident occurs, knots can be used to keep bandages in place or to aid in rescue attempts on the water or in the mountains.

There are dozens of useful knots. By mastering six basic Scouting knots, you'll be ready for just about any situation that calls for tying ropes together, forming loops, and securing ropes to objects. Learning even more knots will add to your problem-solving abilities.

After you have learned to tie a knot, practice it often. Carry a piece of string in your pocket. When you have a few minutes to spare, pull it out and tie all the knots you know. Practice them enough that you can tie them quickly—even with your eyes closed. When you can do that, you will own these knots and be ready to use them whenever they are needed.

Three tests of a good knot:

It should be easy to tie.

It should stay tied.

It should be easy to untie.

 Video instructions for tying various knots are available online. Start at the *Handbook* Web site, *www.bsahandbook.org*.

The Language of Knots

A little terminology can help you learn how to tie knots and understand their advantages.

Running end—The end of the rope that is used to tie a knot. This end is also called the working end.

Standing part—All of a rope that is not the running end.

Overhand loop—Formed when a loop is made so that the running end of the rope is on top of the standing part.

Overhand loop

Underhand loop—Formed when the running end of the rope is placed under the standing part of the rope.

Underhand loop

Bight—Formed by doubling back a length of the rope against itself to form a U. The running end of the rope does not cross the standing part. (If that happens, the shape it forms is a loop, not a bight.)

Bight

Turn—To take a turn, wrap the rope once around a spar or a stake. The friction created by the turn can help you control a line that has tension on it, especially if you are letting out line or taking it in.

Turn

Roundturn—Make a roundturn by wrapping the rope once around a spar or stake and then halfway around again so that the running end of the rope is going back toward the standing part. A roundturn creates additional friction for controlling a line under strain.

Hitch—A knot that secures a rope to a spar or other stationary object.

Roundturn

Dress a knot—To adjust a new knot so that everything is in its place. Dressing a knot ensures that the knot will perform as expected.

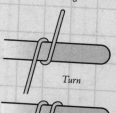

Two Half Hitches

A *hitch* is a knot that ties a rope to something. Friction caused by the wraps of the rope holds the hitch in place.

Two *half hitches* (also called a *double half hitch*) form a loop that can be adjusted to make it smaller or larger.

Step 1—Pass the end of the rope around the post.

Step 2—Bring the end over and under the body of the rope (known as the *standing part*), then back through the loop that has formed. This makes a half hitch.

Step 3—Take the end around the standing part a second time and tie another half hitch.

Step 4—Pull it snug.

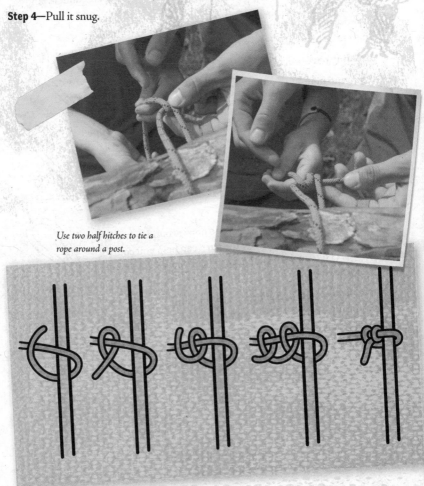

Use two half hitches to tie a rope around a post.

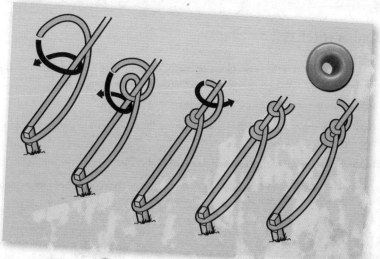

Taut-Line Hitch

The taut-line hitch is used to make a line tight, or taut. It's the knot to use for staking out the guy lines of your tent or dining fly.

Step 1—Pass the line around a tent stake.

Step 2—Bring the end under and over the standing part of the line to form a loop, then twice through the loop.

Step 3—Again bring the rope end under, over, and through a loop but this time farther up the standing part.

Step 4—Work any slack out of the knot.

Step 5—Slide the hitch to tighten or loosen the line.

Timber Hitch

The timber hitch is the perfect knot to use for dragging a log across the ground. It is also the knot that starts a diagonal lashing. Here's how to tie a timber hitch:

Step 1—Pass the end of the rope around a log.

Step 2—Loop the end around the standing part of the rope, then twist the end around itself three or more times.

Step 3—Pull slack out of the rope to tighten the timber hitch against the log.

The hitch will stay secure as long as you are pulling on the rope. When you are done using the rope, the timber hitch is easy to loosen and remove from the log.

Clove Hitch

Clove comes from the word *cleave*, meaning "to hold fast." The clove hitch can be used to start most lashings:

Step 1—Bring the rope end over and under a pole.

Step 2—Take the end around a second time, crossing over the first wrap to form the shape of an X.

Step 3—Bring the rope end around a third time and tuck it under the X.

Step 4—Pull the end of the rope to tighten the hitch.

Another way of tying a clove hitch makes it easy to lay the knot over the end of a pole. This method is especially useful for attaching a line to a bag you will hang from a tree to protect your food from bears or other animals.

Step 1—Make a loop near the end of the rope.

Step 2—Form an identical loop next to the first and a little farther away from the rope end.

Step 3—Without turning over either loop, lay the first loop on top of the second.

Step 4—Place the pair of loops over the end of a pole or over the neck of a bear bag. Tighten the clove hitch.

Bowline

The bowline forms a loop that will not slip. That's just what you want for tying a rope around your waist or around someone requiring rescue. A bowline also works well for securing guy lines through the grommets on a tent or dining fly.

Learn to tie the bowline around yourself, around a post, and in the free end of a rope. With practice, you can even tie it with one hand.

Step 1—Make a small overhand loop in the standing part of a rope.

Step 2—Bring the rope end up through the loop, around behind the standing part, and back down into the loop.

Step 3—Tighten the bowline by pulling the standing part of the rope away from the loop.

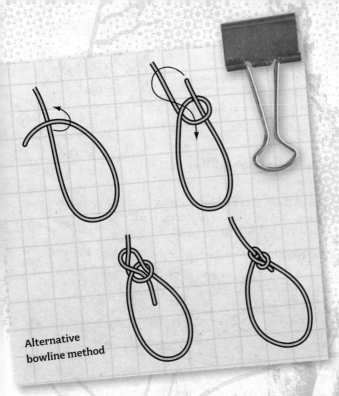

Alternative
bowline method

Here's a faster way to tie the bowline. Try both methods and see which is easier for you.

Step 1—Hold the rope end in your right hand and the standing part in your left. Lay a few inches of the end across the standing part.

Step 2—With the fingers of your right hand, grasp the point where the rope crosses.

Step 3—With your left hand, lift the standing part up and around the rope end, forming a small loop with the rope end inside of it.

Step 4—Pass the rope end behind the standing part and bring the end down through the small loop. Tighten the knot.

Notice the collar-shaped bend of rope in the bowline. To untie the knot, push the collar away from the loop as if you were opening the top on a soda can. That will break the knot so that you can loosen it.

Sheet Bend

The sheet bend is a very good knot for tying together two ropes of the same or different diameters. It is a close relative of the bowline and can be untied in the same way.

Step 1—Put a bend in the end of the thicker rope and hold it with one hand.

Step 2—Pass the end of the other rope through the bend. Then take that end around behind the bend.

Step 3—Bring the end across the front of the bend, and tuck it under its own standing part. (The end does not go into the bend, only under the portion of the rope in front of the bend.)

Step 4—Tighten the knot by pulling the standing part of the smaller line.

A *loop* is formed in a rope when the rope crosses itself.

A *bend* makes a similar shape in a rope, but the rope does not cross itself—it simply bends.

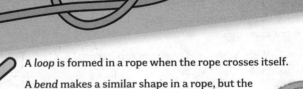

How to Tie a Necktie

Being prepared is about more than learning skills for the outdoors. While it isn't used much in camp, a knot for tying a necktie will come in handy through the years. Here's one way to do it:

Step 1—Put the tie around your neck with the wide end to your right. This end should hang about 12 inches lower than the other end.

Step 2—Lay the wide end across the narrow one and wrap it around the back.

Step 3—Go across the front of the narrow end a second time.

Step 4—Bring the wide end up and under the narrow end next to your neck.

Step 5—Guide the wide end forward and down through the loop in front of your neck.

Step 6—Adjust the shape of the tie as you slide the knot comfortably against your collar.

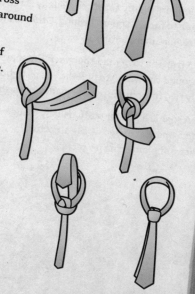

LASHINGS

Bind together two or three poles with a rope and you've got a *lashing*. Add more poles with additional lashings, and you can build pioneering projects that are fun to plan, interesting to put together, and a good way to practice Scouting skills.

Scouts have used lashings to build signal towers, shelters, ladders, and rafts. Lashings were part of canoe building, too. In addition, Scouts used them when building *camp gadgets*—towel racks, tripods to hold water basins, and other smaller pioneering projects that made camp life a little more comfortable.

On today's campouts and backpacking trips, Scouts don't often need to build pioneering projects. But these structures still have their uses. A lashed-together table, for example, will lift food preparation off the ground. At a council Scout camp, your patrol might be able to practice team leadership and problem solving by lashing together a full-sized tower, a bridge, or another classic Scout structure.

The Language of Lashings

The following terms will help you understand how to make lashings.

Wrap—A wrap is a turn made around the two spars to hold the spars tightly together. Usually three wraps are made to form a square lashing. Other lashings might require more wraps.

Frap—A frap is a turn made between the spars. It goes around the wraps to pull the wraps tighter. Usually two frapping turns are made on a lashing.

Spar—A spar is a pole or staff, usually made of wood. Spars are used as the structural members of pioneering projects.

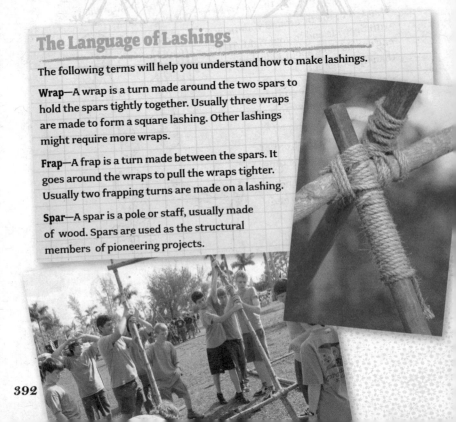

When to Use Lashings

Know how to make good lashings and you'll have a powerful skill that is fun to practice and important to know whenever you need to build a camp structure.

Deciding where and how to construct pioneering projects is an opportunity for you to use ethical decision making. The poles and staves you use should come from a troop or council camp's supply of building materials. If you gather natural materials, be sure you do so in a way that does no harm to the environment. Pioneering projects must not be located in fragile environments where many footsteps in a small area could trample plants and compress soil, making it difficult for the land to recover.

Use the following guidelines to help you decide when you should and should not use lashings.

- Follow Leave No Trace principles to protect the land.

- Use only materials approved for the project.

- Take everything apart when you are done, and leave no evidence that you were there.

- Store poles and staves so that they can be used for future pioneering projects. Coil ropes and cords and store them.

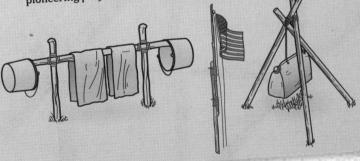

More pioneering projects can be found on the *Handbook* Web site, *www.bsahandbook.org.*

Scale Models of Pioneering Projects

If you don't have the right materials or a good place to construct full-size pioneering projects, practice by building small-scale models. For example, you might make a signal tower that is only 2 feet high or a bridge with a span of just 12 inches. Use straight sticks and strong string to lash together scale models of any rustic structure. Cut sticks to the right length with your pocketknife.

Make your models as real as you can, using the correct scale, knots, and lashings. When you have a chance to build the real thing, you will already know how all the pieces should fit together.

You can use models of pioneering structures to teach other Scouts about knots and lashings. Models also are perfect for school projects, Scout Week window displays, and just for the fun of turning sticks and string into working structures that are correct in every detail.

You can increase your structure's stability by including triangles in its design.

A-trestle

X-trestle

H-trestle

Square Lashing

Use a square lashing for binding together two poles that are at right angles, or square, with one another.

> Frapping adds strength to a lashing.

Step 1—Place the poles in position.

Step 2—Tie a clove hitch around the bottom pole near the crosspiece.

Step 3—Make three tight *wraps* around both poles. As you form the wraps, lay the rope on the *outside* of each previous turn around the top pole, and on the *inside* of each previous turn around the bottom pole.

Step 4—Wind two *fraps* around the wraps, pulling the rope very tight.

Step 5—Finish with a clove hitch around the top pole.

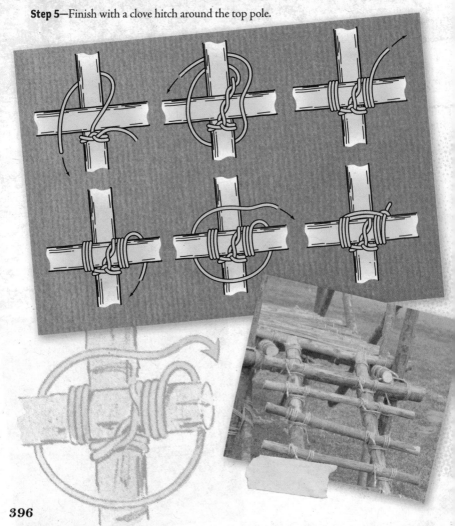

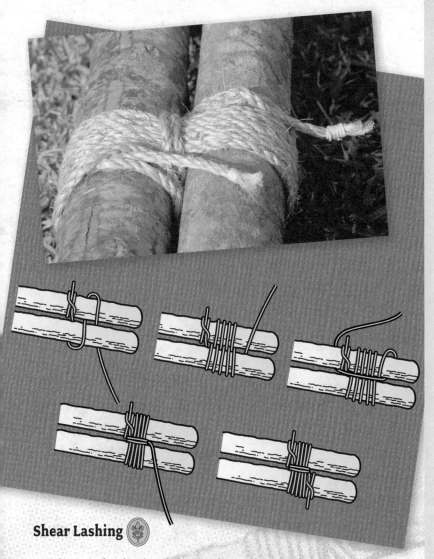

Shear Lashing

Poles secured with a shear lashing can be raised as an A-frame.

Step 1—Lay two poles side by side and tie a clove hitch to one of them.

Step 2—Make three very loose wraps around the poles, and then put two loose fraps between them.

Step 3—Finish with a clove hitch around the other pole.

Step 4—Spread the ends of the poles to form the shape you need. Redo the lashing if it is too tight or too loose.

397

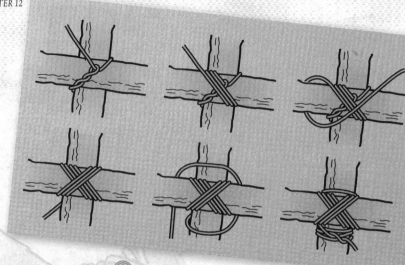

Diagonal Lashing

To bind poles at an angle other than a right angle, use a diagonal lashing.

Step 1—Tie a timber hitch around both poles and pull it snug.

Step 2—Make three tight wraps around the poles, laying the wraps neatly alongside the timber hitch.

Step 3—Make three more wraps across the first three.

Step 4—Cinch down the wraps with two fraps between the poles.

Step 5—Tie off the rope with a clove hitch.

Other Lashings

Learning a few additional lashings will allow you to build special structures or put the finishing touches on a table, tower, or other project.

In Scouting's early days, hiking staffs, or *staves*, were almost a part of the uniform. They could be used as poles in pioneering projects and to make stretchers and splints during first-aid emergencies.

Tripod Lashing

A close relative of the shear lashing, the tripod lashing is used for making a tripod or for joining together the first three poles of a tepee.

Step 1—Lay three poles alongside each other with the top of the center pole pointing in the direction opposite that of the outside poles.

Step 2—Tie a clove hitch around one outside pole.

Step 3—Loosely wrap the rope around the poles five or six times, laying the turns of rope neatly alongside one another.

Step 4—Make two very loose fraps on either side of the center pole.

Step 5—End with a clove hitch around an outside pole.

Step 6—Spread the legs of the tripod into position. If you have made the wraps or fraps too tight, you may need to start over.

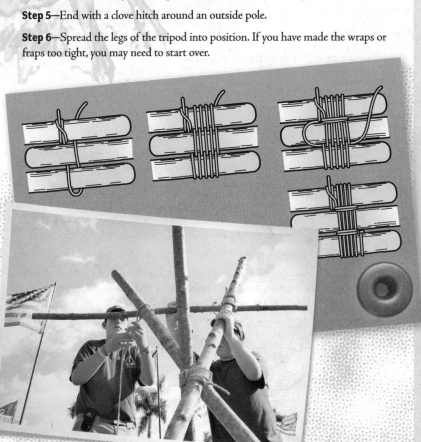

Round Lashing

Round lashings bind two poles side by side.

Step 1—Position the poles beside each other and tie them together with a clove hitch.

Step 2—Make seven or eight very tight, neat wraps around the poles. There are no fraps in a round lashing. The wraps must do all the work, so pull them as tight as you can.

Step 3—Finish the lashing with another clove hitch around both poles.

Step 4—Make a second round lashing farther along the poles to keep the poles from twisting out of line.

Floor Lashing

The floor lashing will tie down the top of a table, the deck of a raft, the floor of a signal tower, or the walkway of a bridge.

Step 1—Lay the poles side by side on top of the *stringers*— the logs or poles on which your platform will rest.

Step 2—Tie a clove hitch around one stringer.

Step 3—Bend the standing part of the rope over the first pole. Pull the bend of rope under the stringer and cast it over the second pole. You may need to lift the end of the pole in order to get the rope over it.

Step 4—Pull the rope tight, then bend it over the third pole. Continue until all the poles are bound to the stringer.

Step 5—Finish with a clove hitch, then repeat these steps to lash the other ends of the poles to the other stringer.

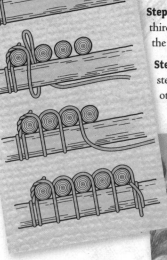

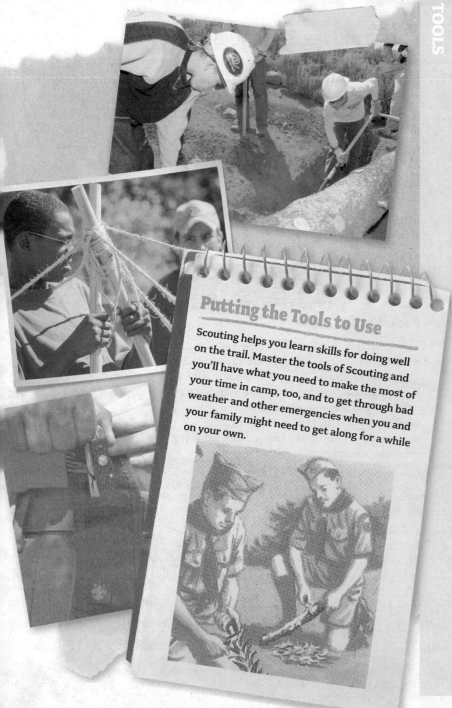

Putting the Tools to Use

Scouting helps you learn skills for doing well on the trail. Master the tools of Scouting and you'll have what you need to make the most of your time in camp, too, and to get through bad weather and other emergencies when you and your family might need to get along for a while on your own.

POCKETKNIVES, SAWS, AND AXES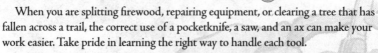

When you are splitting firewood, repairing equipment, or clearing a tree that has fallen across a trail, the correct use of a pocketknife, a saw, and an ax can make your work easier. Take pride in learning the right way to handle each tool.

Just as important as knowing how to use woods tools is knowing when *not* to use them. Carving or chopping into live trees may kill them. Hacking at dead trees and logs can leave ugly scars. Never cut any trees without guidance from a ranger, landowner, or your Scout leaders.

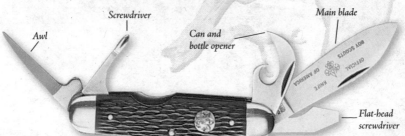

Awl

Screwdriver

Can and
bottle opener

Main blade

Flat-head
screwdriver

Pocketknife

A pocketknife truly is a multipurpose tool with hundreds of uses. It can cut a rope, open a can, whittle a tent stake, punch a hole in a belt, or slice a biscuit for breakfast at a campsite. It's also handy for tightening a screw on a pack frame or camp stove, and for making wood shavings to start a fire. A good general-use pocketknife has a can opener, a screw driver, and one or two blades for cutting.

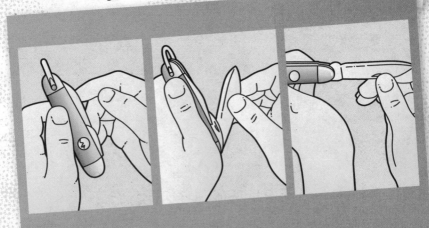

Safe Knife Use

▶ Always keep a knife's blades closed except when you are using them.

▶ Always cut away from yourself, never toward yourself. If the blade slips, you may be injured.

▶ Always close the blades before you pass a knife to someone else.

▶ Always keep your knife sharp. A sharp blade is easier to control than a dull one.

▶ Always obey all regulations about carrying knives in public places, including your school and on airplanes.

▶ Never carry a knife with the blade open.

▶ Never throw a knife.

▶ Never strike a knife with another tool.

▶ Never use the point of a cutting blade as a prying tool. The knife might bend or break.

The Boy Scouts of America does not encourage the use of large sheath knives. They can be heavy and awkward to carry and are unnecessary for most camp chores.

Taking Care of a Pocketknife

Most pocketknives today are made of metal that won't rust. However, dust and lint can collect inside the knife, and normal use will dull the cutting blades.

Cleaning—Open all the blades. Wrap a small bit of cloth around the end of a toothpick, moisten the cloth, and wipe the inside of the knife.

If you have used your pocketknife to cut food or to spread peanut butter and jam, get rid of bacteria by washing the knife in hot, soapy water along with the rest of your dishes.

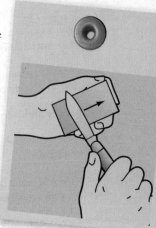

Sharpening—Sharpen your knife with a *whetstone*. Some experts put water on the stone while they are sharpening. Some use light oil, and others want the stone to be dry. The choice depends upon the kind of stone and the traditions of the sharpener.

Step 1—Hold the knife blade against the stone at an angle of about 30 degrees. That is, place the back of the blade so that it is tilted off the stone about one-third of the way to vertical.

Step 2—Push the blade along the stone as though you were slicing a layer off the top of the stone, or move the blade against the stone in a circular motion.

Step 3—Sharpen the other side of the blade in the same manner.

Check sharpness by wiping the knife with a clean cloth and examining the edge of the blade in the sun or under a bright light. A dull cutting edge reflects light and looks shiny. A sharp edge is so thin that it has no shine at all.

Camp Saw

Use a camp saw for most outdoor wood cutting. The blades of *folding saws* close into their handles, much like the blades of pocketknives. A *bow saw* has a curved metal frame that holds a blade in place.

When sawing firewood, brace the piece of wood against a chopping block, sawhorse, or other solid support. Use long, smooth strokes and let the weight of the saw pull the blade into the wood.

Clearing branches and brush from a hiking trail is a conservation service project you might do with your patrol or troop. To saw a branch from a tree, make an *undercut* first, then saw from the top down. The undercut prevents the falling branch from stripping bark off the trunk. A clean cut close to the trunk won't leave an unsightly "hat rack" that might snag the clothing or packs of travelers on the trail. Cut saplings level with the ground so that there are no stumps to trip over.

Check the *Handbook* Web site for video instructions for properly sharpening a knife on a whetstone.

Taking Care of Saws

Treat every saw with the same respect you give your pocketknife. Close folding saws when they aren't in use, and store them in a tent or under the dining fly. Protect the blade of a bow saw with a sheath made from a piece of old garden hose cut to the length of the blade. Slit one side of the hose, fit it over the blade, and hold it in place with duct tape or cord.

The teeth on saw blades are *set*—bent so that they will cut two thin grooves in the wood and then rake out the shavings in between. Even with the best care, the teeth will slowly lose their set and their ability to cut easily through the wood. Saw blades should be replaced when they become dull. Take along a spare blade when you have a lot of cutting to do.

Safe Saw Use

▶ Do sheath a saw when it is not in use.

▶ Do carry a saw with the blade turned away from your body.

▶ Do replace dull blades. Sharp saws are easier to use and to control.

▶ Do use care when passing a saw to another person.

▶ Do wear gloves and protective eyewear.

▶ Don't cut any trees or branches—alive or dead—without permission.

▶ Don't allow a saw blade to cut into the ground. Soil and rocks will quickly dull the teeth.

▶ Don't leave a saw lying around camp.

Ax

The ax has a long and colorful history in America's forests. Pioneers used axes to cut trails and roads through the wilderness. Settlers chopped down trees to make way for gardens and fields. With their axes, people hewed boards and beams for frontier buildings.

Early Scouts often carried hatchets to camp for preparing firewood, sharpening wooden tent stakes, and shaping poles for signal towers, bridges, and other pioneering projects.

Today, Scouts use hand axes or hatchets to split firewood, clear fallen trees from backcountry trails, and complete conservation projects on pathways and in campgrounds. As with all woods tools, handling an ax safely requires good judgment and practice.

Safe Ax Use

Because of its size and the way in which it is used, an ax can be more dangerous than other woods tools. Remove the sheath *only* when you are prepared to use an ax correctly, and then follow this checklist:

- ☐ Safe tool
- ☐ Safe shoes, eyewear, gloves
- ☐ Safe working area
- ☐ Safe technique
- ☐ Safe carrying
- ☐ Safe handling
- ☐ Safe storage

Safe Tool—An ax must be in good condition. If the head is loose, the blade dull, or the handle damaged, don't use it. Bring an unsafe tool to the attention of your Scout leaders and either help repair it or retire it from duty.

Safe Shoes, Eyewear, Gloves—Always wear sturdy boots when you are chopping with an ax. Your boots may not stop a blade from hitting your foot, but they can limit the extent of an injury.

Safe Working Area—You must have plenty of room to swing an ax. Check your clearance by holding your ax by the head and slowly swinging the handle at arm's length all around you. Remove any brush or branches that the handle touches. Be certain other people stay at least 10 feet away while you are cutting.

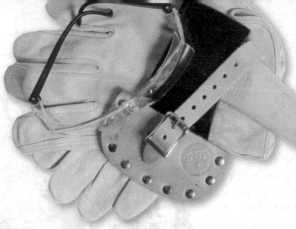

In a long-term camp where you will be using lots of firewood, rope off an ax yard large enough to provide the space you need to work. Enter the yard only to chop and saw wood. Clean up chips, bark, and other cutting debris when you are done.

Safe Technique—Before doing any cutting, get your feet set and your body balanced. Stay relaxed. Pay attention to the work in front of you, and be aware of what is going on around you, too.

Chopping branches off a log is called *limbing*. Stand on the side of the log opposite a branch. Chop close to the base of the branch, driving the ax into the underside of the limb. Keep the log between yourself and your cuts. If your aim is off or the ax skips on a branch, the blade will hit the log rather than your leg.

Limbing

Cutting through a log is known as *bucking*. Begin by holding the ax with one hand near the head and the other close to the knob of the handle. Lift the head above your shoulder, then slide your hands together and swing the bit into the log. Let the falling weight of the ax head do most of the work.

Slide your hand back down the handle to the head, lift the ax, and swing it again. Aim your blows so that you cut a V-shaped notch twice as wide at the top as the log is thick.

Bucking

Splitting firewood is best done on a *chopping block*, a piece of a log that provides a flat, stable surface. A poor swing of the ax will send the bit into the block rather than toward your feet.

To split a large chunk of wood, stand it upright on the chopping block and drive the ax into the end of it. If the wood doesn't split, remove the ax before swinging it again. Don't swing an ax with a piece of wood stuck on the bit. When the ax does go through the wood, the bit should hit the chopping block rather than the ground.

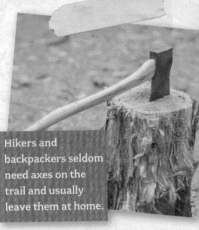

Hikers and backpackers seldom need axes on the trail and usually leave them at home.

Split a small stick with the *contact method* by placing the ax bit against the stick. Lift the stick and ax together and bring them down against the chopping block, forcing the bit into the wood. Twist the ax to break apart the pieces.

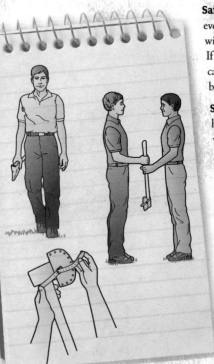

Safe Carrying—Place a sheath over an ax blade whenever it is not being used. Carry your ax at your side with one hand, the blade turned out from your body. If you stumble, toss the ax away as you fall. Never carry an ax on your shoulder where the ax bit could be dangerously close to your neck and head.

Safe Handling—Give an ax to another person by holding the handle with the ax head down. Pass it with the bit turned away from both of you. When the other person has a grip on the handle, he or she should say, "Thank you." That's your signal to release your hold.

Safe Storage—Sheath your ax and store it under a dining fly or in a tent.

Sharpening an Ax

Keep your ax sharp with a *mill bastard file* that is 8 or 10 inches long. The lines across the face of a file are its *teeth*. They angle away from the point, or *tang*. A sharp file will be flat gray, not shiny. A silvery shine means that a file has broken teeth and that it won't work very well.

Wear leather gloves to protect your hands as you sharpen an ax with a file. Make a *knuckle guard* by drilling a small hole in a 3-inch square of leather, plywood, or an old inner tube. Slip the hole over the tang of the file and hold the guard in place with a *file handle*. You can buy a handle at a hardware store or make one from a piece of wood or a dry corncob.

Brace the ax head on the ground between two wooden pegs or tent stakes and a log about 6 inches in diameter. Another Scout can help hold the ax steady. Place the file on the edge of the blade and push it into the bit. Use enough pressure so that you feel the file cutting the ax metal.

Lift the file as you draw it back for another stroke. A file sharpens only when you push it away from the tang. Dragging the file across the blade in the wrong direction can break the teeth and ruin the file.

Sharpen with firm, even strokes. After you have filed one side of the bit, turn the ax over and do the other side. Use about the same number of strokes. Remember that a dull edge reflects light and will look shiny. Keep filing until the sharpened edge seems to disappear.

The Totin' Chip

The Totin' Chip has long been carried by Scouts who have promised to use knives, saws, and axes safely and in the right situations. The card reminds them of their responsibilities whenever they are using woods tools. A Scout's Totin' Rights can be taken from him if he fails in his responsibility.

To earn the Totin' Chip, do the following:

1. Read and understand woods tools use and safety rules from the Boy Scout Handbook.
2. Demonstrate proper handling, care, and use of the pocketknife, ax, and saw.
3. Use knives, axes, and saws as tools, not playthings.
4. Respect all safety rules to protect others.
5. Respect property. Cut living and dead trees only with permission and with good reason.
6. Subscribe to the Outdoor Code.

TOTIN' CHIP

This is to certify that the bearer _____ has read the woods tools use and safety rules from the "Second Class Scout" chapter of the Boy Scout Handbook. He knows that the ownership or use of woods tools means responsibility, and he accepts it. In consideration of the above, he is hereby granted "Totin' Rights."

Scout leader _____

BOY SCOUTS OF AMERICA

Camp Shovel

A small camp shovel or garden trowel is handy for removing and saving earth from a latrine hole. Use a metal shovel to move hot coals while cooking with a Dutch oven or aluminum foil. On winter campouts, a snow scoop or avalanche shovel is ideal for building snow shelters.

Do not dig ditches around tents. Ditches are unnecessary, and they might start erosion.

CAMPFIRES

Campfires have their place, too. A fire can warm you, cook your food, and dry your clothes. Bright flames can lift your spirits

Many Scouts use lightweight stoves on all their camping trips. Stoves are clean, quick to heat water and food, and easy to light in any weather. They leave no marks on the land. A stove in your pack can make it simpler for you to camp without leaving a trace. More information on using camp stoves can be found later in this chapter.

on a rainy morning. At night, glowing embers will stir your imagination.

A good Scout knows how to build a fire, especially in an emergency. He also knows there are often reasons why he should not light a fire. Bonfires are not appropriate.

▶ Campfires can sterilize soil. Vegetation might have a hard time growing again where a fire has been.

▶ Fires burn dead branches, bark, and other organic matter that would have provided shelter and food for animals and plants.

▶ Fire sites can char the ground, blacken rocks, and spoil the appearance of the land, especially in heavily used campgrounds.

▶ Campfires must be closely watched to prevent them from spreading into surrounding grasses, brush, and trees.

Find out ahead of time if the area where you will be camping permits the use of fires. Even where fires are allowed, a lightweight stove is probably a better choice.

How to Build a Campfire

Earlier editions of the *Boy Scout Handbook* celebrated Scouts' ability to kindle a fire. You can use the same methods today to build campfires that are safe, responsible, and kind to the land.

Bare-Ground Fire Site

Protect bare ground from the heat of a fire by making a *bare-ground fire site*. Gather enough mineral soil (sandy earth or other soil without a lot of plant matter in it) to make a raised pad about 2 feet square and 3 inches thick. Kindle your fire on top of the pad. After you have extinguished the blaze and disposed of any unburned wood, take apart and scatter the fire site to erase any sign that you were there. This means crushing the remaining ashes, mixing them with the mineral soil, and returning the soil to the sites from which you borrowed it.

Make a Safe Fire Site—A safe fire site is one on which nothing will burn except the fuel you feed the flames. It's a spot from which fire cannot spread. Many camping areas have metal fire rings, grills, or stone fireplaces. Use these existing fire sites whenever you can.

Otherwise, select a spot on gravel, sand, or bare earth that is well away from trees, brush, and dry grasses. Look overhead and avoid choosing a spot near low-hanging branches that sparks might ignite. Choose a site that is far enough away from rocks and boulders so that they won't be blackened by smoke. Also check that you are not building your fire near tree roots that could be harmed by heat.

Rake away pine needles, leaves, twigs, and anything else that might burn. Save the ground cover so that you can put it back when you are done with your fire. Place a pot or bucket of water close by to put out the flames if they begin to spread.

Gather Tinder, Kindling, and Fuel Wood—Patience is the key to building a fire. You will also need *tinder, kindling,* and *fuel wood.*

> Dead twigs and small branches that are still on a tree might be tempting, but Leave No Trace principles discourage breaking branches off of trees. Gather kindling this way only in emergencies or where it will not harm the environment.

Tinder—Tinder catches fire easily and burns fast. Dry pine needles, grasses, shredded bark, and the fluff from seedpods all make good tinder. Shavings cut with a pocketknife from a dry stick of wood also work well as tinder. Gather enough tinder to fill your hat once.

Kindling—Dead twigs no thicker than a pencil are called kindling. Find enough kindling to fill your hat twice.

Fuel—Fuel wood can be as thin as your finger or as thick as your wrist. Use sticks that you find on the ground. Gather them from a wide area rather than removing all the downed wood from one spot.

> Fuzz sticks can help get a fire going. Cut shavings into each stick, but leave the shavings attached. Prop the fuzz sticks upright in among the kindling.

Lay the Fire—Heat rises. Keep this in mind as you arrange tinder, kindling, and fuel so that the heat of a single match can grow into the flames of a campfire. A *tepee fire* is a good all-around method.

Tepee fire lay

Step 1—Place a big, loose handful of tinder in the middle of your fire site.

Step 2—Arrange plenty of small kindling over the tinder.

Step 3—Place small and medium-sized sticks of fuel wood around the kindling as if they were the poles of a tepee. Leave an opening in the tepee on the side against which the wind is blowing so that air can reach the middle of the fire.

Wet Weather Fire Tips

▶ Before the rains begin, gather tinder, kindling, and fuel wood and store it all under your dining fly.

▶ Keep a supply of dry tinder in a plastic bag.

▶ Split wet sticks and logs with an ax. The wood inside should be dry.

▶ Protect matches from dampness by carrying them in a plastic aspirin bottle with a tight lid.

▶ Store a butane lighter away from heat and moisture, and it will give you a flame in even the wettest weather.

Fireplaces—A fireplace holds cook pots above the flames and allows air to reach the fire.

Three-Point Fireplace—For a single pot or pan, push three metal tent stakes into the embers.

Log Fireplace—Place a log on each side of the fire. The logs should be arranged close enough to hold your pots. The fire will slowly burn through the logs, so keep an eye on your pots whenever you are cooking meals or heating water.

Try resting several old metal tent pole sections or pieces of iron reinforcing bar across the logs as a base on which to rest your pots. You also might use a grill or oven grate for this purpose.

Fire Lighting Methods—When the fire lay is complete and you have a good supply of kindling and fuel wood on hand, ease a flame underneath the tinder. The flame can come from a match or lighter. You might even use a magnifying glass, flint and steel, or a fire-by-friction set.

Practice different methods of lighting a fire during campouts where fires are permitted and appropriate so that you become confident with your fire-building skills. In an emergency, you'll know just what to do.

Tinder for Lighting Fires Without Matches

Very fine tinder is needed for lighting fires with the magnifying lens, flint-and-steel, or fire-by-friction methods. Try shredding the dry inner bark of a cottonwood, elm, or cedar tree. In an emergency, gather the fluff from a mouse nest or chipmunk burrow, if you can find one. You also might use a few squares of toilet paper or tear several pages from a book.

An ideal spark-catcher is *char*—a piece of cloth that has been charred by lighting it on fire and then snuffing out the flame. Dry, crumbling wood from a standing dead tree or a stump also can be burned a little and then snuffed out to make char. Keep char dry in a plastic bag until you need it.

Instructions for lighting a fire with matches, lighters, a magnifying lens, flint and steel, and friction can be found on the *Handbook* Web site, www.bsahandbook.org.

Managing and Putting Out a Fire

Build each fire just large enough for your needs. This will minimize the amount of wood you will burn and can make it easier to erase signs of a fire once you are done.

Take responsibility for every campfire by keeping an eye on it at all times.

Extinguish every fire when you no longer need it or if you won't be around to watch it. Splash water on the embers, then stir the damp ashes with a stick and splash them again. Repeat this process until the fire is *cold out*—cold enough so that when you hold your hand just above the ashes, you do not feel any heat.

Sometimes you will build your fire in a permanent fire site. Clean such sites by picking out any bits of paper, foil, and unburned food. Pack them home with the rest of your trash. If you have made a new fire site, get rid of all evidence that it was ever there. Scatter any rocks, turning sides that have been blackened by soot toward the ground. Spread cold ashes over a wide area and toss away any unused firewood. Replace ground cover. When you're done, the site should look just as it did when you found it.

Camp Stoves

A camp stove gives you a fast, easy way to do your cooking. It produces heat just right for warming a cup of soup or cooking a big pot of pasta. A stove won't blacken rocks and cooking gear or scorch the soil. With a stove, you can camp where there is no firewood or where campfires are not allowed. Stoves work well in deserts, high mountains, and deep forests. They also are ideal for use in storms and on snow.

Many camping stoves burn white gas or kerosene. Store these fuels in special metal bottles with lids that screw on tightly. Choose bright red bottles or mark them with colorful tape so there is no chance of mistaking them for water bottles.

Gas stove

Butane and propane stoves burn gas from small pressurized cans called *cartridges*. Carry cartridges and fuel bottles in the outside pockets of your pack where gas fumes can't get near your food.

 For the pros and cons of different stoves and fuels see the *Handbook* Web site, *www.bsahandbook.org.*

Cartridge stove

Place your stove on a level surface free of leaves, sticks, or other burnable material. A patch of bare ground or a flat rock is all you need. During winter campouts, you can carry a piece of sturdy plywood about 6 inches square. Use it as a platform to hold your stove on top of the snow or to prevent the cold ground from chilling the stove.

Stoves operate in different ways, depending on what kind of fuel they burn. Read your stove's instructions carefully and follow them exactly. In addition, *always* be guided by these stove safety rules:

▶ Use camping stoves only where allowed and only with adult supervision.

▶ Never use a stove inside a tent or cabin. There is a danger of fire and of poisoning by odorless gas fumes.

▶ Before lighting the burner, tighten the stove's fuel cap or tightly screw on the fuel canister. Be sure that containers with extra fuel are stored safely away from the stove. Do not loosen the fuel cap or canister of a hot stove.

▶ Stoves sometimes flare up. Keep your head and hands to one side of a stove as you light and adjust it.

▶ Don't overload a stove with a heavy pot. Instead, set up a grill over the stove to bear the weight of the pot.

▶ Never leave a burning stove unattended.

▶ Allow hot stoves to cool before changing cartridges or filling fuel tanks. Refill stoves and store extra fuel far away from sources of open flames such as other stoves, candles, campfires, and lanterns.

Carry home all empty fuel containers. Don't put them in or near fires. If heated, they might explode.

Your Adventure Continues

"We felt that we had been somewhere! We had traveled through forests where no trail existed, we had traversed a great deal of nearly perpendicular scenery, we had seen wonderful sights, and we had come back safe and well."

—*Thirteen Years of Scout Adventure*, Stuart P. Walsh, 1923

YOUR ADVENTURE CONTINUES

By now, you know that Scouting is full of adventure. You discovered this when you joined your troop. It's been true during patrol activities and on campouts as the skills you've learned have opened doors to great experiences. Your ability to lead and to be of service to others has expanded as you've made your way along the trail to Eagle.

Beyond your troop's local activities and the weekend campouts you enjoy are plenty of bigger Scouting challenges waiting to be explored. Monthly campouts, BSA camporees, and a week at summer camp are just the beginning.

Winter Camp (1986),
by Joseph Csatari

IN THIS CHAPTER

▶ Monthly campouts

▶ Camporee camping

▶ Summer camp

▶ National high-adventure bases

▶ World and national Scout jamborees

▶ National Youth Leadership Training

▶ National Advanced Youth Leadership Experience

▶ The Order of the Arrow

▶ Opportunities for older Scouts

▶ Venturing

▶ Continuing the promise of Scouting

MONTHLY CAMPOUTS

Youth leaders planning a troop's program often build activities toward a monthly campout full of challenge, adventure, and fun. With at least one campout scheduled every four weeks, patrols will become very good at organizing their food and equipment. Scouts can build on what they have learned to become skilled at living in the outdoors any time of the year.

CAMPOREE CAMPING

A camporee is usually a weekend of fun, fellowship, and Scouting activities shared by two or more troops camping together. Your patrol can show its stuff as you take part in camporee activities and share good times and fresh ideas with Scouts from other troops. What are they cooking for meals? How do they pitch their dining fly? Can they teach you the best way to lash together a signal tower?

Perhaps your patrol will lay out an orienteering course that other Scouts can use to test map and compass skills. A knot rack helps everyone learn to handle rope, and an obstacle course can give you and your buddies a real workout. Camporee games encourage members of each patrol to cooperate with one another in order to reach a goal.

419

SUMMER CAMP

The first Boy Scout summer camp was held in 1907. Robert Baden-Powell, the founder of Scouting, brought together 22 Scouts on Brownsea Island off the coast of England. Divided into four patrols—the Wolves, Bulls, Curlews, and Ravens—they set up their tents and cooking areas. Then they devoted seven days to woodcraft, nature study, lifesaving, and other Scout skills. Gathered around evening campfires, they told stories, sang songs, and performed skits. The Scouts agreed their summer camp was a terrific success.

Today, many BSA council camps are tucked into forests or set among high, windy peaks. You'll find others along lakes and rushing rivers. A few are located in deserts or on seashores. Every camp is different, but here's a small sample of what you are likely to find:

▶ Nature hikes with instructors who really know their subjects

▶ Orienteering courses for sharpening your skills with maps, compasses, and Global Positioning System (GPS) receivers

▶ A wood yard for practicing proper use of knives, saws, and axes

▶ Archery and rifle ranges

▶ Conservation projects like meadow repair, trail maintenance, and erosion control

▶ Instruction in Leave No Trace methods of hiking and camping

▶ Project COPE (Challenging Outdoor Personal Experience) courses that improve your balance, fitness, and ability to solve problems

▶ Swimming, lifesaving training, and watercraft programs

▶ Handicrafts areas

Summer camp is a week of living the Scouting life. Your troop leaders will be there to help you enjoy tremendous adventures. A camp staff of adults and experienced older Scouts will offer a helping hand whenever you need it, and you'll have plenty of opportunities to add to your skills and to pass requirements for badges.

For many troops, a week at summer camp is a high point of the year.

NATIONAL HIGH-ADVENTURE BASES

The BSA's national high-adventure bases provide great Scouting challenges beyond your local council. Designed for older Boy Scouts, Varsity Scouts, and Venturers, each base offers training, equipment, and support for wilderness treks that will test your skills, wisdom, and willpower as you explore spectacular environments far from home.

Philmont Scout Ranch

Explore the rugged high country of northern New Mexico on a backpacking trek, as a member of a conservation work crew, or by enrolling in an advanced outdoor leadership program. Covering more than 200 square miles of mountains, forests, prairies, and streams, Philmont invites Scouts to hoist their packs and set off on rugged trails. At backcountry camps, you can try rock climbing, shoot a black-powder rifle, ride horses, and learn about archaeology, wildlife, and the history of early residents. Horseback cavalcades, training courses, and service programs have something for everyone in this legendary landscape.

Learn more about Philmont Scout Ranch and its activities online at www.scouting.org/philmont.

Florida Sea Base

At the Florida National High Adventure Sea Base, you can explore the clear waters of the Florida Keys and the Bahamas by watercraft and sailboat. You also can snorkel and scuba dive among schools of brilliantly colored tropical fish, investigate a primitive island, search for shipwrecks, cast your fishing line in the Gulf Stream waters, practice wind surfing, and study the marine life of North America's only living coral reef.

The home of the BSA's Florida Sea Base is on Islamorada Key, one of the string of islands stretching from the Florida mainland to Key West. Outposts on Summerland Key and on Great Abaco Island, Bahamas, allow Scouts to extend the range of their voyages along shore reefs and far into open water for exciting journeys throughout the year.

Northern Tier

The Sioux and Chippewa American Indians once traveled the northern lake country that is now the Superior-Quetico boundary waters of Minnesota in the United States and Ontario and Manitoba provinces in Canada. French-Canadian trappers followed, their canoes loaded with furs.

Today, this land is part of the BSA's Northern Tier National High Adventure Bases, where you can paddle a canoe across wilderness lakes and down rushing rivers. You can use your navigation skills to find campsites ashore. You might see moose grazing near the shore or find their footprints on portage trails. You can tempt muskies and pike to take the bait as you fish the clear, cold waters. When the lakes freeze and the snow flies, come back to learn the skills of winter camping through the programs of Okpik—Northern Tier's cold-weather camping program.

 Learn more about Florida Sea Base and Northern Tier online at *www.bsahandbook.org.*

WORLD AND NATIONAL SCOUT JAMBOREES

In 1920, Baden-Powell invited Scouts from all nations to attend a jamboree in London. The Scout movement was spreading around the world, and he wanted young people of many countries to camp with each other, share their knowledge, and develop friendships. That first global gathering of Scouts was such a success that world Scout jamborees continue to be held every four years.

National Scout Jamborees

With similar enthusiasm, national Scout jamborees hosted by the Boy Scouts of America bring together thousands of Scouts for a week of fun, learning, and fellowship. The first was held in 1937 in Washington, D.C. Since then, national Scout jamborees have been held at Valley Forge, Pennsylvania; Irvine Ranch, California; Colorado Springs, Colorado; Farragut State Park, Idaho; and Moraine State Park, Pennsylvania. Virginia's Fort A. P. Hill has been the home of the BSA's national Scout jamboree since 1981.

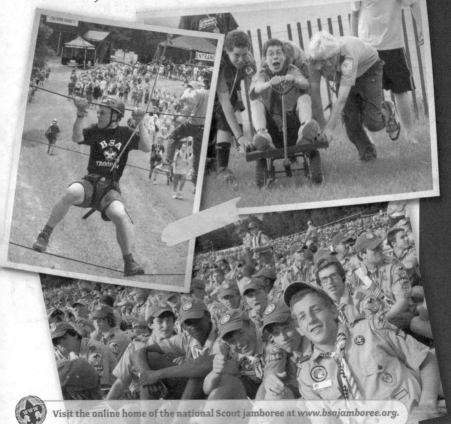

Visit the online home of the national Scout jamboree at *www.bsajamboree.org*.

Locations of World Scout Jamborees, 1920–2015

World Scout jamborees have been hosted around the globe.

1920—Olympia, London, England

1924—Ermelunden, Copenhagen, Denmark

1929—Arrowe Park, Birkenhead, England

1933—Gödöllö, Hungary

1937—Vogelensang-Bloemendaal, Netherlands

1947—Moisson, France

1951—Salzkammergut, Bad Ischl, Austria

1955—Niagara-on-the-Lake, Ontario, Canada

1957—Sutton Park, England

1959—Mount Makiling, Philippines

1963—Marathon, Greece

1967—Farragut State Park, Idaho, United States

1971—Asagiri Heights, Japan

1975—Lake Mjosa, Lillehammer, Norway

1983—Kananaskis Country, Alberta, Canada

1987–88—Cataract Scout Park, New South Wales, Australia

1991—Mount Sorak National Park, South Korea

1995—Flevoland, Netherlands

1998–99—Picarquin, Chile

2002–03—Sattahip, Thailand

2007–08—Hylands Park, Chelmsford, England

2011—Rinkaby, Sweden

2015—Kirara Beach, Yamaguchi, Japan

World Scout Jamborees

At the first international gathering of Scouts in 1920, Robert Baden-Powell hoped that bringing together boys from around the planet would, as he put it, help "to establish friendships among Scouts of all nations and to help to develop peace and happiness in the world and good will among men."

World Scout jamborees continue to be held once every four years, fulfilling Baden-Powell's promise of promoting understanding and brotherhood among Scouts from many countries.

NATIONAL YOUTH LEADERSHIP TRAINING

National Youth Leadership Training is an exciting program designed to help Scouts gain leadership skills and experience they can use in their home troops and wherever else they can provide leadership for themselves and for others. These skills come alive during the week of the program as each patrol sets out on a quest for the meaning of leadership.

Working together and taking part in a wide range of activities, games, and adventures, participants use their improving leadership skills to put the best of Scouting into action. They'll take what they learn home with them to enrich the programs of their home troops, too.

NATIONAL ADVANCED YOUTH LEADERSHIP EXPERIENCE

Combine the backcountry adventure of Philmont Scout Ranch with learning advanced leadership skills and you've got NAYLE—the National Advanced Youth Leadership Experience.

NAYLE draws on elements of Philmont ranger training and methods of search and rescue to teach leadership, teamwork, and the power of selfless service during an unforgettable backcountry experience. Scouts completing NAYLE will find they have greatly improved their abilities as leaders in their home troops and councils.

THE ORDER OF THE ARROW

As Scouting's national honor society, the Order of the Arrow recognizes youth and adults who best exemplify the Scout Oath and Law in their daily lives. Members promote camping, responsible outdoor adventures, and environmental stewardship as essential to every Scout's experience. The OA helps Scouts crystallize habits of leadership and helpfulness into a life purpose of cheerful service to others and to their nation.

Among the OA's national activities are service projects, college scholarships, matching grants for council camp improvements, and leadership seminars. Order of the Arrow Trail Crews completing conservation projects provide invaluable service as they care for the environment at Philmont Scout Ranch and on public lands across America. Similar programs are held at the other national high-adventure bases, too.

The National Order of the Arrow Conference is held every two years at a major university. It is a gathering of OA leaders who are there to sharpen their leadership skills and to enjoy the fellowship of OA membership.

Order of the Arrow members can help strengthen their troops by providing leadership training and by assisting with summer camp promotion, camporees, Scout shows, mentoring, and other activities.

Learn more about what NAYLE can offer you by visiting *www.nayle.org*. The OA's official Web site is *www.oa-bsa.org*. Check it out.

OPPORTUNITIES FOR OLDER SCOUTS

Scouting is packed with challenges for older members. They can take on roles of increasing responsibility as leaders in their troops and work hard to make programs effective and exciting for themselves and for everyone else. The wisdom and experience of older Scouts give a troop its strength. Experienced Scouts can be role models for younger boys and can help them learn skills to take part in campouts and other troop activities.

Scouts up to the age of 18 can continue working on rank requirements and merit badges leading to the Eagle Scout Award. Older Scouts also can set off on expeditions to council and national high-adventure bases, attend national and world Scout jamborees, and be eligible for other BSA opportunities, including Order of the Arrow membership.

Many troops also are associated with Venturing crews or with Varsity Scout teams designed for older Scouts. A troop might also have a Venture patrol to provide older Scouts with program possibilities beyond those available to younger boys.

Venture Patrols

A troop's Venture patrol for older Scouts features exciting and demanding ultimate adventures. For example, a Venture patrol might learn how to paddle and portage canoes, brush up on orienteering, and research the food and gear needed for a long journey. With the skills mastered, they can plan and set out on a canoe camping ultimate adventure—miles of watercraft travel along lakes and rivers, finding their way with map and compass, and pitching their tents each evening on the shore.

 Visit Venturing's online home at *www.scouting.org/Venturing*, or explore Sea Scouting at *www.seascout.org*.

Venturing

Not to be confused with a Venture patrol, Venturing is the BSA's youth development program for young men and women who are 14 (and have completed the eighth grade) through 20 years of age. Venturing's purpose is to provide positive experiences to help young people mature and to prepare them to become responsible and caring adults.

Young adults involved in Venturing will:

▶ Acquire skills in the areas of high adventure, sports, arts and hobbies, religious life, or Sea Scouting.

▶ Experience a program that is fun and full of challenge and adventure.

▶ Learn to make ethical choices over their lifetimes by instilling the values in the Venturing Oath and Code.

▶ Become a skilled training and program resource for Cub Scouts, Boy Scouts, and other groups.

▶ Experience positive leadership from adult and youth leaders and be given opportunities to take on leadership roles.

▶ Learn and grow in a supportive, caring, and fun environment.

What a Venturing crew does is limited only by the imagination and involvement of the adult and youth leaders and members of the crew. They might sail the Caribbean, produce a play, climb a mountain, teach disabled people to swim, or attend the Olympics. All these adventures and many more are being done today by Venturers across the country.

Varsity Scouting

Varsity Scouting is an exciting BSA program for members ages 14 through 17. Each of Varsity Scouting's five fields of emphasis—advancement, high adventure, personal development, service, and special programs and events—is managed by a Varsity team member and by an adult, who work together in a manner similar to that of a player and a coach. Varsity teams also may select a sport, such as basketball or soccer, and spend a season (usually three months) competing among themselves and challenging other teams. Through the year a Varsity team can focus on several sports activities and high-adventure outings.

National Eagle Scout Association

The National Eagle Scout Association is a fellowship of men who have achieved the Eagle Scout rank and who are eager to devote their efforts toward forming the kind of young men America needs for leadership. NESA's objective is to serve Eagle Scouts and, through them, the entire movement of Scouting.

Alpha Phi Omega National Service Fraternity

Founded on the principles of the Scout Oath and Law, Alpha Phi Omega National Service Fraternity is a national college service fraternity active on many campuses. APO's service program encourages its members to continue their Scouting involvement through college connections. Most chapters are coeducational.

"Let the boy remember also that in addition to courage, unselfishness, and fair dealing, he must have efficiency, he must have knowledge, he must cultivate a sound body and a good mind, and train himself so that he can act with quick decision in any crisis that may arise."

—Theodore Roosevelt in *Handbook for Boys*, 1st ed., 1911

Giving Back

Your experiences as a Scout are giving you confidence, skills, and opportunities for terrific adventures. You're also developing friendships that can continue for many years.

As you grow older, you can find many pathways for giving back to Scouting. Adult leadership positions in Scout troops could allow you to continue enjoying outdoor activities while you practice leadership skills that keep the values of Scouting alive. Involvement with Scouting as a district or council leader supports the BSA program for even greater numbers of young people.

Continuing to live by the Scout Oath and Law are important ways to give back to your family, community, and nation. Be true to the values of Scouting in the years to come, and you will know you are always doing your best.

Check out NESA online at *www.nesa.org*, where you will find a list of scholarship opportunities for Eagle Scouts. APO's online home is located at *www.apo.org*.

CONTINUING THE PROMISE OF SCOUTING

A century ago, the first edition of the *Boy Scout Handbook* closed with a letter from Theodore Roosevelt, 26th president of the United States. He encouraged BSA members to do their best and to take full advantage of all that Scouting had to offer.

Millions of boys have been Scouts since Roosevelt penned those words, and they have done exactly what Roosevelt had hoped they would do. They have become better boys who have grown into men able to serve well in their families, communities, and nation. They have trained themselves to be prepared for whatever challenges confront them, and they have thrived on the adventures and achievements of their patrols and troops.

Through the decades, Scouting has made strong promises to those who join its ranks. In return, the Boy Scouts of America asks that you do your best to take part, to learn, and to succeed.

▶ Scouting promises you the great outdoors. You can learn how to camp and hike without leaving a trace and how to take care of the land. You'll study wildlife up close and learn about nature all around you. There are plenty of skills for you to master, and you can teach others what you know. Everybody helping everyone else—that's part of Scouting, too.

▶ Scouting promises you friendship. Members of the troop you join might be boys you already know, and you will meet many other Scouts along the way. Some could become lifelong friends.

▶ Scouting promises you opportunities to work toward the Eagle rank. Scouts learn how to set positive goals for themselves and then follow clear routes to success.

▶ Scouting promises you tools to do your best as a citizen, a student, and a member of your family. The good deeds you perform every day will improve the lives of those around you. You can prepare yourself to aid others in times of need.

▶ Scouting promises you experiences and duties that will help you mature into a strong, wise adult. The Scout Oath and the Scout Law can guide you while you are a Scout and throughout your life.

Adventure, learning, challenge, leadership, and responsibility—the promise of Scouting is all of this and more. It is a doorway to adventure. It is a heritage of service and the development of character.

Scouting's next century is here, and it is beginning with you. Make it great, both for yourself and for those who will follow in your footsteps. Decades from now, Scouts will look back and see that those who launched the second hundred years of the Boy Scouts of America did so with energy, dedication, and joy.

429

AWARDS AND RECOGNITION

In addition to the badges of rank and merit Scouts can earn, there are many other Scouting awards that reflect their achievements. The requirements for these awards are listed in the *Boy Scout Requirements* book, which is updated annually.

Scouting Recognitions

▶ **World Crest.** All members of the Boy Scouts of America wear the World Crest as an expression of world brotherhood.

▶ **Den Chief Service Award.** Den chiefs who complete certain service and training requirements can receive this special recognition.

▶ **Interpreter.** Scouts who wears an interpreter strip can carry on a conversation, write, and translate a foreign language or in sign language.

▶ **Good Turn for America.** Good Turn for America is a national call to service by the BSA to help ensure adequate food and shelter for Americans and to help citizens develop good health habits.

▶ **Organ Donor Awareness.** As a Presidential Good Turn, the BSA set out in 1986 to educate Americans about the importance of organ donation. To learn more about how to become a donor and how to educate others on the importance of donor contributions, contact local donor agencies.

A Scout Is Reverent

Scouts show their faith by doing their duty to God. Some also undertake special service and learning that could qualify them for religious emblems. These are not Scouting awards. Faith groups develop their religious emblems program, including the requirements.

A Scout Is Reverent (1993), by Joseph Csatari

 You can get requirements, application forms, and additional information on all these awards and recognitions from the *Handbook* Web site at www.bsahandbook.org.

Lifesaving Awards

The National Court of Honor presents awards for rare Scoutlike action and for saving life.

▶ **Honor Medal.** The highest special award in Scouting. In cases of *exceptional skill or resourcefulness and extreme risk of life,* the medal is awarded with crossed palms.

▶ **Heroism Award.** Awarded for heroic action involving minimum risk to self.

▶ **Medal of Merit.** Awarded to Scouts who put into practice the skills and ideals of Scouting through some great act of service.

Other BSA Awards and Recognitions

Aquatics Awards

▶ Snorkeling, BSA
▶ BSA Lifeguard
▶ Mile Swim, BSA
▶ Boardsailing, BSA
▶ Scuba, BSA

Environmental/Outdoors Awards and Recognitions

▶ William T. Hornaday Awards
▶ World Conservation Award
▶ Leave No Trace Achievement Award

▶ 50-Miler Awards
▶ Historic Trails Award
▶ Totin' Chip
▶ Paul Bunyan Woodsman
▶ Firem'n Chit

The National Outdoor Awards

The National Outdoor Awards recognize Scouts who demonstrate knowledge and proficiency in outdoors skills. National Outdoor Badges can be earned in Camping, Hiking, Aquatics, Riding, and Adventure, and the National Outdoor Achievement Medal is the highest recognition that a Scout can earn for exemplary achievement, experience, and skill in multiple areas of outdoor endeavor.

Placing all these awards and recognitions on your uniform can be a confusing task. Check the *Handbook* Web site, www.bsahandbook.org, for more information.

431

TENDERFOOT
Rank Requirements

Effective January 1, 2010

✔			Leader initial and date
	1.	Present yourself to your leader, properly dressed, before going on an overnight camping trip. Show the camping gear you will use. Show the right way to pack and carry it. *(Pages 292–293, 297–298)*	
	2.	Spend at least one night on a patrol or troop campout. Sleep in a tent you have helped pitch. *(Page 302)*	
	3.	On the campout, assist in preparing and cooking one of your patrol's meals. Tell why it is important for each patrol member to share in meal preparation and cleanup, and explain the importance of eating together. *(Pages 327, 329–339)*	
	4a.	Demonstrate how to whip and fuse the ends of a rope. *(Pages 380–381)*	
	4b.	Demonstrate that you know how to tie the following knots and tell what their uses are: two half hitches and the taut-line hitch. *(Pages 384–385)*	
	4c.	Using the EDGE method, teach another person how to tie the square knot. *(Page 53)*	
	5.	Explain the rules of safe hiking, both on the highway and cross-country, during the day and at night. Explain what to do if you are lost. *(Pages 279, 282–283)*	
	6.	Demonstrate how to display, raise, lower, and fold the American flag. *(Pages 72–76)*	
	7.	Repeat from memory and explain in your own words the Scout Oath, Law, motto, and slogan. *(Pages 22–27)*	
	8.	Know your patrol name, give the patrol yell, and describe your patrol flag. *(Page 38)*	
	9.	Explain the importance of the buddy system as it relates to your personal safety on outings and in your neighborhood. Describe what a bully is and how you should respond to one. *(Pages 39, 62)*	

Tenderfoot

Downloadable requirements checklists for all ranks and videos to guide you through the Tenderfoot rank requirements may be found on the *Handbook* Web site, www.bsahandbook.org.

	10a.	Record your best in the following tests *(Pages 96–99)*: **Current results**

        Push-ups _____

        Pull-ups _____

        Sit-ups _____

        Standing long jump (_____ ft. _____ in.)

        1/4-mile walk/run _____

30 days later

        Push-ups _____

        Pull-ups _____

        Sit-ups _____

        Standing long jump (_____ ft. _____ in.)

        1/4-mile walk/run _____

10b. Show improvement in the activities listed in requirement 10a after practicing for 30 days. *(Pages 96–99)*

11. Identify local poisonous plants; tell how to treat for exposure to them. *(Pages 138–139)*

12a. Demonstrate how to care for someone who is choking. *(Pages 134–135)*

12b. Show first aid for the following:

- Simple cuts and scrapes *(Page 136)*
- Blisters on the hand and foot *(Page 137)*
- Minor (thermal/heat) burns or scalds (superficial, or first-degree) *(Page 148)*
- Bites or stings of insects and ticks *(Pages 142–143)*
- Venomous snakebite *(Pages 141–142)*
- Nosebleed *(Page 138)*
- Frostbite and sunburn *(Pages 150, 152)*

13. Demonstrate Scout spirit by living the Scout Oath (Promise) and Scout Law in your everyday life. Discuss four specific examples of how you have lived the points of the Scout Law in your daily life. *(Page 30)*

14. Participate in a Scoutmaster conference. *(Page 34)*

15. Complete your board of review. *(Page 55)*

NOTE: *Alternate requirements for the Tenderfoot rank are available for Scouts with physical or mental disabilities if they meet the criteria listed in the* Boy Scout Requirements *book.*

SECOND CLASS
Rank Requirements

Effective January 1, 2010

✔			Leader initial and date
	1a.	Demonstrate how a compass works and how to orient a map. Explain what map symbols mean. *(Pages 354, 360–364)*	
	1b.	Using a compass and a map together, take a five-mile hike (or 10 miles by bike) approved by your adult leader and your parent or guardian.* *(Pages 365–366)*	
	2.	Discuss the principles of Leave No Trace. *(Pages 247–256)*	
	3a.	Since joining, have participated in five separate troop/patrol activities (other than troop/patrol meetings), two of which included camping overnight. *(Pages 444–445)*	
	3b.	On one of those campouts, select your patrol site and sleep in a tent that you have pitched. Explain what factors you should consider when choosing a patrol site and where to pitch a tent. *(Pages 249, 300–302)*	
	3c.	Demonstrate proper care, sharpening, and use of the knife, saw, and ax, and describe when they should be used. *(Pages 402–409)*	
	3d.	Use the tools listed in requirement 3c to prepare tinder, kindling, and fuel for a cooking fire. *(Pages 410–411)*	
	3e.	Discuss when it is appropriate to use a cooking fire and a lightweight stove. Discuss the safety procedures for using both. *(Page 325)*	
	3f.	In an approved place and at an approved time, demonstrate how to build a fire and set up a lightweight stove. Note: Lighting the fire is not required. *(Pages 410–415)*	
	3g.	On one campout, plan and cook one hot breakfast or lunch, selecting foods from the food guide pyramid. Explain the importance of good nutrition. Tell how to transport, store, and prepare the foods you selected. *(Pages 102, 316, 320–323, 326, 329, 339)*	
	4.	Participate in a flag ceremony for your school, religious institution, chartered organization, community, or troop activity. Explain to your leader what respect is due the flag of the United States. *(Pages 72–76)*	
	5.	Participate in an approved (minimum of one hour) service project. *(Pages 84–85)*	

*If you use a wheelchair or crutches, or if it is difficult for you to get around, you may substitute "trip" for "hike."

Downloadable requirements checklists for all ranks and videos to guide you through the Second Class rank requirements may be found on the *Handbook* Web site, *www.bsahandbook.org.*

6.	Identify or show evidence of at least 10 kinds of wild animals (birds, mammals, reptiles, fish, mollusks) found in your community. *(Pages 221, 231)*	
7a.	Show what to do for "hurry" cases of stopped breathing, serious bleeding, and ingested poisoning. *(Pages 162–170)*	
7b.	Prepare a personal first-aid kit to take with you on a hike. *(Page 127)*	
7c.	Demonstrate first aid for the following: • Object in the eye *(Page 145)* • Bite of a suspected rabid animal *(Page 140)* • Puncture wounds from a splinter, nail, and fishhook *(Pages 145–146)* • Serious burns (partial thickness, or second-degree) *(Pages 148–149)* • Heat exhaustion *(Page 150)* • Shock *(Pages 170–171)* • Heatstroke, dehydration, hypothermia, and hyperventilation *(Pages 147–148, 151–152)*	
8a.	Tell what precautions must be taken for a safe swim. *(Page 182)*	
8b.	Demonstrate your ability to jump feetfirst into water over your head in depth, level off and swim 25 feet on the surface, stop, turn sharply, resume swimming, then return to your starting place. *(Pages 190–191)*	
8c.	Demonstrate water rescue methods by reaching with your arm or leg, by reaching with a suitable object, and by throwing lines and objects. Explain why swimming rescues should not be attempted when a reaching or throwing rescue is possible, and explain why and how a rescue swimmer should avoid contact with the victim. *(Pages 196–199)*	
9a.	Participate in a school, community, or troop program on the dangers of using drugs, alcohol, and tobacco and other practices that could be harmful to your health. Discuss your participation in the program with your family, and explain the dangers of substance addictions. *(Pages 113–117)*	
9b.	Explain the three R's of personal safety and protection. *(Page 65)*	
10.	Earn an amount of money agreed upon by you and your parent, then save at least 50 percent of that money. *(Page 25)*	
11.	Demonstrate Scout spirit by living the Scout Oath (Promise) and Scout Law in your everyday life. Discuss four specific examples (different from those used for Tenderfoot requirement 13) of how you have lived the points of the Scout Law in your daily life. *(Page 30)*	
12.	Participate in a Scoutmaster conference. *(Page 34)*	
13.	Complete your board of review. *(Page 55)*	

NOTE: *Alternate requirements for the Second Class rank are available for Scouts with physical or mental disabilities if they meet the criteria listed in the* Boy Scout Requirements *book.*

FIRST CLASS
Rank Requirements

Effective January 1, 2010

✓			Leader initial and date
	1.	Demonstrate how to find directions during the day and at night without using a compass. *(Pages 368–371)*	
	2.	Using a map and compass, complete an orienteering course that covers at least one mile and requires measuring the height and/or width of designated items (tree, tower, canyon, ditch, etc.). *(Pages 346–351, 372–374)*	
	3.	Since joining, have participated in 10 separate troop/patrol activities (other than troop/patrol meetings), three of which included camping overnight. Demonstrate the principles of Leave No Trace on these outings. *(Pages 247–256)*	
	4a.	Help plan a patrol menu for one campout that includes at least one breakfast, one lunch, and one dinner, and that requires cooking at least two of the meals. Tell how the menu includes the foods from the food pyramid and meets nutritional needs. *(Pages 102–105, 316–317, 320)*	
	4b.	Using the menu planned in requirement 4a, make a list showing the cost and food amounts needed to feed three or more boys and secure the ingredients. *(Pages 321–323)*	
	4c.	Tell which pans, utensils, and other gear will be needed to cook and serve these meals. *(Page 324)*	
	4d.	Explain the procedures to follow in the safe handling and storage of fresh meats, dairy products, eggs, vegetables, and other perishable food products. Tell how to properly dispose of camp garbage, cans, plastic containers, and other rubbish. *(Pages 328–329)*	
	4e.	On one campout, serve as your patrol's cook. Supervise your assistant(s) in using a stove or building a cooking fire. Prepare the breakfast, lunch, and dinner planned in requirement 4a. Lead your patrol in saying grace at the meals and supervise cleanup. *(Pages 325–327, 342)*	
	5.	Visit and discuss with a selected individual approved by your leader (elected official, judge, attorney, civil servant, principal, teacher) your constitutional rights and obligations as a U.S. citizen. *(Pages 70–72, 81–82)*	

Downloadable requirements checklists for all ranks and videos to guide you through the First Class rank requirements may be found on the *Handbook* Web site, *www.bsahandbook.org.*

FIRST CLASS

6.	Identify or show evidence of at least 10 kinds of native plants found in your community. *(Pages 212, 215)*	
7a.	Discuss when you should and should not use lashings. Then demonstrate tying the timber hitch and clove hitch and their use in square, shear, and diagonal lashings by joining two or more poles or staves together. *(Pages 386–387, 392–398)*	
7b.	Use lashing to make a useful camp gadget. *(Pages 392–401)*	
8a.	Demonstrate tying the bowline knot and describe several ways it can be used. *(Pages 388–389)*	
8b.	Demonstrate bandages for a sprained ankle and for injuries on the head, the upper arm, and the collarbone. *(Pages 155, 157–161)*	
8c.	Show how to transport by yourself, and with one other person, a person • From a smoke-filled room • With a sprained ankle, for at least 25 yards *(Pages 154, 172–175)*	
8d.	Tell the five most common signals of a heart attack. Explain the steps (procedures) in cardiopulmonary resuscitation (CPR). *(Pages 164–166)*	
9a.	Tell what precautions must be taken for a safe trip afloat. *(Pages 194–195)*	
9b.	Successfully complete the BSA swimmer test.* *(Pages 190–191)*	
9c.	With a helper and a practice victim, show a line rescue both as tender and as rescuer. (The practice victim should be approximately 30 feet from shore in deep water.) *(Page 199)*	
10.	Tell someone who is eligible to join Boy Scouts, or an inactive Boy Scout, about your troop's activities. Invite him to a troop outing, activity, service project, or meeting. Tell him how to join, or encourage the inactive Boy Scout to become active. *(Page 17)*	
11.	Describe the three things you should avoid doing related to use of the Internet. Describe a cyberbully and how you should respond to one. *(Page 51, 61)*	
12.	Demonstrate Scout spirit by living the Scout Oath (Promise) and Scout Law in your everyday life. Discuss four specific examples (different from those used for Tenderfoot requirement 13 and Second Class requirement 11) of how you have lived the points of the Scout Law in your daily life. *(Page 30)*	
13.	Participate in a Scoutmaster conference. *(Page 34)*	
14.	Complete your board of review. *(Page 55)*	

NOTE: Alternate requirements for the First Class rank are available for Scouts with physical or mental disabilities if they meet the criteria listed in the Boy Scout Requirements book.
*See the Aquatics chapter for details about the BSA swimmer test.

			Leader initial and date
✔			
	1.	Be active in your troop and patrol for at least four months as a First Class Scout. *(Pages 34—38, 58)*	
	2.	Demonstrate Scout spirit by living the Scout Oath (Promise) and Scout Law in your everyday life. *(Page 30)*	
	3.	Earn six merit badges, including any four from the required list for Eagle. *(Pages 48—49)* **Name of Merit Badge** _____(required for Eagle)* _____(required for Eagle)* _____(required for Eagle)* _____(required for Eagle)* _____ _____	
	4.	While a First Class Scout, take part in service projects totaling at least six hours of work. These projects must be approved by your Scoutmaster. *(Pages 84—85)*	
	5.	While a First Class Scout, serve actively for four months in one or more of the following positions of responsibility (or carry out a Scoutmaster-assigned leadership project to help the troop) *(Page 58)*: **Boy Scout troop.** Patrol leader, Venture patrol leader, assistant senior patrol leader, senior patrol leader, troop guide, Order of the Arrow troop representative, den chief, scribe, librarian, historian, quartermaster, bugler, junior assistant Scoutmaster, chaplain aide, instructor, troop webmaster, or Leave No Trace trainer. **Varsity Scout team.** Captain, cocaptain, program manager, squad leader, team secretary, Order of the Arrow team representative, librarian, historian, quartermaster, chaplain aide, instructor, den chief, team webmaster, or Leave No Trace trainer. **Venturing crew/ship.** President, vice president, secretary, treasurer, den chief, quartermaster, historian, guide, boatswain, boatswain's mate, yeoman, purser, storekeeper, crew/ship webmaster, or Leave No Trace trainer.	
	6.	Take part in a Scoutmaster conference. *(Page 34)*	
	7.	Complete your board of review. *(Page 55)*	

*Choose any of the 15 required merit badges in the 12 categories to fulfill requirement 3. See requirement 3 in the Eagle Scout rank requirements for a list of badges required for Eagle.

LIFE SCOUT
Rank Requirements

Effective January 1, 2010

		Leader initial and date
✔		

1.	Be active in your troop and patrol for at least six months as a Star Scout. *(Pages 34–38, 58)*	
2.	Demonstrate Scout spirit by living the Scout Oath (Promise) and Scout Law in your everyday life. *(Page 30)*	
3.	Earn five more merit badges (so that you have 11 in all), including any three more from the required list for Eagle.* *(Pages 48–49)* **Name of Merit Badge** _____(required for Eagle)* _____(required for Eagle)* _____(required for Eagle)* _____ _____	
4.	While a Star Scout, take part in service projects totaling at least six hours of work. These projects must be approved by your Scoutmaster. *(Pages 84–85)*	
5.	While a Star Scout, serve actively for six months in one or more of the troop positions of responsibility listed in requirement 5 for Star Scout (or carry out a Scoutmaster-assigned leadership project to help the troop). *(Page 58)*	
6.	While a Star Scout, use the EDGE method to teach a younger Scout the skills from ONE of the following six choices, so that he is prepared to pass those requirements to his unit leader's satisfaction. *(Page 53)* a. Second Class—7a and 7c (first aid) b. Second Class—1a (outdoor skills) c. Second Class—3c, 3d, 3e, and 3f (cooking/camping) d. First Class—8a, 8b, 8c, and 8d (first aid) e. First Class—1, 7a, and 7b (outdoor skills) f. First Class—4a, 4b, and 4d (cooking/camping)	
7.	Take part in a Scoutmaster conference. *(Page 34)*	
8.	Complete your board of review. *(Page 55)*	

*Choose any of the 15 required merit badges in the 12 categories to fulfill requirement 3.

EAGLE SCOUT
Rank Requirements

Effective January 1, 2010

✔		Leader initial and date
	1. Be active in your troop, team, crew, or ship for a period of at least six months after you have achieved the rank of Life Scout. *(Pages 34–38, 58)*	
	2. Demonstrate that you live by the principles of the Scout Oath and Law in your daily life. List the names of individuals who know you personally and would be willing to provide a recommendation on your behalf, including parents/guardians, religious, educational, and employer references. *(Page 30)*	
	3. Earn a total of 21 merit badges (10 more than you already have), including the following: (a) First Aid, (b) Citizenship in the Community, (c) Citizenship in the Nation, (d) Citizenship in the World, (e) Communications, (f) Personal Fitness, (g) Emergency Preparedness OR Lifesaving, (h) Environmental Science, (i) Personal Management, (j) Swimming OR Hiking OR Cycling, (k) Camping, and (l) Family Life.* *(Pages 48–49)*	

Name of Merit Badge   **Date Earned**

_____   _____

_____   _____

_____   _____

_____   _____

_____   _____

_____   _____

_____   _____

_____   _____

_____   _____

_____   _____

**You must choose only one merit badge listed in items g and j. If you have earned more than one of the badges listed in items g and j, choose one and list the remaining badges to make your total of 21.*

Download the Eagle Scout Leadership Service Project Workbook and the Eagle Scout Rank Application from the *Handbook* Web site, *www.bsahandbook.org.*

4.	While a Life Scout, serve actively for a period of six months in one or more of the following positions of responsibility *(Page 58)*:	
	Boy Scout troop. Patrol leader, assistant senior patrol leader, senior patrol leader, Venture patrol leader, troop guide, Order of the Arrow troop representative, den chief, scribe, librarian, historian, quartermaster, bugler, junior assistant Scoutmaster, chaplain aide, or instructor.	
	Varsity Scout team. Captain, cocaptain, program manager, squad leader, team secretary, Order of the Arrow team representative, librarian, historian, quartermaster, chaplain aide, instructor, or den chief.	
	Venturing crew/ship. President, vice president, secretary, treasurer, quartermaster, historian, den chief, guide, boatswain, boatswain's mate, yeoman, purser, or storekeeper.	
5.	While a Life Scout, plan, develop, and give leadership to others in a service project helpful to any religious institution, any school, or your community. (The project should benefit an organization other than Boy Scouting.) The project plan must be approved by the organization benefiting from the effort, your Scoutmaster and troop committee, and the council or district before you start. You must use the Eagle Scout Leadership Service Project Workbook, No. 512-927, in meeting this requirement. *(Pages 84–85)*	
6.	Take part in a Scoutmaster conference. *(Page 34)*	
7.	Successfully complete an Eagle Scout board of review. *(Page 55)*	

AGE REQUIREMENT ELIGIBILITY. Merit badges, badges of rank, and Eagle Palms may be earned by a registered Boy Scout, Varsity Scout, or Venturer. **He may earn these awards until his 18th birthday.** *Any Venturer who achieved the First Class rank as a Boy Scout in a troop or Varsity Scout in a team may continue working for the Star, Life, and Eagle Scout ranks and Eagle Palms while registered as a Venturer up to his 18th birthday.* **Scouts and Venturers who have completed all requirements prior to their 18th birthday may be reviewed within three months after that date with no explanation.** *Boards of review conducted between three and six months after the candidate's 18th birthday must be preapproved by the local council. A statement by an adult explaining the reason for the delay must be attached to the Eagle Scout Rank Application when it is submitted to the Eagle Scout Service. The Eagle Scout Service at the national office must be contacted for procedures to follow if a board of review is to be conducted more than six months after a candidate's 18th birthday.*

If you have a permanent physical or mental disability, you may become an Eagle Scout by qualifying for as many required merit badges as you can and qualifying for alternative merit badges for the rest. If you seek to become an Eagle Scout under this procedure, you must submit a special application to your local council service center. Your application must be approved by your council advancement committee before you can work on alternative merit badges.

A Scout or Venturer with a disability may work toward rank advancement after he is 18 years of age if he meets the guidelines outlined in the Advancement Committee Policies and Procedures.

EAGLE SCOUT
Alternate Requirements

Effective January 1, 2010

✓			Leader initial and date
	1.	The Eagle Scout rank may be achieved by a Boy Scout, Varsity Scout, or qualified* Venturer who has a physical or mental disability by qualifying for alternate merit badges. This does not apply to individual requirements for merit badges. Merit badges are awarded only when all requirements are met as stated.	
	2.	The physical or mental disability must be of a permanent rather than a temporary nature.	
	3.	A clear and concise medical statement concerning the Scout's disabilities must be made by a physician licensed to practice medicine, or an evaluation statement must be certified by an educational administrator.	
	4.	The candidate must earn as many of the required merit badges as his ability permits before applying for an alternate Eagle Scout rank merit badge.	
	5.	The Application for Alternate Eagle Scout Award Merit Badges must be completed prior to qualifying for alternate merit badges.	
	6.	The alternate merit badges chosen must be of such a nature that they are as demanding of effort as the required merit badges.	
	7.	When alternates chosen involve physical activity, they must be approved by the physician.	
	8.	The unit leader and the board of review must explain that to attain the Eagle Scout rank a candidate is expected to do his best in developing himself to the limit of his resources.	
	9.	The application must be approved by the council committee responsible for advancement, utilizing the expertise of professional persons involved in Scouting for the disabled.	
	10.	The candidate's application for Eagle must be made on the Eagle Scout Rank Application, with the Application for Alternate Eagle Scout Award Merit Badges attached.	

In order for a Venturer to be an Eagle candidate, he must have achieved the First Class rank as a Boy Scout or Varsity Scout.

EAGLE PALM
Rank Requirements

Effective January 1, 2010

After becoming an Eagle Scout, you may earn Palms by completing the following requirements:

✔			Leader initial and date
	1.	Be active in your troop and patrol for at least three months after becoming an Eagle Scout or after award of last Palm.*	
	2.	Demonstrate Scout spirit by living the Scout Oath (Promise) and Scout Law in your everyday life.	
	3.	Make a satisfactory effort to develop and demonstrate leadership ability.	
	4.	Earn five additional merit badges beyond those required for Eagle or last Palm.†	
	5.	Take part in a Scoutmaster conference.	
	6.	Complete a board of review.	

You may wear only the proper combination of Palms for the number of merit badges you earned beyond the rank of Eagle. The Bronze Palm represents five merit badges, the Gold Palm 10, and the Silver Palm 15.

Eagle Palms must be earned in sequence, and the three-month tenure requirement must be observed for each Palm.

†*Merit badges earned any time since becoming a Boy Scout may be used to meet this requirement.*

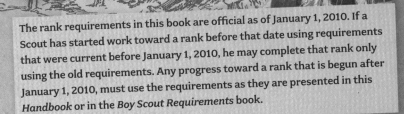

The rank requirements in this book are official as of January 1, 2010. If a Scout has started work toward a rank before that date using requirements that were current before January 1, 2010, he may complete that rank only using the old requirements. Any progress toward a rank that is begun after January 1, 2010, must use the requirements as they are presented in this *Handbook* or in the *Boy Scout Requirements* book.

Scout
CAMPING LOG

Location			Date	Nights	Scoutmaster or Adult Signature
	Depart				
	Return				
	Depart				
	Return				
	Depart				
	Return				
	Depart				
	Return				
	Depart				
	Return				
	Depart				
	Return				
	Depart				
	Return				
	Depart				
	Return				
	Depart				
	Return				
	Depart				
	Return				
	Depart				
	Return				
	Depart				
	Return				

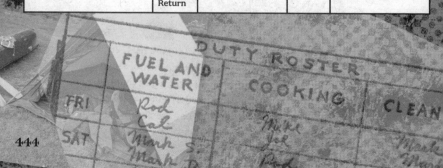

FUEL AND WATER — DUTY ROSTER — COOKING — CLEAN

	FUEL AND WATER	COOKING	CLEAN
FRI	Rod Cal		
SAT	Mark S. Mark D.	Mike Joe Rod	Mark Mark

Scout
SERVICE LOG

Type of Project	Date	Hours	Scoutmaster or Adult Signature

BE PREPARED
TO HELP OTHER
AT ALL TIMES

Scout
CAMPING LOG

Location		Date	Nights	Scoutmaster or Adult Signature
	Depart			
	Return			
	Depart			
	Return			
	Depart			
	Return			
	Depart			
	Return			
	Depart			
	Return			
	Depart			
	Return			
	Depart			
	Return			
	Depart			
	Return			
	Depart			
	Return			
	Depart			
	Return			
	Depart			
	Return			
	Depart			
	Return			

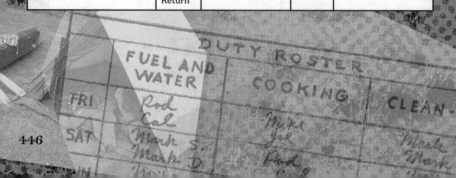

Scout
SERVICE LOG

Type of Project	Date	Hours	Scoutmaster or Adult Signature

BE PREPARED
TO HELP OTHE[R]
AT ALL TIMES

"We never fail when we try to do our duty, we always fail when we neglect to do it."

—Robert Baden-Powell

ACKNOWLEDGMENTS

The Boy Scouts of America gratefully acknowledges the contributions of the following people for their help in preparing the *Boy Scout Handbook*, 12th edition.

Members of the Boy Scout Handbook Task Force: Hector "Tico" Perez, chairman; David L. Briscoe, Ph.D.; Harriss A. Butler III; Andy Collins; W. Stacey Cowles; Jane Grossman; Eric Hiser; Russ Hunsaker; Ki D. Lee; Bob Longoria; Dan Maxfield; Steve McGowan; Wayne Perry; Ben Poole; Thomas E. Reddin; Coleman Ross; Jake Wellman; Dan Zaccara.

National office advisory team: Robert J. Mazzuca, Richard Bourlon, Wayne Brock, Dan Buckhout, Gary Butler, Bill Evans, John Green, Albert Kugler, Fred Meijering, Clyde Mayer, Carey L. Miller, Phillip Moore, Frank Reigelman, Jamie Shearer, Bill Steele, Jim Terry, George Trosko, Stan Willey, James B. Wilson Jr.

Subject experts who provided exceptional assistance: Health and Safety Support Committee; Camping Task Force; Rod Replogle, U.S. Forest Service (retired), former Philmont staff member.

Scouts and Scouters throughout the nation who participated in focus groups, photography efforts, and manuscript reviews.

NATIONAL OFFICE PUBLISHING TEAM

Project director—Joe C. Glasscock, Volunteer Development Team, BSA

Project manager—Richard Luna, Media Studio, BSA

Research and project development—Maria Dahl-Smith, Hispanic Initiatives Team, BSA

Author—Robert Birkby, Eagle Scout, mountaineer, and former director of Conservation at Philmont Scout Ranch

Editor—Elizabeth Laskey

Editor/copy editor—Beth McPherson, Media Studio, BSA

Art director—Laura E. Humphries, Henderson Humphries Design

Lead designer—Stephen Hernandez, Media Studio, BSA

Designer—Jennifer Horn, Jennifer Horn Creative

Concept designer—Jason Gammon, Enventys Creative

Lead graphic specialist—Melinda VanLone, Media Studio, BSA

Graphic specialist—Roxane Galassini, Media Studio, BSA

Print coordinator—Kimberly Kailey, Information Delivery Department, BSA

Illustrator—John McDearmon, John McDearmon Illustration & Design

Photography manager—Michael Roytek, Media Studio, BSA

Digital asset manager—Christy Batchelor, Media Studio, BSA

Production assistant—Justin Garrison

Indexing—Julie Grady, Grady Editorial Services

Senior Web administrator—Eric Brown, Brand Management, BSA

Web development—Randy Piland

Web content development—Mark Ray

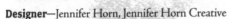

Check out the making of the *Boy Scout Handbook* at *www.bsahandbook.org*.

The eagle on the cover is a juvenile bald eagle photographed at a camporee. Young birds have a mixture of brown and white feathers on their head and tail. It takes about five years for their feathers to turn white.

PHOTO/ILLUSTRATION CREDITS

Cover

Photography

BSA file—*flag*

Brian Payne—*eagle, zip line*

Illustrations

Stephen Hernandez (*design*) and Michael Roytek (*photography*)— *whitewater*

Reprinted from *Boy Scout Handbook*, 6th ed., 4th printing (1962)

Paintings

Joseph Csatari—*All Out for Scouting*

Preface

Photography

Michael Roytek—pages 3 and 8 (*bottom*)

Illustrations

Reprinted from *Boy Scout Handbook*, 3rd ed., 21st printing (1935)— pages 1 and 2

Reprinted from *Boy Scout Handbook*, 6th ed., 4th printing (1962)—page 3 (*flagpole*)

Reprinted from *Boy Scout Handbook*, 8th ed., 1st printing (1972)—pages 6–7 (*Project Soar*)

Introduction

Photography

BSA file—page 14 (*top*)

Daniel Giles—page 16 (*top and bottom*)

Mark Humphries—page 14 (*bottom*)

Brian Payne—pages 16 (*middle*)

Michael Roytek—pages 12 (*both*) and 13

Illustrations

Robert S. S. Baden-Powell/National Scouting Museum—page 12

Stephen Hernandez (*design*) and Michael Roytek (*photography*)— pages 10–11

Reprinted from *Boy Scout Handbook*, 5th ed., 1st printing (1948)— pages 14–15

Reprinted from *Boy Scout Handbook*, 6th ed. 4th printing (1962)—page 13 (*campsite*)

Your Adventure Begins

Photography

BSA file—pages 28, 32, 35, 36 (*bottom*), and 37

Daniel Giles—pages 18 (*bottom*), 19, 29 (*top*), and 38

Brian Payne—pages 23 (*right*), 24, 26 (*bottom*), 29 (*bottom*), and 39 (*both*)

Randy Piland—pages 18 (*background*) and 23 (*left*)

Michael Roytek—pages 20 (*both*), 22, 25, 26 (*top and bottom left*), 29 (*middle*), 30, 31, 33 (*both*), and 36 (*top*)

Wikipedia.org—page 37

Illustrations

Robert S. S. Baden-Powell/National Scouting Museum—page 16

John McDearmon—pages 20, 21 *(all)*, and 32 *(all)*

Reprinted from *Boy Scout Handbook*, 2nd ed., 28th printing (1923)—pages 32–33 *(uniform)*

Reprinted from *Boy Scout Handbook*, 3rd ed., 21st printing (1935)—pages 17 *(This Way to Be a Scout)* and 20 *(salute)*

Reprinted from *Boy Scout Handbook*, 4th ed., 39th printing (1946)—pages page 24 *(Scout Law)*, 25 *(On My Honor and Scout Law)*, 27 *(A Good Turn)*, 28-29 *(Campsite)*, and 34 *(Your Patrol)*

Reprinted from *Boy Scout Handbook*, 5th ed., 1st printing (1948)—pages 18–19 and 22–23

Reprinted from *Boy Scout Handbook*, 6th ed., 4th printing (1962)—pages 30 and 36

Reprinted from *Boy Scout Handbook*, 7th ed., 1st printing (1965)—page 34 *(A Good Turn Daily)*

Reprinted from *Boy Scout Handbook*, 8th ed., 1st printing (1972)—page 26 *(three boys)*

Reprinted from *Boy Scout Handbook*, 9th ed., 11th printing (1988)—page 20 *(handshake)*

Scoutcraft Section

Photography

Randy Piland—page 42 *(injured Scout)*

Michael Roytek—page 42–43 *(whistle)*

Illustrations

Reprinted from *Boy Scout Handbook*, 2nd ed., 28th printing (1923)—page 42 *(hand injury)*

Reprinted from *Boy Scout Handbook*, 3rd ed., 21st printing (1935)—page 42 *(This Way to Be a Scout)*

Reprinted from *Boy Scout Handbook*, 4th ed., 39th printing (1946)—page 43 *(troop)*

Reprinted from *Boy Scout Handbook*, 7th ed., 1st printing (1965)—page 42 *(swimming)*

Reprinted from *Boy Scout Handbook*, 8th ed., 1st printing (1972)—pages 42–43 *(physical health)*

Reprinted from *Boy Scout Handbook*, 9th ed., 11th printing (1988)—page 43 *(advancement)*

Leadership – Chapter 1

Photography

BSA file—page 60 (*all*)

Daniel Giles—pages 47 (*top*) and 48 (*right*)

Mark Humphries—pages 46 and 50 (*bottom*)

Roy Jansen—page 55 (*Eagle Scout Award*)

Roger Morgan—pages 52 (*Baden Powell* and *My Scout Journal*) and 58

Brian Payne—page 50 (*top*)

Randy Piland—pages 50 (*left*), 52 (*Scouts using journal*), 53, 56, 57, and 59

Michael Roytek—pages 49 (*bottom*), 51, 56 (*Silver Buffalo Award*), 62, 63, and 64

Illustrations

Robert S. S. Baden-Powell/National Scouting Museum—page 52 (*sketch*)

Stephen Hernandez (*design*) and Daniel Giles (*photography*)—pages 44–45

Reprinted from *Boy Scout Handbook*, 2nd ed., 28th printing (1923)—page 55

Reprinted from *Boy Scout Handbook*, 4th ed., 39th printing (1946)—pages 55 (*Tenderfoot requirements*) and 64–65

Reprinted from *Boy Scout Handbook*, 6th ed., 4th printing (1962)—page 46

Reprinted from *Boy Scout Handbook*, 7th ed., 1st printing (1965)— page 60–61

Reprinted from *Boy Scout Handbook*, 9th ed., 1st printing (1979)—page 59

Paintings

Norman Rockwell painting produced from copyrighted art from the archives of Brown & Bigelow Inc. and by permission of the Boy Scouts of America—page 47

Citizenship – Chapter 2

Photography

Daniel Giles—pages 79 (*top*) and 82

Mark Humphries—page 87 (*In God We Trust*)

Roger Morgan—page 72

National Archives and Records Administration; http://www.archives.gov/exhibits/charters/charters_downloads.html—page 69 (*top*)

Randy Piland—pages 87 (*mountain and stream*), 88, and 89 (*both*)

Michael Roytek—pages 75, 76, 78 (*maps*), 79 (*bottom*), 83, and 87 (*cliff*)

Illustrations

Stephen Hernandez (*design*) and Michael Roytek (*photography*)— pages 66–67

Reprinted from *Boy Scout Handbook*, 2nd ed., 25th printing (1922)—page 74

Reprinted from *Boy Scout Handbook*, 2nd ed., 28th printing (1923)—page 80

Reprinted from *Boy Scout Handbook*, 4th ed., 39th printing (1946)—pages 70–71 and 84

Reprinted from *Boy Scout Handbook*, 5th ed., 1st printing (1948)—pages 75, 76 (*flag, salute*), 78–79, and 88–89

Reprinted from *Boy Scout Handbook*, 7th ed., 1st printing (1965)—page 68

Reprinted from *Boy Scout Handbook*, 9th ed., 1st printing (1979)—page 81

Fitness – Chapter 3

Photography

Daniel Giles—pages 96 (*right*), 97 (*right*), 98 (*top left and bottom right*), 99 (*landing*), 100 (*thigh stretch, straddle stretch*), 101 (*back stretch, shoulder stretch*), 117 (*all*), 119 (*all*), and 121 (*runners*)

Mark Humphries—pages 102, 103 (*all*), 104 (*almonds, beans, chicken sandwich*), and 107 (*peas*)

Roger Morgan—page 120

Brian Payne—pages 93, 96 (*left*), 97 (*left*), 98 (*top right and bottom left*), 99 (*flex, leap, running*), 109 (*tug-of-war*), 111, and 121 (*crawling, teamwork*)

Randy Piland—page 109 (*rock hopping*)

Michael Roytek—pages 95, 100 (*calf stretch*), 101 (*water bottle*), 105 (*all*), 107 (*pantry, tofu, granola*), 109 (*push-up*), 110, 113, and 118

Illustrations

Daniel Giles (*photography*) and Stephen Hernandez (*design*)—pages 90–91

John McDearmon—page 112

MyPyramid.gov—page 102 (*bottom*)

Reprinted from *Boy Scout Handbook*, 2nd ed., 25th printing (1922)—pages 92, 93 (*Scouts on bicycles*), and 118

Reprinted from *Boy Scout Handbook*, 3rd ed., 14th printing (1931)—pages 102 (*eat to live*), 116–117, and 120

Reprinted from *Boy Scout Handbook*, 3rd ed., 21st printing (1935)—page 93 (*kicker*)

Reprinted from *Boy Scout Handbook*, 6th ed., 4th printing (1962)—page 114 (*lungs*)

Reprinted from *Boy Scout Handbook*, 8th ed., 1st printing (1972)—pages 95, 99, 111 (*right*), and 121

Reprinted from *Boy Scout Handbook*, 9th ed., 1st printing (1979)—pages 97 and 111 (*left*)

Paintings

Norman Rockwell painting produced from copyrighted art from the archives of Brown & Bigelow Inc. and by permission of the Boy Scouts of America—page 94

First Aid – Chapter 4

Photography

Lisa Ames, University of Georgia, *Bugwood.org*, courtesy—page 143 (*brown recluse spider*)

Scott Bauer, USDA Agricultural Resource Service, *Bugwood.org*, courtesy—page 142 (*tick*)

Ronald F. Billings, Texas Forest Service, *Bugwood.org*, courtesy—page 143 (*black widow spider*)

BSA file—pages 139 (*poison ivy*), 150 (*sunscreen*), 157 (*first-aid bandanna*), and 176 (*lifting*)

Daniel Giles—pages 125, 152, and 168 (*top*)

Mark Humphries—pages 132, 133 (*top*), 158 (*top*), 173 (*both*), and 177

Jupiterimages.com—pages 127 (*purple glove*) and 140 (*skunk, bats*)

Kitty Kohout, The Morton Arboretum, Lisle, Illinois—page 139 (*poison sumac in fall, spring*)

Roger Morgan—147 (*top*)

Brian Payne—pages 124, 127 (*closed first-aid kit*), 128 (*blue first-aid kit and troop kit*), 131, 133 (*bottom*), 137, 138, 145, 147 (*bottom*), 151, 154 (*both*), 163, and 171

Randy Piland—pages 127 (*opened first-aid kit*), 139 (*poison oak*), and 160

Michael Roytek—pages 128 (*scissors*), 130 (*both*), 136 (*both*), 144 (*both*), 150 (*Camp Goshen*), 155, 158 (*bottom*), 161 (*all*), 165 (*AED*), 166, 168 (*bottom*), and 175 (*both*)

Marty Welsh—page 146

U.S. Fish and Wildlife Service/Luther C. Goldman, courtesy—page 141 (*coral snake*)

Wikipedia.org—page 141 (*copperhead, rattlesnake, and cottonmouth moccasin*)

Illustrations

Stephen Hernandez (*design*) and Mark Humphries (*photography*)— pages 122–123

John McDearmon—pages 134 (*both*), 135 (*both*), 137, 142 (*both*), 143 (*all*), 146 (*fishhook wound*), 148, 149 (*second-, third-degree burns*), 153, 155 (*sprain wrap*), 156, 157, 159 (*all*), 162, 163, 164 (*all*), 167 (*all*), 174 (*all*), and 175 (*pack-strap carry, two-handed carry, four-handed seat, four-handed carry illustrations*)

Reprinted from *Boy Scout Handbook*, 1st ed., 1st printing (1911)— page 140 (*both*)

Reprinted from *Boy Scout Handbook*, 2nd ed., 28th printing (1923)—pages 124 and 146 (*fishing*)

Reprinted from *Boy Scout Handbook*, 4th ed., 39th printing (1946)—pages 160, 168, and 170

Reprinted from *Boy Scout Handbook*, 5th ed., 1st printing (1948)—pages 126 and 149

Reprinted from *Boy Scout Handbook*, 6th ed., 4th printing (1962)—pages 132, 139, 155 (*right*), and 177

Reprinted from *Boy Scout Handbook*, 7th ed., 5th printing (1965)—page 172

Reprinted from *Boy Scout Handbook*, 8th ed., 1st printing (1972)—pages 128 and 129

Reprinted from *Boy Scout Handbook*, 9th ed., 11th printing (1988)—pages 158, 173, and 175 (*bottom*)

Paintings

Joseph Csatari—page 160

Aquatics – Chapter 5

Photography

Daniel Giles—pages 182, 185 (*back crawl*), 186 (*swimming sign*), 200–201 (*lifesaving sign*), and 201 (*both*)

Kevin Kolczynski—page 196

Roger Morgan—page 181

Brian Payne—pages 186–187 (*swimmer*), 194 (*bottom*), and 200 (*snorkeling, paddle*)

Randy Piland—pages 180, 185 (*Camp Goshen*), and 194 (*top*)

Michael Roytek—page 195

Illustrations

Stephen Hernandez *(design)* and Michael Roytek *(photography)*—pages 178–179

John McDearmon—pages 183–191 *(all)*, 192 *(survival floating, inflating a pocket)*, 193 *(all)*, and 197–199 *(all)*

Reprinted from *Boy Scout Handbook*, 4th ed., 36th printing (1943)—pages 180 and 192–193

Reprinted from *Boy Scout Handbook*, 5th ed., 1st printing (1948)—pages 182–183

Reprinted from *Boy Scout Handbook*, 6th ed., 4th printing (1962)—pages 188–189 *(taking a breath)* and 201 *(Scout paddling)*

Reprinted from *Boy Scout Handbook*, 8th ed., 1st printing (1972)—page 181

Woodcraft Section

Photography

Randy Piland—page 202 *(conifer tree)*

Michael Roytek—pages 202–203 *(binoculars)*

Illustrations

Reprinted from *Boy Scout Handbook*, 1st ed., 1st printing (1911)—page 203 *(raccoon)*

Reprinted from *Boy Scout Handbook*, 5th ed., 1st printing (1948)—page 202

Reprinted from *Boy Scout Handbook*, 6th ed., 4th printing (1962)—page 203 *(conservation)*

Ernest Thompson Seton—page 202 *(fox)*

Nature – Chapter 6

Photography

Dan Bryant—page 229

Vince Heptig—page 235

Istockphotos.com—page 214 *(beech leaf, willow leaf, elm tree)*

Jupiterimages.com—pages 206, 208 *(pinecone, feather)*, 213 *(compound leaf)*, 220 *(cuttlefish)*, 224 *(ptarmigan summer, winter)*, 237 *(both)*, and 240–241 *(star chart)*

NASA.gov—page 240 *(Orion constellation)*

NOAA.gov—pages 232–233 *(weather map background)*

Brian Payne—pages 207 *(waterfall)*, 209 *(biking)*, 210 *(seedling)*, 211 *(broadleaf tree)*, 215 *(both)*, 216 *(biking)*, 217 *(right)*, 218 *(fishing, frog)*, 219 *(snake, falcon, bird watchers)*, 221, 228 *(all)*, 230 *(both)*, and 231

Photos.com—page 209 *(nurse log)*, 212, 213 *(simple, unlobed, toothed edge leaves)*, 214 *(birch leaf)*, 216 *(leaf)*, and 236

Randy Piland—pages 207 *(hiking)*, 211 *(conifer tree)*, 220 *(moose)*, 222, 223, and 232 *(left)*

Michael Roytek—pages 210 *(notebook)*, 216 *(camera)*, 217 *(left)*, 218 *(salamander)*, 219 *(iguana)*, 220 *(butterfly exhibit, bee)*, 225, and 232 *(right)*

Wikipedia.org—pages 214 *(beech tree, birch tree, cherry leaf, cherry tree, elm leaf, willow tree)* and 240 *(Orion drawing)*

Illustrations

Robert S. S. Baden-Powell/National Scouting Museum—pages 206, 212, and 238

Stephen Hernandez (*design*) and Brian Payne (*photography*)—pages 204–205

John McDearmon—208, 210, 211 (*both*), 217 (*both*), 225, 227 (*all*), 233 (*all*), 234 (*cloud formations*), 236, and 239

Reprinted from *Boy Scout Handbook*, 1st ed., 1st printing (1911)—page 220 (*both*)

Reprinted from *Boy Scout Handbook*, 2nd ed., 28th printing (1923)—page 218

Reprinted from *Boy Scout Handbook*, 4th ed., 39th printing (1946)—page 223

Reprinted from *Boy Scout Handbook*, 5th ed., 1st printing (1948)—pages 226, 234 (*background*), and 235

Reprinted from *Boy Scout Handbook*, 6th ed., 4th printing (1962)—pages 230–231

Reprinted from *Boy Scout Handbook*, 7th ed., 1st printing (1965)—pages 222 and 229

Leave No Trace – Chapter 7

Photography

BSA file—page 244

Daniel Giles—pages 250 (*bottom*) and 253

Mark Humphries—page 252

Jupiterimages.com—page 255 (*black bear*)

Bryan Payne—pages 248, 249, 250 (*bottom*), and 254 (*owl*)

Randy Piland—pages 246, 254 (*bison*), and 256 (*hiking*)

Michael Roytek—pages 245 (*bottom*), 250 (*top*), 251 (*top*), 255 (*butterfly*), 256 (*nothing but footprints*), and 257

Illustrations

Stephen Hernandez (*design*) and Brian Payne (*photography*)—pages 242–243

John McDearmon—page 249 (*bottom*)

Reprinted from *Boy Scout Handbook*, 1st ed., 1st printing (1911)—page 255

Reprinted from *Boy Scout Handbook*, 2nd ed., 28th printing (1923)—page 247

Reprinted from *Boy Scout Handbook*, 3rd ed., 21st printing (1935)—pages 256–257

Reprinted from *Boy Shout Handbook*, 6th ed., 4th printing (1962)—pages 244 and 252–253 (*campfire*)

Reprinted from *Boy Scout Handbook*, 7th ed., 1st printing (1965)—page 249

Reprinted from *Boy Scout Handbook*, 9th ed., 1st printing (1979)—page 252 (*lashing*)

Campcraft Section

Photography

Mark Humphries—pages 258–259 (*trail mix*)

Randy Piland—page 258 (*tent*)

Michael Roytek—page 258 (*spiral card*)

Illustrations

Reprinted from *Boy Scout Handbook*, 1st ed., 1st printing (1911)—page 258 (*fire-making tools*)

Reprinted from *Boy Scout Handbook*, 2nd ed., 28th printing (1923)—page 258 (*campfire*)

Reprinted from *Boy Scout Handbook*, 4th ed., 39th printing (1946)—page 258 (*troop*)

Illustrations

Stephen Hernandez (*design*) and Brian Payne (*photography*)—pages 284–285

John McDearmon—pages 302 (*top*), 304 (*all*), and 309 (*top*)

Reprinted from *Boy Scout Handbook*, 2nd ed., 28th printing (1923)—pages 286 and 301

Reprinted from *Boy Scout Handbook*, 5th ed., 1st printing (1948)—pages 295 and 306

Reprinted from *Boy Scout Handbook*, 6th ed., 4th printing (1962)—pages 288, 302–303, 305, and 311

Reprinted from *Boy Scout Handbook*, 7th ed., 1st printing (1965)—page 290

Reprinted from *Boy Scout Handbook*, 8th ed., 1st printing (1972)—pages 296 and 309

Reprinted from *Boy Scout Handbook*, 9th ed., 1st printing (1979)—page 298

Cooking – Chapter 10

Photography

Daniel Giles—pages 319 (*Scout eating*) and 326

Mark Humphries—pages 316, 317 (*all*), 318 (*bottom*), 319 (*corn, green beans, crackers, macaroni*), 328 (*aluminum can*), 329, 330 (*oatmeal*), 332 (*bottom*), 333, 337 (*bottom*), 338, 340 (*all*), and 341 (*top*)

Bryan Payne—pages 318 (*top*), 324 (*dishes*), and 339 (*all*)

Photos.com—page 337 (*bread*)

Randy Piland—pages 315 (*both*), 325, 328 (*straining, disposing of dishwater*), 330 (*eating breakfast*), and 335

Michael Roytek—pages 323, 324 (*pancakes, Dutch oven*), 332 (*top*), 334, 336, 341 (*bottom*), and 345

Illustrations

Stephen Hernandez (*design*) and Brian Payne (*photography*)—pages 312–313

John McDearmon—pages 327 (*boiling water, dish pots*), 328, 331 (*top*), 335, and 343 (*bottom*)

MyPyramid.gov—page 320

Reprinted from *Boy Scout Handbook*, 1st ed., 1st printing (1911)—page 322, 324 (*top*), and 333 (*fish*)

Reprinted from *Boy Scout Handbook*, 2nd ed., 28th printing (1923)—page 336 (*supper*)

Reprinted from *Boy Scout Handbook*, 5th ed., 1st printing (1948)—page 343 (*top*)

Reprinted from *Boy Scout Handbook*, 6th ed., 4th printing (1962)—pages 315 and 330–331 (*bottom*)

Reprinted from *Boy Scout Handbook*, 7th ed., 1st printing (1965)—page 345 (*top*)

Reprinted from *Boy Scout Handbook*, 8th ed., 1st printing (1972)—pages 327 (*bottom*) and 334

Reprinted from *Boy Scout Handbook*, 9th ed., 1st printing (1979)—pages 314, 316–317, 324 (*bottom*), and 340–341

Paintings

Norman Rockwell painting reproduced from copyrighted art from the archives of Brown & Bigelow Inc. and by permission of the Boy Scouts of America—page 344

Navigation – Chapter 11

Photography

Dan Bryant—page 362 (ruler)

BSA file—pages 355 (map symbols), 373 (map), and 374 (map)

Daniel Giles—page 362 (signs)

Mark Humphries—pages 348 (both) and 367

Bryan Payne—page 365

Randy Piland—pages 351, 373 (orienteering), and 375

T. A. Rector, and I. P. Dell'Antonio/ NAOA/AURA/NSF, courtesy— page 371 (moon)

Michael Roytek—pages 346, 352, 356, 357, 358 (right), 360, 361, 364, 366, and 374 (Scout, measuring)

U.S. Geological Survey—page 354 (map)

Wikipedia.org—page 359

Illustrations

Robert Birkby—page 358 (sketch)

Dynamic Graphics; Laura E. Humphries/Henderson Humphries Design; and Julie Moore (photo illustration)—page 369

Stephen Hernandez (design) and Randy Piland (photography)—pages 344–345

John McDearmon—pages 349, 350, 351, 353 (map), 356, 357, 362 (declination), 363 (magnetic north), 368, 370 (both), and 371

Reprinted from Boy Scout Handbook, 4th ed., 39th printing (1946)—page 375

Reprinted from Boy Scout Handbook, 5th ed., 1st printing (1948)—pages 346, 352, and 362

Reprinted from Boy Scout Handbook, 6th ed., 1st printing (1959)—pages 353 and 361

Reprinted from Boy Scout Handbook, 9th ed., 1st printing (1979)—page 347

Reprinted from Boy Scout Handbook, 11th ed., 8th printing (1998)—page 354 (map symbols)

Paintings

Norman Rockwell painting reproduced from copyrighted art from the archives of Brown & Bigelow Inc. and by permission of the Boy Scouts of America—page 347

Tools – Chapter 12

Photography

BSA file—page 402 (pocketknife)

Daniel Giles—pages 378, 382 (right), 383, 385 (both), 392 (top and bottom right), and 408

Roger Morgan—page 415 (middle)

Bryan Payne—pages 379 (both), 380, 381, 384 (both), 398 (lashing), 400 (top), 411, and 412

Randy Piland—pages 392 (bottom left), 395 (all), 396, 397, 398 (tower), 399 (both), 401 (digging), 402 (Scout knife), and 405 (bottom)

Reprinted from Boy Scout Handbook, 10th ed., 5th printing (1990)—page 401 (pocketknife)

Michael Roytek—pages 382 (left), 388, 391, 393, 394 (monkey bridge, trestle), 400 (bottom), 401 (climbing), 403, 405 (top), 407 (both), 414 (both), and 415 (top, bottom)

Illustrations

Robert S. S. Baden-Powell/National Scouting Museum—page 414 (*top*)

Stephen Hernandez (*design*) and Randy Piland (*photography*)—pages 376–377

John McDearmon—pages 380 (*bottom*), 381 (*all*), 383 (*all*), 384 (*bottom*), 385 (*top*), 386 (*middle*), 387 (*right set and bottom*), 388 (*middle set*), 389 (*alternative bowline*), 390 (*middle, bottom left*), 391 (*necktie*), 393–395 (*all*), 396 (*middle set*), 397 (*middle set*), 398 (*top set*), 399 (*tripod lashing*), 400 (*flag pole, round lashing, floor lashing*), 402 (*bottom*), 403, 404 (*top right, bottom right*), 406 (*bottom*), 407 (*all*), 408 (*left*), 409 (*top left*), 410, 412, and 414 (*middle set*)

Reprinted from *Boy Scout Handbook*, 2nd ed., 28th printing (1923)— page 378 (*top*)

Reprinted from *Boy Scout Handbook*, 3rd ed., 21st printing (1935)— pages 380 (*top*) and 384 (*top*)

Reprinted from *Boy Scout Handbook*, 5th ed., 9th printing (1956)— pages 389–390 and 406

Reprinted from *Boy Scout Handbook*, 6th ed., 4th printing (1962)—pages 378–379 (*bottom*), 389 (*right*), 390 (*top right*), 401 (*bottom right*), 402 (*top*), 408–409, and 411

Reprinted from *Boy Scout Handbook*, 9th ed., 1st printing (1979)—pages 396 (*bottom left*), 397 (*bottom right*), 398 (*diagonal lashing*), and 400 (*top center*)

Reprinted from *Boy Scout Handbook*, 9th ed., 11th printing (1988)—pages 382, 385 (*middle, bottom*), 386 (*top right, bottom*), 387 (*top left*), 390 (*bottom*), 392, 399 (*tripod*), 400 (*single-lock bridge*), and 404 (*top left*)

Your Adventure Continues

Photography

BSA file—page 433 (*poison ivy*)

David Burke—page 423 (*right, bottom*)

Mark Duncan—page 423 (*left*)

Daniel Giles—pages 418 (*bottom center, bottom right*), 420 (*top center*), 432, 436–437 (*medical sign*), 438–439 (*swimming sign*), 442 (*bottom left*), and 442–443 (*sailboat*)

Mark Humphries—page 436

Judy Krew, courtesy—page 427 (*backpacking patch*)

Roger Morgan—pages 420 (*top right*) and 434

Bryan Payne—pages 421, 426, 432–433 (*top*), 434–435 (*top*), 437 (*swimmers*), 442–443 (*background*), and 443 (*bottom right*)

Randy Piland—pages 418 (*bottom left*), 420 (*top left*), 425, 428, 438, 439 (*bottom right*), and 444

Michael Roytek—pages 422 (*both*) and 445

Illustrations

Robert S. S. Baden-Powell/National Scouting Museum—pages 418 (*bottom*) and 424

Stephen Hernandez (*design*) and Michael Roytek (*photography*)—pages 416–417

John McDearmon—pages 433 (*foot bandage*) and 434–435 (*swimmers*)

Reprinted from *Boy Scout Handbook*, 2nd ed., 28th printing (1923)—pages 438 (*bottom*), 428, 436 (*top*), and 445 (*bottom left*)

Reprinted from *Boy Scout Handbook*, 3rd ed., 21st printing (1935)—pages 431, 432 (*This Way To Be a Scout*), and 436 (*top*)

Reprinted from *Boy Scout Handbook*, 4th ed., 36th printing (1943)—page 418 (*top*)

Reprinted from *Boy Scout Handbook*, 4th ed., 39th printing (1946)—pages 432 (*top left, bottom left*), 432–433 (*bottom*), 434–435 (*top*), 435 (*top right*), 435 (*bottom*), 436 (*bottom*), 436–437 (*top*), 439 (*top right*), 443 (*bottom*), 442 (*eagle*), and 445 (*bottom right*)

Reprinted from *Boy Scout Handbook*, 5th ed., 1st printing (1948)—pages 434 (*top*), 440 (*top*), 443 (*top*), and 438 (*top*)

Reprinted from *Boy Scout Handbook*, 8th ed., 1st printing (1972)—pages 419, 422, and 444 (*bottom*)

Reprinted from *Boy Scout Handbook*, 9th ed., 1st printing (1979)—pages 421, 440 (*bottom*), and 444 (*top*)

Paintings
Joseph Csatari—pages 419 and 430

Acknowledgments/Index

Photography
BSA file—pages 452, 456, and 477

Robert Birkby—page 449

David Burke—page 461

Daniel Giles—pages 448 (*both*), 459, 476, and 478

Mark Humphries—pages 458, 463, and 466

Brian Payne—pages 450, 453, 455, 457, 467, 470, 474, and 475

Photos.com—page 479

Randy Piland—pages 454, 460, and 471

Michael Roytek—pages 451, 462, 465, 469, 472, and 473

Illustrations
Reprinted from *Boy Scout Handbook*, 1st ed., 1st printing (1911)—pages 472–473

Reprinted from *Boy Scout Handbook*, 2nd ed., 25th printing (1922)—page 477

Reprinted from *Boy Scout Handbook*, 3rd ed., 14th printing (1931)—pages 468 and 470

Reprinted from *Boy Scout Handbook*, 4th ed., 36th printing (1943)—pages 454 and 474

Reprinted from *Boy Scout Handbook*, 5th ed., 1st printing (1948)—pages 462–463

Reprinted from *Boy Scout Handbook*, 5th ed., 9th printing (1956)—pages 448 and 462 (*top*)

Reprinted from *Boy Scout Handbook*, 6th ed., 1st printing (1959)—pages 449, 457, 459, 464, 467, and 478

Reprinted from *Boy Scout Handbook*, 6th ed., 4th printing (1962)—page 451

Reprinted from *Boy Scout Handbook*, 9th ed., 1st printing (1979)—page 460

Reprinted from *Boy Scout Handbook*, 10th ed., 1st printing (1990)—pages 452–453

"We must depend upon the Boy Scout movement to produce the men of the future."

—Daniel Carter Beard

INDEX

A

Achilles tendon and calf stretch, 100

Addiction, 113, 115

Adult leadership positions, 428

AED. *See* Automated external defibrillator (AED)

Aims of Scouting, 15

Airway, 163

Alcohol, 115, 116

Allergies, 144

Alpha Phi Omega National Service Fraternity, 428

Aluminum foil, cooking in, 340

American flag, 72–76

 displaying, 75

 flying, 74

 folding, 75

 at half-staff, 74

 hoisting, 74

 lowering, 74

 retiring worn-out, 76

 on uniforms, 76

American's Creed, 87

Amphibians, 218

Anaphylactic shock, 143, 144

Animal bites, 140–142

Animals. *See* Wildlife

Ankle drag, 174

Aquatics, 180–201

 opportunities, 200–201

 swimming, 180–193, 200

 water rescues, 196–199

 water safety, 194–195

Aquatics awards, 431

Armed forces, 71

*ArrowCorps*⁵, 23

Arthropods, 220

Asking, for information, 50

Athens, 68

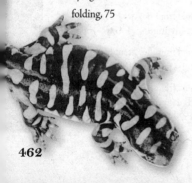

Atmosphere, 232

Automated external defibrillator (AED), 165

Aims of Scouting, 15

Awards and recognition, 430–431

Axes, 406–409

B

Back crawl, 185

Backpacker's lunch, 332

Backpacks, 297–299

Backstroke, 187

Bacon, 330

Baden-Powell, Robert

    Brownsea Island camp of, 37

        on ethical decision making, 117

        founding of Scouting by, 60

        jamborees and, 423, 424

        journal of, 52

        on knots, 382

        on navigation, 371

        on patriotism, 88

        on physical fitness, 109, 121

        summer camp by, 420

Bare-ground fire site, 410

Barometric pressure, 233

Bar scales, 354

Beans, 104

Bear bags, 309

Beard, Daniel Carter, 60

Bears, 255, 308–309

Bedrolls, 299

Bee stings, 143

Bentsen, Lloyd, 84

Big Dipper, 240, 368

Bight, 383

Bill of Rights, 70

Biodegradable toilet paper, 250

Bird feeders, 225

Birds, 219, 223–225

Biscuit mix, 337

Biscuits, 337, 338

Black widow spiders, 143

Blanket drag, 174

Bleeding, 167

Blisters, 137

Blogs, 52

Boards of review, 55

Body weight, 108–109

Books, 50–51

Boots, hiking, 275–276

Bowline, 388–389

Boyce, William, 27

Boy Scouting, 15. *See also* Scouting

Boy Scouts of America (BSA)

    founding of, 27

    joining requirements, 17

    mission of, 15

    programs of, 15

Bread, 337–338, 341

Breakfast, 329–331

Breakfast drinks, 331

Breaststroke, 188

Breathable fabrics, 274

Breathing, rescue, 164

Breathing hurry cases, 163–165

Broadleaf trees, 211

Broiling, 334

Broken bones (fractures), 156–161

Brown recluse spiders, 143

BSA. *See* Boy Scouts of America (BSA)

BSA Safe Swim Defense, 182

BSA Safety Afloat, 194–195

BSA swimmer test, 190–191

Buddy system, 39

Bullying, 62

Bunche, Ralph, 56

Burns, 148–149

C

Caffeine, 105

Campcraft, 258–259

Campers, respect for other, 256

Campfires, 301, 410–414

    building, 410–413

    for cooking, 325

    managing and putting out, 414

    minimizing impact of, 253

    in wet weather, 412

Camp gadgets, 392

Camporee camping, 419

Camp saw, 404

Camps/camping, 286–311

    backpacks for, 297–299

    camporee, 419

    choosing campsite, 300–301

    cleanliness while, 307

    on durable surfaces, 248

    first campout, 39–41

food protection, 308–309

Leave No Trace, 310

merit badges, 310

monthly campouts, 419

overnight, 288

planning camping trips, 290–297

Scout camps, 289

Scouting and, 310–311

sleeping, 305–306

summer, 420

tarps, 304

tents, 302–303

Camp shovels, 409

Camp stoves, 253, 301, 325, 414–415

Canned foods, 319

Carbon monoxide poisoning, 170

Cardiopulmonary resuscitation (CPR), 164, 165

Carnivores, 221

Casts of animal prints, 228

Catholes, 249

Cereal, 330

Char, 413

Chase, Salmon D., 87

Chicken, 334, 340

Chigger bites, 143

Chivalry, 118

Chlorine Free Products Association, 7

Chlorophyll, 210

Choices

    ethical, 92, 117–120

    making good, 61

Choking, 134–135, 162

Chopping blocks, 408

Circulation, 165

Cirrus clouds, 234

Citizenship, 68–89
    community, 77–83
    duties of, 71–72
    merit badges, 72
    rights of, 70
    service projects and, 84–85
    world, 88–89
Civil War, 71
Clark, William, 290
Cleanliness, 307
Clean up, after meals, 327–329
Closed fractures, 156–157
Clothes drag, 174
Clothing
    cold-weather, 273
    extra, 265
    for outdoor adventures, 270–276
    using as life jacket, 192–193
    warm-weather, 272
Clouds, 234–235
Clove hitch, 387

Coiling ropes/cords, 381
Cold fronts, 233
Cold-related injuries, 150, 152–153
Cold-weather clothing, 273
Colors, on maps, 355
Community
    government, 81–83
    knowing your, 77–78
    leaders, 81–82
    maps, 78
    neighbors in, 78–79
    world, 88–89
Compass, 266
    measuring widths using, 351
    using, 361–364
Compass game, 372
Conifer trees, 211
Constellations, 239–240, 369
Constitution, U.S., 68–71
Constitutional rights, 70
Contour lines, on maps, 355, 356
Convenience foods, 319
Cooking, 314–343. *See also* Meals
    in aluminum foil, 340
    cook kits, 324
    eating kits, 324
    meal planning, 316
    menus for, 320
    outdoors, 317–319
    sharing kitchen duties, 325–326
    spices for, 323
    stoves and campfires, 325
    without utensils, 341
Cooking notebook, 343
Cook kits, 324
    Coral snakes, 141

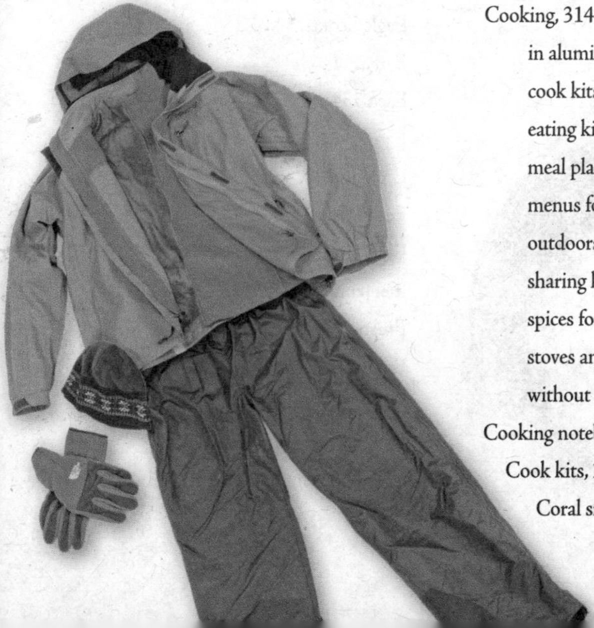

Cords, coiling, 381

Corn, 340, 341

Cotton, 270

CPR (cardiopulmonary resuscitation), 164, 165

Cravat bandages, 157

Cross-country hiking, 278–279

Crunches, 98

Cub Scouting, 15

Cultural diversity, 79

Cumulus clouds, 234

Cuts and scrapes, 136

Cyberbully, 61

D

Declaration of Independence, 69

Declination, 362–363

Defibrillation, 165

Degrees, 358

Degrees of declination, 362

Dehydration, 147

Den Chief Service Award, 430

Desserts, 338–339

Diagonal lashing, 398

Diet, 102–107

Digital leaf collections, 216

Disabilities, 79

Disease, protecting against, 112

Dishwater, 250, 328

Distances, measuring, 348

Double half hitch, 384

Dress a knot, 383

Dried/dehydrated foods, 318

Drinking water, 101, 267, 301, 322

Driving while intoxicated, 115

Drugs, 115, 116

Dumplings, 338

Durable surfaces, 248

Dutch ovens, 338

Duty rosters, 326

E

Eagle Palm rank requirements, 443

Eagle Scout Award, 426

Eagle Scout rank requirements, 440–442

Eagle Scouts, 54, 428

Ears, 111

East, 354

Eating kits, 324

Ecology, 208

Ecosystems, 208

Eggs, 330

Elementary backstroke, 187

Emancipation Proclamation, 71

Emblems, patrol, 38

Emergencies. *See also* First aid

    fire-related, 172

    phone numbers for, 64–65

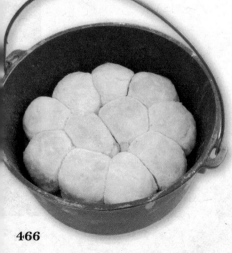

Emergency-preparedness kits, 129

Emergency services, 131

Environment. *See* Nature

Environmental Choice
    Program, 7

Environmental/outdoors awards
    and recognitions, 431

Epinephrine, 144

Equal-length shadow method, 371

Equator, 357

Ethical decisions, 92, 117–120

Exercise, 95–101

Eyes

    caring for your, 111

    objects in, 145

F

Fabrics, 270, 274

Fair-weather signs, 238

Faith, 430

Family, leadership and your, 62–65

Fats, 104

Federal holidays, 86

Felling method of measurement, 349

50-Miler Award, 310

Filters, water, 267

Fire. *See* Campfires

Fireplaces, 413

Fire-related emergencies, 172

Fire starters, 266

First aid, 124–177

    animal bites, 140–142

    basic, 136–161

    bleeding, 167

    blisters, 137

    broken bones (fractures), 156–161

    burns, 148–149

    cold- and
    heat-related injuries, 150–153

    CPR, 164, 165

    cuts and scrapes, 136

    dehydration, 147

    goals of, 125

    heart attacks, 166

    hurry cases, 132, 162–171

    hyperventilation, 148

    importance of, 125

    moving ill or injured
    person, 172–175

    neck and spine injuries, 153

    nosebleeds, 138

    object in eye, 145

    poisoning, 169–170

    poisonous plants, 138–139

    puncture wounds, 145–146

    self-protection during, 168

    shock, 170–171

    spider and insect bites, 142–143

    sprains and strains, 154–155

First-aid kits, 127–129

    for hiking, 264

    home or patrol/troop first-aid
    kits, 128

    personal first-aid kits, 127

First Aid merit badge, 176

First-aid method, 129–135, 168

First class rank requirements, 436–437

First-degree burns, 148–149

Fish, 333, 335, 340, 341

Fishhook wounds, 146, 218

Fitness, 92–121

    defining, 92

    diet and nutrition, 102–107

    exercise and, 95–101

    hiking and, 277

    lifelong, 121

    mental, 92, 117

    moral, 118–120

    protecting against injury and disease, 112

    sleep and, 110

    steps to better, 95

    tobacco, alcohol, and drugs and, 113–117

    vision of, 93

    weight and, 108–109

    500-yard walk/run, 99

Flags

    American flag, 72–76

    patrol, 38

Flashlight, 265

Floating, 191–193

Floor lashing, 400

Florida National High Adventure Sea Base, 422

Food. See also Cooking; Meals

    canned, 319

    convenience, 319

    cost per person, 323

    dried/dehydrated, 318

    for hiking, 266

    leftovers, 328

    nonperishable, 318

    for outdoors, 317–319

    repackaging, 323

    safety, 326, 333

    serving sizes, 321–322

    storage, 308–309, 329

    trail, 266

Food allergies, 107

Food guide pyramid, 102–104, 320

Footgear, 275–276

Forest Stewardship Council, 7

Fossett, Steve, 46

Founding leaders, 60

Four-handed seat, 175

Fractures, 156–161

Frap, 392

French toast, 331

Fresh foods, 317

Friends, judgment in choosing, 61

Front crawl, 184

Fronts, 233

Frostbite, 152

Fruits, 103, 329, 340

Frying, 334, 335

Frying pan bread, 338

Fuel wood, 411

Full-thickness burns, 149

Fusing, 381

Future plans, 48–49

G

Gaiters, 274

Gear. *See also* Tools

    backpacks, 297–299

    footgear, 275–276

    rain, 265, 274

Geocaching, 367

Giving back, 428

Global Positioning System (GPS)
    receivers, 366–367

Goals

    long-term, 55

    personal, 48–49

    reaching your, 54–55

    short-term, 55

Going (swimming) rescues, 198

Gold Award of the Permanent Wild Life
    Protection Fund, 245

Good Turn, 27

Good Turn for America, 430

Government, community, 81–83

GPS. *See* Global Positioning System
    (GPS) receivers

Grace, 342

Grains, 103

Granola, 330

Great Bear, 240, 368

Grilling, 334, 335

Ground cloth, 305

Group size, for camping trips, 292

H

Half hitches, 384

Ham, 330

Hamburger, 340

Handshake, Scout, 20

Hats, rain, 274

Hazing, 62

Head injuries, 155

Heart attacks, 166

Heat exhaustion, 150

Heat-related injuries, 150–151

Heatstroke, 151

Heights, measuring, 349

Height/weight charts, 108

Herbivores, 221

Heroism Award, 431

High-adventure bases, 421–422

Highways, hiking on, 279

Hikers, respect for other, 256

Hiking, 262–283

    clothing for, 270–276

    cross-country, 278–279

    essentials for, 264–266

    fitness and, 277

    food for, 266

getting lost, 282–283

on highways and roads, 279

Leave No Trace, 277

pace, 277

safety, 279

in stormy weather, 280–281

trail manners, 278

trip plans, 268–269

Hiking boots, 275–276

Hiking sticks, 276

Hitches, 383, 384

Home or patrol/troop first-aid kit, 128

Honor Medal, 431

Hornaday, William T., 245

Hornet stings, 143

Hot spots, 137

How to Protect Your Children from Child Abuse (BSA), 34

Human waste, disposal of, 249–250

Hurricanes, 237

Hurry cases, 132, 162–171

Hygiene, 307

Hyperventilation, 148

Hypothermia, 152–153

I

Illegal drugs, 61, 115, 116

Index lines, 356

Information, researching, 49–53

"In God We Trust," 87

Inhaled poisons, 170

Injuries. *See also* First aid

moving injured person, 172–175

protecting against, 112

Insect bites and stings, 142–143

Internet, 51, 61

Interpreter, 430

Invertebrates, 218, 220

Isobars, 233

J

Jamborees, 423–424

Joining knot, 21

Joining requirements, 17

Journals, 51–52

Judgment, 61

K

Kabobs, 341

Kephart, Horace, 286

Key, Francis Scott, 73

Kindling, 411

Kitchen duties, 325–326

Knots, 382–391

bowline, 388–389

clove hitch, 387

necktie, 391

sheet bend, 390

square (joining), 21

taut-line hitch, 385

terminology, 383

timber hitch, 386

two half hitches, 384

Knuckle guards, 408

L

Land managers, 246

Landmarks, identifying, 366

Lashings, 392–400

diagonal, 398

floor, 400

round, 400

shear, 397

square, 396

terminology, 392

tripod, 399

when to use, 393

Latitude, 357–358

Latrines, 250

Leaders/leadership

community, 81–82

family and, 62–65

leading others, 56–57

patches, 58–59

patrol, 38, 57

Scouting's founding, 60

self-leadership, 46–55, 92, 94

stages of, 57

Leading EDGE, 59

Leaf ink prints, 217

Learning opportunities, 48–49

Leave No Trace

beyond, 257

camping, 310

hiking, 277

principles of, 206, 247–256

Scouting and, 244–245

stalking and, 229

LED flashlights, 265

Leftovers, 328

Leopold, Aldo, 257

Level, measuring, 352

Lewis, Meriwether, 290

Libraries, 51

Life jacket, using clothing as, 192–193

Lifelong fitness, 121

Lifesaving awards, 431

Life Scout rank requirements, 439

Lifting, 112

Lightning, 236, 280–281

Lincoln, Abraham, 86

Line tender water rescues, 199

Listening, 50

Local councils, 16

Log fireplace, 413

Longitude, 357–358

Long jump, 99

Long-term goals, 55

Lost, 282–283

Lower back stretch, 101

Lunch, 332

Lungs, 111

M

Macaroni and cheese, 336

Magnetic north, 354, 362–363

Mammals, 220

Map key, 354

Maps

    community, 78

    contour lines on, 355, 356

    following routes on, 365

    for hiking, 266

    longitude and latitude on, 357–358

    for navigation, 353–360

    orienting, 364, 365

    topographic, 353

    using, 365–366

    UTM system, 359–360

    weather, 233

Map symbols, 354–355

Matches, 266

Meal planning, 296, 316

Meals. *See also* Cooking; Food

    bread, 337–338

    breakfast, 329–331

    cleaning up after, 327–329

    desserts, 338–339

    lunch, 332

    as special events, 342

    supper, 333–337

Measuring, 346–352

    distances, 348

    heights, 349

    level, 352

    time, 352

    widths, 350–351

Meat, 104, 333, 334

Medal of Merit, 431

Medical alert bracelets, 144

Mental fitness, 92, 117

Menus, 296, 320

Meridians, 257, 358

Merit badges, 49, 241, 257, 310

Methods of Scouting, 15

Mile Swim Award, 180

Milk, 103

Mill bastard file, 408

Minutes, 358

Moleskin, 137

Mollusks, 220

Monthly campouts, 419

Moon, navigating by, 371

Morally straight, 118–120

Motto

    Scout, 25

    U.S., 87

N

Names, patrol, 38

National Advanced Youth Leadership Experience (NAYLE), 53, 425

National anthem, 73

National Court of Honor, 431

National Eagle Scout Association, 428

National high-adventure bases, 421–422

National Order of the Arrow Conference, 425

National Scout jamboree, 423

National Weather Radio, 234

National Youth Leadership Training (NYLT), 53, 424

Nature, 206–241

    caring for, 241

    ecosystems, 208

    learning about, 207

    plants, 209–217

    stars and constellations, 239–240

    weather, 232–238

    wildlife, 218–231

Navigation, 346–375

    compasses, 361–364

    GPS receivers for, 366–367

    maps for, 353–360

    measuring, 346–352

    by moon, 371

    orienteering courses, 372

    orienting skills, 373–374

    by stars, 368–369

    by sun, 370

    tools, 353–360

    using skills of, 373–375

Neckerchief, 32

Neckties, 391

Neighbors, 78–79

New-Scout patrols, 37

Nicotine, 113

Nonbreathable fabrics, 274

Nonlatex gloves, 127

Nonperishable foods, 318

Nonvenomous snakebites, 141

North, 354, 362

Northern Tier National High Adventure Bases, 422

North Star, 368–369

Nosebleeds, 138

Nutrition facts labels, 106

O

Oatmeal, 330

Observation skills, 50

Older Scouts, 426–428

Omnivores, 221

One-pot stew, 336

Open fractures, 156

Order of the Arrow (OA), 425

Organ Donor Awareness, 430

Orienteering courses, 372

Orienting maps, 364, 365

Orienting skills, 373–374

Orion (Hunter), 240

Outdoor Code, 28, 245

Outdoors. *See* Nature

Overhand loop, 383

Overnight camping, 288

P

Pack-strap carry, 175

Pancakes, 331

Partial-thickness burns, 149

Pasta, 336

Patrol leaders, 38, 57

Patrol leaders' council, 38, 57

Patrols, 36–38

Peach cobbler, 339

Peer pressure, 61

Permission, for camping, 301

Personal first-aid kits, 127

Personal hygiene, 307

Philmont grace, 342

Philmont Scout Ranch, 421

Photosynthesis, 210

Physical examination, 94

Physical fitness, 93–117

    diet and nutrition, 102–107

    exercise and, 95–101

    protecting against injury and disease, 112

    sleep and, 110

    tobacco, alcohol, and drugs and, 113–117

    weight and, 108–109

Pioneering projects, 252, 394

Pit vipers, 141

Planning

    camping trips, 290–297

    Leave No Trace and, 247

    meals, 296, 316

Plant keys, 212–214

Plants, 209–217

    evidence of, 216–217

    identifying, 212–215

    photosynthesis by, 210

    poisonous, 138–139

    role of, 209

    trees, 211

Pledge of allegiance, 19

Pocketknife, 14, 264, 402–403

Poisoning, ingested, 169–170

Poisonous plants, 138–139

Polaris, 368

Poncho, 274

Potatoes, 340, 341

Pots and pans, 324

Preparation, Leave No Trace and, 247

Pressed leaves, 217

Prime meridian, 357

Privacy, 301

Projects, pioneering, 252, 394

Protein, 104

Pull-ups, 97

Puncture wounds, 145–146

Push-ups, 96

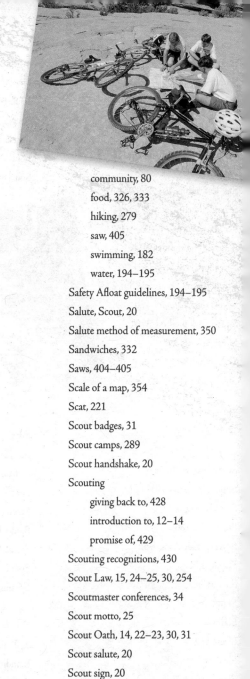

R

Rabid animals, 140

Rain covers, 298

Rain gear, 265, 274

Rain pants, 274

Rain parka, 274

Ramen noodles, 337

Ranger cobbler, 339

Reaching water rescues, 197

Reading, 50–51

Recovery position, 171

Regular patrols, 37

Reptiles, 219

Republic, 69

Rescue breathing, 164

Rescue signals, 283

Research, 49–53

Revolutionary War, 69

Rice, 336

RICE (Rest, Ice, Compression, Elevation), 154

Roads, hiking on, 279

Roosevelt, Theodore, 428, 429

Ropes

    coiling, 381

    fusing, 381

    whipping ends of, 380

Round lashing, 400

Roundturn, 383

Rowing water rescues, 198

Running end, 383

S

Safe Swim Defense, 182

Safety

    ax, 406–408

    camping, 300

    community, 80

    food, 326, 333

    hiking, 279

    saw, 405

    swimming, 182

    water, 194–195

Safety Afloat guidelines, 194–195

Salute, Scout, 20

Salute method of measurement, 350

Sandwiches, 332

Saws, 404–405

Scale of a map, 354

Scat, 221

Scout badges, 31

Scout camps, 289

Scout handshake, 20

Scouting

    giving back to, 428

    introduction to, 12–14

    promise of, 429

Scouting recognitions, 430

Scout Law, 15, 24–25, 30, 254

Scoutmaster conferences, 34

Scout motto, 25

Scout Oath, 14, 22–23, 30, 31

Scout salute, 20

Scout sign, 20

Scout slogan, 26

Scout spirit, 30

Scout troops, 16–17, 34–35

Scout uniform, 32–33, 76

Second class rank requirements, 434–435

Second-degree burns, 149

Seconds, 358

Self-leadership, 46–55, 92, 94

Senior citizens, 78

Service projects, 84–85

Services, community, 80–81

Serving sizes, 321–322

Seton, Ernest Thompson, 60, 283

Sexual responsibility, 120

Shado-stick method, 370

Shear lashing, 397

Sheet bend, 390

Shock, 132, 143–144, 170–171

Shoes

    camp, 276

    hiking, 275–276

Short-term goals, 55

Shoulder stretch, 101

Shovels, 409

Sidestroke, 186

Silver Buffalo Award, 56

Sitting, 112

Sit-ups, 98

Skin care, 110

Slavery, 71

Sleep, 110

Sleeping bags, 305

Sleeping pads, 305

Slings, 160–161

Slogan, Scout, 26

Smellables, 308

Smoking, 113–114, 116

Snakebites, 141–142

Soap, 251, 328

Socks, 276

South, 354

Souvenirs, 251

Spaghetti, 336

Spar, 392

Sparta, 68

Special diets, 107

Spices, 323

Spider bites, 142–143

Spinal cord injuries, 153

Splinting, 158–159

Sprains and strains, 154–155

Square knot, 21

Square lashing, 396

Stalking, 229–230

Standing long jump, 99

Standing part, 383

Star charts, 239

Stars, 239–240, 368–369

Star Scout rank requirements, 438

"Star-Spangled Banner, The," 73

States, 86

Stationary fronts, 233

Stews, 334, 336, 340

Stick method of measurement, 349, 350

Stings, 142–143

Storms, 236–237, 280–281

Stormy-weather signs, 238

Stoves, 253, 301, 325, 414–415

Stovetop oven bread, 338

Straddle stretch, 100

Stratus clouds, 234

Stretching, 100–101

Sugar, 105

Summer camp, 420

Sump holes, 328

Sun, navigating by, 370

Sunburn, 150

Sun protection, 266

Superficial burns, 148

Supper, 333–337

Support, community, 80

Survival floating, 191, 192

Swimming, 180–193, 200

BSA swimmer test,
    190–191

        floating, 191–193

        learning to swim, 183

        safety, 182

        strokes, 184–189

Synthetics, 270

T

Tarps, 304

Taut-line hitch, 385

Teaching, 53

Teaching EDGE, 53

Teeth care, 110

Tenderfoot fitness checklist, 96

Tenderfoot rank requirements, 432–433

Tents, 302–303

Thigh stretch, 100

Third-degree burns, 149

13th Amendment, 71

Three-point fireplace, 413

Thriftiness, 206

Throwing water rescues, 197

Thunderheads, 236

Thunderstorms, 280–281, 352

Tick bites, 142

Timber hitch, 386

Time, measuring, 352

Tinder, 411, 413

Tobacco, 113–114, 116

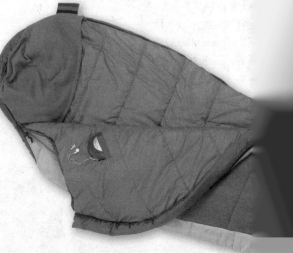

Toilet paper, 250

Tools
    axes, 406–409
    camp shovel, 409
    camp stoves, 414–415
    knots, 382–391
    lashings, 392–400
    navigation, 353–360
    pocketknife, 402–403
    ropes, 380–381
    saws, 404–405
    of Scouting, 378–415

Topographic maps, 353

Tornadoes, 237, 281

Totin' Chip, 409

Tracking, 226–229

Trail food, 266

Trail manners, 278

Trees, 209, 211

Trekking poles, 276

Trip books, 51

Tripod lashing, 399

Trip plans, 268–269, 290–291

Troops, 16–17, 34–35

Trudgen stroke, 189

True north, 354, 362–363

Turn, 383

Two half hitches, 384

Two-handed carry, 175

U

Underhand loop, 383

Uniform, Scout, 32–33, 76

United States Geological Survey, 353

United States of America, 86
    founding of, 69–70
    motto of, 87

Universal Recycling Symbol, 7

Ursa Major, 240, 368

U.S. Constitution, 68–71

U.S. territories and commonwealths, 86

UTM (Universal Transverse Mercator)
    system, 359–360

V

Varsity Scouting, 15, 427

Vegetables, 103, 335

Venomous snakebites, 141–142

Venture patrols, 37, 426

Venturing, 15, 427

Vertebrae, 153

Vertebrates, 218–220

Vision statement, 68

Volunteer organizations, 83

W

Walking assist, 174

Warm fronts, 233

Warm-weather
clothing, 272

Wasps stings, 143

Waste disposal,
249–250

Watch method of
navigation, 370

Water
dishwater, 328
drinking, 101, 267, 301, 322
soap residue in, 251, 328
for washing, 307

Water bottle, 265

Water rescues, 196–199

Water treatment tablets, 267

Waypoints, 357, 367

Weather, 232–238
clouds and, 234–235
hurricanes, 237
lightning, 236, 280–281
signs, 238
stormy, 236–237, 280–281
time and, 352
tornadoes, 237, 281

Weather maps, 233

Weight, 108–109

West, 354

West, James E., 60

Whipping, 380

Widths, measuring, 350–351

Wildlife
birds, 223–225
classification of, 218–220
evidence of, 221–222
identifying, 231
respect for, 254–255
stalking, 229–230
tracking, 226–229

William T. Hornaday Award, 245, 257

Woodcraft, 203

Wool, 270

World community, 88–89

World Crest, 430

World Scout jamborees, 88, 424

Wounds
fishhook, 146
puncture, 145–146

Wrap, 392

Writing, 52

Y

Yells, patrol, 38

Youth Protection, 3 R's, 65

On the trail to high adventure...

you do the planning, we supply the gear!

The Supply Group is ready to be your trail partner. You can depend on us for the latest in lightweight, durable, quality gear that will meet and surpass your toughest requirements. Visit your local Scouting retailer to see the latest in official outdoor gear.

To find the Scouting distributor near you or to browse the complete online BSA catalog, visit the BSA Official Retail Catalog Web site at

www.scoutstuff.org

With Supply Group, YOUR SATISFACTION IS GUARANTEED. If for any reason any item fails to meet your expectations, you can either exchange it for a replacement or return it for a refund.

Subscribe to *Boys' Life* magazine to keep up to date with the latest adventures in Scouting! *www.boyslife.org*

SATISFACTION
SUPPLY GROUP
GUARANTEED